W9-BDZ-678

**MARRIAGE
AND FAMILY
RELATIONSHIPS**

Marriage
and Family
RELATIONSHIPS

RICHARD H. KLEMER
Professor of Child Development and Family Relations
University of North Carolina at Greensboro
and Clinical Professor of Family Studies
Bowman Gray School of Medicine

HARPER & ROW, PUBLISHERS
New York/Evanston/London

**Marriage
and Family
Relationships**

Copyright © 1970 by Richard H. Klemer

Library of Congress Catalog Card Number: 78-95841

CONTENTS

PREFACE

T HIS book has the hopeful intention of offering students of the 1970s a way of studying marriage and family relationships that can have direct pertinence in their own living experiences. To achieve some of this personal significance, the "empathetic approach" is introduced early in this volume and is used extensively. This is a modified case study method that although not wholly unique in its concept, will be a new way of learning for many students. The empathetic approach can be an exciting experience that promises an active partnership for the student in the process of learning and furthering learning.

To assure a more complete understanding of the empathetic approach, the first two chapters contain discussion of its techniques and rationale. It is hoped that each reader will examine these chapters carefully and critically, for much of his ability to deal with the cases that follow will depend both on his familiarity with the basic principles of case analysis and on his self-generated conviction that he can grow toward educational and social fulfillment by his own personal insights and his own perceptive sensitivity, as well as by the absorption of knowledge from a teacher and a textbook.

A few words of explanation about the case reports that follow are appropriate here. Although the "cases" are founded on actual experiences, they are now hypothetical to the extent that all names, places, and occupations, and some circumstances, have been changed. In many instances, behaviors and attitudes from several different interpersonal relationship situations have been rearranged and recombined to form a single new "case." Moreover, although the cases are often reported in a conversational, first-person style, it should not be inferred that these are the words the participants really used. Actual case interviews often are rambling, confused, vague, and hesitant, and short excerpts rarely express the real meaning of the participants. Consequently the first-person style used in this book represents condensed and synthesized recreations of attitudes manifested—sometimes over long periods of time—by the participants.

My list of acknowledgments must begin with the many scholars in the social and behavioral sciences who created the knowledge on which this book is based. I am also indebted to the many students and research respondents who have led me to new insights and understandings of today's marriage and family problems; and to my mother, Dora H. Klemer, one of the pioneer marriage counselors and family life educators, who encouraged my early interest in relationships.

More immediately, I am inestimably grateful for the help and advice of Robert H. Coombs and Rebecca Smith, who reviewed the entire manuscript for this book. Carl M. Cochrane, Barbara James, Herbert Otto, Sarah Shoffner, Mary Stegall, and James Walters supplied guidance for various parts. Evelyn Freeman and David Klein, graduate students while I was at the University of Washington, and Nancy Taylor Coghill, Roswell Cox, Irene Johnson, Polly Lewis, and Charles Snow, recent graduate students here at the University of North Carolina at Greensboro, provided invaluable research and editorial assistance. Trudy Voogd and Firth Fabend also made very important research and editorial contributions, and a large measure of appreciation must be reserved as well for Donna Humphreys, Joan Haynes, Sally Shelton, Ann Smith, and Karen Judd, whose technical skills prepared the manuscript for publication.

Further, I am also especially appreciative for the help of Anthony Mellor and his successor as editor in the College Department at Harper & Row, Mike Mattoon. It was Tony Mellor's early vision and his continuing support that made this book possible.

Finally, I am grateful to my wife, Margaret Grim Klemer, and my daughter, Caralea Klemer, who gave up some of the family life that was ours so that this husband and father could write to other family members about improving family relationships. In a very real way, though, our family has already made back its loss, for now that the job is done, the satisfaction is infinitely more satisfying because it can be shared.

RICHARD H. KLEMER

1

STUDYING
RELATIONSHIPS
IN MARRIAGE
AND THE FAMILY

This is a different kind of textbook about marriage and family relationships. It is based on the empathetic approach to learning.

The empathetic approach assumes that much of your understanding about relationships comes to you in a breakthrough moment of insight when you all at once perceive new meanings and new cause-and-effect associations. The young mother who suddenly recognizes that her little daughter is threatening a doll in exactly the same tone and inflection that the mother had used just minutes before in threatening the child may have an important learning experience in family relationships even though she has gained no new knowledge in the usual textbook sense.

Such dramatic changes in perceptions often take place as a result of your own day-to-day living experiences. They can also take place vicariously through studying the experiences of others. For that reason, a large part of this book will be devoted to case presentations that realistically portray the attitudes, conflicts, and adjustments of present-day marriage partners and their family members. It is intended that you will empathize with (feel with) the family members in the case illustrations to the point where you will get the insights, draw the inferences, and figure out the possible alternatives that could lead to the solutions of the problems presented. Inasmuch as these insights, inferences, and solutions will be in keeping with your own value system and your own personality, they can have immediate meaning in your own living experience. Indeed, often they will have greater meaning for you than other people's generalizations and interpretations might have had.

Just as your understanding of man–woman and parent–child relationships did not begin with the present course you are taking, it will not end when you have completed this book. It has been—and will be—a continuous process throughout your lifetime. Your ongoing progress in understanding the dynamics of human relationships and adjusting to them will have a crucial effect on your success, your happiness, and your emotional health. Perception and skill in interacting with others is a large part of being what psychologist Abraham Maslow has called a "self-actualizing" person—a self-respecting, achieving individual whose manifest adjustment to living makes him pleasant to be with.[1] On the other hand, poor understanding of the dynamics of interpersonal relationships is often a prelude to emotional breakdown. Modern students of psychopathology since the time of Harry Stack Sullivan have tended to put increasing emphasis upon the individual's interpersonal relationships ability as a criterion of his emotional health.[2]

It is very important to recognize, though, that no one learns about relationships *entirely* through the dramatic process of insight. You have learned much about personal interaction from your parents' deliberate teaching and from the modifying instruction and correction you got from your teachers, your peers, and your social groups. At least some direct teaching was involved in your "internalizing" all the customs, attitudes, values, and expectations that now strongly affect all your living experiences and all your relationships.

(Because customs, attitudes, values, and expectations are so important, they should be defined and differentiated right here at the book's beginning. Customs, including role behaviors, are the "proper" ways of any cultural group. Attitudes are the beliefs that predispose an individual to think or act one way or another.[3] Values are the enduring criteria that the individual uses to make judgments. Value judgments result from the use of values in making choices. Expectations are the individual's anticipations that people and events will and should behave and occur as he imagined they would. When these anticipations become strongly emotionalized, they become emotional needs.)

Ever since your first elementary-school course in social studies, you have been learning about relationships, including your own, through a study of what psychologists, sociologists, anthropologists, home economists, and other scientists have found from their research data. This "relationships education" may have been a very important factor in your social growth. But more is needed, for, without further study of the psychosocial data that have been accumulated by behavioral scientists, your insights, inferences, and solutions could reflect only your present attitudes and your present knowledge. This is not enough—it can lead you into perpetuating old behavioral habits because you are unaware of new ones.

So, along with the many illustrations and cases that appear on the following pages, there will be a considerable amount of social history, research data, and theoretical interpretation. There will also be some value judgments for your critical examination and evaluation. As a matter of fact, this whole book is based on two crucial value judgments.

The first major value judgment is that marriage and family living are continuing "goods" in our changing society. In times past, this judgment might have been so universal and so taken for granted that there would have been no

---

[1] Abraham H. Maslow, *Motivation and Personality,* New York, Harper & Row, 1954, p. 218.

[2] Harry Stack Sullivan, *The Interpersonal Theory of Psychiatry,* New York, Norton, 1953.

[3] As Milton Rokeach suggests, the concept of "attitude" in social psychology has been plagued with ambiguity. Rokeach's own definition is this: "An attitude is a relatively enduring organization of beliefs around an object or situation, predisposing one to respond in some preferential manner." See *Beliefs, Attitudes and Values,* San Francisco, Jossey-Bass, 1968, p. 112.

need to make it explicit. But in this era of contraceptives and cafeterias, when young men and women might live as efficiently—even though not as effectively —as single adults, the very continuation of the family as we have known it becomes the subject of controversy. As we shall see in the following chapters, there are now those who propose that both marriage and family living are anachronisms, undesirable vestiges of middle-class conventionality.

While an absolutely impartial examination of the pros and cons of the continuance of the family as a social institution may serve the purposes of the social theorist, it does little or nothing for the person who is seeking functionally meaningful help in improving his own relationships ability. Marriage and the family in our time should be (and shall be) critically examined. But to be more than just academically stimulating to a concerned individual, that critical examination must be done with the intent of improving—not just debating—the worth of both marriage and family living *and* that individual's unique relationships within them. Just as the physician does not examine the patient with objective impartiality about whether that patient should live or die, but rather with a transcending value commitment to health improvement, so this book begins with marriage and family living as conceded values and goes on from there.

The second major value judgment is that the empathetic approach offers a good way to study the very personal and very crucial relations between men and women and between parents and children. Reasons why this value judgment may be valid are given throughout this book. You are urged to evaluate them carefully. If any or all of the cases and concepts that follow improve your sensitivity to the feelings and behaviors of others and so improve your understanding of marriage and family relationships, this book will have achieved its purpose.

2
THE EMPATHETIC APPROACH

Empathy occurs when one person completely identifies with the perceptions and sensations of another person. For the time being, he *is* that other person.

The empathetic approach to the study of marriage and family relationships involves the thoughtful and feelingful examination of people and their problems. Ideally, you should be able to experience vicariously the conflicts, attitudes, and perceptions of the people involved in each relationship situation. Hopefully, you will be able to identify with *all* the partners in a relationship—sometimes with each in turn, sometimes with several simultaneously. You can actually sharpen your empathizing ability to the point where it is possible to feel not only with the mate of your own sex, but also with the mate of the opposite sex and even with the children in the situation. Then, by using all available knowledge, by introspective evaluation, by group discussion, and by insight, you can arrive at some solution for the problem acceptable to *you*. Sometimes this may not be the textbook's solution, or the instructor's solution, or even the group's solution. But because it is your own solution, it can constitute important learning.

The empathetic approach is an adaptation of the case-study method used effectively for many years in studying business administration, law, and other people-oriented specialties. The empathetic approach shares two of the major advantages of the case-study method. First, it takes the student out of the role of passive absorber and makes him a partner in the learning process. Second, the empathetic approach opens free channels of communication among students and between students and professors. It enables a student to make a contribution to the understanding of the whole group. This, in turn, encourages all students to think purposefully and to work harder.

But there are reasons for suggesting that the empathetic approach may be even more significant in the study of marriage and family relationships than the case-study method is in many other disciplines. For one thing, marriage and family relationships deal with the extraordinarily delicate but legally permanent interpersonal arrangements between individual men, women and children. There is more to it than that, though. To understand fully the significance of the use of the empathetic approach in relationships education, it is necessary to examine the recent history of relationships education itself.

MARRIAGE AND FAMILY RELATIONSHIPS EDUCATION

Courses expressly designed to help students with their own marriage and family relationships—later called "functional" courses—were introduced into American colleges and universities in the early 1920s. Although there was a wide variation in the quality of these courses, much of the writing and teaching of early family relationships educators and value-oriented advice aimed at perpetuating traditional middle-class customs and attitudes. As Richard Kerckhoff has pointed out, many of the writers' and teachers' undocumented assertions, both to their students and to their professional colleagues, went unchallenged.[1] Whether there was complete agreement that this was the way things really were or not, most people generally believed that this was probably the way things ought to be or, at least, that this was the way that young people should be told they ought to be.

But in the 1930s, 1940s, and 1950s, depression, war, and social crises not only turned up glaring value contradictions and agonizing value dilemmas, but also brought about large-scale mixing of people from differing value systems, with a consequent dilution of positive value judgments. *Cultural relativism*, with its implication of no absolute right or wrong, good or bad, (since these vary from culture to culture) became more fashionable, and dogmatic conviction became less so. At about the same time that young adults began to reject and ignore many traditional teachings, their parents and teachers became more doubtful about them, too. As America moved into the second half of the century, traditional value-filled education in the home, in the school, and especially in higher education was clearly on the defensive.

In the hallways of the universities, there was new emphasis on avoiding value judgments. There was also a new stress on creating scientific, value-free knowledge in the behavioral sciences and on eliminating any teaching that smacked of the earlier parochialism.[2]

Furthermore, change had become clearly established as a value in itself—perhaps the highest value. That which was traditional had become suspect. People wanted new things; they wanted 1961 cars in 1960—definitely not 1959 cars. And, although there were wide regional and cultural differences, a there-must-be-something-better spirit affected thinking about relationships as well as about automobiles.

[1] Richard K. Kerckhoff, "Teaching Ethical Values Through the Marriage Course: A Debate (Con)," *Marriage and Family Living*, **19** (November, 1957), 330–334.
[2] For a good review of the value versus nonvalue controversy in academic sociology, see R. C. Hinkle, Jr., and G. J. Hinkle, *The Development of Modern Sociology*, New York, Random House, 1954, ch. 2. For specific reference to values in marriage and family relationships education and research, see Harold T. Christensen, ed., *Handbook of Marriage and the Family*, Chicago, Rand McNally, 1964, ch. 24.

A few interpreted "something better" as meaning the rejection of every-thing old or traditional, forgetting C. C. Bowman's succinct warning: "Noting that the mores contain irrationalities, gross generalizations and many other illogi-cal elements, one may easily fall prey to the unwarranted conclusion that dia-metrically opposed beliefs will be rational, logical, scientific."[3]

But there were other, more thoughtful scholars who believed that "some-thing better" involved the application of scientific, reliable knowledge gained in a purified, value-free atmosphere to the problems of interpersonal relationships in marriage and the family. Since most reliable knowledge in the behavioral sciences is obtained by statistical investigations, citing research findings on how some other people behaved became the popular *modus operandi* in relation-ships education. Those students who were seeking academic knowledge as such, without particular reference to its personal significance or usefulness, benefited by this new approach. But for many students faced with individual problems, it turned out to be little more personally enlightening and little more acceptable than the old-style moralizations.

Statistical studies, however well validated and useful in generalizations, can rarely encompass all the complexities of a unique personal situation with enough relevance to clarify an emotional dilemma. For example, knowing the statistics on the number of females who engaged in premarital intercourse at the University of Florida in the 1950s, provides very little meaningful guidance for the young woman who is struggling with an immediate decision in a parked automobile in Seattle. Statistical research is extremely useful, but what the Seat-tle girl's dilemma clearly demonstrates is that *statistical research does not sub-stitute for value judgments in all cases where decisions are needed.* There are at least five reasons why this is so:

Inappropriate Actuarial Research. The first reason is that much of the social research presently being done is of the actuarial type. Although such re-search provides dependable predictions in large numbers of cases, it may pro-vide no prediction whatsoever when applied to a single case. It does not follow, for example, that because 75 percent of married couples have trouble with their in-laws, any particular couple has a 75 percent chance of having in-law troubles.[4] A particular couple has a 100 percent certainty of not having in-law troubles or a 100 percent certainty of having in-law trouble. If all the attitudes and feelings bearing on the relationship of a particular couple and their in-laws were known in advance, it might be possible to predict what the outcome would be. The chance of having trouble is determined by the personalities involved and the patterns of the relationship, not by any frequencies found in the population at large.

In relationships as well as individuals, causation is always personal and never actuarial. As Gordon Allport has said, "The only way to make a certain prediction of effect from cause is to study the life in which the causes operate and not a thousand other lives."[5]

Allport's statement is especially important in a mobile, changing hetero-

[3] Claude C. Bowman, "Hidden Valuations in the Interpretations of Sexual and Family Relationships," *American Sociological Review*, **11** (October, 1946), 543.

[4] A physician lecturing a medical-school class pointed out that in 99 out of every 100 cases, a certain disease was nonfatal. "But," he quickly added, "to each in the other percent, it isn't a 1 percent loss, but a 100 per cent loss."

[5] Gordon W. Allport, *The Use of Personal Documents in Psychological Science*, New York, Social Science Research Council, 1942, p. 157.

geneous society such as ours. In other societies, where patterned role relationships remained relatively stable over hundreds or thousands of years, it might have been possible to predict individual behavior more accurately. For example, in some older societies, a daughter-in-law would have been so rigidly conditioned to be subservient to her mother-in-law that in-law trouble would never have arisen.

Inapplicable to the Specific Situation. A second reason why any indiscriminate substitution of statistical research for value judgments is often unwise is illustrated by the case of the girl in Seattle. Many of the most quoted research studies are both out of date when they are quoted and unrepresentative of the experience of the people to whom they are quoted. Winston Ehrmann's classic study of premarital intercourse at the University of Florida was made in the 1950s and may or may not have any relationship to the situation on the campus at Gainesville today.[6] Moreover, even if it should still be valid there, the chances that it is descriptive of present conditions on a small midwestern campus or at the University of Washington in Seattle is even less probable. Furthermore, even if Ehrmann's statistics had present validity for college students everywhere, they would have, as Kinsey and his associates have clearly shown, almost no meaning for the vast majority in America's noncollege-educated population.[7]

Conflicting Conclusions. A third major problem in the substitution of statistical findings for value judgments in decision-making situations is the question of *which* findings to try to substitute. Reuben Hill, one of the leading advocates and outstanding exponents of family research, pointed out wistfully in 1967 that some of the most highly respected authorities and scholars in the family field have arrived at conflicting conclusions concerning many important family questions.[8] Although such disagreement may be a healthy sign of scholarly growth, it creates severe dilemmas for the student who is seeking personal guidance from research results.

Sometimes it is possible for a sophisticated research specialist to decide which is the more scientifically acceptable of two or several conflicting findings by reference to certain well-established standards of methodology. Often,

[6] Winston Ehrmann, *Premarital Dating Behavior,* New York, Holt, Rinehart and Winston, 1959.
[7] Alfred C. Kinsey, W. B. Pomeroy, and C. E. Martin, *Sexual Behavior in the Human Male,* Philadelphia, Saunders, 1948.
[8] Reuben Hill, "Status of Research About Marriage and the Family," address to the American Association of Marriage Counselors, Washington, D.C., October, 1967. Hill started his list of eleven propositions on which important scholars disagree with "(A.) People tend to marry people like themselves rather than opposites." Here are two other examples from Hill's list and the citations that go with them.
"(E.) The economic factor is not significant in divorce or marriage adjustment. Burgess and Cottrell (Ernest W. Burgess and Leonard S. Cottrell, Jr., *Predicting Success or Failure in Marriage,* Englewood Cliffs, N.J., Prentice-Hall, 1939) and Locke (Harvey J. Locke, *Predicting Adjustment in Marriage,* New York, Holt, Rinehart and Winston, 1951), *for;* Goode (William J. Goode, "Economic Factors and Marital Stability," *American Sociological Review,* **16** (December, 1951), 803–811, Williamson (Robert C. Williamson, "Socio-economic Factors and Marital Adjustment in an Urban Setting," *American Sociological Review,* **19** (April, 1954), 213–216), and Monahan (Thomas P. Monahan, "Divorce by Occupational Level," *Marriage and Family Living,* **17** (November, 1955), 322–324), *against.*
"(G). American families are becoming democratic companionships. Burgess and Locke (Ernest W. Burgess and Harvey J. Locke, *The Family: From Institution to Companionship,* New York, American Book, 1953), *for;* Hill (Reuben Hill, "The American Family: Problem or Solution?" *American Journal of Sociology,* **53** (September, 1947), 125–131) and Johnson (A. L. Johnson, *A Study of the Applicability of Selected Marital Success Criteria in Certain Population Groups,* Minneapolis, University of Minnesota, 1953, Ph.D. dissertation), *against."*

though, this is all but impossible. So it has become classic in modern relationships textbooks, occasionally even in this one, to cite all the studies that the author can find on both sides of the question and let the student choose for himself which is closer to scientific knowledge and thus, presumably, more helpful to him. This has the seeming respectability of being democratic, permissive, and nonbiased. Unfortunately, however, if one is really dependent wholly on facts to make his decision (no value judgments), then not knowing which are the facts can be a disaster.

Prevalence Confused with Excellence. A fourth major consideration in the substitution of statistical research findings for value judgments is the problem of confusing prevalence with excellence. It has been suggested that objective discussions of research findings in our contemporary society, although not intended to do so, sometimes lead people to adopt behavior that they might otherwise have avoided or rejected.[9] "Everyone is doing it" and "It's the latest thing" are very convincing arguments in our modern, fad-conscious, security-needing society.

Curiously, this sometimes puts statistical research in the completely unwanted position of being a "bandwagon technique," one of the very antiintellectual symptoms that those who opposed the teaching of values previously sought to eliminate. This time, however, the presumed values seem to get their authenticity not from being ordained by God or by tradition, but rather from having been statistically blessed by the computer.

Yet, even when a certain behavior can be clearly shown to be both practiced by a majority and brand new to the American scene, its elevation to the status of decision controller only for those reasons is highly questionable. The Nazi debacle in Germany is just one recent confirmation of the historically indisputable proposition that not everything prevalent is good and not every change is progress. This premise is especially true in the area of marriage and family relationships. Some tired old folkways and platitudes may have outlived some of their usefulness, but at least they have the respectability of having been demonstrably workable at one time. In this, they are often more reliable than untested fads and more rational than indiscriminate change seeking.

Emotional Impediments. The fifth reason why statistical research is often an inadequate substitute for value judgments is somewhat the opposite of the fourth. Many people, far from being stampeded by new statistical norms, are emotionally incapable of accepting them even when they are relevant and up to date and might well lead to an improvement in relatability. As we shall see repeatedly throughout this book, each individual carries with him the deeply embedded customs, attitudes, values, and expectations that were conditioned into him in childhood. This emotional conditioning frequently takes precedence over any logical reasoning or any statistical research finding in difficult decision-making situations. These inner compulsions to behave in certain ways *are* the person as he exists at the present moment. Any attempt to change him *immediately* by citing what other people have done, however valid the research, often can lead to further frustration rather than to the resolution of a particular difficulty. The person who says "I am in no mood for logic" is probably right.

Despite these five objections to substituting statistical research for value

---

[9] Harold T. Christensen, "The Intrusion of Values," in Harold T. Christensen, ed., *Handbook of Marriage and the Family*, Chicago, Rand McNally, 1964, p. 982.

judgments, it should be pointed out once more that the problem is not with the research itself. Moreover, when the behavioral-science research that exists today is properly used, it can be a helpful adjunct to the decision-making process even in specific individual situations. For example, knowing that mixed marriages usually require more difficult adjustments than homogamous marriages may help one to prepare himself even though he decides to go through with a mixed marriage anyway.

The most important function of statistical research is validating generalizations—*when generalizations are important.* Curiously, Willard Waller, one of the most respected figures in the history of family studies, questioned this. Said Waller: "No generalization can be so clearly buttressed by facts as one which is definitely supported by one or two well understood cases; generalization from statistics is ever more tenuous and inconclusive than generalization from persons."[10] But few behavioral scientists agree with Waller these days. Most, including myself, feel that ordinarily dogmatic generalization from one case is extremely hazardous. When generalization is appropriate, it is wise, if possible, to discover its limits of generality by statistical techniques. This does not, of course, rule out initial speculation, without which there would be no research hypotheses to test. Nor does it rule out common sense and the manifest evidence of folk behavior without which we would face the ridiculous task of proving and reproving billions of commonly accepted premises from one moment to the next.

It is hoped that in the following pages a neat balance can be achieved by using both case reports for the particularization they can provide and statistical research, where available, to verify the degree and extent of behaviors that comprise our cultural interaction.

THE CASE FOR
THE EMPATHETIC APPROACH

Although the postwar move from advice to statistics may have been a real advance, most students today want something more. They want some definitive criteria by which they can guide their own lives. This has been validated repeatedly, both by research and by clinical interviews. It was a major finding of a study of student attitudes I made in 1962.[11] But modern students don't want those guidelines to be presented as dogmatic advice. Nor do they want equivocations or sterile statistics about other people's behavior. Rather they want to find their own criteria, and make their own decisions, using their own reflective insights.

This leads directly back to the singular importance of the empathetic approach in studying and improving relationships. The empathetic approach tends to diminish didactic lecturing and preaching markedly. Moreover, while it makes use of reliable scientific knowledge, it avoids the necessity of substituting statistical findings for value judgments when decisions have to be made. The empathetic approach also enables each person to arrive at his own direction and conviction through personal insights that are compatible with the emotional residue of the value system he has carried over from childhood. Such new in-

[10] Willard Waller, *The Old Love and the New*, New York, Liveright, 1930, p. 316.
[11] Richard H. Klemer, "Student Attitudes Toward Guidance in Sexual Morality," *Marriage and Family Living*, **24** (August, 1962), 260–264.

sights are usually more easily interpolated into the student's own living experience than the admonishings and urgings of other people.

For all these reasons, the empathetic approach seems to offer real advantage in better preparing the individual for a lifetime of relationships with other people—in marriage, in the family, in the community, and in the individual's professional life. It is training in a scientfic approach to problem solvng that combines the best elements of objectivity and subjectivity. But more, it is practice in "sensitivity," the art and science of perceiving how others feel. As most leaders in business, politics, and human relations will attest, there is no more valuable learning than this.

The idea of using the case method in relationships education is by no means new. In its earliest informal application it antedates all other methods of teaching about family relationships. Willard Waller, as far back as the 1920s, was a strong advocate of the use of personal documents in teaching family relationships. In 1958, Jessie Bernard, Helen Buchanan, and William Smith published an excellent book containing both personal documents and excerpts from fiction that were adapted for case-study use.[12] In 1966, Rose Somerville, Val Clear, and Laurence Smarden published reports of their use of stories, novels, and plays in marriage and family relationships education.[13] These are only a few of those people who have written of their work or expressed their interest in the use of individual situation reports in relationships education in the past two decades.

Some Disadvantages
of the Empathetic Approach

The empathetic approach, like the case method, is not without its disadvantages. For one thing, it takes much more time to arrive at a personally acceptable conclusion than it does to adopt and repeat someone else's generalization or conclusion. In the process of classroom discussion, a good deal of time is often taken with statements by other members that are irrelevant, repetitious, or even mistaken. Sometimes students may express feelings about cases that are unacceptable to other members of the class; there will be more about this later.

The long conditioning that many students have had to the traditional notion that their teacher will provide them with the "right" answers to all problems—including their own—is another difficulty in using the empathetic approach. Some students feel that, having once paid the tuition, they are entitled to all the knowledge the teacher possesses regardless of how inappropriate it may be to the solution of the personal problem under discussion. Even if they recognize that there is no right or wrong answer, they would like, at least, to have the teacher's opinion about every case. Sometimes such a request is not altogether unreasonable; a teacher's opinions can be valuable when they enlarge the student's own insight.

There are still other difficulties with the empathetic approach. Sometimes the problems presented are unsolvable, and sometimes the only solutions are

[12] Jessie S. Bernard, Helen E. Buchanan, and William M. Smith, Jr., *Dating, Mating and Marriage*, Cleveland, Howard Allen, 1958.
[13] Rose M. Somerville, "The Literature Approach to Teaching Family Courses," *Journal of Marriage and the Family*, **28** (May, 1966), 214–216; Val Clear, "Marriage Education Through Novels and Biography," *Journal of Marriage and the Family*, **28** (May, 1966), 217–219; and Laurence Smarden, "The Use of Drama in Teaching Family Relationships," *Journal of Marriage and the Family*, **28** (May, 1966), 219–223.

markedly less than desirable. Using the empathetic approach occasionally can be shattering to romantic illusions and disappointing to cherished ideals.

Yet using the empathetic approach is stimulating and exciting to the degree that it does make relations between people very honest and very real. For this positive reason alone, using the empathetic approach is an adventure in understanding, communication, and personal growth.

What the Empathetic Approach Is Not

It is a great temptation to jump right into the empathetic approach by examining some melodramatic husband–wife conflict that would almost immediately capture the student's interest. However, before one tries out the empathetic approach it is important to be aware of how it differs from some of the common methods of dealing with relationships problems. Let's take, for example, the newspaper advice columns. In addition to being entertaining, these columns provide, in their own way, some useful public services. They help many people to feel better by knowing that others have similar problems, and they offer their letter writers at least some outlet for pent-up frustrations that otherwise might fester. But the empathetic approach has very little in common with newspaper advice, as the following example makes clear.

A letter-writer who identified herself as "Bewildered" wrote to Abigail Van Buren, the well-known newspaper columnist. Said the letter:

> Everyone tells me how lucky I am to have this jewel. Now here's the rub: Bruce (I'll call him) was a bachelor, living with his mother when I married him. I agreed to keep my job until we could afford a nice home. Now, a year later, I have bought all the groceries and paid the rent. Bruce doesn't have one suit of clothes at our apartment. He shaves and showers at his mother's, keeps everything there except his socks and underwear. He even gets his mail there.
>
> I have never seen a bank statement, a paycheck, or a canceled check. All his personal papers and records are locked up in a strongbox at his mother's. When I mention these things to him he just smiles. If I pursue it further he walks away and ignores me. The newspaper is the one thing he buys, and he reads your column, so please print this, and tell me what to do.
>
> Bewildered

The columnist reacted with hard-hitting directiveness. She did what she was asked—she told Bewildered what to do.

> Dear Bewildered:
> Did you marry this little boy, or adopt him? Tell your good-natured "jewel" that he is about to be polished off unless he faces the responsibilities of marriage like a man. And if he doesn't, send his socks and underwear over to his mother's, and add his walking papers with the rest of his "records."[14]

There appears to be much poetic justice in Abby's advice. Most of her readers would nod their heads in thorough approval. And, in the end, this might be the only thing that could be done in the situation.

But the student trained in the empathetic approach to family relations would certainly want to evaluate a great many other alternatives if he were to consider the case of Bruce and Bewildered. First he would try to get more

[14] Abigail Van Buren, "Dear Abby," *Seattle Times*, September 28, 1966, p. 30.

facts. One of the great tragedies of all human relationships (and especially marriage relationships) is that people tend to make important judgments before they know all the details of a situation. In the case of Bruce and Bewildered, the alert student would immediately ask, "What would Bruce have had to say?" We will never know, but let us speculate that his reply might have been something like this: "Bewildered knew that I had obligations to my mother when I married her. As a matter of fact, I protested that we oughtn't to get married when we did because of my financial situation, but she offered to keep working until we could afford everything we wanted. Now she wants to know every last detail of my business. I try to be pleasant about it, but she wants to make a fight out of it. I never was able to disagree with any woman, especially my mother. So I do my best to avoid stirring up hostilities with either Bewildered or my mother, since this would only cause deterioration in the situation rather than improve it."

All these speculations might be justified from what Bewildered said in her letter. And these are speculations that only *defend* Bruce. He might have a hundred charges to make against Bewildered if we ever were able to talk with him.

Even without knowing another thing about Bruce, the insights we can get from Bewildered's letter, combined with what we know and what we shall learn from the work of psychologists, sociologists, and family relationships specialists in the coming chapters, should help us to get some new understanding of the problem involved. For example:

1. Bewildered is a rather insecure person. She is impressed by what "everyone" tells her. She asked Abby to tell her what to do.
2. She really doesn't want to leave Bruce. In fact, she may possibly have been offended by Abby's advice that this might be best. She makes this clear when she tells Abby that she wants Bruce to read Abby's reply. In effect, she is saying, "Please tell him to change, *so that I don't have to leave.*"

But would Bruce change under any circumstances? He almost certainly would not because of being told to, *either* by Bewildered *or* by Abby. His patterns of behaving are, as we shall see in later chapters, the result of deep conditioning processes. Just telling him to change is going to have no effect on him, except perhaps to antagonize him further, and make him sure that his mother was right in the first place. It is almost axiomatic that the only person Bewildered can change is Bewildered.

But does this mean that there is no hope that Bruce might ever change? No, not necessarily. The facts we do have suggest that Bruce is dependent on his mother and neurotic in his inability to break away from her. It is possible that psychotherapy with a skilled professional therapist could help him to reorient his personality needs so that he could cut some of the apron strings. Unhappily, he will probably never seek psychotherapy. Like many other people, he is probably unable to recognize that he needs it. Except for the persistent nagging of Bewildered, which Bruce would undoubtedly see as *her* problem and not his own, he is probably fairly satisfied with the way things are.

Bewildered probably doesn't think she needs psychotherapeutic help either. All she thinks she needs is someone to tell her husband what he should do.

Even without psychotherapy, Bruce will undoubtedly change some over the years. Everyone changes as he grows older. Whether these changes make his personality more flexible or less flexible can depend to some extent on the congeniality and security of the environment in which he is growing older. Bruce could be helped to need and love Bewildered more as the years go by if she will create the climate in which this can occur. Then, when Bruce's mother dies, as she inevitably will, both Bruce and Bewildered could find their needed security in each other.

A third major area that students using the empathetic approach would want to look into would be the inadequate communication between Bruce and Bewildered. As we shall see repeatedly throughout the book, only through genuine communication can there be any understanding. Neither Bruce nor Bewildered has ever developed the ability, desire, security, and selectivity that can make possible real communication between marriage partners. She nags and he ignores, and neither one of them behaves in a manner satisfactory to the other. For most people, nagging is the equivalent of rejection (you don't behave the way you should; therefore you are "bad"). Walking away is obvious rejection. These mutually rejecting behaviors often lead to absolute hostility.

Sometimes, of course, even though nagging is detrimental to interpersonal relationships, it is effective. In cases like Bruce and Bewildered, though, the fact that repeated applications of this treatment have not worked might convince other people that such behavior is never going to work and, therefore, is not conducive to problem solving. But these two apparently persist in their efforts to solve the problem by means that are obviously bankrupt.

It should be recognized, however, that Bewildered's letter to the columnist is at least an *attempt* to do change her tactics. It could be the beginning of some reevaluation on her own part. Yet, even in her letter her communication was inadequate in that she never did make it clear to the columnist that she didn't want to leave Bruce. As one develops more security in communication, one learns to say what he means. We shall see in Chater 17 that it is sometimes necessary to help your listener by expressing your true intent; it is also necessary for your listener to help you by listening to your meaning instead of to your words.

There are several other things that could have been learned from the empathetic approach to Bewildered's problem. First of all, an alert student would have been interested in the fact that Bruce was a bachelor (perhaps too long a bachelor) and would have looked into the professional literature on hard-core bachelors. He would find that there is a tendency for bachelors to have emotional problems to begin with.[15] This is not, of course, true of every bachelor, but the fact that some men resist constant and consistent social and biological pressures toward marriage makes them statistically unusual, even if not psychologically so.

Moreover, the student of the empathetic approach would also have consulted studies of the varieties of ways in which people divide up family spending. It is somewhat unusual to have the wife buy all the groceries and pay all the rent from her salary. Yet there are undoubtedly people who have been able to adjust to this pattern. Why is Bewildered *now* unable to accept her unusual

[15] Genevieve Knupfer, Walter Clark, and Robin Room, "The Mental Health of the Unmarried," *American Journal of Psychiatry,* **122** (February, 1966) 841–851; Paul Popenoe, "The Old Bachelor," *Family Life,* **15** (May, 1953), 1; Edith Lederer, "Bachelors More Unhappy," *Science News Letter,* **87** (May 29, 1965), 342; Eleanor Harris, "Men Without Women," *Reader's Digest,* **78** (February, 1961), 88–90; "Study Disputes Image of Happy Bachelor," *Science Digest,* **49** (June, 1961), 22; and Elisha M. Rallings, "Family Situations of Married and Never Married Males," *Journal of Marriage and the Family,* **28** (November, 1966), 485–490.

role in marriage? Did Bewildered forswear the traditional patterns when she agreed to work in the first place? These are interesting questions that will recur time and again as we examine changed role and financial arrangements between men and women in the problem situations discussed in the following chapters.

Ordinarily in the later cases there will be more feelings and/or facts available than in the case of Bruce and Bewildered. But the process of learning remains the same. It is first important for the student to identify with the *feelings* of the people in the case. Then, using all the psychological, sociological, and family relationships knowledge available to him, he can arrive by his own insights and his own considered evaluations at the most adequate solutions to the problems presented.

Below is a typical relationships problem. Although there are no right and wrong answers to this problem in the usual, mathematics-textbook sense, certain concepts important to the establishment of good relationships should be readily apparent as the student reads through this case.

CASE 1

Mary is now twenty and Al is eighteen. She came from a well-to-do banking family in Spokane; he is from an ex-coal miner's family in Black Diamond, Washington. He is a freshman and she a junior at the University of Washington. Al and Mary knew each other for only three months when they decided to get married. Mary's family, shocked and disappointed, forbade her to marry. So Al and Mary went to Coeur d'Alene, Idaho, on a weekend and were married anyway.

After they were married Mary's parents seemed to become resigned to the idea. Al wanted to drop out of school and go to work in Black Diamond, but Mary's parents offered to pay all the college expenses for both of them and even to provide money for an apartment in Seattle if they would both continue in school. Al didn't think much of that (the truth was that he was failing in several subjects anyway), but because it seemed to be what Mary wanted, he agreed to it.

Al is very close to his family. Al's mother, a plump and friendly woman, has always done everything for the men in the family, picked up their clothes and kept her little house immaculately clean. She feels this is a woman's role, as do her menfolk. Al's mother goes to church regularly and she talks a great deal about religion and what's right, although her grammar is poor and some of her ideas are a little vague. Al's father is a quiet, bashful man who works hard and doesn't like to dress up in city clothes, but who believes in being the boss in his house.

For the first few months of the marriage everything seemed to go well. On the weekends when Al's folks didn't come to visit, Al and Mary traveled the 20 miles to Black Diamond to see them. (Mary's parents rarely came, because Spokane was 290 miles away). But Mary began to get a little tired of Al's folks and their talk about hard-shelled religion. Besides, when Al's mother was around, Mary always felt as if she didn't do enough for Al. His mother would scrub the apartment when she came and bake and sew for Al. Al's people never offered to help pay any of the young people's expenses, even though Mary felt they could provide a token now and then. Whenever Mary mentioned this to Al, he got quite angry and told her he was going to quit school and go to work in Black Diamond.

A month ago, Al reminded Mary that his mother's birthday was coming on the twenty-first of the month and said he had invited his folks over for that weekend. He gave Mary a little money and asked her to buy his mother a fancy nightgown. Mary was fed up by this time and said some ugly things about Al's people coming over all the time. But she got the gown with the money Al had saved, and Al didn't say much more. A week later Mary's people wrote that they would be in Seattle on the twenty-first en route to a resort in Las Vegas. Since the apartment was small, Mary asked Al to uninvite his folks. "After all," she said, "they come all the time." Al refused. Mary got the nightgown and tore it to shreds. Al stamped out.

Three days later, Al came back. He said he had talked with his mother, and she had sent him back to apologize and resume his Christian duty to his wife. He also said that his folks would not be coming to stay overnight. Mary was relieved and immediately invited some of her college friends to meet her parents on the twenty-first.

On Sunday afternoon the twenty-first, just as Mary was serving tea, Al's folks pulled up in their 1959 Plymouth. Al had told them it wouldn't be convenient to stay overnight, but he hadn't said they shouldn't come at all.

Mary blew her top. She screamed at Al's folks and told them exactly what she thought of them. Al told her to shut up. This made her even more furious and she kicked him. Al didn't say any more; he just took his mother by the arm and walked out.

It is now five days since Al left. Mary is tearful; she really loved Al, she protests. She thinks she should stay on in the apartment, wait for him to come back, and then apologize. But her parents have urged her to go with them to Las Vegas and get a quick divorce. She wants your advice.

What would you say to her? What would you say to Al? What should Mary's parents have done? What should Al's parents have done? What could be done to avoid situations like this? What principles of marriage relationships can be extrapolated from this case?

In using the empathetic approach, several additional guidelines may be helpful. First of all, in making your own private analysis, it is very important to analyze the cases, using all the feelings and facts. Avoid, if you can, reading the cases too lightly; stop and make a note of the significant factors as you go along. Remember that using the empathetic approach requires thoughtful concentration and much self-guided reasoning. The following steps are adapted from a list of E. Jackson Baur's techniques for analyzing and interpreting case material in the social sciences.[16]

1. Become as familiar as you can with the concepts and theories of the general field in which you are working. The empathetic approach draws most heavily on concepts from family relations, child development, psychology, and sociology. Many of these concepts will be discussed in this book before cases involving them are presented, but outside reading is helpful.

2. After you have read the case carefully, mull it over. Play with the ideas that flow through your mind, and imaginatively manipulate the facts without rational restraint; generate a "brainstorm."

3. After the preliminary free manipulation, critically sort out the tenable from the untenable insights. Retain those that fit and are consistent with the other facts in the case.

4. Look for hidden meaning in people's statements. Words may conceal unconscious feelings. They may not express what the person really intended. Try to "put yourself in his place" and "feel out" meanings.

5. Distinguish facts from inferences. No case ever contains all the facts that are needed for conclusive interpretation, so to complete the interpretation

[16] E. Jackson Baur, "A Student Guide for Interpreting Case Material," Improving College and University Teaching, 8 (Summer, 1960), 104–108.

you may have to make some assumptions about things that are not reported in the case. Interpolate or extrapolate from the facts that are present or add hypothetical facts that you imagine are probably there because they seem reasonable and plausible. But be careful to identify these as assumptions or inferences.

6. Write out an interpretation for yourself relating the abstract ideas to the concrete events reported in the case. Whenever you use a concept or theory, refer to the concrete facts in the case to which it applies.

7. If the case is very complicated, break it up into smaller units. Then analyze each unit separately and later bring them together. Draw general conclusions from these separately related parts of the case.

A second major guideline for using the empathetic approach is to try to empathize *completely* with all the people in the cases. In the beginning, you may have a tendency to identify only with the person of your own sex or of your own age group. If you continue this, you will be reinforcing old patterns of thinking and relating, and you will be learning nothing new. Practice taking the other's point of view.

A third major guideline is to reemphasize constantly to yourself that rarely, if ever, is any one participant in the situation wholly right or wholly wrong. Even if it were possible to determine it, discovering who is right does not solve a problem. The only constructive analysis of a situation leads to a decision about *what can be done about it now*.

Another guideline is to avoid jumping to conclusions. Very often a case will contain some revealing implications toward the beginning that will trigger an immediate insight. There is a temptation to fix judgment at this point and to go no further. Yet there may be other points later in the case that are not so obvious but that must be taken into account.

It is also important to avoid passing premature judgment of approval or disapproval of a participant in the case. This includes labeling someone's behavior with a common psychiatric term. It doesn't help, for instance, to characterize one of the participants as, say, paranoid. The important thing to know is *why* the person is disturbed and to figure out what can be done to help him.

The fifth guideline is to remind yourself constantly that, in analyzing and discussing cases, although it is wise to know the facts of the particular case and as much as you can about what authorities have said, it is also important not to overlook the value of "common sense." Common sense is one of the important tools in the empathetic approach. Fritz Heider, a leading scholar in the field of social psychology, points out in his book *The Psychology of Interpersonal Relations* that

> In interpersonal relations, perhaps more than any other field of knowledge, fruitful concepts and hunches for hypotheses lie dormant and unformulated in what we know intuitively. . . . Actually, all psychologists use common sense ideas in their scientific thinkings; but they usually do so without analyzing them and making them explicit.[17]

Professor Heider also quotes Alfred North Whitehead, the philosopher, mathematician, and educator:

> . . . Science is rooted in what I have just called the whole apparatus of common sense thought. That is the datum from which it starts, and to which it must

[17] Fritz Heider, *The Psychology of Interpersonal Relations*, New York, Wiley, 1958, p. 5.

recur. . . . You may polish up common sense, you may contradict it in detail, you may surprise it. But ultimately your whole task is to satisfy it.[18]

The sixth guideline is to speak up when the time comes for class discussion of the cases. At first you may find this difficult. Students who have been accustomed to a lecture format and who have been expected only to receive and repeat facts and ideas contained in the lectures and textbooks are often at an intellectual and emotional loss when they must do all the thinking themselves. Professor Charles I. Gragg of Harvard, one of the strong advocates of the case-study method in business administration, has put it this way:

> Not all students can bear the strain of thinking actively, of making independent judgments which may be challenged vigorously by their contemporaries. Many people will always prefer to have answers handed to them. . . . The inherently dramatic and challenging character of the case system, however, although it may produce anxiety and confusion for the newcomer, also arouses his deep interest and leads him to make the effort required for adjustment.[19]

The adjustment to the empathetic approach, as in other case-type learning situations, is usually made in three progressive steps. In the first step, the student discovers that he is unable to think of everything that all his fellow students can think of. He may find it very discouraging to have spent time, thought, and effort considering a particular case and then realize, in listening to his fellow students, that there were many angles that hadn't occurred to him.

This problem usually corrects itself quickly as the student takes the second step: recognizing the need for accepting help from others. As each student gains security, he derives more and more pleasure from cooperative discussion and analysis.

The third and final step toward case-study maturity comes with the recognition that other students and instructors do not necessarily know the "best" answers. Even when they do, each student is still free to disagree. This is especially true in analyzing interpersonal relationships. Because relationships are highly individual matters governed by the values of the individual, the "best" answer for any particular individual is the best answer for *him*. Even though others may see different things than you may see, those that have significance for you are, in your frame of reference, the best.

In class discussion or in your own private discussion with yourself, don't be afraid to make your values explicit. Throughout history, people who have believed strongly in something have accomplished a great deal more than people who did not. Often the believers also had better relationships with other people, for regardless of how we may disagree with someone else, we are usually made more secure by knowing the other person's patterns of thinking and feelings (provided, that is, that those thoughts and feelings don't threaten us directly). Although you have a social responsibility not to monopolize the class hour, you also have a responsibility to contribute your unique viewpoint to the learning experience of the whole group.

Moreover, you can learn much about your values by restating them. You can also learn much about yourself. Why did you feel compelled to contradict at one point? Why were you afraid to speak up at another point? Why did you

---

[18] Alfred North Whitehead, *The Aims of Education and Other Essays*, rev. ed., New York, Macmillan, 1959. p. 159.
[19] Charles I. Gragg, "Because Wisdom Can't Be Told," in Kenneth R. Andrews, ed., *Human Relations and Administration*, Cambridge, Mass.: Harvard Univ. Press, 1955, p. 9.

feel hostile when somebody said so-and-so? Why were you privately gratified when somebody else said such-and-such? Think about it after each class.

In addition to making your values explicit, it is also important to make your assumptions explicit. In no case, either in this book or in real life, will you ever have all the facts about a particular situation. It will be necessary for you to speculate a great deal about how other people involved in the case might be thinking or feeling. But when you use these assumptions, you should clearly recognize that they are assumptions and so label them for the people with whom you are discussing the case. For example, it is best to start out by saying quite frankly, "Assuming that John really was having an affair with Mary, then his wife Betty probably should . . ."

Most of the cases that will provide the largest amount of practice in the empathetic approach will be found in the latter chapters of this book. Preceding them will be significant background information and discussion of the cultural environment in which people live in contemporary society. This too is part of the empathetic approach, because a "frame of reference" and a store of accurate information are, along with insight, necessities for recognizing and evaluating possible solutions to relationships problems.

3

WHAT'S HAPPENING
TO MARRIAGE
AND THE FAMILY?

Relationships can best be understood when they are examined in the context of social history and the predisposing cultural experiences of the individuals concerned. So before examining more cases, let's take a look at what has been happening to marriage and the family.

All the professional observers of the American family agree that there have been many changes in recent times in family experiences and family roles. There most agreement ceases. As America approached the middle of the twentieth century, William Ogburn and Meyer Nimkoff asked eighteen of the best-known family experts to list the most significant changes in the American family in their professional lifetimes.[1] The lack of unanimity in the replies was impressive. The group reported a total of sixty-three changes, but only one change, the increasing divorce rate, was reported by all. Only eight changes were mentioned by at least half the experts.[2] About two-thirds of the reported changes were mentioned by only one or two persons. Said Ogburn and Nimkoff, "That so many changes should be reported is not surprising because the family is a complex social institution with many inter-relations with other institutions, all of which are undergoing extensive changes in our time."[3]

Many of the changes that Ogburn and Nimkoff's experts proposed in the

---

[1] William F. Ogburn and Meyer F. Nimkoff, *Technology and the Changing Family*, Boston, Houghton Mifflin, 1955.
[2] The eight changes were (1) increasing divorce rate (mentioned by all eighteen); (2) wider diffusion of birth control and/or decline in family size (mentioned by twelve); (3) decline in authority of husbands and fathers (mentioned by twelve); (4) increased sexual intercourse apart from marriage (mentioned by eleven); (5) increase in the number of wives working for pay (mentioned by eleven); (6) increasing individualism and freedom of family members (mentioned by ten); (7) increasing transfer of protective functions from family to state (mentioned by ten); (8) decline of religious behavior in marriage and family (mentioned by nine).
[3] Ogburn and Nimkoff, *op. cit.*, p. 6.

late 1940s appear to be still in progress. These include the decline in the authority of husbands and fathers, the increase in premarital and extramarital sexual intercourse, the increase in the number of wives working for pay, the increase in individualism and freedom of family members, the decline of relig- ious behavior in marriage in the family, and the transfer of family functions.

The decline in family size, which the second largest number of experts mentioned, did not materialize as expected, and the birth rate continued to rise until 1956, when it reached a peak and began to decline. By 1968, the rate in the U.S. had dipped to the lowest recorded in modern times.

The divorce rate, the only item universally cited by all of Ogburn and Nimkoff's experts, is now on a slowly rising curve after dropping markedly from an all-time high at the end of World War II. There were 301 divorces per thou- sand marriages in 1945, 231 per thousand in 1950, 246 in 1955, 258 in 1960, 266 in 1965, and 279 in 1967. It should be noted that, although such figures for divorces reflect marriages made in earlier decades, if these rates continue for another generation, over a quarter of those who marry will be divorcing. See Table 3–1.

Even when measured in terms of divorces per thousand population, the rate of divorce increase is substantial. The divorce rate per thousand population rose from 2.2 in 1957 to 2.7 in 1967—more than a 20 percent increase in the rate in the decade.

The sharp dip from the inflated divorce rates in the post–World War II years and the relatively slow rise led some sociologists in the 1950s and 1960s to hypothesize that perhaps a realistic minimum rate consistent with our present "happiness-oriented" marriage value had been reached. The divorces were seen by these observers as "safety-valve" escapes for those who did not find the hap- piness they expected and thus were socially valuable.

This conclusion, however, ignores the fact that while the rate per thou- sand population may be down since 1946 and has risen only slowly in the past decade, the percentage of divorces involving people who have children is up dramatically—from 42 percent in 1948 to 60 percent in 1967.[4] Moreover, there are significantly more separations, more desertions, and more annulments than

Table 3–1
Divorce Rate per 1000 Marriages

Year	Marriages	Divorces	Divorce Rate per 1000 Marriages
1940	1,595,879	264,000	165.42
1945	1,612,992	485,000	300.68
1950	1,667,231	385,144	231.00
1955	1,531,000	377,000	246.24
1960	1,523,000	393,000	258.04
1965	1,800,000	479,000	266.11
1966	1,844,000	494,000	267.89
1967	1,913,000	534,000	279.14

Source: U.S. Department of Health, Education and Welfare, *Monthly Vital Statistics of the United States: Annual Summary*, Washington, D.C., 1967, and *Vital Statistics of the United States, 1965*, vol. 3.
Note: Figures include annulments as well as divorces.

[4] U.S. Department of Health, Education and Welfare, *Monthly Vital Statistics Report*, **18** (supplement), April 16, 1969; and Paul Jacobson, *American Marriage and Divorce*, New York, Holt, Rinehart and Winston, 1959.

ever before. In many large American cities (Los Angeles, for example), more people seek to break marriages legally than seek to make marriages legally in most months out of the year. In some recent years such diverse areas as Oklahoma County in Oklahoma and San Mateo County in California actually have reported marriage "deficits," because more people actually did get divorces, annulments, and separations over the entire year than got married. Neither of these places was a "divorce haven" with easy laws designed to encourage out-of-state divorce. San Mateo County, just south of San Francisco, has many of the characteristics that epitomize affluent space-age suburbia. Such figures from an area reputed to be where the fad-makers live is an ominous sign for family stability.

So, despite the seemingly slow rise in the national divorce rate over the past half-century, American marriage is becoming increasingly fragile in fact and possibly even more so in attitude. Alan Hoehler, writing in *Harper's Bazaar*, observed in 1966 that the divorcing woman of the space age is merely conforming to "another tack of fashion." Moreover, "divorce puts her in the driver's seat. It's almost better to have loved and lost, period."[5]

Marriage disruption has some of the characteristics of an endemic disease. First, it is a problem, ranging from inconvenience to tragedy, for those who are affected by it, regardless of what percentage of the population they represent. To the million or more children affected by their parents' divorce or separation in any recent year, the fact that they are part of a statistic that is rising only slowly is of very little comfort.

Second, like any infectious disease, divorce tends to breed divorce. Often people who have been divorced tend to rationalize their behavior both to themselves and to their married friends. Some consciously or unconsciously begin to act as missionaries and propagandists for divorce by enlarging on the joyfulness of being single again. Other divorcées give prestige to divorce without ever expressing their feelings. Just the fact that *they* were divorced gives tacit stature to divorce in their friends' eyes. Occasionally, people who might otherwise have been able to work through their own responsibilities and problems to a full and happy later married life are so affected by their divorced "friends" that they abandon their efforts to make their own marriages work.

To continue the analogy, marriage dissolution, again like a disease, tends to leave a residue that cannot help but cost the community. Just as desertion is notorious for increasing the public-welfare costs, many legally divorced people also become public charges when ex-breadwinners skip to other states. Often, though, financial cost is the least expensive part of the heavy divorce cost; for, whereas some people do experience relief after divorce, for others the price in emotional distress and unhappiness is all but unmeasurable.

SCHOLARLY ANALYSES
OF THE CHANGING FAMILY

The changes in modern marriage and family life have been defined, classified, and explained in many ways. Well-known scholars have written erudite books and developed elaborate theories. Notable among them is the cyclical theory of Carle C. Zimmerman. In his *Family and Civilization*, Zimmerman traced the life cycle of family systems throughout the history of Western civilization. He de-

---

[5] Alan Hoehler, "The Gay Divorced," *Harper's Bazzar* (November, 1966), 182.

scribed a regular pattern or movement from the "Trustee Family," in which all individual rights are subordinated to the welfare of the family group, to the "Domestic Family," in which family control is weakened although the family remains essentially a strong unit. From the Domestic Family there is a predictable movement to the "Atomistic Family," in which familism is replaced by individualism. The Atomistic Family is both the cause and the effect of decay in social life. In its latter stages, there is little real meaning in the marriage ceremony, widespread adultery, acceptance of sexual permissiveness, easy divorce, childlessness, and delinquency.[6]

Zimmerman clearly believed that, like Greece and Rome before us, the United States was in the final stages of the evolution to the Atomistic Family. The best hope for renewed greatness, or even survival, he thought, was to swing back toward the Domestic Family and toward the social strengths associated with it.

Another of the classic theories of family change is the structure-function theory for which Talcott Parsons is a well-known spokesman. Instead of believing that we are headed toward destruction as a result of recent changes in our marriage and family behavior, Parsons has suggested that the changes were functional adaptations to the increasing specialization of other institutions in our society. He believed that the modern family is doing the only thing it can to meet the requirements of a changing society.[7]

Although these comprehensive systematic theories of marriage and family change have important usefulness to the professional sociologist, the student interested in the practical relationships problems of modern relationships needs more limited and more directly applicable explanation.

It seems to me that much of what has happened to the marriage relationship in this century can be subsumed under one of two headings: (1) the change in determination to stay married or (2) the loss of satisfaction in marriage because of unrealistic marriage expectations. We will examine each of these areas in detail (determination in this chapter, satisfaction in the next), because they will provide a frame of reference for the entire empathetic approach. Although the emphasis will be on the changing relationship between the marriage partners, some discussion of family structure and function will be involved as well.

THE CHANGE
IN DETERMINATION

It is probable that the primary reason for the continuing increase in the fragility of marriage is that happiness has replaced stability as the major goal of marriage partners. Since happiness is more elusive and less easily measured than stability, it is now much easier to convince oneself that a marriage has failed.

A hundred years ago the most important values in marriage were staying married, producing children, and continuing to exist in spite of merciless natural forces that made existence difficult. Generally, both partners took satisfaction and pride in this.[8] In those days a man needed a wife. She was an economic

[6] Carle C. Zimmerman, *Family and Civilization*, New York, Harper & Row, 1947.

[7] Talcott Parsons, "The Social Structure of the Family," in Ruth N. Anshen, ed., *The Family: Its Function and Its Destiny*, New York, Harper & Row, 1959, pp. 241–274.

[8] Not always, though. William Goode warns against the tendency to stereotype the "good old" American farm family of the past. The interested student should read William J. Goode, *World Revolution and Family Patterns*, New York, Free Press, 1963, ch. 1.

asset to him in many ways. Not only did she cook and clean, but she also put up the vegetables that made it possible for him to live until the next harvest. Additionally, she produced children, and they, too, were economic assets. It was said that a good catch for a young bachelor before the Industrial Revolution was a healthy widow with six children, for he would have suddenly acquired fourteen hands to help him.

For the woman, too, there was a satisfaction in a stable marriage relationship and in working hard to make the marriage stable. A woman's very existence depended upon her husband, and her emotional satisfaction came from serving him and seeing to it that he had cleaner shirts and better food than the neighboring husbands.

Today, the marriage ideal is "happiness" for each of the marriage partners, and this happiness is often expected to come with the marriage. Since it is no longer absolutely necessary for people to spend their entire lives grubbing out a marginal existence, happiness *is* a more realistic goal than it ever was before. The important question, though, is how that happiness is achieved. If each partner is expecting to receive bountiful happiness from the marriage without giving anything to it, someone is bound to be disappointed. For marriage is a giving relationship—especially after the children arrive. This has not changed. It is as true today as it was a hundred years ago.

In every relationship between two people, inevitably there will be some less ecstatic moments. In the past, these were more often tolerated or shrugged off, but today they have become moments for decision about whether or not to continue the marriage. With divorce as an easy alternative, the modern couple's toleration level has declined dramatically.

This change in determination to stay married has been greatly increased by some recent and often overlooked social changes. For an example, now we live in a society where a woman is not dependent upon some man, be it husband, father, or brother, for her very existence. Today a woman can leave her husband, settle down a thousand miles away, and support herself in some culturally approved activity. Often she can make more money than the man she left.

This has given women the same kind of tacit threatening power that men have always had. A wife *can*, with relative security, say to her husband, "If you don't behave like the lover I want, I will leave you." And usually a permissive society will allow her to do just that.

The editors of *Newsweek*, in commenting in 1967 on the modern woman's relative lack of determination to stay married, said:

> What underlies the failure of so many mature marriages is not a new form of friction—but a new unwillingness to tolerate the old frictions. In the age of the pill, the sexual revolution and the feminine mystique, the notion that happiness takes precedence over family solidarity has clearly captured the female imagination.[9]

MORE INTERSEX CONTACTS

There are other reasons, too, for the modern loss of determination. One is the more frequent contact of married partners with friends and co-workers of the opposite sex. Today a modern young wife who works outside the home may

---

[9] "The Divorced Woman—American Style," *Newsweek*, **69** (February 13, 1967), 65.

see more attractive men in a week's time than her great-grandmother back on the farm saw in a lifetime. Moreover, the modern young woman may work side by side with some of these men at a task requiring close cooperation that is more interesting than the routine work she must do (with or without the presence or assistance of her husband) when she returns home at the tired end of the day.

CASE 2

"My marriage is breaking up," Molly told the counselor. "I know exactly what is happening, yet I don't seem to be able to do anything about it. It isn't me and it isn't my present husband, Chuck—it's just the way of modern living. I'm as guilty as Chuck is because I was the reason he broke up his first marriage. But if it happens again, it's just going to compound the tragedy for everybody.

"I married Ross, my first husband, while we were both in college. With a little help from our parents, we both managed to finish. Then he got a job in personnel work at a department store and did fairly well. We decided not to have a family right away so we could have some fun for a while. We had a nice apartment in a big complex in Los Angeles where there were a lot of other young couples. There were many expenses, though, especially because of the weekend parties and skiing trips.

"At first I didn't work. I cleaned up the apartment for an hour or so in the morning and spent much of the rest of the day around the swimming pool. But after a while I got very bored. Most of our friends began having babies and moving away. So when I was offered a job with a broadcasting network as a typist, I decided to take it. We needed the money right then.

"I started working in the typing pool. But I did very well and soon was assigned to be Chuck's private secretary. He was a rising young executive, married, with two children. He was a fine, straightforward, clean-cut guy and he still is. At first, our only interest in each other was that he was the boss and I was the secretary. But he was a hard worker, and he knew just how to handle me. Before you know it I became terribly interested in doing my work well and in working *with* him. Inside of a year I had more to talk about with Chuck in the eight hours we spent together each day than I did with Ross in the few hours we had together before bedtime.

"I met Chuck's wife several times. She was mostly interested in talking about her children and what she did at the bridge club. She didn't know very much about what was going on at the office, and she didn't seem at all interested.

"Well, you can guess what happened. Before long I fell in love with Chuck and he with me. I really don't think it was our fault. It was just the way things are today. So we each asked for a divorce. Ross didn't raise much of a fuss. I think he was already interested in a girl at his office, because he married her within a few weeks after our decree became final.

"But Chuck's wife threw a fit. She threatened to contest the divorce, and she said an awful lot of nasty things about me and about Chuck's lack of responsibility. He wound up having to pay her a lot of alimony and child support. I don't think the money part bothered him as much as having to give up his children, although he never talks about that now.

"But the money part bothered *me*. Now that we are married I resent having to give up a large part of our income to keep that woman. Moreover, now Chuck and I have three children of our own, and I have to deny them some things because Chuck's first wife is too lazy to support herself.

"The worst part about all this is that now I see it happening all over again. Chuck and I don't have very much in common anymore. I stopped working at his office five years ago, and he stops listening when I talk about children and the things that happen to me at home. But that's all I have to talk about now. I know that some women can't talk about anything else besides their children, but I don't think I'm that bad. I try very hard to keep up with current events and the news. But I have a feeling that I'm losing out to his new secretary. I've met her several times, and the same things that attracted *me* to Chuck are attracting *her* to him. He's a leader, and she's married to an inadequate, mousy little guy. I've confronted Chuck with my fears several times, but he just tells me I'm imagining things. What am I going to do?"

What can she do? What might she have done?

CHANGING LAWS
AND ATTITUDES

The liberalization of the divorce laws and changing public opinion about divorce have contributed to the increasing fragility of the marriage relationship in modern times. In the past, some people were obliged to stay married because they had no legitimate grounds for a divorce in their state and no stomach for deserting their spouse. Ordinarily the legal problems could be surmounted, either by manufacturing evidence (as was common practice in New York State before 1967, when the only grounds was adultery), or by moving to a state where more easily proved grounds, such as incompatibility or mental cruelty, were accepted. Nevertheless, the stricter divorce laws in some states were probably a deterrent to divorce, if only because it was expensive to move or to manufacture evidence.

Public opinion was also a deterrent in times past. As recently as two generations ago, divorce was looked upon in some areas as a sin, and mothers lowered the shades when a divorcée walked past the house so that the children would be protected from the sight of evil. I was told of a case as late as 1966 in which a high-school principal in a modern industrial city suggested to one of his teachers that she not tell the students that she had been divorced lest the parents protest that their childen were being taught by a divorcée.

In general, however, today's new ease and casualness about divorce have led many, especially many young people, to take a "let's-try-it-and-see" attitude toward marriage. Determination to make it work is downgraded from the very beginning. It is tacitly understood by both partners that, if their happiness is not increased—or at least maintained—by marriage, they will end the relationship.

In her remarkable book *Advice from a Failure,* Jo Coudert made a strong plea for some reversal of this trend.

> The worst piece of advice I have ever been given was: "Go ahead and get married. If it doesn't work out, you can always get a divorce." It made marriage sound so easy, like accepting a job that has been offered because if you do not like it you can quit and do something else. Even at nineteen, I should have known better, but, alas. . . .
>
> Marriage is not a job, and divorce is not two weeks' notice and out. There is no hell like a bad marriage; divorce, although it may be a relief when it comes, is a highly public and painful admission of failure; and after divorce, you are not simply single again, back where you were before marriage. If a nineteen-year-old were to ask my advice now, I would say the opposite of

what I was told, that is, that marriage should be contemplated as though there were no such thing as divorce. The possibility should be shut out of mind completely, and all the years of a life with this person envisioned: locked in, no escape hatch, forever committed. Is it a bearable thought, or is the prospect of marriage only intriguing because there is a way out if the going gets rough?

If the latter, remember this: until you can squeeze through the trapdoor, you are locked in, and two people can do each other serious and lasting damage in the enclosed space of a marriage. Wounds are inflicted the scars of which are borne for a lifetime. Far more anxiety and depression are involved than could have been predicted. There is ugliness. There is unexpected trauma. It is impossible to escape unscathed, or even lightly scathed, from a marriage. Between in and out, there is a bruising road to travel, and it is infinitely preferable to reconnoiter the road sanely before setting foot on it than to embark on it casually and take a chance on what lies around the bend.[10]

It is important to note Coudert's deliberate reference to the relief some get from divorce. There are people who are manifestly happier when they are released from intolerable relationships. But without arguing the merits of any particular divorce action, the importance of avoiding a "try-and-see" attitude before marriage can be emphasized. Consider the following case.

CASE 3

John and Margaret were persuaded to come to the marriage counselor by her mother, even though Margaret thought that it would be simpler just to continue with the divorce. They had been married for three years and had two little children. "It's very simple," Margaret said. "We just don't love each other any more. I guess the marriage just never should have been. As a matter of fact, I had some doubts about it even before we got married, but it just seemed simpler to go through with it and try it out."

Then she went on, "We just don't like to do the same things. I like to go out to exciting places and do things in the evening, and all he wants to do is sit at home and watch television. In the beginning I tried to interest him in modern art and music, but he just brushed me off, and I soon decided it wasn't worth it. Why bother? I have seen lots of attractive men. As a matter of fact, I know one right now who is very interested in me. He works where I do and we have a great deal in common. He's exciting when he talks and he's interested in almost everything.

"I have a very good job and it's never dull," she continued. "I get paid well enough so that I can easily support the children, and with the child-support money the court will make him pay, I can have enough household help so that life will actually be easier than it is now. He never did make very much anyway, and he isn't very ambitious. I guess I married him because I felt a little sorry for him. It seemed like the whole world was against him and I wanted to help him. But I soon found that he really didn't want my help; he just wants to live the way that he wants to.

"I really don't know what I'm doing here talking to a marrage counselor. I don't love him anymore, and it would be silly to continue the marriage. I think it would be best to get out now while I am still young and still attractive and can easily get another husband if I want to. If we go on living together, we will just compound our problems for both of us and might even have more children to hurt when we finally did separate."

Now his side of the story: "She's got that fancy job and all sorts of social life at the office where she works," he said. "She's constantly nagging me to do things that I don't want to do and, believe me, it's just plain hell. I'm not opposed to going out if there's any good reason for going. But she doesn't want to do the things I want to do, like going to football games. I'd even take her to her stupid old operas once in a while, but that isn't enough for her. She says I have to *enjoy* it or it isn't worthwhile for her. I want a good old-fashioned wife who stays home and takes care of the kids and lets me do the providing. Instead I get a wife who wants to go out all the time and expects me to come home and help her with the housework.

"You know," he went on, "she wasn't at all like this when we were going together. She let me think that she wanted to do all the things that I wanted to do, and that all she wanted to do in life was to help me. I still love her and I love my children. I don't want a divorce."

If you were the judge, would you grant these people a divorce? Would you do so if they had only been married for three months and had no children? What would you do if you were Margaret? If you were John?

THE EFFECT OF CHANGING
FAMILY FUNCTIONS

Of the many social changes that have affected people's determination to stay married, none is more important than the loss of the traditional family functions. It is classic among family sociologists to point out that the family has lost or greatly diminished its production function, its educational function, its protective function, and much of its recreational, governmental, and child-care function.[11]

Practically everything consumed in the family in our early agricultural society was produced in the family—food, clothing, and shelter. Today, however, relatively little is produced in the urban or suburban family, except on a hobby basis. Sewing, baking, and woodworking, which used to be regular responsibilities of the family members, have now been turned over to bakers and manufacturers. Today, the bread mixes and do-it-yourself kits are often more recreational than functional.

The educational function has also dwindled to a shadow of its former self. Formal education has been turned over to the school, and vocational education is now often the responsibility of industry. In this technological age, very few parents are equipped to prepare their sons and daughters for the profession in which they will earn their living. Religious education has been turned over to the church (if, indeed, the child gets any religious training whatsoever). Even family-life education, including sex education, has tended to become a province of other institutions because of family default in this area.

There has been a transfer of the protective function outside the family as well. In the early days, the father protected the family from intruders, human

[11] William F. Ogburn authored the best-known exposition of the loss of functions in the American family and the dilemma that was thereby caused. He postulated seven lost functions—economic, status-giving, educational, religious, recreational, protective, and affectional—and indicated that only the affectional remains vigorous in modern times. Recently Clark Vincent pointed out that Ogburn probably had in mind that it was the *traditional content and form* of the functions that were lost; the basic functions themselves were merely changed. For example, the economic production function was changed to the economic consumption function. See Clark E. Vincent, "Mental Health and the Family," *Journal of Marriage and the Family*, **29** (February, 1967), 18–39.

and animal, with his rifle, and the mother's home remedies were the only protection the family had against disease. Without police and without many doctors, this was the way it had to be. Now, most families rely almost exclusively on outside professionals for their protection.

The extent to which the family has forsworn its recreational function is debatable. Those who romanticize the "good old days" insist that almost all family recreation occurred in or near the bosom of the home. They think of the nostalgic scene of father and mother and all the children singing around the old parlor piano. It is undoubtedly true that, because of the difficulties in transportation and the sparsity of neighbors, much of the recreation did take place in the family. However, in the urban complexes that developed after 1800, there was a considerable amount of visiting to the public house by the male adults and a considerable amount of group activity among the children. In the early twentieth century, as public transportation developed and as such public recreation facilities as the movies began to spring up, more family members sought recreation outside the home.

Since the advent of television and the thirty-five-hour workweek, the typical space-age family (not including the teenagers, who generally want to get away by themselves) may be spending more time at home than they used to. This is not to say that they are spending that time together: They may have three or four different television sets going in different rooms, or they may each be enjoying separate hobbies. At any rate, the typical modern family is not going to the movies or visiting with friends as much as it was a few decades ago.

Those who do enjoy going outside the home for recreation are doing so much more frequently than formerly, a trend initiated by the two- or multi-car family and encouraged by the wide variety of recreational enterprises available. Attendance at all sporting events is up enormously. This may be accounted for in part by prosperity among socioeconomic groups who formerly could not afford to do anything but sit at home. Moreover, the automobile makes possible quick and easy transportation to the many commercial recreation sites. Various family studies have indicated that the "most enjoyable" recreation for the family is recreation outside the home.

In addition to maintaining and protecting its children, the family has a major function in socializing them. In some parts of the world, there is a trend toward more and more public upbringing. Although this is not yet a significant trend in the United States, here there is a tendency toward the lengthening of school hours and the establishment of preschools, day-care centers, and federally sponsored programs like Head Start that provide both education and outside-the-home care for the children of working mothers. In many communities, because of this lengthening of the school day, outside-the-home feeding has become a part of public education.

Another function of the American family that has changed considerably is the governmental function. As in most other societies, the American family is the first social group exercising control over the individual. However, American families now generally impose fewer restrictions on their offspring than before and deliberately allow them more independence. In part, this may be caused by parental reaction to the confusion over what is right and what is wrong in child rearing, but in part it may be an effort to train children to make decisions and so become self-reliant. Whatever the cause, the immediate effect is apparent: Modern American boys and girls have much more independence and much less control then they did previously.

SOME FUNCTIONS
HAVE BEEN ENLARGED

The same series of technological changes that have diminished the need for some of the traditional functions of the family have also increased the need for other functions. For example, the *executive* function of the family has been enormously increased in recent years. Although it is no longer necessary for the family to produce the goods in a direct way, it is now very necessary to plan the consumption and make a myriad of quantity and quality decisions.

William Goode has pointed to the family's *mediating* function, in which the family is a buffer between the individual and the larger society. Clark Vincent has suggested that the family has an *adaptive* function. He sees the family as being an important agent for translating the demands of other social institutions into the child socialization process.[12] Vincent points out that, because the family lacks the institutional organization with which to resist changes thrust upon it, it must adapt itself and help its members to adapt to a changing society.

It seems reasonable to speculate, however, that the greatest proportionate increase in family function in recent years has been in the affectional function. In our modern, tension-filled society with fewer primary group contacts (that is, contacts with family friends, neighbors, and relatives), the family has in some cases become a greater source of solace, comfort, and vital personal attention. Today American men have their wives as friends to a degree that is unusual throughout the rest of the world. In other times and in other places, men more often sought companionship not at home but in the local pub or in the boudoirs of their mistresses. The affectional relationship, both romantic and companionate, is now a major function and cohesive force that provides the determination to hold most American families together.

There are those who believe that the family is finished as a social institution. Barrington Moore contends that the family is no longer functionally necessary and that it is probably disfunctional in a modern industrial society.[13] He thinks that the current theories of the survival of the family are merely projections of middle-class hopes. Since kinship is obsolete, says Moore, there is no longer any obligation to give affection, and there is no reason to fear the transfer of responsibility for the children from parents to professionals. He argues that aristocrats have always turned the responsibility of child rearing over to servants; now, in the space age, it is possible for all of us to be aristocrats.

Moore has few followers in modern social thought. Although the experts agree that the family has changed and will continue to change, most authorities see the family as a continuing institution in our society. In fact, there are some, like myself, who believe that in our modern, computerized, impersonal society, it is more important than ever that each person have someone who is loyally committed to him and who will provide warmth, acceptance, and understanding. Robert Coombs points out that most people desperately need someone who will bandage up a bruised ego at the end of a day and who will genuinely believe that "you must have been right; it was he who was wrong."[14] It is even more satisfactory when the loyal companion is of the opposite sex and the rela-

[12] William J. Goode, *The Family*, Englewood Cliffs, N.J., Prentice-Hall, 1964, p. 2; and Clark E. Vincent, "Family Spongia: The Adaptive Function," *Journal of Marriage and the Family*, **28** (February, 1966), 29–36.
[13] Barrington Moore, *Political Power and Social Theory*, Cambridge, Mass., Harvard Univ. Press, 1958, pp. 160–178.
[14] Robert Coombs, "Problems in Mate Selection," address to the Seminar on Family Problems, University of North Carolina, Greensboro, N.C., June, 1968.

tionship is enriched by the warmth of sexual love. And there is still greater richness when a man and woman have the mutual satisfaction of overcoming difficult problems in guiding dependent children. It is very improbable that Moore or anyone else is going to find an emotionally significant substitute for this biologically and culturally conditioned affectional function in the near future.

A FINAL NOTE
ON DETERMINATION

Toward the end of the report of their monumental study of *Sexual Behavior in the Human Male,* Dr. Kinsey and his associates swing away from their in-depth analysis of sexual behavior long enough to make a revealing comment—almost an aside—on marriage. After examining 6000 marital histories, nearly 3000 divorce histories, and after having reported 544 laborious pages of technical data, the sex researchers agree that their research "suggests that there may be nothing more important in a marriage than a determination that it shall persist. With such a determination, individuals force themselves to adjust and to accept situations which would seem sufficient grounds for break-up, if the continuation of the marriage were not the prime objective."[15]

The importance of determination in making marriages successful would be hard to overestimate. A great many successfully married people have reported that, if it weren't for a rugged determination on the part of both partners to make it succeed, their marriages would have failed. A final appropriate footnote to determination is added by one young woman who quite candidly conceded that the only reason she had a happy and successful marriage now was that her mother died not long before her marriage and her father was overseas for an extended period. "I couldn't go running home the way my friends did," she said. "I thought it was a tragedy then. Now I see it was the best thing in the world. It made me work to solve our problems. Some of my friends weren't so lucky. They are divorced now."

[15] Alfred C. Kinsey, W. B. Pomeroy, and C. E. Martin, *Sexual Behavior in the Human Male,* Philadelphia, Saunders, 1948, p. 544.

4

SATISFACTION
IN MARRIAGE

Despite the present dedication to the pursuit of happiness in marriage, many people appear to lose satisfaction when they marry. Understanding why this is so becomes much simpler if you accept one postulate: In order to achieve satisfaction in anything (and especially in marriage), you must first know what you expect, and also what is expected of you; then you must do what is expected better than others expected you could. If too much is expected, if what is expected of you is not made clear, or even if not enough is expected, it is not probable that you will get very much satisfaction. All three of these conditions—too-great expectations, confused expectations, and inadequate expectations—are present in modern marriage and family relationships. We will take a look at each of them in turn.

TOO-GREAT
EXPECTATIONS

Most young men have always had to compete with a variety of fantasy heroes for their true love's affection. But in the past, the competition has never been as it is now. Today the typical young husband is constantly compared to the best athlete's manliness and the finest gentleman's manners. Television and the broad contacts of modern social living make this inevitable. Unhappily, however, relatively few of our young males can consistently stand up to this kind of comparison. Although this expectation problem usually develops after marriage, it has its roots in childhood and adolescence, when some of the marriage expectations are formed.

This very evening, for example, millions of girls and young women all over the country will watch the latest television hero perform in an idealized setting and act in a manner deliberately calculated to stir emotions. As they watch, these young women will be developing attitudes and ideals. They will be consciously or unconsciously developing expectations about the men they will marry and the marriages they will have. In these fantasies, *their* men will have all the resoluteness, decisiveness, intelligence, perception, good looks, and wealth of the television hero. In addition, *their* men will naturally have all the desirable attributes of the girls' fathers. Almost imperceptibly these dreams will become internalized—that is, they will become fixed expectations—whether the girls know it or not.

Clearly, it is not only television that creates all the expectations, nor is it only females who develop unrealistic expectations. All over the country tonight young men will watch glamorous television heroines and will dream about the wives they will one day have. *Their* wives will be paragons of beauty, charm, poise, and elegance; they will be sweet, kind, tender, and loving, and, in addition, they will have unquestioned skills as homemakers, mothers, and sex partners. They will also be fine cooks, appliance mechanics, chauffeurs, purchasing agents, accountants, child psychologists, and psychiatrists for their husbands. Moreover, they will be warm and tender, submissive, agreeable, and adaptable, and their goals in life will be to fulfill their husbands' every wish.

The fact that these attitudes and expectations are acquired in childhood increases the importance of their effect on later satisfaction in marriage, for childhood expectations—like childhood attitudes and values—have a way of becoming conditioned to the point where they attain emotional dominance over later intellectual learning. By the time many young people are in high school, their expectations for the roles and behaviors of their prospective mates are already well established.

Marie Dunn, in her study of high-school boys and girls in Louisiana, found that in her sample it was not uncommon for high-school boys to have expectations of how their wives would behave that differed markedly from the way in which girls in the same high school expected to behave as wives. And vice-versa. Likewise, the girls had expectations of the way their husbands would behave different from the boys' expectations of how they would behave as husbands.[1] Obviously, the seeds of marital discord were already planted.

If television were the only source of internalized attitudes, its effect might be only to create similarly unrealistic expectations in both boys and girls, because both would be exposed to some of the same playacting. But expectations derive from a randomly ordered combination of highly emotional attitudes and values gained from one's family living *and* his peer-group experiences, as well as from the world of make believe. An overindulgent family, for example, can create as many—if not more—unrealistically high expectations as can the picture tube and the printed word.

How Expectations
Affect Marriage

Often, marriage dissolution starts with the early disenchantment that results when a partner first discovers that his mate is incapable of meeting his expectations. Peter Pineo has pointed out that men often suffer disenchantment earlier in marriage than women, perhaps because their expectations are more unreal-

---

[1] Marie S. Dunn, "Marriage Role Expectations of Adolescents," *Marriage and Family Living*, **22** (May 1960), 99–104.

istic in the first place. But which is the first to be disillusioned is unimportant. Sooner or later one partner's disillusionment will affect the other, and the entire relationship will suffer.[2]

Some years ago, Sidonie Gruenberg and Hilda Kretch suggested that, as far as the reality of expectations was concerned, the less-advantaged girls were often luckier than those brought up in luxury. Having had less-pampered childhoods, the less advantaged were likely to be much more aware of the realities of the modern marriage relationship, including the long hours of routine involved in actual homemaking and the limitations on one's social life when small children must be cared for.[3]

In this same general vein, I recall that while I was walking through the waiting room of a large marriage counseling clinic, I was struck with the over-representation of beautiful women waiting for help with marriage problems. In later discussion with other colleagues, the hypothesis was developed that the plain or average-looking young women might have possessed more realistic expectations of what the marriage relationship would provide them in terms of attention from *one* husband, because before marriage they had not been accustomed to a great deal of attention from large numbers of males.

MARRIAGE ROLES

Satisfactions in marriage have been decreased, not only by unrealistically high expectations, but also by the downgrading of the respective roles of husbands and wives. The typical young father today, while still having responsibility for the welfare of the family, often finds that he has responsibility without much authority. His pride in being a "good provider," which was a strong motivating force in bygone generations, has been undermined by a frantic effort to "keep up with the Joneses." This is always a frustrating game, because there are always higher-statused Joneses to keep up with.

Many young fathers have also lost the ego-building satisfaction of knowing more than anyone else in the family. Today the wife is liable to have had more schooling than her husband, and, even in well-educated families, the children are often better informed than the parents, as a result of watching television and the increasing emphasis in the schools on current events and social problems.

The status of many young fathers today might well be summed up in the tongue-in-cheek statement of the teenage girl who said, "We always try to make Father feel as if he were a member of the family."

Within the same society that has downgraded the role of the husband and father, there has been a simultaneous upgrading of both the status and the rewards of the bachelor life. In colonial times, bachelors had a comparatively greater disadvantage economically. Not only did they not have wives to help them, they were even taxed for being bachelors.

Not so today. Now the marriage resistor is apt to have a "plush pad" and an easy life with multiple rewards, both economic and biologic, unavailable to the married man. Once scorned, the bachelor is now envied not only by

[2] Peter C. Pineo, "Disenchantment in the Later Years of Marriage," *Marriage and Family Living*, **23** (February, 1961), 3–11.
[3] Sidonie M. Gruenberg and Hilda S. Kretch, *The Many Lives of Modern Woman*, Garden City, N.Y., Doubleday, 1952, pp. 36–50.

married men but by young women as well. Even though some of his pleasures may be illusory and in the long run self-defeating, his way of life represents something of a threat to the American marriage tradition.

The Wife-Mother Role

The role of being *just* a wife and mother has also been downgraded. Some of the neo-feminists complain that a smaller percentage of college women are now getting advanced degrees, a smaller percentage want full-time careers, and many more educated women appear to be settling for the traditional wife-mother role. This is true. But it is also true that being "just a housewife" is still somewhat demeaning.

In recent times, an increasing number of women have been able to combine homemaking with outside employment. In 1920, only about one-third of the women working outside the home were married; today about two-thirds are. How many of these women are really more satisfied and "fulfilled" because they work outside the home? Those who have stimulating professional jobs and cooperative husbands may have found additional satisfaction. But there are millions of other women with routine jobs in offices, factories, laundries, and restaurants who dislike working and who feel guilty because they may be doing a less-than-adequate job at home besides. For these women, the "feminine mystique" has a very hollow ring. On the other hand, women who do not work outside the home often suffer a loneliness for adult social interaction as they find themselves tied down to a small apartment or house with one or more small children, day after day, and week after week.

Moreover, some direct satisfactions have now been eliminated from homemaking. For example, the joy of competing for blue ribbons at the county fair is now limited to a small proportion of the population. Even the competitive satisfaction of being the first woman on the block to get the wash out on the line on Monday mornings has been eliminated by the automatic dryer.

Thus, as the expectation of the role that the other person will play in modern marriage has greatly increased, often the satisfaction that is provided by one's own role in marriage has considerably diminished for both sexes. This is not to say that there are not many creative partnerships in which the partners have found increasing satisfaction. There are. But these days this requires both more realistic expectations and more creative initiative from both oneself and one's mate.

In addition to too-great expectations of the marriage partner's performance and too-great expectations of one's own role satisfactions, in recent years difficulty has resulted from too-great expectations of marriage itself. Some individuals expect marriage to provide the happiness that they have never before had in their lives. In many cases, young people go into marriage expecting that they will find new freedom, or new security, or an escape from whatever problems had plagued them before marriage. Usually, though, such people find that marriage only adds to their problems. Marriage is a status, not a cure. It provides an opportunity to give love; it is not a remedy for unhappiness.

CONFUSED EXPECTATIONS

Social roles have been changing so rapidly that it is sometimes difficult to identify what are the proper expectations for role performance. This, too, diminishes satisfaction. For example, today many women are unsure whether or not they should work outside the home, especially if they have children. This is a far cry from the old days when woman's role was highly structured. Elizabeth Cady Stanton, Lucretia Mott, and the others who gathered in 1848 to draw up the manifesto for women's rights did not foresee that once women got the right to work outside the home they might be expected to do so most of the time. Nor did they foresee that the very need for making a choice in a world with less highly structured roles might create emotional difficulty. Today, because of confused expectations, some women feel guilty if they do work outside the home; some others feel guilty if they do not. This kind of confused expectation leads to psychological ambivalence, which, in turn, can preclude marital satisfaction.

Of all the confused role expectations that plague modern marriage, though, none is more difficult than the family-leadership problem. Most American women are intellectually conditioned to expect a husband to be reasonably democratic, permissive, and equalitarian. He will consult them about important matters, solicit their advice, and sometimes look to them to make decisions.

But the *emotional* conditioning of some of these same young women is very different. They grew up in homes where Father was the undisputed leader, and emotionally they are conditioned to expect that they will marry a resolute, courageous leader who will tell them what to do and make them like it. It is not that they expect the husband to be the boss because he is a man, but rather that he should earn the right to be boss by demonstrating his superior leadership ability. Not uncommonly, many of these young women give their new mates a little harder time than they need to just so that they can enjoy the feeling of his having earned the right to dominate.

In modern marriages, the two sets of conditioning sometimes come into conflict. Sometimes a wife wants recognition as her husband's equal in decision making and planning, and sometimes she wants him to make the decisions and carry them out. Sometimes she doesn't know what she wants. If she is confused, think how much more confused her husband is. If marriage partners had substantial agreement on role expectations, most marriages might be more stable than they are.

NOT ENOUGH
EXPECTATION

In recent times, some family members have been denied satisfaction because their roles have not provided *enough* expectation. Medical doctors are familiar with cases of both men and women who, without children or responsibility, have too much leisure and too little challenge. People with too much time on their hands sometimes become introspective and develop psychosomatic illnesses.

Although there are relatively few idle young adults in our society, there is a much larger group of family members for whom expectations are too limited to provide adequate satisfactions. In our space-age culture, we have no structured role for Grandmother. In other cultures and in other times, Grandmother received satisfaction in her role as household administrator, wise old counselor, or, at least, babysitter. Today, however, the young married couple usually establishes a separate household and one that may be many hundreds or even thousands of miles away from the grandparents' home. This leaves Grandmother (and sometimes Grandfather) with no role to play in the young people's household, and it leaves Grandmother, often because she is a widow, without much of a role in her own home either.

To understand the magnitude of the change in the Grandmother role, it is necessary to look back only a few generations. As recently as a hundred years ago, the typical woman married at about age twenty-two. She had her children more or less spaced throughout her childbearing period. Because of high mortality rates, and because the last child was often born late in her child-bearing years, the typical mother frequently died before her last child left home. She had the structured role of mother right up to the end of her days.

In recent times, however, the typical woman has married at about age twenty, has had her two or three children early in marriage, and is through childbearing by age twenty-six. She is a grandmother by age forty-four. She then has a life expectancy of some thirty years, of which for the last eight or ten she will probably be a widow.

How to get satisfaction in this last thirty-year period is a problem that is causing many women great difficulty. One answer is, of course, to go to work outside the home. The large increase in employed women in recent years has resulted in great part from the needs of young grandmothers.

But the kinds of work outside the home for which older homemakers are qualified, because they often have neither the education nor the experience with which to compete with career women in the business world, are often unac-ceptable to them. Volunteer work is always a possibility, but it can have the appearance of routine busy work. Until our society finds some more creative use for their talents and energies, many of our younger grandmothers are going to want for feelings of satisfaction and of fulfillment.

Another major group to miss satisfaction because of not enough role expectation is the children. Years ago, when children were working members of the family team with the full knowledge that they were helping to provide for the common welfare, there was far more opportunity for them to develop the adult-type satisfaction. Today satisfaction through achievement, if any, is more often associated with activities outside the home, such as athletics, schoolwork, and recreational groups.

In our modern child-centered homes, the child is often delegated the role of family pet with the expectation that his major satisfaction will come from receiving *things*. As parents lavish more and more material things on their children, the children learn to get all of their satisfactions from receiving. In addition, the children see on television and read in magazines that marriage is a wonderful state from which they will one day *receive* additional satisfactions. When they grow up and marry someone who was conditioned in the same way, both partners expect that they will continue to *receive* satisfactions as a result of the behaviors of their mate. But, as has been pointed out earlier, marriage is a *giving* relationship. Unless either one or both of this newly mar-ried pair learns to make the transition from getting satisfactions through receiv-ing to getting satisfactions through giving, their marriage is in trouble. I esti-mate that fully 30 to 40 percent of the people I saw in my marriage-counseling practice were having difficulty because either one or both of the partners never learned to make the transition from getting satisfactions through receiving to getting satisfactions from giving.

THE MARRIAGE PARTNERS'
DIFFERING EXPECTATIONS

Too-great expectations, confused expectations, and not enough expectations are only a part of the expectations problem in modern marriage. Of equal importance is the problem of the *differing* expectations that the partners bring to the marriage relationship. These differing expectations sometimes cause not only misunderstanding, but also a complete lack of understanding between the marriage partners.

Because of the differential conditioning given male and female children, men and women have always had a difficult time understanding each other's behavior in the marriage relationship. It is not unusual for a young man to say to the marriage counselor, "I don't understand the woman I married. She expects me to do things for her that she could easily do for herself, she expects me to do things for her that she hasn't told me she wanted me to do, and sometimes, in fact, she expects me to do things for her that she has denied she wanted done." One young man described being away from his new bride on a business trip. Each night he called her from the city where he was staying. One night she said to him, "Now let's try and save money so that I can go with you on the next trip. Don't call me tomorrow night. All right?" The young man, pleased with his wife's thrift and foresight, agreed. When he did call her two days later, she was angry. Why was she angry? He hadn't called her the night before!

The classic example of this kind of behavior is often seen in the sexual relationship. Typically the young man complains to the marriage counselor that he doesn't understand the woman he married. "I wanted to make love to her last night and she rejected me. So, being a considerate fellow, I turned over and tried to go to sleep. Then she sat up crying half the night." When the marriage counselor talks with the young wife, she claims that she should have been so irresistibly fascinating that he would have persisted despite any obstacles she put in his path. "Obviously," she said, "he doesn't love me enough."

The young man was quite right when he said he didn't understand her. He didn't understand the conditioning that made persistent reassurances of her desirability so important to his wife. This conditioned need, in its extreme form, causes some young women to continually be asking their husbands, "Do you love me?" or "Are you sure you still love me?" It is a product of competition in the love-oriented society that most girls experience. To be successful is to be loved and to be irresistibly desirable. The young man has not ordinarily experienced this kind of security-need to the same degree.

Lack of understanding of the opposite sex is by no means limited to men. Often a marriage counselor will see a young woman who will say, "I don't understand the man I married. He went out and bought a brand-new automobile when we could hardly pay for the good car we already had."

What she is saying in effect is that she doesn't understand the depth and extent of conditioned need for prestige and the symbols of success that were built into that particular young man in the success-oriented male society. Perhaps if she had been raised as a boy in his home she would have understood it. But she wasn't.

This kind of lack of understanding between men and women probably goes back to the caveman, but social change has given it a new dimension.

In our modern, mobile, cosmopolitan society, people are marrying other people from widely differing backgrounds—differing nationality backgrounds, differing ethnic backgrounds, differing religious backgrounds, differing socioeconomic backgrounds. Each partner brings to the marriage not only his conditioned male or female expectations, but also an entire series of internalized customs, attitudes, and values that are sometimes extremely important to him emotionally whether he is aware of it or not. Yet these customs, attitudes, and values may be so foreign to his mate that they are looked upon as silly whims or notions that are quite unreasonable.

diverse environment socialized them into

CASE 4 *2 different ways of handeling money*

"I've been married to Susan for seven years," Rudolph said to the marriage counselor, "and in all that time she's never been able to hold on to a nickel for more than a few hours at a time. Money goes through her hands like water, and she can't save either. She won't even mend a rip in a torn sheet!"

When the counselor talked to Susan, she said, "Rudolph is the cheapest, the tightest, the most miserly man there ever was. Why, he even expects me to mend torn sheets! Can you imagine that?"

While it was clear to the counselor that this wasn't the only problem in this marriage, it was also evident that the torn sheet symbolized the deep division in the couple's emotional attitudes toward spending family income. After airing some other overlying resentments, Rudolph volunteered the following information: He was the son of a widowed mother from New England. He grew up with his four brothers in a small, semicircle community whose values were "use it up, wear it out, make it do." His mother constantly impressed upon the developing consciousness of her five boys that a good husband—not a wastrel and a profligate like their late father had been—should save his money for the inevitable rainy day. These attitudes acquired in childhood had intense emotional significance for Rudolph.

In due course, Rudolph grew up, went into the army, was sent to California, and there met and very quickly married the happy-go-lucky daughter of a happy-go-lucky Glendale family. In Susan's neighborhood "gracious living" was an important value. The popular attitude was "spend your money, that's what it's for." It was important to keep up with the Joneses. Moreover, those people who did spend (sometimes beyond their means) for houses often made a substantial profit in the California real-estate market and therefore had even more money to spend.

Each of these partners thought his mate was trying to punish him with silly notions that were contrary to the best interests of the family. "But I'm only trying to save it for my family's future," Rudolph said emphatically. Susan pleaded, "We are entitled to some kind of adequate living now when we are young enough to enjoy it." Susan and Rudolph had been to see divorce lawyers, who recommended that they consult a marriage counselor.

Should Susan sew up holes in torn sheets? Should Rudolph have been forced to spend more money? Would it help to know all the details of their budget?

Although Rudolph and Susan came from very different sections of the country, this regional difference is often far less important in the United States culture than the attitudes of the family in which the marriage partner grew up. Consider the following case:

CASE 5
Joe and Carolyn were both from Illinois. Joe was the son of a downstate farmer

who was doing the best he could to eke out a living on a small farm. Joe had three brothers. The men in his family worked hard. When they wanted recreation, they went off together for days at a time hunting and fishing.

Joe's mother was a hard-working farm wife who took pride in keeping the house spotless and the backyard garden watered and free of weeds. She left all the decisions to her husband. Joe's father was the boss, and she wanted it that way. Having enough money was a constant problem for Joe's family, and spending decisions were made on the basis of what was absolutely necessary to continued survival.

Joe went off to the University of Illinois on the G.I. Bill after he had completed his army service. There he met Carolyn, the daughter of a Chicago banker. They fell in love and were married.

Carolyn had grown up in a large, well-appointed suburban home. In her family, "recreation" meant that father and mother would go off to the theater or a concert together, and the children would gather for Ping-Pong or tennis at a friend's house. Father consulted Mother on the major decisions and often accepted her suggestions on what should be done. Spending the family income was never much of a problem, although Father sometimes did have difficulty in deciding which was the better investment opportunity.

Joe and Carolyn had been married only seven months when she came to see the marriage counselor. They had had a fight, and Joe had left home two weeks ago. She wanted the counselor's help in inducing Joe to return. Joe talked to the counselor reluctantly. "I sure don't want to go back now, and I'm not sure that I ever do," he said. "Our honeymoon came to an abrupt end early last fall when I wanted to go off on a few days' hunting trip with my brother. 'What!' she screamed. 'You're going to leave me at home all by myself?' In the end I didn't go; it wasn't worth it to fight with her. But now I kick myself all over the place. I should have been man enough to go anyway. She wants to control me. I can't go out with a friend for a glass of beer by myself. She always wants to know how much money I have, and she thinks she ought to manage the checkbook. That isn't right. And even if it were right, I couldn't trust her with it. She spends money for almost anything. She went downtown and bought a coat at a fancy specialty shop and paid $150 for it when they had the same coat—I swear it was the same coat—at Sears for $85. Why should I go back to that?"

When Carolyn came back to see the counselor, she cried profusely. "I just don't understand it," she said. "He doesn't even want to talk with me about it. Do you think it was right for him to want to go away and leave me in a strange house all by myself after we'd been married just three weeks? I don't like hunting (that is, I don't think I like hunting, though I've never been), but the least he could have done would be to have offered to take me along. Besides, it wasn't only those two days. Sometimes he's away for a whole evening when he's just told me he's going to see a friend for a few minutes. And then he doesn't want to explain where he's been when he comes back. I admit that I'm not a fussy housekeeper, but I do a lot of volunteer work at the Junior League, and he doesn't even want to help me with the housework.

"I know he thinks I'm extravagant," she continued. "But it pays to buy a good thing. That coat I bought will last me for years, and a cheap coat would have fit me poorly and gone out of style quickly. He really doesn't know anything about spending money because he never had any to spend. I want you to try to make him understand."

Should the counselor try to make *him* understand? Or should he try to make *her* understand? How can he help both of them come to a common understanding?

ROLE THEORY AND
SYMBOLIC INTERACTION

The theory that differing role expectations account for all or most of the difficulties in marriage has fascinated sociologists for many years. One of the early expressions of marital role theory was by Leonard Cottrell.

> First, marriage adjustment may be regarded as a process in which marriage partners attempt to re-enact certain relational systems or situations which were obtained in their own earlier family groups. Or, in other words, marriage partners tend to play the habitual roles they evolved in their childhood and adolescence.
>
> Second, the kinds of roles that marriage partners bring to the marriage will determine the nature of their marriage relationship and the degree of adjustment that they will achieve.
>
> Third, . . . maladjusted marriages may be regarded as the results of the failure of the marriage situation to provide the system of relationships called for by the roles which the marriage partners bring to the marriage.[4]

Closely related to this role theory of marital adjustment is the sociologic conceptual framework of *symbolic interactionism*.[5] The interactionists make important use of the individual's "self-concept" and "definition of the situation," in addition to his perception of marital roles. In general, it is postulated that the greater the congruence of the perceptions that each partner has of himself and his marriage roles with the perceptions of his mate, the more satisfactory the marriage.

Testing these concepts, A. R. Mangus hypothesized that marriage problems resulted from the presence or absence of "harmony, consistency, and congruity among the role expectations of those participating in marriage." He concluded that "It is believed that the most pressing, inter-personal problems in marriage arise out of the disparities among the role concepts and self concepts that are pertinent to the marriage situation."[6]

In 1960, Eleanore Luckey reported that in her studies she had indeed found a significant and positive association between marital satisfaction and the congruence of perceptions of self and the perception of self by spouse.[7] In 1966, Robert Williamson went even further. He said: "In fact divorce may be considered basically the outcome of role conflicts. There is a breakdown in the image of the other person and in his or her ability to personify the role desired."[8]

In addition to role theory, however, many marriage counselors who work directly with individuals who have marriage problems refer regularly to concepts of personality development emerging from clinical psychology. They use the theories of human motivation that, in addition to stressing the importance of roles and self images, put emphasis on psychological needs and the concept of behavioral games. These will be discussed in the next chapter.

[4] Leonard S. Cottrell, Jr., "Roles and Marital Adjustment," *Publications of the American Sociological Society*, **27** (May, 1933), 109.

[5] As Sheldon Stryker suggests, there is some disagreement over the exact differentiation between "role theory" and "symbolic interaction theory." Some writers use them interchangeably; other writers insist on distinction. Stryker has an excellent chapter for the interested student on "The Interactional and Situational Approaches" in Harold T. Christensen, ed., *Handbook of Marriage and the Family*, Chicago, Rand McNally, 1964.

[6] A. R. Mangus, "Role Theory and Marriage Counseling," *Social Forces*, **35** (March, 1957), 206.

[7] Eleanore Luckey, "Marital Satisfaction and Its Association with Congruence of Perception," *Marriage and Family Living*, **22** (February, 1960), 49–54.

[8] Robert C. Williamson, *Marriage and Family Relations*, New York, Wiley, 1966, p. 535.

5

THE IMPORTANCE
OF PERSONALITY
IN RELATIONSHIPS

It sometimes appears that the concept of unmet role expectations might be stretched to cover any malfunction in human relationships, especially in marriage. It could be said, for instance, that any wife who divorced her alcoholic husband did so because he didn't meet her social expectation, that a husband who left his frigid wife did so because she didn't meet his sexual expectation.

Frequently, there is more to it than this. "Expectation" usually connotes accurate awareness by the individual of his own motivations and attitudes. But not everyone really knows why he behaves the way he does, because some behavior is directed by unconscious feelings and conflicts. For example, a wife who urges her husband to take a Sunday afternoon nap because this satisfies her unconscious need to feel martyred would find it hard to define her unmet expectation. She probably couldn't tell you whether she "expects" that a wife should play the role of self-abnegating helpmeet who is subservient to her husband's pleasures or whether she "expects" that a husband should be an energetic, aggressive fellow who would not take naps on Sunday afternoon even if he were urged to do so.

When unconscious needs are involved, as they often are, it is important to look beyond the individual's present role expectations to those patterns of thinking and behaving that formed his personality. The concepts of role expectation and personality needs exist side by side, and, in any one case, one concept may provide a more satisfactory explanation of the situation than another.

Personality is the configuration of an individual's characteristics and behaviors. It is the pattern of thinking, feeling, and behaving that usually (but not always) predetermines and preselects an individual's way of adjusting to the pleasures, frustrations, and insults of living. Some marriages result in the harmonious synchronization of two personalities. Some marriages exist in spite of (or, as we shall see later, perhaps *because* of) the differing personalities of the partners. Some marriages are torn apart by the irreconcilable attitudes and living patterns of the marriage mates. To understand the working of any marriage relationship, it is necessary to know something of the personalities of the individuals concerned.

THE DEVELOPMENT
OF PERSONALITY

Personality develops from physical structure, cultural conditioning, and individual unique experience. Any human being's physical structure affects his personality in several ways. Characteristics such as the ability to talk and smile permit him to develop the individual expressiveness that promotes the differential reactions of other people to him and thus initiates the process of personality development. Equally as important are the basic physical needs—to eat, to sleep, and, later, to have sexual activity,—that each person is born with. The individual's unique adaptation to these physical needs both conditions and may be conditioned by his personality. Thus, while some people are grouchy because they are hungry, there are others who eat because they are unhappy.

Another way that physical structure affects personality is through the individual differences in bodily activity that result from one's genetic structure. For example, a man who has inherited an unusually active thyroid gland from his great-grandfather will be more active than other people and will tend to have a lively temperament. If, on the other hand, he has inherited an underactive thyroid from his great-grandmother, he may well be a lethargic and submissive personality type. A person who inherits the tendency toward dyspepsia may have a low frustration tolerance and thus a grouchy disposition.

Still another way in which physical structure affects personality is through body image. In our culture, a tall, lean, athletic man usually will have greater feelings of self-respect than his short, fat, clumsy neighbor. These feelings often help the athletic-type male to have better relationships with other men as well as with women, who admire not only his physique and athletic ability but also his self-confidence.

Types of body build and consequent social relationships condition personality even in the child. J. R. Staffieri and Boyd McCandless reported in 1966 that even some four-year-old children know what their body build is. If it is short and thick, they tend to describe it unfavorably and in a socially rejecting way.[1] There is an excellent discussion of body image and its effect on the development of personality in Boyd McCandless's *Children: Behavior and Development.*[2]

Body image can be even more important to a female. A beautiful girl will develop a different personality from a plain girl. She may also have living experiences that make her life a much more pleasant one and consequently make her personality more pleasing. A beautiful girl may also feel so sufficiently admired that she can afford to reject compromises with her value system; a

---

[1] J. R. Staffieri and Boyd R. McCandless, "A Study of Social Stereotype of Body Image in Children," paper presented at the fiftieth annual meeting of the American Educational Research Association, Chicago, February, 1966.

[2] Boyd R. McCandless, *Children: Behavior and Development*, 2nd ed., New York, Holt, Rinehart and Winston, 1967, pp. 395–414.

plain girl may have to decide whether she will be promiscuous or prudish. There will be more about the effect of body image on personality in a subsequent chapter.

THE IMPORTANCE
OF CULTURE

The second major influence on the development of personality is the culture in which the person grows. This includes both the large national or regional culture and the subculture of the family unit.

A classic example of the effect of culture on personality is the legend about Quaker parents traveling in New Guinea who became separated from their infant son. The child was found and raised by a tribe of head-hunters. Would the boy turn out to be a gentle Quaker or a head-hunter? The answer is obvious—he became a head-hunter—with all the aggressive personality characteristics of his foster family. A Japanese girl is taught to be submissive and self-abnegating, whereas a middle-class American girl is taught to be independent and self-expressing. The effect of these cultural conditionings on the personalities of the individual concerned is both large and relatively permanent.

Within the larger national culture we have many subcultures that have an important role in the development of any child's personality. A boy from a disadvantaged group may learn to be aggressive in order to exist in the slum; a young woman raised in genteel Southern society may learn to be demure. The disavantaged boy was not necessarily born aggressive, nor was the Southern girl born demure.

Individual family differences play a large role in the conditioning of the child. A child from a family whose highest value is the accumulation of material things might turn out to be a grasping, clawing individual, even though he might sometimes adopt certain superficial patronizing behavior in order to disguise his ulterior purpose. Another boy reared in a family where helping other people was the highest family value might turn out to be a social-work-type whose satisfactions are derived through altruism. Of course, it does not always follow that every child adopts the family values as his own; some children reject them completely. Ordinarily, though, the family is a powerful conditioning factor.

In every period of life, and especially in childhood, parental and family teaching is modified by outside groups. If the child plays with other children who are from families where similar customs, attitudes, and values are observed, much of his role learning will be reinforced. When someone says, "Let's play house," a boy knows that he is expected to be either the father or the brother. If he makes a mistake in his role-appropriate behavior, he will quickly be corrected: "No, no, Silly. The father doesn't bake the pie; the mother does!" If his playmates come from various cultural backgrounds, he may start learning for the first time that different families have different customs, attitudes, and values. Then he is in for a long period of agonizing effort in reconciling what his peers tell him is proper and what his parents have prescribed. He soon learns that his relationships both with his parents and his peer group may be affected by the kind of adjustments he makes to these ambivalent expectations.

In earlier times, it is probable that parents and peer groups played a greater part in establishing a child's behavior patterns than they do today. In modern America, parents are much more permissive, often, as will be seen, because of their own perplexity in a changing society. Moreover, play groups are often more temporary. Considerably more of the child's behavior is subject to confirmation and modification by other influences—especially by the school. It is also often subject to challenge and confusion by television, radio, newspapers, and magazines. The child learns from his parents, for example, that guns are "bad," but, on television, people do shoot guns. He also learns that, although the gunslinger is ordinarily the "bad guy," under certain circumstances he can become the "good guy." More important to future marriage and family relationships, however, are the differing patterns of family-role behaviors the child learns. A girl child, for example, may observe that in her home her father is invariably the boss and makes all the decisions, but on television millions of other homes are represented in family dramas in which the mother has the dominant role or is, at least, equal in fact as well as in fancy to her husband.

How well the child accepts his early socialization and how carefully he integrates these cultural standards into his behavior depends in some measure on other aspects of his personality. If, for example, he is aggressive and hostile, he may reject prescribed patterns. If he is mischievous, he may pretend to reject them. If he is obsessive or insecure, he may overreact to all the prescribed patterns in a frantic endeavor to conform absolutely. All of these ways of behaving not only affect the child's current relationships but also have a manifest effect on his later dating, marriage, and family relationships.

UNIQUE EXPERIENCES

A third major determinant of personality is the unique experiences of the individual. Two children raised in the same family in the same culture may turn out very differently. An undeterminable part of these differences is the genetic, but another part, and possibly a more important part, is that each child had different environmental influences with which to contend. The first child born into a family is exposed to different parental attitudes than the second one, if only because the first was first. A second child arriving in a family has a differing living experience because he already has a sibling with whom he must share attention and affection. Moreover, most siblings have different playmates, different teachers, different accidents and experiences along the way.

Other circumstances can intervene, too. A child who grew to age ten in a poverty-stricken farm family in Oklahoma might have entirely different attitudes about himself and an entirely different self-image than his brother who was born after a rich source of oil had been found on their little farm. Some years ago Carpenter and Eisenberg observed the different self-esteem levels of girls raised in wealthy homes when compared with the self-esteem levels of those raised in poverty.[3] The rich girls were more poised, aggressive, and self-confident, in part, at least, because their fathers' financial security transferred feelings of worth to them.

Having examined the development of personality in general, it now becomes important to look closer at two vital aspects of it: self-image and needs. All three of the major determinants of personality—physical structure, culture,

[3] June Carpenter and Philip Eisenberg, "Some Relations Between Family Background and Personality," *Journal of Psychology*, **6** (July, 1938), 115–136.

and individual experiences—affect the development of any individuals' self-image and his emotional needs. Self-image and needs are the prime effectors of both a man's behavior and his relationships with other people.

THE SELF-IMAGE

A newborn infant makes no distinction between himself and the things outside himself. As he grows, however, self-perception is one of his earliest achievements. He becomes aware of imaginary ability to get outside of his body and look back at himself. This phenomenon was described by sociologist Charles H. Cooley as "the looking-glass self," because the individual perceives himself as he assumes other people will perceive him.[4] This is the beginning of self-image or self-definition. Soon the child begins to make certain very important assumptions about what he is like, and he tends to structure his behavior in accordance with those assumptions.

In the earliest years, it is the family group that provides the experiences in the form of both praise and criticism that give the individual some basis for his self-image. If a child's parents make him feel loved and wanted and treat him as if he is acceptable and good, he more often comes to see himself as adequate, competent, and lovable in a world that is friendly and secure. Later he is likely to turn out to be an emotionally healthy person who has the self-confidence to undertake new experiences and the flexibility to modify his behavior and learn from those experiences. William Morrow and Robert Wilson found that a child who is given self-confidence by accepting parents tends to be a high-achieving adult.[5]

If, on the other hand, the childhood home is deficient in either love or security, and if the child is not helped to develop adequate self-confidence, he may grow up with an inadequate self-image. Unloving or inconsistent parents may make him so confused that he loses all confidence in his ability to interpret experiences. A child who is constantly belittled may grow up feeling that he is incapable of dealing with his relationships and so will avoid new experiences, because he is always afraid they will turn out badly.

Robert Coombs and Vernon Davies, after citing W. I. Thomas's classic observation, "If a situation is defined as real it is real in its consequences,"[6] suggested that, in the context of the school world, a student who is defined as a "poor student" (by significant others and thereby by himself) comes to conceive of himself as such. He gears his behavior accordingly, and the social expectation is realized.[7]

In the process of developing a self-concept, a child may, and often does, make false assumptions about how other people—especially his peers—feel about him. Sometimes these are in a positive direction: I love myself; therefore

[4] Charles H. Cooley, *Human Nature and the Social Order*, New York, Scribner, 1902, pp. 152–153.

[5] William R. Morrow and Robert C. Wilson, "Family Relations of Bright High-Achieving and Under-Achieving High School Boys," in Gene R. Medinnus, ed., *Readings in the Psychology of Parent-Child Relations*, New York, Wiley, 1967, pp. 247–255.

[6] William I. Thomas, "The Persistence of Primary-Group Norms in Present Day Society," in H. S. Jennings, et al., *Suggestions of Modern Science Concerning Education*, New York, Macmillan, 1917, pp. 159–197, and *The Child In America*, New York, Knopf, 1928, p. 572.

[7] Robert H. Coombs and Vernon Davies, "Self-Conception and the Relationship Between High School and College Scholastic Achievement," *Sociology and Social Research*, **50** (July, 1966), 468.

others must love me. Sometimes they are in a negative direction—often as a result of the ideas that the child himself has about *other* people. For example, the child who is insecure about his own appearance is often critical of others. Then he turns around and assumes that others are criticizing him, even though this may not be the case at all. This tendency to assume that other people will be critical is pronounced among those who have an inadequate self-image.

Adequate self-image development is even more difficult for the person (male or female) with some uncorrectable body impairment or physical difference. He *has* to learn to live with whatever physical handicap he has. Often this leads him to withdraw from social contacts and drastically affects his ability to relate to others. Acne, for example, can be one of the most serious tragedies to afflict the young human being, for it is a damager of self-image at just the time in his social development when he needs all the self-confidence he can get.

There is, however, no one-to-one relationship between the actual physical impairment and the attitude that the individual has about it. It is not how bad the handicap really is that matters; nor is it how bad the impairment really appears to others. It is how bad the individual himself *thinks* it is that causes all the difficulty. This will be illustrated by a case in the next chapter.

A damaged self-image can result from feelings of inadequacy as well as from physical handicaps, and a poor self-image resulting from a disadvantaged home situation is one of the great problems faced by those who work with minority-group children.

In the process of developing his accepted self-image, the child also develops an *ideal* self-image. This is the self the child wishes he could become, and he frequently judges his actual appearance and conduct against this ideal self-image. If his real self closely approximates his ideal self, he is likely to be a self-confident, secure person who is well liked by others. If his real self-evaluation is widely divergent from his concept of an ideal self, he is likely to be an unhappy person who is difficult to get along with.

The child's concept of himself will vitally affect his motivation, both positively and negatively. If, for example, there is a close congruence between his present self-definition and his ideal self, he will be motivated to try to close the gap. A young man who has a secure image of himself as a good student will do everything he possibly can to maintain (and even improve) that self-image. Coombs and Davies, in a study of Washington State University freshmen, found that those who had loftier conceptions of their scholastic ability expected to obtain high college grades and usually did so.[8]

But what happens if an individual overresponds in an effort to live up to his ideal? He may be always on the defensive, making elaborate and unnecessary explanations of any behavior on his part that he feels falls short of the high standards he sets for himself. Many highly motivated individuals are constantly trying to prove to themselves and to others that their real self-images approximate their ideal self-images.

EMOTIONAL NEEDS

As a result of his self-image, an individual tends to develop certain emotional needs. For example, if a young man is to maintain or enhance his self-image as

[8] *Ibid.*, p. 468.

a good student, he needs to be constantly reassured by excellent grades. Thus, he may come to develop a rather large need for recognition. If he has any doubt about his self-image, he may have an even greater need for recognition. Or if, in growing up, a woman develops a self-image of being inferior and subservient, she may also develop a masochistic need for abuse in order to feel adequate to her low self-image. The satisfaction of being congruent with her self-image gives her greater emotional pleasure than the physical or emotional punishment gives her pain. Thus, we have the woman who is happy when her husband beats her, because this gives her the security of having conformed to her image of herself as the abused wife.

Needs are important aspects of motivation. Although they may grow out of self-image, they have an independent status in almost all theories of human motivation and behavior.

Men are motivated—indeed impelled—by incessant inner proddings that have been variously labeled as wishes, desires, drives, and, more recently, needs. Some have made a distinction between these impulses. For example, drives are sometimes spoken of as "pushes" from within the individual, whereas needs are goals or objectives or, you might say, "pulls." But in the end the effect is the same whether it is from within or without. The needs, as we shall call them, are the motivational factors in human behavior. They develop concurrently with the self-image.

First of all, and earliest of all, the human being manifests his physiological needs. The sucking reflex and evidences of hunger appear almost immediately after birth. So does the need to sleep and the need for sensory stimulation.

Although young children have sex feelings and impulses, no one is exactly sure when the sex impulse can be defined as *need*. The time most observers assign to it is the onset of puberty.

As the child develops, and as his self-image develops, he acquires even more needs. He *needs* to feel secure both physically and socially in order to protect his self. He *needs* to be publicly recognized in order to promote his self and perpetuate its integrity. He *needs* to be constantly and consistently loved in order to reassure his self of its worthiness.

Throughout this century, there have been attempts by various psychologists to define and classify human needs. In 1923, William I. Thomas proposed a very simple list of what he called "wishes" in his classic study of unadjusted girls.[9] He suggested that human individuals, in our culture at least, have needs for security, response, recognition, and new experience.

This list has severe limitations, because it obviously ignores some of the more complex needs, like the need for power and the need for self-abuse, but it does have the advantage of simplicity.

In 1954, Abraham Maslow postulated that all psychological needs subsume from three basic needs that were very similar to Thomas's.[10] Maslow suggested that the basic psychological needs were for safety, love, and self-esteem. Directly from these needs, he said, came a fourth need—the need for self-actualization—the need to fulfill the best that is in you.

Just how these needs affect the behavior of individuals in relationship situations will be pointed out in the next chapter. Here it is sufficient to suggest that an individual's needs are basic to the reasons why he behaves as he does

[9] William I. Thomas, *The Unadjusted Girl*, Boston, Little, Brown, 1925, p. 4.
[10] Abraham H. Maslow, *Motivation and Personality*, New York, Harper & Row, 1954, pp. 84–92.

in any relationship. The young man who shows off on a date has a basic need for recognition. The boy who is shy and retiring has a great need for security. There is a wide variation in the intensity of needs. Some men spend every waking hour seeking response from other people; other men willingly go off alone to hunt or to prospect for days, weeks, months, or even years at a time.

Although a person's needs tend to fall into precedence patterns, one special need may take overwhelming precedence over another at any one particular moment. The young man who feels impelled to show off by driving a hundred miles an hour may be fulfilling his need for recognition at the same time as he is subverting his need for security or safety. At times, physical needs may dominate psychological needs, or vice versa. A person who is hungry may not that minute be interested in recognition, although a need for recognition is one of the main driving forces in his life. A security-needing person who is sexually excited may lose some of his concern for security. On the other hand, an insecure person may endure severe discomfort because he is unwilling to ask directions to the toilet, or a devoutly religious person may take vows prohibiting any sexual activity.

Actually, the relationship between physical and psychological needs is very close. Repeated emotional-need frustrations can have serious physical consequences, just as repeated physical-need frustrations can have emotional consequences. The chronically insecure man may develop stomach ulcers; the starving person may literally go berserk.

The relationship between emotional needs and physical needs is very important in the study of human relationships. It can be demonstrated that physical contacts and emotional relationships between human beings are not only desirable, they are actually necessary to the continuance of life itself. Infants deprived of handling by another human being over a long period of time sink into irreversible decline and often succumb. Adults deprived of sensory stimulus may become emotionally unbalanced. Eric Berne suggests that all humans need "stroking" as a result of their inborn infantile stimulus hunger. In later life, he said, the stroking may consist of subtle, symbolic forms of handling, such as recognition in place of intimate physical contact.[11] Berne sees the infantile stimulus hunger (a physiological factor) as being transformed into something that may be termed "recognition hunger" (an emotional need). As the individual matures, Berne feels, he seeks recognition to replace the original need for physical contact. An actor, for example, may require hundreds of "strokes" per week from anonymous and undifferentiated admirers "to keep his spinal cord from shriveling," whereas a scientist may keep his physical and mental health on one "stroke" per year from a respected master.

Because each individual brings to every relationship a series of predeveloped needs, those needs cannot help but affect every relationship into which he enters. This is especially true since needs are often unknown to the person who has them. Even when they are in his awareness, he may deliberately seek to hide them. A basically insecure man may shout and bluster because he knows he is so insecure. Moreover, because many of the needs are unconscious ones, they may serve as channels for all other needs as well. As Maslow has pointed out, a person who thinks he's hungry may actually be seeking comfort more than food.[12] A woman who thinks she wants love may actually be seeking security.

[11] Eric Berne, Games People Play, New York, Grove, 1964, p. 13.
[12] Maslow, op. cit., p. 81.

Each person, in order to try more perfectly to meet his physical and emotional needs while at the same time maintaining and enhancing a self-image, develops a series of strategies or defense mechanisms. These protect his tender ego while simultaneously helping him to greater need satisfaction.

THE DEFENSE MECHANISMS

Each individual reacts differently to insults to his self-image and to frustrations of his emotional needs. In fact, reactions can differ in the same individual from one situation to the next. Generally, though (and this is the major reason why understanding self-image and needs is so important to the understanding of human relationships), individuals have unconscious or semiconscious patterns of behavior that they adopted in childhood and that they continue to use as adults. Sometimes these patterns are neither logical nor problem-solving in a particular situation. But because they were learned in childhood, they are now compelling even if self-defeating. For example, a girl who learned as a child that by crying she generally got what she wanted may as an adult cry when she is frustrated. Even though her husband is repulsed by her crying and is even more intent on denying her when she does cry, she persists in this behavior. If she were asked why she cries, she would say, "I just can't help it."

Certain defense mechanisms or unconscious patterns of adjusting to insults, conflict, and frustration occur so frequently in so many individuals that they have been sorted out and labeled: Rationalization, projection, identification, reaction formation, repression, and compensation are some of these typical defense mechanisms. Before discussing them, it should be pointed out that these reactions are alternatives to either direct aggression, which is probably the most frequent response to frustration, or withdrawing, which is another common method of handling conflict. In addition to direct aggression, such as hitting or threatening, there is also passive aggression, such as negativism or noncooperation. There are also indirect withdrawals. The most common way of withdrawing is through fantasizing or daydreaming, but there are other ways, such as denying response and inattentiveness.

The classic defense mechanisms involve ways to maintain or enhance self-esteem and at the same time to escape or defend against anxiety without using either direct aggression or complete withdrawal. They were emphasized by Sigmund Freud in his account of the unconscious ways in which people react to conflicts and frustrations. All of the defense mechanisms have in common the quality of self-deception, and all are found in the everyday behavior of normal people. Most people probably could not live with themselves without them. It is only when one of these mechanisms is used so frequently that it interferes with the individual's ability to function adequately that it becomes an impairment to his emotional health.

Rationalization. Rationalization is the process of assigning logical reasons to (or plausible excuses for) behavior that we do not wish to acknowledge to ourselves in its total reality. Examples of such self-deception are legion: "I didn't get good grades because the teacher didn't like me." "I wouldn't have gone to the dance even if I had been invited because I heard they were having a terrible combo."

Projection.   Projection is assigning one's own undesirable qualities, in exaggerated amounts, to other people. This justifies one's own tendencies and removes the stigma of bad qualities by minimizing them in oneself and exaggerating them in others. Typically, a person who is critical or unkind to others but who has a self-image of being a "good guy" will convince himself that those around him are critical and unkind and that the harsh treatment he gives to others is based on justifiable retribution, not on any bad qualities of his own. The classic projection in marriage is that of the unfaithful husband who accuses his innocent wife of having been unfaithful. His emotional mechanics operate something like this: I have been unfaithful and I feel badly; but if I, who am so good, have been unfaithful, then my wife might also have been unfaithful." It is a very short jump from "might also have been" to "has been" when such a projection will relieve the guilt of the unfaithful husband and so protect his self-image.

Identification.   Instead of assigning one's own bad qualities to other people, in identification one often takes other people's desirable qualities as his own. To polish up his own self-image, an individual will identify with important groups or well-known people and by such association (actual or fantasied) improve his own self-stature. If you have ever watched another couple in the theater audience, you have probably seen identification at work. When the hero bent forward to kiss the heroine on the stage, you may have seen both of the audience partners purse their own lips.

In a marriage, one partner or the other often identifies with his childhood family group in an effort to buoy up his own position in his marriage. Or one mate may identify with the hero or heroine role in a television serial in an effort to get his mate to behave like his opposite number on the serial.

Reaction Formation.   Reaction formation is concealing a motive in one's self by giving a strong expression to its opposite. Women who are secretly consumed with passionate desires are sometimes overstrict in curbing any sexual impulse in their children. Feeling guilty over their own sex desire, they seek to atone by downgrading sex. In other family relationships, this tendency toward reaction formation is not uncommon. A mother with an unwanted pregnancy may later be overindulgent with the child in order to assure herself that she is good mother.

Repression.   Repression is the mechanism of protecting the self-image from ideas and impulses that are incompatible with it. Repression is different from suppression in that repression is unconscious control, whereas suppression is a conscious control that keeps impulses and tendencies in check. A person is aware of a suppressed idea or impulse, but he may go for years without recognizing his repressed thoughts and desires. Usually, however, repression is not complete, and thoughts and impulses find indirect expression.

A classic but oversimplified illustration of repression is the case of a twenty-five-year-old woman who was walking along the street and was suddenly troubled when someone looked her in the eye. Later being looked in the eye became so upsetting that she actually fainted in the street. After several years of psychotherapy she was finally able to recall a repressed incident that took place in her early childhood. She had been to visit her aunt for a week. Her aunt had told her that she might look anywhere in the house except in the bottom drawer of the bureau in the front bedroom upstairs. As soon as Auntie was out of sight, the little girl went upstairs and into the bottom drawer of the bureau. There, on a piece of gauze in the corner, was a glass eye. The child was frightened.

If she had not been forbidden to go to the drawer and had just stumbled on the glass eye accidentally, the little girl might have run downstairs and told her aunt what she had found. Her aunt would have reassured her and reduced some of the traumatic anxiety. At the end of the week, she might have gone home and told her parents what she had found. They too would have reassured her, and her anxiety would have been further reduced. Then she might have told all her playmates about it. By the time she had told her last playmate, she would have completely reduced the fright and tension that accompanied the incident. She might even have been able to laugh about it for the rest of her life.

But she was not able to do any of these things because she thought she had done something wrong. Therefore, instead of being able to extinguish the fright and anxiety that went with the original incident, she compounded it with guilt. Since she was unable to cope with all of this emotional trauma, she did the only thing she could: She repressed it, pushed the incident down deep inside her. Later it returned to trouble her in the form of the street fainting. She was able to do in psychotherapy what she should have done as a child. She was able to repeat the incident over and over again to another person and so reduce her anxiety and her guilt about it.

Every person brings to his relationships with other people a great many repressed thoughts, ideas, and behaviors. Some minor repressions will trouble some individuals more than some severe repressions will trouble others. There is no rule about the intensity of the repression versus the intensity of the reaction. But those who must live with other people, especially in a relationship as intimate as marriage, must recognize and accept the existence of repressed and unconscious thoughts and behaviors—their own as well as their mate's.

Compensation.   Compensation is the effort to make up for a deficiency in one area by excellence in another. The classic example is the boy who fails in athletic events and so studies diligently and achieves recognition through success in schoolwork. Usually this defense mechanism is the process of making up for weakness in one activity by excellence in another. However, there is another kind of compensation in which the individual attempts to deny or correct his inadequacy by continuing to try to excel in that particular area. Theodore Roosevelt, sickly as a child, showed tremendous determination to become a physically rugged outdoorsman. Often, weak, poorly developed men are spurred by their own weakness into building themselves up to superior performance. In such cases, overcompensation has a positive value, but there have been many instances throughout history in which overcompensation has led to an undesirable result. Many power-mad dictators, for example, were overcompensating for their lack of power in childhood.

As pointed out earlier, defense mechanisms are regularly used to salve and protect the tender self-image. Ordinarily, a person has well-developed patterns of defense by the time he marries. He brings all of his defense mechanisms with him to the new relationship. Often, as we shall see when we come to further examination of cases, these defense mechanisms are fairly easy to spot in someone else's behavior. But the individual who is using them may have had them for so long that now he is almost as unaware of his defenses as he is of the original unconscious feelings that caused him to adopt them.

PERSONALITY DISORDERS

To use the empathetic approach effectively, it is often necessary to remember that there are some people who are repetitively maladaptive. If they can change at all, they can change only after long-term psychotherapy. Their problems and relationships cannot be solved either by changing their environment or by telling them what they ought to do. These individuals are usually diagnosed by psychiatrists as having character or personality disorders. Psychiatrist Joan Hampson has described four classic examples, which are designated as psychosocial immaturity, the hysterical personality, the sociopathic personality, and the obsessional personality.[13]

Psychosocial Immaturity. As an example of psychosocial immaturity, Hampson suggests the case of a woman who was "fixated" at the childish level. She had a weak sense of responsibility that could be superseded by any reasonably acceptable excuse. People at this level expect complete reliability in others but alibi for themselves. They are obsessed with achieving praise or fixing blame. Hampson illustrates as follows:

> An attractive, thirty-five-year-old woman complained that her life was made miserable by her husband's inconsiderateness. She felt sexually unresponsive because her husband was "not romantic . . . pre-emptory, and oversexed." Though a conscientious mother to her two children, she felt trapped by domestic responsibility but childishly held out the expectation that most of her problems would be solved if only her mother would babysit for her more often and "just give me a little sympathy." Once, while her parents were out of town and her husband was at work, she naively invited the local supermarket manager to go with her to her parents' home and help her feed the cats for whom she was acting as temporary custodian. She was only mildly surprised when her invited guest seduced her. Later she rationalized to the psychiatrist, "After all, my husband won't be romantic, no one can blame me if I fall for a guy who will be." The marriage was an on-again, off-again affair, with both husband and wife alternately stalking out of the house and declaring themselves through.[14]

Clearly, neither one of the partners in this marriage was psychotic (out of touch with reality) or so neurotic that he needed to be institutionalized. Equally clearly, although they both knew they needed help with their marriage, the underlying problem was their persistent and immature personality patterns —a problem unlikely to be resolved either quickly or easily by attending to the alibis that both partners gave.

Hysterical Personality. The hysterical personality is described by Hampson as an immature and shallow person, self-absorbed to the point of egocentricity. Some such individuals can be singled out by their flair for the dramatic in manner, dress, and speech. They are emotionally capricious. A female hysteric is often a caricature of the "sexsational"—dressing and acting in a sexually provocative manner but, paradoxically, becoming frightened and perplexed when her behavior provokes a masculine response. Such women are often highly suggestible and are often adept at presenting fantasy as fact.

Sociopathic Personality. Under the heading of the sociopathic personality

---

[13] Joan G. Hampson, "The Effect of Character and Personality Disorders on Marriage Relationships," in Richard H. Klemer, ed., *Counseling in Marital and Sexual Problems: A Physician's Handbook,* Baltimore, Williams & Wilkins, 1965, p. 44.
[14] *Ibid.,* p. 45.

Hampson describes a person of average or sometimes unusually high intelligence. He often has great personal charm and an easy social manner. His freedom from the socially inhibiting effect of anxiety allows him to excel for a while in all of his human relations, including his work and studies. Inevitably and repeatedly, however, he manages to sabotage his life, lose his job, alienate his friends, and often appear in the office of the doctor or the marriage counselor on the verge of losing his wife and children as well. Some sociopathics are passive and inadequate, but others repeatedly commit aggressive and antisocial acts. They are the thieves, check forgers, and swindlers who become involved in common-law marriages, bigamy, and sexual escapades. Sometimes they are involved in more shocking crimes and usually with little or no provocation. Also in this classification are the child beater, the wastrel, the alimony evader, and the irresponsible nonprovider.

Obsessive-Compulsive Personality. The fourth in Hampson's categories of personality disorders is the obsessive-compulsive person. These people are over-meticulous, overorderly, and sometimes overpersistent and inflexible. They live by routines and are upset if the routine is disturbed; they are fond of discipline, adhering to a set of regulations themselves and expecting the same precise performance in others. They are perfectionists and are never able to leave well enough alone; some are always busy, others are procrastinators because they feel that they cannot perform well enough. Fearful of error, such people are often indecisive, insecure, hesitant, and dependent upon the opinion of others, even though they try to hide their uncertainty and, paradoxically, may give the illusion of being self-possessed and confident to the point of appearing smug.

The effect that people in any one of Hampson's four categories can have on a marriage relationship is readily apparent, even to the casual observer. Unhappily, it is not always so obvious to the young person who believes he is in love and who is willing to believe that the other person will change after marriage ("I can *help* him!"). It is difficult enough to establish deeply congenial relationships with relatively normal people. With those who have psychological problems, it is often impossible.

Before turning to a case illustrating the importance of personality factors in marriage relationships, it might be well to point out again that even people who are psychologically normal, relatively mature, problem-solving individuals have self-images, needs, and defense mechanisms. Moreover, many people who are motivated by unconscious repetitive impulses are not automatic candidates for the psychiatrist's couch. The test of psychological health is whether the individual maintains and improves his relationships or whether he persistently deteriorates them by his behavior.

There is a second caution to be stored for future reference. In using personality concepts in the empathetic approach to relationships problems, one should remember that, although personality patterns forecast that an individual will act *more or less* predictably in most situations, this is not always true. In interpersonal situations, behavior is frequently the product of the reciprocating interaction between the two people involved. A person may behave differently in the presence of one person than in the presence of another. An army sergeant may be very tough in the presence of men in his squad, very submissive in the presence of the captain, and very gentle in the presence of his wife. Is the "personality" of the army sergeant, then, tough, submissive, or gentle?

Both the relationship between the individuals concerned and the situation in which they find themselves can set aside usual patterns of behaving. Two people who might easily get along in a relatively calm social situation may have violent difficulty when they are placed under extreme emotional tension. In other words, personality factors, while they are usually predictive of tendencies, are not absolute predictors of behavior.

Now it is appropriate to look at a somewhat complex case that illustrates many of the personality dynamics we have been discussing. Try using the empathetic approach, applying all that has been discussed up to now.

CASE 6

Richard came to see the marriage counselor less than three months after he had been married. In the very first interview, he said emphatically that he no longer loved his wife, he couldn't stand to touch her sexually, and he wanted the marriage counselor to tell his wife that *she* should divorce *him*. Richard said that he couldn't take the initiative in getting the divorce, first of all because his wife had never done anything to hurt him and, secondly, because he belonged to an evangelical church that would frown on his breaking up his marriage. This was the beginning of a long series of counseling interviews for Richard during which the following facts emerged.

Richard was an unwanted child born to an alcoholic mother who had severe personality difficulties and who despised her husband. From his earliest recollections Richard felt rejected. This was even more true after a brother was born whom his mother obviously favored. Despite repeated rejections, Richard continued to try to win his mother's affection.

As he grew, it soon became apparent to everybody—including Richard—that he was an ugly duckling. He had poor vision and consequently had to wear thick-lensed glasses. Other children laughed at him and called him "four eyes." Moreover, he had very poor muscular coordination and wasn't very good at games. When the teams were chosen, the other kids would say: "Aw, do we have to take *him*?" Since he rarely got a chance to play, he was very fumbling and unskillful when he did, and his ineptness provoked further critical comments from the other children. Soon he began withdrawing from games whenever he could. He invented all sorts of reasons, from illness to excuses about his mother needing him. When he got away from the group, he hid in a dark corner and fantasied that he was the game's hero, defeating all the other children.

At home, however, he read and studied a good deal and was proud of his stamp collection. He also took a very great interest in Sunday-School activities at the evangelical church. He came to believe that, even if no one else loved him, God did, and this was comforting. His strong religious orientation made him even more curious in the eyes of the other children. He ate a very great deal, especially between meals. This, too, was comforting. He soon grew overweight; this compounded his difficulties in relating to the other children. Now they taunted him even more, and they were less willing to let him play with them.

When he got to high school, Richard encountered more social problems. The girls didn't want to be with him any more than the boys did. He had almost no social skills and consistently embarrassed any girl he was with even for a moment. He had almost no opportunity for dates or participation in intersex activity. Here again, after several awkward experiences he withdrew to his reading, his stamp collection, and his church activities.

Finally, his unhappy high-school days behind him, he went to the university. Although the studies and the environment at the university were a little better than they had been in high school, his social life remained poor. He continued to overeat, which not only increased his obesity but aggravated a poor complexion as well.

Richard did exceptionally well in university classes and was admitted to medical school. Here he had his first opportunity to relate to people in a protected, professional relationship. Although his bedside manner left a great deal to be desired, at least he began to learn some of the fundamentals of social interaction. After completing medical school, he was inducted into the army as a medical officer.

Then things began to happen to Richard in rapid succession. First of all, the army slimmed him down with some basic-training exercises. As he lost weight, he gained motivation to lose more, and he dieted his way down to normal. As a matter of fact, he cut a rather handsome figure in his army uniform. When he added contact lenses, the results were astonishing. Not only did other people look at him differently, he began to look at himself differently. Soon he was seeing a great deal of the women who frequented the bars near the army base. His relationships with them provided some of the social experience he needed, for these women, less discriminating than most of the girls he had known previously, gave him a kind of acceptance that built up his self-confidence.

In due course, his army tour was completed, and Richard accepted an offer of a residency in pathology at a large metropolitan hospital in San Francisco. In this particular hospital there were almost 200 young women of marriageable age and marriageable inclination—nurses, technicians, dieticians, secretaries, and others—all of whom were excited and interested in the arrival of the new young resident in pathology.

Richard found himself the center of a great deal of attention. He was smiled at, flirted with, and courted as he had never been before. In one large rush he tried to make up for all the time lost. His diary now began to report a quantity of social and sexual activity that would have made Dr. Kinsey blanch.

Richard, like so many other people, was able to pigeonhole and rationalize his moral values. His activities at the hospital were not allowed to interfere with his church work—and of course, vice versa. He never missed a Sunday at church, and he soon became one of the pillars of the local congregation.

As time went by, the older women of the church began to suggest—at first subtly and later insistently—that it was time he found himself a nice girl, married her, and settled down to the sober family life the Lord had intended for him. Richard didn't really want to do this, but at length he was persuaded that it was, in fact, his Christian duty.

He picked out a demure young nurse named Linda, who had a reputation for wide-eyed sexual innocence, and set about courting her. She was immensely flattered, for it was obvious to everybody that she had won the prized male. It was also obvious that he had a kind of reverent esteem for her and her presumed sexual innocence that was far different from the attitude he had toward most of the other girls he dated. She was very careful to foster this image by appearing incensed at the slightest off-color remark and by actually walking out of a slightly risqué movie. Before long, Richard proposed marriage, and a wedding date was set some six months in the future.

Long before the wedding date arrived, Richard had second thoughts. One night, three months or so before the ceremony, he told Linda that he really didn't think he loved her, and he suggested that perhaps it would be better if they didn't get married. She couldn't bear the thought of telling the other 199 girls that she had lost the prized catch, so she explained to Richard that all bachelors get cold feet before marriage, and even if he didn't love her now he would learn to love her as their marriage progressed. Besides, she emphasized, she loved him in a way that his mother never had. She tried to do everything for him that she could possibly think he might want done. Richard thought he ought to feel reassured and went ahead with the wedding plans, even though he had a nagging, half-conscious suspicion that he would like it better if she let him try to please her more often instead of trying to please him all of the time.

On the appointed date, they were married, and after the marriage they moved into his former bachelor apartment. From the beginning, their life together was difficult. In most of the sexual relationships that Richard had previously had, the women had taken the initiative, and this had given him the security of feeling that sex was "all right." His new bride, however, was still playing the role of the demure innocent, and she wanted Richard to be the aggressor. When she coyly rejected some of his timorous advances, Richard began to feel ashamed and guilty, and before long he didn't want to touch her. The madonna image of her he had built up made sexual relationships impossible. When she tried to correct this by being a little more aggressive, he was even further repulsed.

Other aspects of their married life were equally distressing. She continued in her job and was often up early and gone until late in the afternoon. When she came home, she had little energy left for homemaking chores. Consequently, his married life was not much different from his bachelor life.

Although he had few of the pleasures, he now had all of the responsibilities and restrictions of a married man. Before long, he began to think of the "good old days" when all the girls were crazy about him. Soon he came to the conclusion that he had made a bad mistake and that all he wanted to do was to get out. However, he recognized that he had no real complaint against his new bride except, perhaps, that she wouldn't stop working and stay home. Linda argued that not only did they need the money, but also that she needed to keep her job more than ever, since he was hinting that their marriage might break up.

In this dilemma, Richard tried several ways of solving his problem. He thought of applying for reinstatement in the army, but he almost immediately abandoned that idea, for it occurred to him that he would assuredly be sent to Vietnam. Then he tried leaving his unexpurgated diary out where Linda could find it. His hope was that she would read this diary, which she did, and then divorce him as a cad. However, Linda could still not admit that she had failed and lost the prize. Besides, she still believed she loved him, even if he did not want her.

In desperation, Richard went to a marriage counselor, hopeful that the counselor would tell his wife that she should divorce him.

What can be done in this situation? What might be done to help Richard? What might be done to help Linda? Should Linda be urged to divorce Richard? Should Richard be urged to divorce her? On what basis could the marriage possibly continue? Is it worth it? Which "defense mechanisms" were illustrated in this case?

6

WHY SHOULD
THEY FALL
IN LOVE WITH YOU?

In our culture, love is the predominant factor that creates families and holds them together. Most textbooks in the field of family relationships have a chapter on love that either starts or finishes with a definition. Love isn't easy to define, because, like electricity, love can be described by its results but it is hard to pin down exactly *what* it is. Almost every author tries it, though. Love is looked at sociologically, psychologically, physiologically, anthropologically, psychoanalytically, romantically, and even cynically.

Robert Bell gives a modern and brief definition of conjugal love as a "strong emotion directed at the opposite sex and involving feelings of sexual attraction, tenderness and some commitment to the other's ego needs."[1] Robert Winch defines love as the

> positive emotion experienced by one person (the person loving, or the lover) in an interpersonal relationship in which the second person (the person loved, or the love object) either (1) meets certain important needs of the first, or (2) manifests or appears (to the first) to manifest personal attributes (beauty, skills, status) highly prized by the first, or both.[2]

Sociologist Joseph Folsom once described the symptoms of "cardiac-respiratory" love, in which being in love involved "a deep sigh and a feeling about the heart as if it had stopped, followed by palpitation or rapid beating, and a feeling akin to fear." Folsom went on to suggest that

> shivering and trembling sometimes accompanies these reactions. Then there is the thrill reaction, which may be a kind of muscular trembling, or a circu-

[1] Robert R. Bell, *Marriage and Family Interaction*, rev. ed., Homewood, Ill., Dorsey, 1967, p. 111.
[2] Robert F. Winch, *The Modern Family*, rev. ed., New York, Holt, Rinehart and Winston, 1963, p. 579.

latory disturbance. Introspection localizes it in the chest, abdomen, and arms; it seems to involve a sudden increase of energy due possible to liberation of endocrine hormones into the blood.[3]

The behavioral scientists are latecomers to the business of describing love. In 1805 Sir Walter Scott epitomized a viewpoint of all the romantics who have ever believed love to have incomparable power over men's lives:

Love rules the court, the camp, the grove,
And men below, and saints above;
For love is heaven, and heaven is love.

Cynics as well as poets have also looked at love. Francis Bacon contended that among all the great people of history "there is not one that hath been transported to the mad degree of love." H. L. Mencken described love as a "state of perpetual anesthesia."

After taking a long look at the work of those who have written on love— from poets and philosophers to behavioral scientists—Morton Hunt concluded sadly that "most of the learned people who write about love seem to equip themselves in advance with a special theory; with this as a kind of butterfly net, they then sally forth and attempt to capture cases to prove or exemplify their point."[4]

Although he may have overstated the case, and although there have been some modern students of love for whom his blanket indictment is inappropriate, Hunt's statement is, in general, hard to refute. Most analyses of love to date have been diverse, contradictory, sometimes esoteric, often meaningless, and usually poorly validated. William Goode has suggested that definitions of love are notoriously open to attack because individual value judgments are implicit in most of them.[5]

Most students aren't really very much interested in knowing more about what love is. Again the analogy to electricity is cogent. Most people, even very knowledgeable people, are not concerned by science's inability to define exactly electrical energy: It seems far more important to them that they be able to use it to light and improve their living experiences. Besides, William Kephart reports that the great majority of college students already think they know what love is. Some 82 percent of males and 87 percent of females in his study of a thousand college students were either relatively sure or dead certain about the meaning of love.[6]

However, although most students may not be too interested in pursuing any elaborate philosophical discussion of the intrinsic characteristics or meaning of love, almost all of them are eager to participate in it. The real burning issue is not "what is love?" but rather *how does one obtain love?* What are the characteristics of true attractiveness that cause some people to be popular lovers and others to be romantic rejects? In other words, why should they fall in love with you?

In an effort to answer these questions, I have conducted a series of studies extending over a period of two decades. At the outset, I had one additional objective as well: to confirm Manford Kuhn's suggestion that by study-

[3] Joseph Folsom, *The Family*, New York, Wiley, 1934, p. 68.
[4] Morton M. Hunt, *The Natural History of Love*, New York, Knopf, 1959, p. 8.
[5] William J. Goode, "The Theoretical Importance of Love," *American Sociological Review*, **24** (February, 1959), 41.
[6] William M. Kephart, *Family, Society and the Individual*, Boston, Houghton Mifflin, 1961, p. 321.

ing the unmarried, much might be learned about factors favorable and unfavorable to relationship success in marriage.[7]

The first study, done in Florida, was a comparison of a matched group of single and married women, designed to filter out differences in background, circumstances, and personality factors between those who married and those who did not.[8] Women were chosen only because, outside of the military services, single women are easier to find in large groups, at universities in the summertime, for example. Single men tend to lose themselves in the anonymity of the city or on faraway ranches. However, later counseling and observational studies have convinced me that most of the basic generalizations about personality factors in marriageability that can be drawn from the Florida study of women can be adapted to apply to men. In fact, in many cases, personality factors inhibiting marriage and love might be even more demonstrable in men, since some studies have shown that older unmarried men have an even greater tendency to be maladjusted and socially inadequate than unmarried women.[9]

The Florida study provided several interesting and significant findings. First, it was clear that the single women in the Florida sample were on the average equally as attractive physically as the married women. In fact, some of the single women were more attractive than most of the married women. Second, more of the single women were at the extremes of the personality characteristics for which they were measured. For example, more of the single women were extremely aggressive and extremely shy. The married women tended to cluster in the center of the continuum between aggressiveness and shyness. (It could be, of course, that personality changes took place *after* marriage. Some women could have become less shy as a *result* of the social opportunities and confidence gained in marriage, and some women could have become less aggressive as a result of the satisfactions of their marriages.)

Third, *married* women had been more social and more romantic in their growing-up years. The married woman had had more dates, love affairs, and romances than the single woman had had. In fact, the average age at which the two groups had started dating was significantly different. The single women delayed the start of private intersex social activities well beyond that of the girls who did get married. In more recent counseling with single women, I have found this to be a consistent pattern.

Although these three findings from the Florida study were interesting, they did not fully answer the fundamental question: Were circumstantial factors (such as the sex ratio in the individual's community) or personality factors (such as an inability to make others feel comfortable) more controlling to the love, romance, and marriage chances of any particular person?

This is an important question. At the time of the Florida study, the research evidence on circumstantial versus personality factors was thin and obscure. Many people urged their single friends to move to areas where the sex ratio was more favorable to their chances of marrying. Women were advised to go West, where the statistics said there were more men than women. Many were steered toward Alaska, which has about 120 men for every 100 women.

[7] Manford F. Kuhn, "How Mates Are Sorted," Howard Becker and Reuben Hill, eds., in *Family, Marriage and Parenthood*, Boston, Heath, 1948, p. 249.
[8] Richard H. Klemer, "Factors of Personality and Experience Which Differentiate Single From Married Women," *Marriage and Family Living*, 16 (February, 1954), 41–44.
[9] Genevieve Knupfer, Walter Clark, and Robin Room, "The Mental Health of the Unmarried," *American Journal of Psychiatry*, 122 (February, 1966), 841–851.

On the other hand, almost everybody could point to instances in which a warm and friendly young woman seemed to attract men even where there were no men available for miles and then date them on her own terms, while another girl, seemingly no less physically attractive, couldn't get a date at a YMCA convention. How important was opportunity? How important was personality?

Later, in teaching at a women's college, I studied these questions again. The college provided a good "laboratory" situation, for "opportunity" was somewhat controlled. Each year all of the new students started out with almost the same opportunity, since all were away from home, and very few of them had automobiles. In a few months, some young women were dating frequently and others were dating occasionally, but some had no dates at all. Indeed, at the end of the four years there were still some girls who had not had a single date. It was difficult to escape the conclusion that in this situation personality factors were preeminent.

Accepting the priority of personality factors over circumstantial factors has a theoretical importance far beyond its actual demonstration, for, unlike either the sex ratio or the individual's physical appearance, both of which may depend upon totally uncontrollable circumstances, the ability to relate to people of the opposite sex, the ability to love and be loved, and the characteristics that make a person more marriageable *can be learned*. They can be learned or relearned or improved by almost anyone who is motivated to work at it. A person's love-ability quotient can be increased in time by study, practice, self-evaluation, and, in some cases, counseling with a professional in the field. It is not always easy, particularly if deep-seated habit patterns or emotional blocks are involved, but often a little quiet introspection and a few insights can start a person on the way.

Of course, personality is not *always* to blame. There undoubtedly are some people whose circumstances absolutely prevent them from having the love, romance, and marriage they desire. There *are* some whose obligations to care for parents or relatives prevent them from even considering marriage. One of the most frequently overlooked social changes in the last century has been the change in the status of an older unmarried daughter from that of a dependent to that of a supporter of dependents. But there are some people who have such obligations who fail to realize that they *needed* to stay home close to Father and Mother *before* their parents became dependents.

Physical handicaps are another often-cited reason for failing to find love and marriage. Yet there are many physically handicapped people who are married. In our beauty-conscious society, major deviations from accepted standards of beauty are very real impediments to social success. But often the deviation itself is not the problem, but rather the damaged self-image that results from the real or presumed handicap.

Almost everybody has some physical imperfection, but little blemishes sometimes impede the romance chances of some people more than big ones do other people.

Think about this illustration: "I have been crippled since I was four-and-a-half," Elaine told the counselor. "But I never really believed that I wouldn't get married. Todd chose me over three other girls I know he could have had. I think that was because I had a better self-image than some people without any physical problems have. Once I was talking to a beautiful twenty-seven-year-old secretary in Todd's office. She wasn't married and she said she wanted to be. She spotted my crutches and began to talk as though we had something in common. She mentioned her 'handicap' several times. After several puzzled minutes I asked, 'But *what* handicap?' 'Why,' she said in a shocked tone, 'I wear glasses!' "

A lack of opportunity to meet people of the opposite sex is often mentioned as another reason why some people fail to find love, romance, and marriage. Many people, particularly young women, are discouraged by the national sex-ratio statistics, which indicate that there are now about 3 million more women than men in the United States. At first glance, it might appear that American girls are at a great disadvantage, but the statistics don't convey that the great excess of women over men is in the older age groups. In every age group under the age of fifty, there are more single, never-married men than single women. In the childbearing age groups, there are many more single, divorced, and widowed women in total. Thus, there are more marriage-eligible men than marriage-eligible women. This results from the fact that about 105.3 boy babies are born for every 100 girl babies. An even larger number of boy babies are conceived, but more boy babies are miscarried.

It is true that these statistical factors do not take into account these social factors that bear on male–female relationships. For example, single women who remain unmarried by their late thirties tend to be from upper social and educational groups, but, by the time a woman is in her late thirties, she will find that the remaining unmarried men in her age group are predominantly from lower socioeconomic and educational echelons. Consequently, there exists a matching problem for women, even if there isn't a statistical one.

Actually, national sex-ratio statistics have very little effect on anyone's chances of finding love, romance, and marriage. Such statistics have no more relation to *your* opportunity for love and marriage than the national average income has to the amount of money you earn. Your motivation to seek love and marriage, your flexibility, and your skill in relationships will determine your success. These are the major factors that control the number of friends (and consequently opportunities for romance) in your own little social world. It is the size and composition of *that* social world that does have an important relationship to romance chances.

MOTIVATION

If you ask, almost all young single people will tell you that they would like love and, sooner or later, marriage. Desire for love and marriage was nearly universal at the women's college where I conducted studies, and other investigations have shown that it is nearly universal on coeducational campuses as well. And yet, many young people behave in a manner that indicates that other things are more important to them. At the women's college, some of the students professed to want romance, but when an opportunity for romance came along, they were too busy to take advantage of it. Soccer practice or glee club or studying was more important at the moment. Their motivation wasn't strong enough to push everything else aside. Why not? For many, the answer was fear, conscious or unconscious. Others had never achieved the "goal-set" necessary to make love and romance their primary interest. Some of the students had developed relationships that provided substitute satisfactions to dating. Still others had never learned to love.

Fears

Many of the college women and many of the single women and men who later came for counseling in Los Angeles knew they were afraid of love and marriage. Sometimes they realized exactly why they were afraid; sometimes their fears were unreasoned. Sometimes, major fears, such as a fear of sex, had been deliberately built into them in childhood by anxious parents who were trying to control their children's later moral behavior. The parents might have realized that this could inhibit the later sexual life of their children, even after marriage, but they probably believed their proscriptions were more valuable than the problem of some future inhibition. In other cases, the parents were completely unaware of the harm they were doing.

Fears are easily conditioned. Many fears are learned by the child before he is old enough to remember how he got them. For example, many people are afraid of spiders; yet very few can remember ever having been bitten by a spider. Spider-fear is learned by the child from the reactions of those around him. It does not have to be a dramatic and hysterical scene that a frightened mother plays at the sight of a spider; more often she may give only a small alarm, but her reaction is perceptible enough so that the child comes to understand that he is supposed to be afraid of spiders.

A fear of spiders is unlikely to harm one's chances of love, romance, and marriage, unless one's prospective mate is an arachnidologist. But there are other fears that children acquire that can have an injurious effect on their later social lives. Fears of the other sex or fears of sexual experience can be completely love-inhibiting.

Some of the fears most damaging to marriage chances are often not thought of as fears at all. These are the conditioned insecurities that make a young person overly afraid of doing or saying something improper or inaccurate. Kept within reason, these little fears make the world a livable place, because they predict how other people (who also fear disapproval) will behave. But for some people, the fear of being socially disapproved of—especially by their peers—becomes unreasoned and destroys their ability to live creatively.

Such people have difficulty handling normal human relations. Sometimes they are so shy that they cross the street to avoid meeting other people. Often they are extremely sensitive to criticism, real or imagined. They defend themselves elaborately. Disapproval is traumatic for them, and they may become agitated at the mere hint that their activities are being evaluated. Some overrespond to flattery and reassurance and will do almost anything for compliments and praise. Sometimes they demean others in the hope of appearing superior by comparison.

These fears and insecurities not only destroy present relationships but also lead to other problems. A person who feels unloved will not reach out to love anyone else. In turn, no one will love him. Finally he becomes permanently unloved and a first-class candidate for the psychiatrist's couch.

Goal-Set

A nonlove, nonmarriage "goal-set," the second major reason for lack of motivation, is also implanted early in childhood. It may start when a parent, catering to his own emotional needs, dreams himself into the future life of his newborn infant. For example, parents may envision their infant girl as a great woman of magnificent achievements, a glamorous actress, an important career woman, or even a pious and virginal saint. They may see her as a substitute for a son, as a provider and breadwinner for their old age, a devoted lifelong dependent, or in any one of many roles that satisfy their own yearnings. Such parents can often make their dreams come true by consciously or unconsciously downgrading one role and lauding another as the child grows and develops. Consider Roberta: "Nobody actually said I had to be a physician, but my parents made an awful fuss whenever I showed any interest in dolls or in working around the house. I never really tried to oppose them, though. I was supposed to be a boy —that's what my father wanted—and I did everything I could to make up to them for being the wrong sex. I worked hard in school. They expected me to! I don't ever remember thinking very much about romance; I was too busy. I didn't date at all. I used to think that going on into medicine was all my own idea. But as I look back, I can see that I was gently steered that way from the very beginning."

Certainly the parents are not always solely responsible for a particular goal-set or personality malfunction. As we will see in Chapter 24, sometimes the best-intentioned parents are thwarted by environmental circumstances or the child's temperament. The three factors, the parents, the child, and the environment, interact to condition the child's development. But the parents are usually the primary influence in the initial development of the attitudes and values that will guide much of the child's later behavior.

Once a particular goal-set is established, it often becomes self-enlarging. The individual "sells" himself on the idea that his present role direction is his destiny. He tends to play his self-conceptualized role to the hilt. He searches out meanings in the comments of others that verify the appropriateness of his performance.

One of the common goal-set problems that diminishes later opportunities for love, romance, and marriage occurs when the child develops an overwhelming need to demonstrate superiority. "I know," Lynn said. "It isn't really opportunity; it's me, Lynn. I see lots of men and I talk with many of them, but somehow it is more important to me to be superior than to win a friend. I see it in the first-graders I teach: Some of them just have to be first all the time. I'm like that, too. The only time I'm happy is when I have just shown up somebody. It's ironic that here I am, a woman who is denied love because she is deliberately seeking it. As a child, being superior brought me love and admiration from my mother and her friends. I felt especially good when I was better than my three brothers. I know intellectually that people don't like me when I am openly superior to them. But I still seem compelled to seek satisfaction by being the best. It has brought me competitive successes but it hasn't brought me the warm relationships I am hungry for."[10]

Men as well as women have goal-sets that diminish their love and marriage motivation. Sometimes with boys, as with girls, this nonlove, nonmarriage goal-set was not deliberately intended by the parents. It may be, for example, that a reserved atmosphere and an absence of overt affection in the home, the parents' normal pattern, were absorbed into the personality of the developing boy. But at times, there can be a deliberate attempt to steer the boy away from romance. To placate their personal emotional needs, some mothers stress the advantages of the boy remaining at home or not becoming involved with

[10] Richard H. Klemer, *A Man for Every Woman*, New York, Macmillan, 1959, pp. 72–73.

women on the grounds that women might injure his career opportunities by insisting on marriage. Unhappily married fathers and unmarried friends can also prejudice the young man against romantic commitment. The free, idyllic joy of the bachelor apartment can be made to appear much more attractive when compared to the responsibilities that follow from love and marriage.

"Why get involved?" Christopher asked. "I've seen a lot of very unhappy men who got tangled up in love and marriage—including my father. So I'm playing it casual. I get all the sex I want with no commitments. If a fellow lets himself get serious and sentimental, first thing you know he has a wife and then he's trapped. A woman can get out easily, but for a man there's a big financial risk. A man making $12,000 a year can barely support himself and have any fun these days. If he gets burned by one woman, then he might have to pay alimony and lose half his income. It isn't like in the old days when a woman helped you. Women don't want to be housekeepers anymore. Now all they want to do is sit around doing nothing or else to be going out spending your dough."

A normal sex drive is of major importance to a goal-set toward love and marriage. Those who have healthy heterosexual interests take a more active part in all kinds of male–female relationships, even if they reject love and marriage itself. Romance has no greater enemy than apathy, and there is no greater romantic apathy than that of the sexually disinterested person. As one discouraged young woman put it, "A girl has more trouble with the sheepishness of the sheep than she does with the wolfishness of the wolves."

The hows and whys of sexual interest among men and women will be discussed in later chapters. Here it is enough to note that some people, especially women, who typically realize their maximum sexual drive at a later age than men in our society, don't understand their sexual desire until it is too late. For physical or psychological reasons, as yet poorly understood, some people mature sexually later than others. When at last they are mature enough to have desire, they may have organized their lives around patterns, religious or secular, that preclude sex.

Substitute Satisfactions

Closely allied to the nonlove and nonmarriage goal-set as a reason for lack of motivation to love and marry is having one's needs—physical, emotional, or sexual—met in other ways. Occasionally, twins, very close siblings, and even warm friends lack interest in finding a romance partner or a marriage mate because they already have someone who meets many of their needs in some sufficient degree.

Some of these relationships are undoubtedly homosexual. Kinsey and his associates found that, of the men in their sample, 10 percent were exclusively homosexual between the ages of 16 and 55, and 4 percent were exclusively homosexual throughout their lives.[11] The Kinsey group reported that less than half as many females in their sample were exclusively homosexual, at least in their behavior. The researchers speculated that the widespread belief that there are more practicing homosexual females than males probably arises from the more open affectional responses of females to each other, which is often inter-

[11] Alfred C. Kinsey, W. B. Pomeroy, and C. E. Martin, *Sexual Behavior in the Human Male*, Philadelphia, Saunders, 1948, p. 651.

preted by males as indicative of some deep psychosexual interest.[12]

But many people who lack romance motivation, even if they engage in some homosexual activity, are not homosexual in any permanent sense. The Kinsey group reported that some 50 percent of all the males in their sample and 28 percent of all the females had had some homosexual experience in their lives.[13] Many people who have a poor self-image and low self-esteem think they are unable to compete for attention from the opposite sex. Discouraged and starved for affection, they turn to someone of their own sex, more for solace than for stimulation. Some such people later develop satisfactory heterosexual relationships.

There are many varieties of substitute satisfaction. One of the major satisfactions of any human relationship is being needed. When this need is met by taking care of an aged mother, a friend, or even a stray cat, motivation to establish a new relationship that might lead to romance is reduced in some degree, however slight. Motivations to love and to marry are functions of emotional hunger—good, normal, emotional hunger. Substitute satisfactions reduce the hunger and consequently the motivation.

Never Learned
to Love

A fourth major reason for lack of marriage motivation in many young people is that they never really learned to love appropriately. That is, they never learned to love any person other than their parents, relatives, or friends of the same sex.

The ability to love is learned. The learning process starts early. By the age of two or three, some of the attitudes that will affect patterns of adult love behavior—and, incidentally, sex behavior—are probably already formed.

The majority of parents do a very good job of teaching their children to love, but some do not. Some children have no good example from which to learn because of hostile conflicts between their parents. Sometimes the parents belittle love and denigrate the importance of affectional relationships with other people. By their reserved attitudes toward each other and toward the children, some parents create a "cold" atmosphere in which a warm, loving response is downgraded.

Parents may go in the opposite direction. Abnormal amounts of highly charged affection from the parents can lead to an excessive attachment and overdependence on the part of the child. Some parents give their children an overabundance of love or attention with a recognized or unrecognized intent that the child will respond with an excessive amount of love in return. In the beginning, this may result in only a little spoiling: The child is unhappy whenever he is alone or when he is not the center of attention. Later, the overdependent child often finds it difficult, if not actually impossible, to form other relationships. Many such parents are delighted that their children continue in a dependent relationship long after the time has come for them to leave the nest.

Sigmund Freud's theory of the Oedipus complex presumes that a child develops an unconscious sexual love for the parent of the opposite sex as a part of the normal process of growing up. In psychoanalysis, an adult who does not love appropriately is often found to have become "fixated" in this Oedipal

[12] Alfred Kinsey et al., *Sexual Behavior in the Human Female*, Philadelphia, Saunders, 1953, p. 475.
[13] *Ibid.*, p. 474.

stage. If the subject is male, he is believed to be still in love with his mother and to fear unconsciously that his father will castrate him in jealous rage. If the subject is female, it is believed that she still loves her father sexually and unconsciously wishes to murder her mother and have a child by her father.

This theory may be appropriate in some cases, for it is true that there are many romanceless people whose relationship to the parent of the opposite sex is unnaturally close. In many cases, though, there appears to be more reason to suspect that a parent has consciously or unconsciously conditioned his pliable and easily suggestible child to meet some of his own unrequited need for attention and affection than there is to assume that the child had a psychological problem to begin with.

As a matter of fact, in our society, a neurotic need for affection on the part of a parent is not uncommon. Sometimes this need is relatively simple and the damage it does is readily apparent.

CASE 7

"My father divorced my mother when I was only two-and-a-half," Stanley told the counselor. "I guess I was her only real happiness after that. She never remarried, and I was the only child she ever had. Sometimes when I was little I wasn't sure if I really did make her happy. She cried a lot, and it was very hard for me to distinguish whether she was crying because my father was gone or whether she was crying because she was happy I was there. She was always very 'sensitive.' Things other people said hurt her, and even when I was just growing up, she turned to me for solace. It seemed to make her feel better to tell me her problems even though she knew that I, as a child, could do nothing about them.

"She tried to do everything she could for me. She went without clothes herself so that I could have everything I needed. She worked long hours, and part of the time she had a second job doing work at home. I used to feel terribly guilty about it, but she would always say, 'There, there, you are my little boy to take care of now, but someday you will be my big man to take care of me.'

"We were very close. I started sleeping in her bed soon after my father left. I still do. I don't tell anybody that, because they would think it was mighty queer for a grown man to be sleeping with his mother. But there's nothing sexual about it. I guess it's habit. I don't like to sleep alone any more than she does.

"When I got to high school I didn't have many dates. I was sort of shy and not very athletic. I didn't have much chance to play with the other boys. I'd been too busy with my studies because that's what Mother encouraged me to do. The girls didn't pay much attention to me. I turned out to be 'sensitive' too, and my feelings were pretty easily hurt. They still are.

"In my senior year in high school Mother started getting sick. I had talked some about going away to the state university. But when I found out that the anxiety connected with my leaving made her even sicker, I decided not to do that, and I went to college right here in town.

"But she continued to have some manifestations of illness. The doctors have never decided exactly what it is, but anything that upsets her now puts her to bed for a few days.

"While I was in college, I went out with a few girls. I might have gone out more often, but I couldn't stand to think of Mother sitting home alone.

"When I got to graduate school I met Ruth, and for the first time I think I had some real feelings of love. But it upset Mother terribly for me to talk about her. Mother didn't like her. She pointed out to me a lot of things that I probably should have seen myself about Ruth. Ruth was from a different background, and she was very selfish. Anyway, I broke up with Ruth after about a year. That was eight years ago.

"Mother is much older now, and I am her only source of support—both economically and emotionally. She literally lives for me. Recently I met a girl named Beatrice, and I have been going with her for about six months. Mother is starting to talk about her the same way she talked about Ruth, only worse. Beatrice says that I have to choose between her and my mother. I just can't do that. What am I going to do?"

What can Stanley do? How could this situation have been avoided? Or was it unavoidable?

Stanley's case is bad enough, but sometimes a neurotic parent's needs and the responses they evoke in a child are far more complex.

CASE 8

Jenanne was an attractive twenty-eight-year-old fashion illustrator who found something wrong with every young man she went out with more than a few times. "I like to have a good time," Jenanne said, "but after I go with a fellow for several weeks I begin to see how many faults he has, and just about that time he begins to get serious and wants to paw me or both.

"I have a well-paying job and a beautiful car. My life is convenient and well planned. I have always said to myself, 'Why should I marry someone just for the sake of being married?' The other girls tried to make me feel as if I were missing something, but I thought I knew better. I'm still sure I know more about love and more about men than most of them will ever learn.

"My mother was married twice, and both times it was to an irresponsible man who failed to provide for us. My father was the first one. He was a remorseful alcoholic with an overwhelming need for affection and response. He tried all the time to beg, demand, or buy my response. Even as a tiny child, I had to live with complex emotional problems. I had to learn to see through and sometimes to give deceptive satisfactions to his impossible demands. I knew all about the weaknesses of men long before I had my first formal dress.

"My father didn't stop when my mother divorced him. In fact, I think it got even worse. He needed me more than ever, and he used to call me long distance when I was in school. I didn't know what to say to him, then, and I don't now. I just try to do the best I can. But that's never been enough.

"After my father left, my mother married someone just like him. It would almost be funny if it weren't so tragic. She used to swear that if she ever got out of the situation she was in, she would never look at another man for as long as she lived. But she wasn't unmarried a year before she found another man to abuse her. In many ways, he was much worse to both of us. One thing about him, though, when I left home he let me alone.

"Anyway, now I am thirty-three. It has hit me all of a sudden that in another ten years or so I'll be too old to have children and that I don't have much to live for right now. Last week for the first time in a long while a man was really serious about wanting to marry me. Tim is a nice guy—not very exciting—but nice. I don't really love him. But I think I am fond—yes, that's the word—fond of him.

"I know, though, that if I do marry Tim, I'll be looking for his faults from the wedding day forward. I just can't seem to help myself. And I will probably manipulate him, terribly. I can do it. I've had lots of parctice. I might be good for him, though. I really think he needs me. I know just how to cheer him on and make him feel successful. What shall I do?"

What should Jenanne do? Is it possible she might learn to love Tim? Could she really be "good for him"?

It is small wonder that Jenanne never really learned to love. She couldn't: Hers was the greatest learning difficulty of all; she never had a hero.

After many years as a counselor, I would be among the last to suggest that anyone love "blindly." Good marriages are made when the two people involved know themselves, know each other, and know before they marry that they can adjust to each other's faults. The love that leads to good marriages is a love in which two human beings respect each other and are actually drawn close together, despite their mutual recognition that neither is perfect. But learning to love in this manner involves preparation and practice. The lover has to know how to look up to an ideal. He or she has to learn as a child to value —and, in a sense, to overvalue—some member of the opposite sex, be it parent, sibling, friend, or movie star. To be a great lover it is necessary to have practiced a little harmless hero worship.

Real love is not for cynics, pessimists, or critical analyzers and worriers. Real love requires being able to see the best—not the worst—in the other person from the beginning. It includes having a reasonable amount of trust and faith that your partner will turn out for the best—after you are sure you could adjust even if he didn't. It demands a kind of courage to put aside your fears of "what will happen" that often distort the vision of those who have seen too much of life's unpleasantness.

Some courageous optimism is necessary, not only for a person to love and marry at all, but also to keep a love and to keep a mate. Positive trust is often rewarded by its own expectation. The man or woman who has faith in his partner's ability may help that partner grow toward the desired goal. The man or woman who lacks faith actually helps to make his worries come true.

No one can really love another unless he has self-respect—self-love in its finest sense. For most people, learning to love means learning to love themselves to the point where they believe in themselves, in their own judgment, and in their own desirableness. Then, and only then, they can love someone else exquisitely.

FLEXIBILITY

Equally as important as motivation to the individual's chances for love and marriage is his flexibility: How willing and able is he to adapt to the realities of the social situation in which he finds himself? Some men are notoriously inflexible, insisting that they will date only a rich girl or only one with a perfect figure. So are some women. Mary Jones had always believed that a girl looked silly with a boy who was shorter than she. As a result, she turned down all dates with boys who she knew in advance were not as tall as she was. Not so with Jane Smith. Jane dated the shorter boys and then met their taller roommates. It was that simple.

Intellectual and emotional inflexibility may increase as a person grows older. Moreover, an individual may cling to rigid attitudes and patterns of behavior, even though these attitudes and behaviors do not achieve his objective, as the following illustration makes clear. Susan was a well-educated young woman who had a Master's degree in fine arts and a great loyalty to the church of which she was a member. As a matter of fact, she insisted that any man who could really interest her would have to be a member of *her* church and also have a Master's degree in fine arts. She maintained this, despite the fact that she had grown up on a prairie-state farm where few people knew the difference between a Picasso and a Cézanne. Several people also pointed out to her how improbable it was that she would find a young man with these specific qualifications in the small California city to which she had moved, but she persisted in rejecting the men who did try to be friendly with her because they did not meet her rigid qualifications.

Finally, despairing of ever finding the man she wanted in California, she moved to Alaska on the theory that she would find many more men available there. This was, of course, true, but very few of them had a Master's degree in fine arts. However, when she got back to the invigorating, pioneering atmosphere of the wide open spaces, the values that she had held as a girl back on her prairie farm seemed to take on a new importance. Ultimately, she met and fell in love with a young potato farmer who not only didn't have a Master's degree in fine arts, he hadn't even been to college. Because they had similar basic value systems, Susan and her husband had the kind of mutual understanding in which love can grow. Even more important, she was flexible enough to reevaluate her own attitudes.

Certainly there is nothing wrong with having high standards. This is a mark of self-respect upon which the self-love that makes other love possible is invariably based. Moreover, it is almost axiomatic that the more common attitudes, values, and expectations the engaged couple share, the more readily they will be able to adjust to each other in marriage. But the inflexible person who can settle for nothing less than perfection in romance is probably defeating his own objective. He or she could very well pass up potential love and marriage partners because of his overly rigid specifications. As in all other areas of human interaction, there is an area of moderation in which the individual should attempt to protect his basic values, but he should also allow some latitude for reevaluating his attitudes in order to grow. This is flexibility, and it is one more answer to the question, "Why should they fall in love with you?"

BUT SHOULD EVERYBODY BE MARRIED?

There is general agreement among mental-health professionals that everyone needs love, but whether or not everyone needs marriage is something else again. As pointed out earlier, there are those whose physical or emotional handicaps make marriage impossible and those who, despite their motivation, cannot increase their marriageability. It is unhappily true that if a woman hasn't been asked by a suitable partner by the time she is a certain age, she probably won't be. In a society that values marriage so highly, this is a real tragedy, especially since some of these women are among the best educated, best behaving, and, therefore, in one sense, the most deserving in our society.

There are many others, both male and female, who could be married if they wished to, but, like Christopher on page 64 and Jenanne on page 67, they have decided against it for various intellectual and emotional reasons.

Will they be sorry? Maybe Yes, maybe No, depending on their personalities, the depth of their conditioning against marriage, and a variety of unforeseeable later experiences. In prior generations, the story might well have been different, but today the evidence indicates that some people live out their lives in relative satisfaction with their single status.

In a sample of unmarried professional women, Luther Baker, Jr., found that 90 percent expressed contentment with their pattern of living. Said Baker:

> The never-married subjects in this investigation expressed no feelings of frustration, no sense of not being a "whole person" as a consequence of being unmarried. Their sense of personal worth comes not from their biological function as a female but from their social function as a human being, from what they perceive as a creative contribution to their significant society.[14]

It has been suggested that many of these women sometimes feel that their greatest problem is to convince their married friends that they are really happy. This is understandable. However, Hortense Glenn and James Walters quite properly suggest that those who value marriage should also value a person's right to choose not to marry.[15]

The age of an unmarried person may well have something to do with his or her satisfaction with singleness. Robert Weiss and Nancy Samelson found in their study of the social roles of American women that whereas almost a third of the older unmarrieds had no feelings of usefulness or importance, none of the young unmarrieds felt that way.[16]

Some unmarried people are probably wise in staying so. Evelyn Ellis, after a study in the early 1950s, reported that there was some evidence to suggest that single, hard-driving, career-minded women probably would not make good marriage partners anyway.[17] The studies of hard-core bachelors previously cited indicate that many bachelors have habit patterns that wouldn't go well with marriage either.

Now that getting married isn't as necessary as it once was, the decision to seek marriage can depend—and probably should depend—on a large and complex group of personal attitudes, values, and expectations. Some of these feelings concern the motivation and the flexibility just discussed. But many more have to do with "relatability," the subject of the next chapter.

[14] Luther G. Baker, Jr., "The Personal and Social Adjustment of the Never Married Woman," *Journal of Marriage and the Family*, **30** (August, 1968), 473–477.

[15] Hortense M. Glenn and James Walters, "Feminine Stress in the Twentieth Century," *Journal of Home Economics*, **58** (November, 1966), 703–707.

[16] Robert Weiss and Nancy Samelson, "Social Roles of American Women: Their Contribution to a Sense of Usefulness and Importance," *Marriage and Family Living*, **20** (November, 1958), 358–366.

[17] Evelyn Ellis, "Social Psychological Correlates of Upward Social Mobility Among Unmarried Career Women," *American Sociological Review*, **17** (October, 1952), 558–563.

7

RELATABILITY:
THE "KNOW-HOW"
OF ESTABLISHING
RELATIONSHIPS

Relatability is the skill and know-how involved in developing close relationships with other people. For some it seems almost natural, as if they had been born with it. The chances are, though, that they learned it.

It is true that some marginally genetic factors, such as intelligence and temperament, are involved in relatability. One has to be perceptive enough to be able to see how to interest other people and active enough to want to. But some less-than-brilliant people are more skillful in human relationships than some geniuses, and some passive and slow-moving people are more attractive than some hyperactive ones.

Since much of relatability is learned, the quality of it can usually be improved by almost anyone who is really motivated to work at it. There are many ways of doing this. Some will be suggested in this chapter. But in order for an individual to know how to improve his relatability, he needs to know something about the whole process of developing a love relationship, for only then can he know how to apply his improved skills.

The process by which a love relationship ordinarily develops has been variously analyzed by many behavioral scientists over the years. One of the more recent theoretical formulations was by Ira Reiss in 1960.[1] He described a progression to love as starting with rapport (feeling at ease with each other and being relaxed and eager to talk about oneself and learn about the other person). Rapport leads to intimate self-revelation, which in turn leads to mutual dependency (each comes to depend on the other to fulfill his expectations) and, finally, to personality need fulfillment.

This chapter will look at the process of love development in a slightly

[1] Ira L. Reiss, "Toward a Sociology of the Heterosexual Love Relationship," *Marriage and Family Living*, **22** (May, 1960), 139–145.

different way, a way that I have found practical and effective in counseling and teaching. Although I agree with Reiss about the progression from initial rapport to need fulfillment, I see the process as containing three steps rather than four. First, one must make a good first impression on the other. Second, one must become a "sex-appropriate" friend. Third, one must become emotionally indispensable to the other person.

These steps ordinarily should be taken in this order, for taking them out of order can seriously affect the growth of a depth relationship. The man or woman who tries to become emotionally indispensable on the first date is probably not going to create conditions conducive to enlarging the relationship. But the person who is still trying to make an impression when the time has come to be emotionally indispensable is not going to succeed either.

THE FIRST IMPRESSION

Usually a good first glance is requisite to a good first impression. Most human beings have been conditioned to *temporal extension,* the process of judging what *will* be by what *is* through stereotyped attitudes over a lifetime. If, for example, one person sees another frowning, he assumes that the other has the full-time personality of a cold fish. On the other hand, if he should happen to catch the other smiling, he is likely to judge him as a warm, friendly person he would like to know.

The importance of the smile in social relationships in America is hard to overestimate. A smile is a gesture of response that immediately makes people feel accepted. If one withholds this symbol of friendliness and good humor, he is almost immediately stamped as an undesirable prospect for a deeper relationship. Some years ago, students at Arkansas State University were asked to describe an "old maid" they had known. The students listed many diverse characteristics, but the one thing most commonly noted was that an old maid never smiles.[2]

There are other stereotypes that condition first-glance deductions about people. Paul Secord and John Muthard presented a collection of twenty-four pictures of women to a group of 140 college men and asked them to predict the personalities that went with the photographs.[3] There was a surprising amount of agreement in the reactions of the young men. One opinion was that widened eyes were associated with good moral character and traits like kindness and faithfulness. Eyelids that drooped slightly, a jauntily tilted head, and narrowed eyes were presumed to be indicative of those who were conceited, demanding, and attention-loving. It was the girl who had a well-groomed look and a smiling mouth that attracted the young men in Muthard and Secord's sample of conservative, highly educated Southern men. She was judged to be the truly socially adjusted type: gay, intelligent, refined, likable, and a good mixer.

Such studies in stereotyping demonstrate the often underestimated importance of dress, manner, and smile. The stereotype for what is acceptable or desirable varies, of course, with the previous cultural conditioning of the judging

[2] H. K. Moore, "A Comparison of Unmarried and Married Women," paper presented at the annual meeting of the Arkansas Psychological Association, Conway, Ark., Nov., 1950.
[3] Paul F. Secord and John E. Muthard, "Personalities in Faces: IV. A Descriptive Analysis of the Perception of Women's Faces and the Identification of Some Physiognomic Determinants," *Journal of Psychology,* **39** (April, 1955), 269–278.

person and with the current styles in dress and behavior within the culture. But the principle is the same. If the first impression is a good one, it often meets the other person's role expectations, and this, in turn, is the foundation for a successful relationship.

The good first glance is not, however, synonymous with the complete good first impression. The relationship of any two personalities is complex, but it is probably safe to generalize that the one thing that epitomizes the total good first impression is the self-confidence of the one who does the impressing.

THE IMPORTANCE
OF SELF-CONFIDENCE

In attempting to establish some hypotheses about students' relative effectiveness in social relationships in the studies at a women's college, I attended many college dances and social gatherings. I watched what happened when a young woman was about to be introduced to a young man. Later, I talked with the participants. The two following composite pictures emerged as plausible descriptions of the emotional mechanics of typical social introductions situations.[4] If the person who was about to be introduced had self-confidence, he or she was far more likely to be successful in the introduction procedure. For example, a self-confident girl, when she was introduced, did not keep saying to herself all the time, "I wonder how I look? I wonder what he is thinking about me now?" Instead, she was thinking to herself, "I wonder what I can do to make him feel more comfortable?"

Because she was able to do this, the boy *did* feel more comfortable, and because he liked the comfortable feeling, he liked her. In turn, because he liked her, she felt even more desirable and self-confident, and she was able to be even more gracious. Consequently, her popularity tended to pyramid.

But when a young woman who had no such self-confidence was about to be introduced to a boy, she would say to herself, "Now I know he won't like me, so I won't take any initiative or he'll think I'm aggressive, and I won't say too much to him or he'll think I'm dumb."[5]

The young man who was being introduced to this unself-confident girl would try at first to be pleasant. He would ask her several questions, but to each of these she would give a one-word reply. Thereupon, he would conclude that she really didn't want to talk with him. Feeling rejected, he would slink off to nurse his wounded ego. Then the girl would say to herself, "Now, see, I knew he wouldn't like me!" As she lost more and more of the little self-confidence she did have, her popularity tended to decline.

A decade after I reported these observations, Robert Coombs did a statistical study of social participation, self-concept, and interpersonal evaluation.[6] Coombs's sample consisted of 220 male and 220 female college students paired by a computer. His observational setting was a college dance attended by all 440

---

[4] These were reported in Richard H. Klemer, *A Man for Every Woman*, New York, Macmillan, 1959.

[5] A classic study by Mirra Komarovsky indicated that many young women feel they have to "play dumb" to attract a man. See "Cultural Contradictions and Sex Roles," *American Journal of Sociology*, **52** (November, 1946), 184–189.

[6] Robert H. Coombs, "Social Participation, Self-Concept, and Interpersonal Evaluation," paper presented at the annual meeting of the American Sociological Association, Boston, August, 1968.

participants. For six months he studied the interpersonal responses of the partners and the effect of previous dating participation and self-concept on those responses. He found validation for all of his six hypotheses. (1) Those who were favorably evaluated by their dating partners, as compared to less-successful persons, more often conceived of themselves as having been successful in receiving favorable ratings. (2) Those who conceived of themselves as having been favorably evaluated by their dating partners, as compared to less-confident persons, more often participated in additional dates with their partners. (3) Those who had had experience in dating situations were more often favorably evaluated by their dating partners than were less-experienced persons. (4) Those persons who were most experienced in dating situations, as compared to the less-experienced persons, more often came to the dance possessing favorable views of themselves as dating partners. (5) Those who were favorably evaluated by their partners, as compared to less-successful persons, more often participated in additional dates with their partners. (6) Those who came to the dance possessing favorable concepts of their own dating desirability were more often favorably evaluated by their dating partners than were less-confident persons.

In a way, the sixth hypothesis says it all. Coombs adds, however, that

> In general, the more confident a person was prior to the dance with regard to his appearance, dancing ability, and popularity with the opposite sex, the more likely his partner was to desire future dates with him. A time analysis shows that the relationship was more pronounced immediately following the dance than it was six months later. A comparison of male and female responses indicates that a positive self-image increased a girl's chances of being desired for further dates more than it did a boy's.[7]

It is extremely hazardous to describe anything as "human nature." The modifying force that cultural conditioning has on human drives is overwhelming. But in every culture and in every situation, the self-confidence that puts other people at ease, whether by saying the "right" things easily or by properly passing the peace pipe, is the essence of the good first impression. It meets the other person's need for security right from the beginning.

BECOMING
SEX-APPROPRIATE FRIENDS

If developing a deeply romantic relationship with another person is the objective, then making a good first impression and becoming *just* friends is not enough. The buddy-buddy or brother–sister type of friendship may be very desirable for some relationships but it can sometimes be actually detrimental to romance. There must be sex-role appropriateness if the relationship is to move toward romantic love.

It is at this point that my analysis of the love progression differs from Reiss's. Reiss suggests that revealing one's intimate feelings and experiences is the second step in the progression to love. In some cases, this is undoubtedly true; being trusted with another's intimate secrets can be a moving and love-enriching experience, but only under circumstances in which the other has already been identified as a sex-appropriate love object. Many people, both men and women, have close personal friends of the opposite sex who know all

[7] *Ibid.*

their secrets but whom they do not love romantically and would never consider marrying.

The identification of an appropriate other for developing romance, like the good first impression, is culturally conditioned. A female love object in one culture might be obese; in another she might wear a bone through her nose. In one culture, a desirable woman is aggressive; in another culture, she is reserved. This cultural variation is equally true for men.

Appropriate others can vary within the subcultural groups of a larger culture, too. A romance-stimulating woman in Hollywood might be heavily made up, bejeweled, and aggressive. An ideal love object among the Amish of central Pennsylvania might be unadorned, hard working, and reticent.

The one thing that is universal about the love object is that he arouses the potential lover's romantic emotions. To do this he must be appropriate to the particular other's personal sex-role expectation. In other words, when a woman looks at a potential lover, she should be able both to think and to feel romance. She should be able to suggest to herself that this man is or could be, in fact, her hero. Similarly, the way *she* looks and acts should consciously (or subconsciously) stimulate romantic feelings within her male partner. In the late 1960s, there were some writers, notably Marshall McLuhan, who suggested that we have been moving away from differentiated sex roles and, consequently, away from romantic love altogether.[8] The prevalence of young men wearing long hair and beads and women in tight pants and loose shirts led McLuhan to conclude that being a masculine man or feminine woman was becoming less important in our society. He has even suggested that, as sex-role importance decreases, the frequency of sexual intercourse might decrease, because there would be no need for the male to be sexually aggressive in order to prove his masculinity either to his partner or to himself.

Many other observers, however, while conceding that there have always been and probably always will be minor fads and fashions in sex-role observances, see no complete loss of sex differentiation in the foreseeable future. Both McLuhan and his critics agree that sex role and romantic love are highly correlated. Those who wish to believe in romantic love and wish to perpetuate it, at least in their own lives, are going to find that sex-role appropriateness is a large part of the package.

Until very recently, there has been a tendency for some writers in the family-relationships field to downgrade romantic love and sexual attractiveness as sound bases for lasting relationships on the theory that the violent emotional upsurges produced by such feelings are not conducive to building permanent relationships. It is true that rushing headlong into marriage because of a physical attraction increases the probability of marital failure, but it is also true that excitement of romantic love is often responsible for enabling the partners to surmount some of the difficult adjustments of the early months of marriage. In many instances, if the partners were not so much in love, they might never survive the first year of living together.

Moreover, it isn't necessarily true that all romance must be lost from the relationship as it matures. There are many long-married couples who still have the excitement and pride in being together that they shared in the early days of their courtship. Although, as we shall see, disillusionment is fairly common after marriage, it is not necessarily universal, nor does it have to be complete.

[8] Marshall McLuhan and George B. Leonard, "The Future of Sex," Look, **31** (July 25, 1967), 56–63.

Having made a first impression and become sex-appropriate friends, there remains for those who wish to establish a deep relationship the most important process of all—becoming emotionally indispensable to the other person.

BECOMING EMOTIONALLY INDISPENSABLE

Some years ago, Oliver Ohmann pointed to a curious fallacy to which many modern Americans cling. The fallacy is that, by dressing up their appearance and manner, they can become so irresistible and fascinating that other people will naturally fall in love with them.[9] It isn't that way at all. A person falls in love because he *needs* the other person. The wisest course for the one who wishes love, therefore, is to meet the emotional needs of the other person, thereby making himself emotionally indispensable. Meeting the other person's emotional needs is not only the best way to get and keep another person's love, in the long run it is the only way.

But what *are* the other person's needs? How can you identify them?

Let's go back for a moment to the four needs postulated as universal by William I. Thomas: the needs for recognition, response, security, and new experience.[10] Although this short list is not complete, and although needs vary in intensity from person to person, it and the following illustration can serve as a starting point for our discussion.

Hank was a high-school junior. He had been looking forward for months to the junior prom to which he was going to take his classmate Mary. On the Saturday morning of the dance, Mary's mother called to say that Mary had the mumps and couldn't go to the dance. Hank was terribly disappointed.

Upstairs in the same apartment house lived Jane, an attractive career girl of twenty-five. She had dates, many of them, with men of her own age. Although Jane thought they had had a good time, the men usually said goodnight to her at her door and never called her again. Jane had a date for Sunday evening, but she didn't have one on the night of the junior prom. So when she heard about young Hank's disappointment, she offered to go with him to the dance. To say that Hank was surprised was putting it mildly, but the more he thought about it, the more he liked the idea, and soon he agreed.

At the end of the evening, when they got home from the dance, Hank was completely in love with Jane. Yet the next night, when Jane went out with a man of her own age, the usual thing happened. Although she thought they had had a good time on the date, the man said goodnight to her at the door, and she never heard from him again. Why did Jane engender an affectional response in Hank, yet arouse no response whatsoever in the older men?

You could say it was a matter of maturity. But that explains almost nothing. What actually happened was this: When Jane started off to the dance with Hank, she expected—and *expected* is the key word—that she would meet his needs. When he talked about himself and what a good football player he was, she listened intently, thereby meeting his need for *recognition*. When he complimented her, she accepted his praise demurely and immediately returned the

[9] Oliver Ohmann, "The Psychology of Attraction," in Helen Mougey Jordon, ed., *You and Marriage,* New York, Wiley, 1964, pp. 13–39.

[10] William I. Thomas, *The Unadjusted Girl,* Boston, Little, Brown, 1923, p. 4.

conversation to him. When he fumbled with the change at the refreshment stand and spilled his drink all over the table, she was the picture of poise and easy helpfulness. She gave him a *security* in the social situation that Mary, ten years younger, was not yet mature enough to know how to do. Jane *responded* to Hank and met his need for a *new experience*. Thus, it was almost inevitable that he would reward her with his love feelings.

But what happened the next night? The next night Jane expected—and again *expected* is the key word—that since the older man had asked her for a date he would meet *her* needs. Since Jane was intelligent as well as attractive, she knew that the male of the species requires a certain amount of flattering attention, so she perfunctorily complimented him on his accomplishments. But the genuine giving feelings she had had with young Hank were not evident, and the man quickly sensed her insincerity.

After all, Jane thought (and her attitude betrayed), why should *she*, intelligent and attractive Jane, subordinate *her* personality needs to those of the man she was out with? Didn't he ask *her* for a date? Was she expected to subserve herself in the manner of a Japanese housewife? No, indeed, Jane rationalized; he should be happy merely to be out with an entertaining woman who was sophisticated and impressive.

But was he? No. Are other men? Generally not, although there are, of course, some men whose personality needs for recognition or new experience could be fulfilled by a coldly impersonal but exquisitely beautiful woman, just as there are some other men who need to be dominated in order to feel secure. Most men, however—and most women, too—have less complex personality needs that are better satisfied by genuine recognition, response, security, and new experience.

Almost always it is a serious mistake to believe that cosmetics or glamour can do more than get a relationship to the sex-appropriate-friend stage. From there on, building a love relationship is a matter of becoming indispensable to the other person by a genuine sensitivity to his emotional needs and a genuine desire to meet them.

It is equally important that a man meet a woman's needs as that a woman meet a man's. There is no sex priority in need-meeting. A deep love relationship follows from a casual acquaintance when there is an unusual ability on the part of one individual to sense and to fulfill the psychological needs of the other. Fancy clothes, expensive automobiles, and after-shave lotion are relatively impotent when compared to the addicting power of being able to understand, reassure, and respond to another person.

This suggests one more definition of love: *An individual is in love when meeting the emotional needs of his beloved becomes an ultimate emotional necessity for him.* When one clearly perceives the other's basic personality needs—some to a fault—and still feels he wants to help that other find satisfaction for those needs more than anything else in the world, then he is in love.

From this definition it is clear why the process of continuing love relationships is as difficult as it is. First, it takes a great deal of perception to know what an individual's needs really are. Although it may be easy to see, for example, that a boastful person has a large need for recognition, it is often more difficult to see that the retiring person has an even greater need: He demands that you meet his need for security before he will even talk with you.

Moreover, a person's real needs sometimes differ from what even he thinks they are. Later you will read the case of a woman who wanted the counselor to tell her husband that he should put his arms around her and comfort her when she had a temper tantrum. The counselor asked her if she was sure this would really help. The woman pondered for a while and finally concluded that if her husband did try to comfort her, it would only make her feel worse, for then she would know for sure that she had something to feel bad about. What she really needed, she decided, was a secure husband who would tell her to "shape up," for such a man could make her feel better by his very strength.

There are many other examples. For instance, it doesn't necessarily follow that a man will fall in love with the cook at the luncheonette he patronizes simply because she meets what he feels is his primary need for food. Nor will he necessarily fall in love with a casual pickup simply because she meets what he feels is his primary need for sex.

Another part of the difficulty in recognizing needs results from the fact that, although all people have needs, these needs differ in intensity. For example, some men need response so badly that they spend all their waking hours seeking it. Others can go off hunting or fishing or even prospecting for years at a time without apparently needing or missing response from another person.

Still another difficulty about meeting needs is that not everybody can outwardly express his love feelings in return for having his needs met. The need-meeting may be very satisfying, but the individual whose needs are being met is unable to communicate his pleasure. This inability may betray his greatest need: for someone who will understand how he feels without his having to make it explicit.

There are, of course, people who can absorb need-meeting like a sponge and never feel or give anything in return. These selfish people are a dead end as far as any true love relationship is concerned. They are probably still a minority in our culture (although they may be becoming increasingly less so). Such people can be helped to know and understand love themselves only through psychotherapy.

To illustrate the problems involved in need-meeting, we might consider what happened to Linda. As a young child, Linda worshipped her father but was rejected by her mother. She had no dates until she was far beyond the usual age for starting to date. When she got to college, she met Ted, a handsome young man who, by the very fact that he looked in her direction, seemed to meet Linda's easily discernible needs for affection, recognition, and security. By giving Linda a very little attention, Ted won her undying affection.

But Linda didn't know how to go about meeting Ted's real needs. She didn't realize that Ted was a demanding, highly self-centered individual, from a different subcultural group where exploitation of another individual was a casually accepted custom. The woman who became a physical outlet for his sex tensions was not, by any stretch of the imagination, meeting his emotional needs. Ted demanded and got submissive intercourse from a large number of women, including Linda. He needed a secure, determined girl who would meet his emotionally conditioned expectation that he would marry only a virgin who refused him premarital intercourse even though he insisted on it. He needed a courageous, aggressive, protecting, and dominating mother-figure who could give him the security that he had known briefly as a child but that had been snatched from him by his mother's early death. Because of her limited experience in dealing with people, Linda never even got to know Ted's real needs, let alone to meet them.

NEEDS CHANGE

The fact that an individual's needs may change as he moves from place to place and from time to time is, as Bernard Murstein, among others, has pointed out, another major stumbling block in need-meeting.[11] Some needs change in well-patterned progression as the person grows older. Typical adolescents want less response from their parents and more recognition from their peers. Older people want fewer new experiences and more security.

But sometimes there are changes in the direction and intensity of needs that, unless recognized in advance by the love partner, can be seriously damaging to the relationship. Consider the following classic case, which has come to be known as the medical-student problem. Actually, medical students are probably no more prone to this need-change difficulty than students in other specialties, but they have gained a widespread reputation for it.

CASE 9

Sally and Ronald grew up together. They came from the same neighborhood in a small town, went to school and church together, and started going steady in high school. When the time came, they went off to the same college. By the time they were juniors, they decided that they could no longer wait to be married. After the wedding, Sally quit going to school and took a job as a typist so that Ron could complete his education.

In due course, Ron was graduated from college and admitted to medical school. Sally and Ron moved into a small housing project originally designed for low-income families. Sally, of course, continued to work, but she resented that, besides typing for eight hours a day, the household chores were largely her responsibility as well. In the few hours that Ron was home, he usually had some studying to do. Sally sometimes suspected that he could have done his studying at school, but then he would have missed the cafeteria conversation and the occasional bridge games with the other students.

Finally the great day came, and Ron was graduated from medical school and accepted as a resident at a nearby hospital. There was still very little money to spare, so Sally continued to work, but at long last she persuaded Ron to start a family. Before his residency was complete, they had a child. Sally quit her job and seemed to be very happy with her new life. Getting started in practice meant more lean years. Moreover, another baby was born. With two in diapers and a house to take care of, Sally was always tired. But she loved Ron and she believed Ron loved her.

Within a few years, Ron's practice began to prosper. In fact, before long, Sally and Ron had money for all the material things they wanted. At first Ron worked very hard to pay off the debts and to build up an investment income. After a while, however, he began to take an increasing amount of time off to play golf at the country club. Sally went to the country club once or twice, but she was a small-town girl and felt out of place there. The women there talked about golf and bridge, neither of which she played. Ron kept urging her to try, but finally he gave up. With increasing frequency, he went to the country club by himself.

Meanwhile two more children had arrived, and Sally was ever busier with home-making activities. At the country club, Ron met a great many people, including some attractive young divorcées who had grown up in the atmosphere of the country club. Sophisticated and charming, they had gone to élite Eastern women's colleges

[11] Bernard I. Murstein, "The Complimentary Needs Hypothesis in Newlywed and Middle-Aged Married Couples," *Journal of Abnormal and Social Psychology*, **63** (July, 1961), 194–196.

and seemed able to anticipate exactly what Ron wanted even before he himself realized it.

One day Ron came home and, in effect, said to Sally: "I have found that the women at the country club meet my needs better than you do. I've changed. I need someone who is gay and sophisticated. I am sure you wouldn't want to have me spend the rest of my life with you, knowing that I didn't love you. You are a good woman and would make some other man a good wife, but you and I no longer have common interests. I will always take care of you and the children financially, but I want a divorce."

What should Sally do? What should she have done? Would you advise Ron to press for a divorce? Or should he be forced to stay with his wife?

WHOSE NEEDS?

After all is said and done, the biggest difficulty in meeting other people's needs, and so engendering their love, results from the difficulty of putting one's own needs aside in order to meet the other person's needs first. This can be rather easily illustrated. Suppose a group of young women were asked to list the things they didn't like about the young men they dated. The list, which would probably be very long and very thorough, would undoubtedly contain the following:

1. They're conceited.
2. They're fickle.
3. They don't hold car doors for us.
4. They make too many sex advances.
5. They call too late for a date.
6. They suggest the same old places to go on a date.

Now suppose the young women were asked to analyze the needs involved in these complaints and—more importantly—whose needs were involved. On the assumption that the frequency of repetition is related to the intensity of need, it might be speculated that the boys who talk about themselves excessively have a deep need for recognition and response as well as a need for the ego security of knowing that they are worthy persons. It might also be a valid deduction that fickle men have a greater-than-average need for response from a large number of persons. The response need might also tend to explain the behavior of the "wolves," though, in their case, biological drives enter the picture and so does the fact that there is a recognition value accorded to the young man who can report back to his friends that he has been victor in another sex adventure.

But what about the other items on the list? What of the young men who didn't hold car doors, who called too late for a date, and who always took them to the same old places? Obviously somebody's needs were not being met, but whose? Not the young men's, but rather the young women's! The men who didn't hold the car doors were not giving the young women recognition as worthy and desirable females. The men who called too late for a date were neither meeting their partners' needs for security nor recognizing them as popular and important young women. The men who took their dates to the same old places were not meeting their partners' needs for new experiences.

This part of the analysis often comes as a surprise to those who, because they have been catering for many years to their partners' obvious needs, have felt that they have therefore been completely self-sacrificing. Many men and many women do not realize how demanding they are about having their own needs met.

Usually before he is ready to see how he can be more attractive by placing the first emphasis on meeting another person's need, the romance seeker must have many insights about his own needs. Many people are so conditioned to look to their own status and prestige that they play games intended to make the other person put himself in the giving position first. If the objective is immediate ego satisfaction—and nothing more—that is probably exactly all the winner of the game will net. But if the objective is to promote a real, deep emotional feeling on the part of the other person, then meeting his needs first is more logical and more effective. The relationships that continue to grow richer with the passing of the years are those in which each person can recognize and meet both the permanent and the changing needs of the other.

Giving need satisfaction first is an evidence of strength that only the weak and selfish cannot afford. Indeed, it is only those people with superior self-respect, or "self-love," in the finest sense who can meet the other person's needs at all.[12] The insecure individual is too busy looking out for his own tender self.

It should be made eminently clear that meeting another person's emotional needs does not imply that one should become a self-abnegating jellyfish. A sense of personal worth and integrity is absolutely necessary, or it will be impossible to meet any other person's needs for very long. People want their needs to be met by secure, positive others and not by fawning, supplicative, "try-too-harders." Experiments with rats have led some psychologists to believe that most animals, including humans, do not want all of their needs satisfied too easily. As Leon Festinger says it, "Insufficient reward does lead to the development of extra preference. . . . Rats and people come to love things for which they have suffered."[13]

As we shall come to see in the later chapters on adjustment, the husband who tries to do everything his wife might possibly want him to do is not always the most successful of husbands, for he deprives his wife of the opportunity and challenge of working for his love. Here again, perceptive analysis of a partner's true emotional dynamics is a critical factor in need-meeting.

CASE 10

Laura, an attractive, twenty-year-old college junior, had been going with Rolf for about two years. She was beginning to wonder if she loved him enough to marry him, which he was eager that she do. "He's a wonderful fellow and most of the time I enjoy being with him. We have fun together," she said. "But I'm beginning to wonder if I am affectionate enough for him. I come from a sort of reserved family. My father and mother never outwardly express affection toward one another, and I am a little uneasy when I see people mushing over each other. But he is from an excitable, foreign-born family and he expects—in fact he demands—a great many evidences of love all the time. I can't figure out whether he was denied enough response or whether he just got used to having too much.

[12] There is an excellent discussion of self-love in Erich Fromm, *The Art of Loving*, New York, Harper & Row, 1956, pp. 57–63.
[13] Leon Festinger, "The Psychological Effects of Insufficient Rewards," *American Psychologist*, **16** (January, 1961), p. 11.

"Anyway, Rolf is always telling me how much he loves me in such elaborate ways that I am embarrassed. He keeps trying to coax me to say that I love him, and sometimes I just can't. It isn't that I don't think I do (or is it?). It's just that I get embarrassed around that sort of talk.

"He is always coming over to my house, even when I'd rather he didn't. I really don't have enough time to study. He brings me gifts and presents. He almost smothers me. I think the times when I was most happy was when we first started going out together. Rolf was then interested in another girl, and I had to compete with her in order to get him to call me at all. Last week for three days he didn't come over to the house. I began to get a little uneasy, so I went to see him. On the way over I got sort of a thrill for the first time in a long while. It was nice to be able to do something for him that I wanted to do.

"Now Rolf wants to get engaged. It isn't enough for him to go steady. I've always wanted to have a career after I finished college. Not a long one; I want to get married some day. But I do want to have some freedom. Please don't misunderstand me, though. Rolf is awfully nice, and I would hate to lose him. I've gone with a lot of other boys—some were the kind who push you around—and I wasn't really very happy with them, either. I'm afraid that if I tell him we won't get engaged, he'll find some other girl. He really needs affection, and I think he really wants to get married. What shall I do?"

What shall she do? Knowing just this much about the situation, what can we deduce about Rolf's needs? What about Laura's? Will Rolf and Laura be able to continue to meet each other's needs? Do you think Laura's needs will vacillate less as she grows older?

IMPROVING RELATABILITY

If you are really motivated to improve your relatability, and if you accept the theoretical formulation that real love develops in steps from the good first impression to becoming sex-appropriate friends and is brought to completion by becoming emotionally indispensable to the other person, then perhaps the following suggestions will help you.

Most of the easy generalizations about the good first-glance impression have already been made: Smile, respond easily, and keep your appearance within the expectation tolerance of those you wish to impress. In connection with the last point, find out all you can about the group you are preparing to enter and about the people you are about to meet. The more you know about the group's (and the individual's) expectations, the more confidence, poise, and relaxed security you can have.

Since self-confidence is so important to the total first impression, anything that can be done to build your self-confidence and reduce your initial tension will be helpful. Some of the following suggestions may work for you; some may not. (1) Many people find that they can make a better impression by *trying* to be calm and relaxed. Practice "loosening up" beforehand. (2) Remembering that the other person is probably just as concerned as you are may help. If you can understand that he is quiet not because he doesn't like you but because he is tense too, perhaps you can get the courage to take the lead in the conversation and thus win his friendship. (3) Not trying too hard sometimes helps, too. You may feel that you must impress the other person with your accomplishments. The less he seems to respond, the harder you try. Actually, he may have been very impressed, but you may not have given him an opportunity to say so in his own way. Usually, people hear and see you, even when you are not sure they do. (4) Listen carefully. Listen to the other person's name and what he has to say. Ask discreet questions and get to know where he is from, what he has done, and what his family was like. All these things can give you invaluable clues in talking further with him. (5) Assume that he likes you. As a matter of fact, assume that everybody likes you, until it is proved otherwise. If you behave as if everybody likes you, they probably will. (6) Think of the other person's needs and his *likes*, remembering that this will probably make him want to reciprocate. Don't overdo it; there is a time to receive as well as a time to give. (7) When you can no longer appropriately talk about the other person, talk about those things you are most enthusiastic about—with the exception, of course, of other opposite-sex friends. He will be interested in almost anything that really interests you, provided you can project that interest to him by your own enthusiasm. (8) Be positive when he asks for your opinion. Not knowing what you think often contributes to the other person's insecurity. For example, if he asks if you would like to go to the movies and you say "I don't know" or "It doesn't matter," you are adding to his insecurity. If, however, you are enthusiastic about your likes and are willing to express your dislikes openly, he can feel contented that *he* has made the right decision by taking you where you want to go. (9) Try not to worry about your first-impression failures. The first thing a good salesman has to learn is that he can't make a sale every time. If he lets himself get discouraged over the last sale he didn't make, he is sure to muff the next one.

Increasing your relatability in the sex-appropriate-friend stage is more difficult, for it often may involve changing some of your customs, attitudes, values, and expectations in order to accept some of his. First, *can* you change? Second, is it worth changing? Sometimes it is easier and better to find someone whose ideal you can be without too much alteration on either's part.

If you do decide that you do want the other person enough to change, remember that it must be an honest change. Usually the only person you can change is yourself, and you can't do it by adopting a new set of tricks or techniques all of a sudden. Any change in your personality involves a lot of motivation, a lot of self-discipline, a lot of practice, and a lot of patience.

Even if there were techniques and tricks available, using them might be self-defeating. Words and phrases seductive to one person may turn out to be repulsive to another. Pressure techniques that force some people into the desired action motivate others toward undesired behavior.

Moreover, do you want a person you can trick? Or would you, in reality, feel a little contempt for him? If, in fact, he has to be guided to a decision, is he the decisive individual you want? Or will you have to decide little things for him for the rest of his life?

In the very process of exploring whether or not you can meet his expectations of a sex-appropriate friend, you may well have started on the process of becoming emotionally indispensable to him, for, in order to understand his expectations, you will have to try to understand him and his cultural conditioning. That very interest on your part may meet one of his most important needs.

But the chances are that he has other needs too, and if you decide that you do want him, you are going to have to determine what those needs are. The best way to do this is to observe and to listen. Some people are trying to tell others about themselves all the time, even when they are being overly quiet.

Merely *knowing* another's emotional needs isn't enough. If you want to become emotionally indispensable, you have to be able to meet those needs as well. This is something you can practice, even when you aren't trying to develop a deep emotional relationship. The butcher, the baker, and the candlestick maker have emotional needs, too. You can start learning to improve your emotional-needs-meeting ability by analyzing your roommate. Watch closely how he or she reacts. Give him or her medium doses of recognition, response, security, and new experience, and study the results. Then try it on a tougher case: that grouchy fellow in your chemistry lab perhaps.

But, remember that your feelings have to be genuine. If you start developing close relationships, it will be because you have genuinely changed, and others are reacting to that change. And remember, too, you have a social responsibility not to encourage a deeper relationship than you are prepared to continue.

8

SOCIAL FACTORS
IN MATE SELECTION

Need-meeting may explain why people fall in love, but it does not necessarily explain why two particular people get married. A person may have many loves. Many other people could meet his needs. Why then does he marry the one he does?

There are usually *many* reasons (and some unreasoned feelings) that control both the opportunity to marry and the final decision to take the step. These reasons and feelings have been divided into sociocultural factors, which sociologists have emphasized, and personal and emotional factors, which are usually thought of as being in the psychologist's jurisdiction. We will presently take a look at the sociological concepts of propinquity, exogamy and endogamy, and the psychological concepts of needs and neurotic interactions,

In any *particular* marriage relationship, however, all these factors together may not answer the question "Why did they marry?" for there are an infinite number of chance meetings, capricious impulses, accidents, coincidences, impressions, *faux pas,* missed opportunities, and deliberate schemes that prevent or encourage the marriage of two individuals. Although most marriage partners are aware of at least some of the reasons why they married, in many cases the deciding factors are unconscious to one or both of them.

It is important, nevertheless, that every student of the empathetic approach give careful examination to factors in mate selection, for, as we shall see when we get to marriage adjustment, the best way to ensure good relationships in any marriage is to improve the choice of marriage mates in the first place. What can be done to ameliorate marriage difficulties *after* marriage is limited; what can be done to avoid marriage difficulties *beforehand* by wise selection of partners is infinite.

This chapter will be devoted to background information useful to the cases and discussion of present-day mate selection in the three chapters that follow it.

PROPINQUITY

One of the reasons why people marry the mate they do is because the mate is *there*. Someone who is close at hand is a more probable candidate, even in this space age, than someone who is far away.

An early sociological study of *residential propinquity* (the tendency to marry the boy next door) was made by James Bossard in Philadelphia in 1931. After examining some 5,000 marriage licenses, Bossard concluded that roughly one-sixth of the applicants lived within a block of each other, approximately one-third within five blocks, and more than one-half of the total resided within twenty-five blocks of each other.[1]

In the years since Bossard did his original study, other studies have confirmed the tendency for people to marry mates who live near them. These later studies, however, indicated that nationality, ethnic, religious, and other social groupings were greatly responsible for the tendency to choose a mate living in the same area, at least prior to World War II.[2] Apparently the residential propinquity Bossard found was not necessarily a *cause* of marital choice but rather the *effect* of social considerations that caused people with like interests and like backgrounds to live in the same neighborhoods. Since most people do choose— sometimes with considerable parental help—mates with similar subcultural backgrounds, in the past they were more likely to find them close to home.

Things are somewhat different in America today. In the first place, cities and suburbs are much more likely now to have culturally mixed backgrounds. Moreover, in modern society, more Americans choose mates who were reared hundreds of miles away. More young people have automobiles, more marriageable young men are sent to far-distant places in the armed services, more students go away to college, and 20 percent of American families move every year. People still tend to marry partners who are close in distance, but the closeness is more likely to be as of right *now* rather than as of their childhood homes.

But even the new closeness has to be somewhat continuous for a marriage to result. J. Richard Udry points to studies that show that separation or lack of propinquity during courtship is one of the most frequent reasons for breaking engagements; he says: "Specifically, the more time a couple spends together during courtship, the more likely they are to marry. The further they are apart, the harder it is to spend time together."[3] It may be helpful to have this authoritative sociological validation, but most lovers have known it for a long time. The line in a popular song of the 1960s, "When I'm not near the one I love, I love the one I'm near," may not be applicable in every case, but there is certainly a tendency in that direction.

EXOGAMY AND ENDOGAMY

Stated succinctly, *exogamy* means marrying outside one's own tribe. In some times and in some parts of the world, members of the same clan were forbidden

[1] James H. S. Bossard, "Residential Propinquity as a Factor in Marriage Selection," *American Journal of Sociology,* **38** (September, 1932), 219–224.

[2] A. C. Clarke, "An Examination of the Operation of Residential Propinquity as a Factor in Mate Selection," *American Sociological Review,* **17** (February, 1952), 17–22; G. J. Schnepp and Lewis A. Roberts, "Residential Propinquity and Mate Selection on a Parish Basis," *American Journal of Sociology,* **58** (July, 1952), 45–50.

[3] J. Richard Udry, *The Social Context of Marriage,* Philadelphia, Lippincott, 1966, p. 209.

to marry. In the recent past in China, for example, individuals who bore the same surname could not intermarry, even if their original clan connection was remote. Exogamy exists in the American culture in the form of incest laws and taboo. Were it not for those, we might have more brother–sister marriage or, at least, more cousin marriage.

In the United States, as in most cultures, we have patterns of *endogamy* (marrying within one's tribe) as well. Indeed, several states still have laws on their books *requiring* marriage within the same race, even though a 1967 Supreme Court decision makes attempted enforcement of these laws improbable. But *cultural* endogamy, the subtle pressures of group customs and group values, still has a significant effect on our mate-selection patterns.

Throughout this chapter and the next two, the term *endogamy* will be used to describe mate selection in which people with group-related similarities, such as race, religion, and socioeconomic status, marry. In Chapter 11, where we will be discussing psychological factors in mate selection, we will use the term *homogamy* to describe marriages in which two people with similar personal characteristics select each other for marriage.

THE HISTORY
OF MATE SELECTION

To understand the nature of American endogamous mate selection patterns, it is necessary to look at the history of American mate selection. Our colonial ancestors brought to the New World the traditional European philosophy that marriages should be arranged by the parents, but in the American wilderness, there was very little opportunity for the formality that had existed in the more structured European cultures. Of all the colonists, the Puritans of New England were probably the most strict with regard to mate selection and premarital practices.[4] They resurrected the old Hebrew custom of betrothal as a precontract and celebrated it as a solemn occasion. The precontract ceremony involved a solemn promise to marry heard by at least two witnesses.

In all the colonies, though, it was necessary for a young man to secure permission from the girl's parents before beginning his courtship. There is considerable difference of opinion about how difficult the permission was to obtain. William Kephart believes that parents did not ordinarily withhold their permission, because marriage was so necessary for a woman.[5] Stuart Queen, Robert Habenstein, and John Adams, on the other hand, suggest that such permission was not always easy to obtain.[6] At any rate, the bachelor who tried to woo his beloved without obtaining the necessary consent came up against a law against "inveigling," and the hasty swain could be marched off to jail.

In addition to obtaining parental approval to court, it was necessary to have a second parental consent before a marriage could take place. Marriage was an economic transaction, and contracts detailing property rights and financial arrangements were common. This is not to say that there was no romance in colonial marriage. Women were in the minority, since more men than women

---

[4] William M. Kephart, *The Family, Society and the Individual,* Boston, Houghton Mifflin, 1961, p. 145.
[5] *Ibid.,* p. 145.
[6] Stuart Queen, Robert W. Habenstein, and John B. Adams, *The Family in Various Cultures,* 2nd ed., Philadelphia, Lippincott, 1961, pp. 276–277.

tended to migrate to the New World. This stimulated competition to the point where romantic behavior, traditionally more important to women, became the order of the day.

Some interesting courtship customs and rituals developed. One that often receives more attention in history than its incidence probably warrants was "bundling." Bundling was the practice of the fully clothed courting couple going to bed together either separated by a center board or with the girl stuffed neck high into a "bundling bag." There were no sofas and few chairs in colonial times, the houses were cold, and firewood was sometimes hard to come by. Bed was a practical place to be. That it was sometimes too practical is very probable. However, the parents were always in the house and usually in the same room, and there was, as Kephart puts it, "less likelihood of premarital sexual indulgence than there is today in the parked automobile."[7] Moreover, even when premarital pregnancy did occur, the responsibility was rather easily fixed. Then, as now, the wedding date was sometimes moved up a little.

As time went by in early America, romance continued to flourish. Women remained in short supply, and on the frontier especially they were highly sought after. In addition to being sex partners and romantic love objects, women had a practical value; they were a great economic asset. Not only could they themselves produce much more than they consumed, they also could bear children who were, in turn, economic assets.

After 1800, cities began to increase in size, and a middle class with social aspirations came into being. Formality increased. So did parents' interest in improving their own statuses by supervising their daughters' and sons' marriages. Moreover, in the cities, the sex ratio began to change as the supply of women increased.

Things remained catch-as-catch-can on the frontier, though. It is reported that, in the mining camps of the booming West, there developed what might be called serial polyandry, women having many husbands consecutively. Some of the frontier women would live with one mate only so long as he pleased them. When he failed to do so, they would move on to the next miner's shack.

In the later years of the nineteenth century, as America became more and more urbanized, the middle class continued to grow and to imitate the upper-class socialites by adopting rules for courtship behavior. Moreover, the new immigrant groups from Europe again brought with them formalized customs of older societies. These almost invariably involved considerable parental control of courtship behavior. Whereas some parents used direct methods of control, including strict chaperonage, others influenced the mate-selection probabilities of their children by such devices as moving into neighborhoods inhabited by others with the same ethnic or social-class background.

In the years following World War I, social changes spelled the beginning of the end of direct parental control. The automobile encouraged dating away from home and enlarged "outside-the-group" associations. The new freedom of the flapper era and the popular emphasis on parental permissiveness in child rearing combined to make the strict parent feel somewhat guilty. In turn, the so-called flaming youth of the 1920s rebelled even more aggressively against parental controls over courtship behavior. Coincidentally, or perhaps causally, romance was being sold in large doses by the movies. According to Arthur Schlesinger, Jr., "The invention of the movies gave romantic love its troubadours

---

[7] Kephart, op. cit., p. 148.

and its temples of worship. . . . The contagion was irresistible."[8]

Not all parents abandoned all efforts to influence the selection of their children's mates by any means. As we shall presently see, there are many mate-selection practices today that could result only from parental pressures, albeit more subtle now. As Robert Coombs puts it, "This more subtle means is not unimportant, for although a child may rebel against domination, he cannot escape the ideas conditioned in him from his childhood."[9]

Most children today, though, are exposed to cross-cultural influences, whether their parents like it or not. Now almost 90 percent of our young people enter high schools, and, even in suburban areas, the high school is more cross-cultural than ever before. Some 40 percent of these young people go on to college. There, too, they find that, despite the vestiges of traditional social conformities maintained by some sororities and fraternities, there is a wide heterogeneity of backgrounds among the students. Campus life today, especially at large universities, often encourages the associations of people with diverse cultural and subcultural origins.[10]

Even so, there is abundant evidence that, among the total American populations, endogamous courtship and marriage are still the rule rather than the exception. We will examine just a few of the classic areas in which social endogamy is operative.

RACIAL INTERMARRIAGE

Race is undoubtedly the most strongly continuing endogamous norm. There are surprisingly few studies of interracial marriage, and many of these are out of date, but there is some evidence that interracial marriage is on the increase.

A study of Los Angeles marriages in both 1952 and 1962 found that the rate for all racial intermarriage (including Orientals as well as whites and Negroes) had more than doubled in that period, although such marriages still amounted to only about 1.5 percent of all marriages.[11] But because Los Angeles has a greater variety of racial and ethnic groups than most other cities in the United States, these statistics may be somewhat misleading. Barnett reported that, in all California, the interracial marriage rate was 1.4 percent in 1959, the last year, incidentally, that California law required that race be recorded on the marriage license.

The Negro–white rate in California is considerably lower than the rate of all interracial marriages. Of all the white California males marrying in 1959, fewer than 0.1 percent married Negroes, and of the white California females marrying that year, fewer than 0.3 percent married Negroes. The great preponderance of interracial marriages in California was between whites and non-Negroes or between non-whites.[12] More recent data in the two states for

[8] Arthur Schlesinger, Jr., "An Informal History of Love in the U. S. A.," *Saturday Evening Post,* **239** (December 31, 1966), 30–37.
[9] Robert H. Coombs, "Reinforcement of Values in the Parental Home as a Factor in Mate Selection," *Marriage and Family Living,* **24** (May, 1962), 157.
[10] Gerald R. Leslie and Arthur S. Richardson, "Family Versus Campus Influences in Relation to Mate Selection," *Social Problems,* **4** (October, 1956), 117–121.
[11] J. Burma, "Interethnic Marriages in Los Angeles, 1948–1959," paper read at the American Sociological Association, Washington, D.C., August, 1962.
[12] Larry D. Barnett, "Research on International and Interracial Marriages," *Marriage and Family Living,* **25** (February, 1963), 105–107.

which they are available show the Negro–white marriage rate to be about 0.1 percent in Michigan and about 0.001 percent in Nebraska.[13]

The following generalizations are adapted from Larry Barnett's review of the available studies on interracial marriage:

1. Whites appear to be more willing to engage in interracial marriage with Orientals than with Negroes.
2. Among whites, it is Protestant and Catholic males and Jewish females who most frequently marry members of other races.
3. Religiously less devout persons more often marry interracially than the religiously more devout.
4. Persons who have experienced disorganized and stressful parental families are more likely to marry members of other races than those who were raised in cohesive and stable families.
5. Persons living in urban areas are more likely to marry interracially than persons living in rural areas.
6. In interracial marriages, the spouses more often come from different religions and from different socioeconomic levels, although one study suggests that the majority of mates in interracial marriages come from the same socioeconomic group.
7. In interracial marriages, it appears that the nonwhite male has a higher-than-average economic status, and the white male and female and the nonwhite female have a lower-than-average socioeconomic level.
8. In Negro–white marriages, the Negro is more often the male spouse, but in Oriental–white marriages, the white male more frequently marries a Japanese female and the Chinese male marries a white female.
9. Among those who undertake an interracial marriage, a greater-than-average number have been married previously
10. Foreign-born white males more than native white males and native white females more than foreign-born white females undertake Negro–white marriages.
11. In Negro–white marriages, the family of the Negro spouse seems to be more willing to accept the couple than does the family of the white spouse.
12. American males and females marrying out of their racial group are generally older than average at the time of marriage.[14]

Most writers agree that Hawaii is a special case among the states. Freeman has suggested that interracial or interethnic marriages are the preferred type there. But Freeman believes that in Hawaii, as in the continental United States, most of those young people who enter into interracial and interethnic marriages appear to be in overactive rebellion against their parents or against their social group.[15]

Although racial intermarriage may have been slowly increasing in the United States in recent years, the future rate of increase is obscure. Udry suggests that it seems unlikely that there will be a large increase in interracial marriage in the near future, and Heer finds it hard to imagine that any large-scale Negro–white intermingling will take place within the next hundred years.[16]

An Associated Press survey found that, in the first full year after the Supreme Court nullified the states' legal bars to interracial marriage in 1967,

[13] David M. Heer, "Negro–White Marriages in the United States," *Journal of Marriage and the Family,* **28** (August, 1966), 262–273.
[14] Barnett, *op. cit.,* 105–107.
[15] Linton Freeman, "Homogamy in Interethnic Mate Selection," *Sociology and Social Research,* **39** (July, 1959), 369–377.
[16] Udry, *op. cit.,* p. 215; and Heer, *op. cit.,* p. 273.

less than a hundred interracial marriages took place in all of the seventeen states that previously had laws banning such marriages.[17] However, some investigators believe that the gradual increase in school integration, which will hasten interracial association, will have a considerable effect on increasing intermarriage. E. A. Thomas Barth, a University of Washington sociologist, pointed out in 1967 that, "In our segregated society young people have not been in contact with other ethnic groups at the dating period. But contacts have been increasing. We can expect the rate of interracial marriage to increase. People do, after all, tend to marry people they know."[18]

RELIGIOUS ENDOGAMY
AND INTERFAITH MARRIAGE

At midcentury, August Hollingshead proposed that, next to race, religion is the most decisive social factor that American males and females consider in defining those who are eligible marriage partners. At that time, in his study in New Haven, Connecticut, he found that 97 percent of the marriages involving Jews were religiously endogamous. So were 94 percent of the marriages involving Catholics and 74 percent of the marriages involving Protestants.[19]

Very few sociologists believe that Hollingshead's findings are pertinent today. Although almost all the investigators agree that marriage within one's own religion is a greater-than-chance occurrence, there now is a great deal of disagreement about the exact nature and degree of religious endogamy. Data in this area are sparse, because only one state, Iowa, asks about religious affiliation on marriage-license applications. When special studies are made, it is usually found that there are wide regional differences in the rate of interreligious marriage in the United States. John Thomas, a Jesuit sociologist, found that interreligious marriages involving Catholics varied from 70 percent in Raleigh and Charleston to 10 percent in El Paso.[20] Moreover, deciding which is an interreligious marriage is often difficult. There are greater differences among some Protestants than there are between some Catholics and some Protestants. Then, too, people often change their religious thinking throughout their lifetimes. Should a bride who converted from Protestantism to Catholicism six months before she married a Catholic be counted as a Protestant or a Catholic?

The following generalizations are supported by research evidence:

1. Most interreligious marriages in the United States involve Protestant–Catholic combinations. When Jews enter interreligious marriages, they appear to select Protestants or Catholics with approximately equal frequency.
2. In Jewish–Gentile marriages, generally it is the Jewish male who marries a Gentile female, but there are no consistent findings for which sex most frequently is involved in Catholic–Protestant marriages.
3. Interreligious marriages are more frequent among persons who are remarrying than among persons entering first marriages.
4. Interreligious marriages are more frequent among the young and among people who are marrying at older ages.

[17] *The New York Times*, July 28, 1968, p. 35.
[18] "People Who Intermarry: Pioneers or Protestors?" Seattle Urban League Special Report, Seattle, Wash., April, 1967, p. 6.
[19] August Hollingshead, "Cultural Factors in the Selection of Marriage Mates," *American Sociological Review*, **15** (October, 1950), 622.
[20] John L. Thomas, "The Factor of Religion in the Selection of Marriage Mates," *American Sociological Review*, **16** (August, 1951), 488.

5. Interreligious marriages are more frequently characterized by an out-of-state residence of the bride and by a civil wedding.
6. There is strong evidence that the proportion of a religious group in any community is probably the single most influential factor for predicting interreligious marriage rates: The smaller the group, the larger the probability of intermarriage. The more a minority-group member associates with people of different religions, the more possibility there is that he will marry someone of a different religion.
7. Attitudes toward interreligious dating are more favorable than attitudes toward interreligious marriage.[21]
8. Males tend to have less opposition to interreligious dating or marriage than females.[22]
9. Young people from lower-status homes (as measured by father's occupation) have more favorable attitudes toward interreligious dating or marriage.[23]
10. The greater the church attendance, the stronger the opposition to interreligious dating and marriage.[24]

It appears that interreligious marriage is becoming more common. John Thomas suggests that almost half of all marriages involving Catholics are interfaith, including both those marriages not sanctioned by the Church and those interfaith marriages that the Church considers valid.[25]

Jerald Heiss found strong support for the hypotheses that parents of his total group of interreligious partners were less tied to their religion, that the interreligiously married were more likely to report dissatisfaction with their earlier relations with their parents, and that the interreligiously married were more likely to report tenuous ties to the family when they were young. Among Catholics, he also found strong support for the hypotheses that the interreligiously married were more likely to report strifeful family interaction when young, and that the interreligiously married were more likely to have been emancipated from their parents at the time of their marriage.[26]

SOCIAL CLASS
AND SOCIAL STATUS

Many of the recent studies indicate that both men and women tend to marry close to the occupational status of their own families. Leslie and Richardson, however, have noted a difference when the partners meet and marry in college. Those who met before attending college showed greater status endogamy than those who met while they were away from home.[27]

Over the years, many sociologists have suggested that, when and if social class lines are crossed, the man tends to marry down and the woman tends to marry up. This has been termed the "mating gradient" and is classic in most textbooks on mate selection. A recent study by Zick Rubin has suggested that

[21] Points 1 through 7: Lee G. Burchinal, "The Premarital Dyad and Love Involvement," in Harold T. Christensen, ed., Handbook of Marriage and the Family, Chicago, Rand McNally, 1964, p. 650.
[22] H. F. Hoover, "Attitudes of High School Students Toward Mixed Marriages," Catholic University of America Educational Research Monograph No. 15, 1950.
[23] Burchinal, op. cit.
[24] Ibid.; Hoover, op. cit.; and Prince, op. cit.
[25] Thomas, op. cit., p. 489.
[26] Jerald Heiss, "Premarital Characteristics of the Religiously Intermarried in an Urban Area," American Sociological Review, 25 (February, 1960), 52.
[27] Leslie and Richardson, op. cit.

such a tendency is not as universally applicable as was previously believed. Rubin found some indication that upper-middle-class women tend to marry up, but no strong tendency in the lower-middle class and lower class.[28]

Since social mobility is most easily achieved by a woman when she can marry a higher-status male, the idea of women marrying up seems quite logical. A man gains status through his career, but a woman's status is more often conferred on her by her husband. John Finley Scott puts it somewhat cynically:

> Insofar as she responds to the American dream of upward mobility, every unmarried American girl has a bit of the golddigger in her. . . . The pressure for marrying up in women produces a kind of imbalance in marital bargaining, to the advantage of high status men and low status women and the disadvantage of low status men and high status women. A low status man has little wealth or prestige to offer for a wife. In addition, he must compete for wives not only with others in his own station but with higher ranked men as well.

> A well-born woman, if she is to maintain through marriage the status conferred on her by her parents, must marry a man at least equally well born but for such men she faces a deadly competition from lower status women who also regard them as desirable husbands. As a result, low status men are more likely to remain bachelors, and high status women are the more likely to remain spinsters. This is the "Brahmin problem," so named because it reached its most extreme form among the high castes of Hindu India (but it can be observed among the Boston Brahmins as well).[29]

The greater employment of women has affected the mating gradient in recent years. Sundal and McCormick found that, among brides who were employed, the status level of the bride's occupation was more closely related to that of the groom's than to that of her father.[30] Working side by side may in the future be an important factor in increasing occupational-status endogamy.

AGE, EDUCATION, AND MARITAL STATUS

Americans tend to marry mates similar in age, education, and marital status. There has been an increasing tendency for the differences in the ages of bride and groom to narrow in recent years, even though a gap still exists.

For a period of a few years in the late 1960s, this trend toward age similarity was accelerated. Paul Glick, a statistician for the Census Bureau, has pointed out that young women usually marry for the first time between the ages of eighteen and twenty-two; young men usually marry for the first time between the ages of twenty and twenty-four. In the late 1960s, there were still more males than females at the same young-adult levels, but a marriage squeeze resulted from the fact that the girls born in the postwar baby boom of the 1940s became of marriageable age (statistically speaking) sooner than the boys.[31]

[28] Zick Rubin, "Do Americans Marry Up?" American Sociological Review, 33 (October, 1968), 750–760.
[29] John Finley Scott, "Marriage Is Not a Personal Matter," The New York Times Magazine (October 30, 1966), 70. © 1966 by The New York Times Company. Reprinted by permission.
[30] A. Philip Sundal and Thomas McCormick, "Age at Marriage and Mate Selection: Madison, Wisconsin, 1937–1943," American Sociological Review, 16 (February, 1951), 43–44.
[31] Robert Parke, Jr., and Paul C. Glick, "Prospective Changes in Marriage and the Family," Journal of Marriage and the Family, 29 (May, 1967), 249–256.

Men who marry at a relatively young age tend to choose women only a few months younger, but men who marry later are ordinarily considerably older than their brides. In 1960, husbands over 55 years old were an average 3.6 years older than their wives, whereas husbands under 35 were only 1.9 years older.[32] The marriage age has been declining for both men and women for the past century. In 1890, the median age for grooms was 26.1 and for brides 22, but in 1967 the median age of the groom's first marriage was 23.1 and the bride's was 20.6.[33]

There is a strong tendency for Americans to select a marriage mate with equal or almost-equal education. This tendency is strongest in the college population, with college men showing an overwhelming preference for women with similar education. Americans tend also to marry people with a similar marital status; that is, singles tend to marry singles, divorced to marry divorced, and widows to marry widowers.

Thus, it can be seen that, in American mate selection, cultural and background similars, not opposites, attract. But why? Udry identifies three factors that he feels tend to produce marriages that are endogamous with respect to social characteristics.

First, he suggests that society is organized into groups with similar social characteristics; therefore those who are socially similar are the most likely to meet and interact with one another frequently. Second, Udry feels that there are social values that encourage persons to marry those with similar values and discourage marriage with those who are socially different; groups holding these values bring pressure on individuals to encourage endogamous selection and discourage exogamous marriages. Third, Udry thinks that differences in behavior, attitudes, mannerisms, and vocabulary tend to make interaction between socially dissimilars difficult and unsatisfying.[34]

So far we have been talking primarily about mate selection in the impersonal, group-statistical terms of the research sociologist. We have avoided the really important question each individual faces (or ignores) in the selection of his own mate: What is best for me? The next two chapters deal with some of the pros and cons of endogamy.

[32] Ibid., pp. 251–253.
[33] U.S. Department of Commerce, Current Population Reports, series P-20, no. 170, February 23, 1968, p. 4.
[34] Udry, op. cit., pp. 343–344.

9

FOR OR AGAINST ENDOGAMY?

Current movements toward social integration and ecumenicalism in religious thought have given new vigor to an old dilemma for young Americans. Which is the more important value: to maintain the traditional endogamous patterns of mate selection and thus to align one's self with parental desire and a statistically greater probability of marriage success, or to break through cultural barriers in the ultimate demonstration of independence and democratic idealism and have the supposedly exciting experience of marrying someone "different"?

Alert students will immediately point out that very few people have to make this kind of cognitive decision when they are about to marry. By the time people are ready for marriage, they are usually deeply in love, and the decision to marry or not to marry is a matter of satisfying or denying emotional fulfillment, with very little reference to any social decision.

But, somewhere along the line, from the first date to the morning of the wedding, a decision *does* have to be made. "Endogamy, yes or no" is an intellectual choice (albeit sometimes a gradual and semiconscious one) before it ever becomes subordinated and obviated by love. Disillusioning as it may seem to the romantics, we do allow ourselves to fall in love—or not to—by establishing a field of eligibles. For example, except in very rare instances, no one permits himself to "fall in love" with his brother or sister, regardless of how common the bond or how close the relationship. On the other hand, a disenchanted husband may permit himself to fall desperately in love with his secretary after he has decided that he has every right to her love since he is so misunderstood at home. Those who do fall in love with heterogeneous others have allowed this to happen. The question then becomes: Should they have allowed it? Or, more importantly, should *you*? This chapter will present the case for endogamy; Chapter 10 will present the case against it.

THE CASE
FOR ENDOGAMY

The case for endogamy is most often put in terms of what happens if you *don't* marry within your own cultural background. Let's examine an extreme case.

> **CASE 11**
>
> Sarah was a middle-class Protestant girl from a Bible-belt town in South Carolina. When she was a sophomore at the University of Florida, she met Abdul, an education major from Iraq. Abdul was a good-looking young man who spoke English well and loved American games—football especially. On one occasion he went to New York for two weeks and saw three professional football games. Sarah and Abdul went steady together for about six months and then decided that they could no longer wait to be married, despite the objections of both his Moslem family in Baghdad and the frantic protestations of Sarah's family back in South Carolina. They were married by a Presbyterian minister, and Abdul joined the Presbyterian church. Sarah dropped out of school and took a typing job. Abdul continued his college work.
>
> Soon, however, Sarah became pregnant, and even though she worked up until the eighth month, the eight weeks she was off having the baby created financial hardship for the young couple. Abdul, however, got a job, and they managed to get by. They seemed fairly happy, and, after he received his bachelor's degree, he went on and got his master's degree. Only then, however, did the full realization come to the young couple that he could not teach in the Florida schools because he was not a citizen. No matter, he got a job in Tampa. Soon a second child was on the way.
>
> One day Sarah and Abdul received a letter that contained what seemed to be exciting news. He was offered a job teaching English in Baghdad. They accepted quickly and within a few weeks were on their way to Iraq.
>
> Less than a year later, however, Sarah was back home. She left Iraq so precipitately that she merely picked up the children, leaving their clothes and belongings behind. She could stand it no longer. What could possibly have happened?
>
> For the first few weeks after the arrival in Baghdad, everything went well. It looked as if the young couple were finally headed toward success. Soon, however—in fact very soon—Abdul's friends observed that Sarah didn't act like a "normal" woman. Instead of staying in a corner with the other women, she circulated through the room and talked with the men. When the women began to notice these breaches of custom and tradition, they began to gossip among themselves, saying, in effect, "What kind of woman is this?" Meanwhile, the men were urging Abdul to treat his wife the way a wife should be treated. One day Abdul came home and said to Sarah, "From now on you must behave like an Iraqi woman. I know this isn't the way that you were raised, but when in Rome we must do as the Romans do." At first Sarah tried to go along, but there were too many things that she felt she couldn't accept without compromising her integrity. "He wanted me to live like a poor Arab woman, including sitting on the floor and eating with my bare hands," Sarah said. "When I refused, he got angry and I got slugged, shoved, spat at, and cursed at. In the eleven months I was in Iraq, I lost thirty pounds—both from the food I couldn't eat and from nervous tension. It turned out he wasn't really a Christian at all—he was still a Moslem. The blowup finally came when he insisted that our daughters be raised in the Iraqi manner. I just couldn't take that."

What happened in this marriage? Did Abdul deliberately deceive Sarah when he lived in the United States? Or did he absorb the superficial customs of the society in which he lived, believing he was a Christian until he got back into the environment in which social pressures forced him to behave like the others in the environment behaved? What should Sarah have done?

Subcultural Differences

Very few young Americans will ever be faced with the type of intercultural marriage situation that Sarah and Abdul faced. But many young Americans will have to cope with the more subtle differences that arise from the diverse subcultures within the larger cultural environment. These small differences can sometimes be as insidious and destructive to marriage as large intercultural differences.

As a result of the mass media and the various leavening movements at work in our society, some of these subcultural differences appear to be diminishing. Often, though, childhood-indoctrinated attitudes, values, and expectations remain, and, whether the individual knows it or not, they dominate his behavior. On occasion, under severe emotional stress, attitudes and behaviors that an individual thought he had rid himself of years ago come back to afflict or even destroy his relationship with his marriage partner.

One major way in which Americans differ is in the childhood conditioning they had as a result of the socioeconomic group in which they were raised. From the very beginning, middle-class and lower-class children are reared differently. Some differences in breast feeding, toilet training, and discipline practices, which were earlier identified by researchers, appear to be wearing out.[1] But there are still differences in food, amusement, and aesthetic preferences, and differences in the choice of words and symbols used.

Some of the more important differences are in sexual behavior, spending the family income, expressing aggression, and raising children. In my experience as marriage counselor, these areas give rise to the problems most often responsible for marriage problems.

Few middle-class children have any idea what it is like to be reared as a lower-class child. As a matter of fact, very few middle-class adults, including teachers, have any real concept of family life in the lower socioeconomic groups. Lower-class children are often equally as ignorant of the real problems middle-class boys and girls face in trying to live up to all the social expectations that confront them. Even television, for all of its seeming realism, fails to portray either the defensive hostility of much lower-class social interaction or the spirit-crippling anxiety that some middle-class children have about violating social expectations.

Allison Davis, in discussing the differences in the aggressive and sexual behavior of lower-class and middle-class adolescents, had some insightful comments. He pointed out that, with regard to most goals, what is rewarding to a middle-class adolescent is not rewarding to a lower-class adolescent. What they fear, what they abhor, what they desire, what they crave, what they will work for, fight for, or consider valuable or sacred differs in almost every area of human relationships:

[1] Eleanor Maccoby and Patricia Gibbs, "Methods of Child-Rearing in Two Social Classes," in Celia B. Stendler, ed., *Readings in Child Behavior and Development,* 2nd ed., New York, Harcourt, Brace & World, 1964, pp. 272–287.

In the middle class, aggression is clothed in the conventional forms of "initiative," or "ambition," or even of "progressiveness," but in the lower class it more often appears unabashed as physical attack, or as threats of and encouragement to physical attack. In general, middle class aggression is taught to adolescents in the form of social and economic skills which will enable them to compete effectively at that level. It may be full of personal hostility and insecurity, or it may be realistic and socially directed. The lower classes not uncommonly teach their children and adolescents to strike out first with fist or knife and to be certain to hit first. Both girls and boys at adolescence may curse their father to his face or even attack him with fists, sticks, or axes in free-for-all family encounters. Husbands and wives sometimes stage pitched battles in the home; wives have their husbands arrested, and husbands try to break in or burn down their own homes when locked out. Such fights with fists or weapons, and the whipping of wives occur sooner or later in many lower class families. They may not appear today or tomorrow, but they *will* appear if the observer remains long enough to see them.

The important consideration in regard to aggression in lower class adolescents is that it is learned as an *approved and socially rewarded* form of behavior in their culture. . . . In such lower class groups an adolescent who does not try to be a good fighter will not receive the approval of the father, nor will he be acceptable to his playgroup or gang. The result of these cultural sanctions is that he learns to fight and to admire fighters. The conception that "aggression and hostility" are neurotic or maladaptive symptoms of a chronically frustrated adolescent is an ethnocentric view of middle class individuals. In lower class families in many areas, physical aggression is as much a normal, socially acceptable and inculcated approved type of behavior as it is in frontier communities and in war.[2]

Davis points out that sexual behavior and sexual motivation are far more direct and uninhibited in the lower-class than in the middle-class adolescent. The sexual drives and behavior of lower-class children are not regarded as undesirable. Mothers may try to prevent their daughters from getting pregnant before they are married, but the example that the daughter sees all around her is quite often to the contrary. At a very early age, the child learns about extramarital relationships by observing the men and women in his own family. As Davis puts its:

He sees his father disappear to live with other women, or he sees other men visit his mother or married sisters. While none of his siblings may be illegitimate, the chances are very high that sooner or later his father or mother will accuse each other of having illegitimate children; or at least one of his brothers or sisters will have a child outside of marriage. His playgroup, girls and boys, discuss sexual relations frankly at age 11 or 12 and he gains status with them by beginning intercourse early.

With sex, as with aggression, therefore, the instigations and the goal responses of adolescents who live in these different cultures are opposite. The middle class adolescent is punished for physical aggression and for physical sexual relations; the lower class adolescent is frequently rewarded, both socially and organically, for these same behaviors. The degree of anxiety, guilt or frustration attached to these behaviors, therefore, is entirely different in the two cases. One might go so far as to say that in the case of the middle class adolescent such anxiety and guilt with regard to physical aggression and sexual intercourse are proof of their normal socialization in their culture. In lower class

[2] Allison Davis, 'Socialization and Adolescent Personality," in Nelson B. Henry, ed., *The Forty-Third Yearbook for the National Society for the Study of Education: Part I, Adolescence*, Chicago, Univ. of Chicago Press, 1944, pp. 209–210.

adolescents in certain environments, they are evidence of revolt against their own class culture, and therefore of incipient personality difficulties.[3]

The implications of Davis' writings are very important to the case for endogamy. Although a marriage partner who was reared in a lower socio-economic group may outwardly adopt middle-class norms, he may, under stress-producing situations, revert to earlier forms of behavior. In marriage-counseling practice, it is not uncommon to see a middle-class wife who previously found psychological satisfaction in the aggressiveness and sexual self-confidence of her lower-class husband become outraged when he hits her and insists that he "has a right to" extramarital relationships. Often she describes this behavior as "crazy" and demands that he get psychological help. But, as Davis pointed out, he is behaving quite normally for the group in which he was raised. The difference, then, is not really a matter of psychopathology but rather a matter of background conditioning.[4]

Social-class differences in attitudes toward spending money and rearing children often appear after marriage, too. Ordinarily, middle-class people were taught as children to postpone immediate enjoyment in favor of accumulating savings for future security. Maintaining (and raising) one's present status is very important to middle-class Americans. In lower socioeconomic classes, on the other hand, children learn to spend what little they have today for today's necessities or enjoyment. Marriage counselors often listen to middle-class husbands and wives complain bitterly because their mates from both lower and upper socioeconomic groups cannot seem to curb their impulse to spend. Some disadvantaged people, long starved for things that money can buy, are impelled to spend now, and some upper-class people, never knowing the insecurity of not having plenty of money, spend as a matter of habit. Divorces can and do result from just such differences in conditioned values.

In child-raising practices, too, attitudes conditioned into parents as a result of *their* childhood experiences can vitally affect their marriage relationship. Moreover, it can also affect the emotional stability of the child, because consistency in parental attitudes has long been held to be an important factor in sound child development. Generally speaking, lower-class spouses tend to be oriented toward physical punishment for the children. Marriage of such a man to a middle-class wife who believes in reasoning with her children rather than spanking them makes some husband–wife conflict almost inevitable. Marriage counselors listen to wives charging their husbands with unfeeling brutality, while the husbands counter that their wives are spoiling the children beyond belief.

Some sociological studies have confirmed that a similarity of social-class background can be an important factor in marriage success. As long ago as 1939, Ernest Burgess and Leonard Cottrell stated that the more similar the spouses were in social-class family background, the better their marital adjustment would be.[5] Later, Julius Roth and Robert Peck, working with the Burgess and Cottrell data, found that substantially more couples who married within their own social class were better adjusted than those who married outside their

[3] *Ibid.*, p. 211.
[4] Theodore Ferdinand has particularized the differences in sexual attitudes among all social class levels in his excellent essay "Sex Behavior and the American Class Structure: A Mosaic" in the *Annals of the American Academy of Political and Social Science,* **376** (March, 1968), pp. 76–85.
[5] Ernest W. Burgess and Leonard S. Cottrell, Jr., *Predicting Success or Failure in Marriage,* Englewood Cliffs, N.J., Prentice-Hall, 1939.

own class, and that the greater the difference in class level, the more likely it was that there would be poor adjustment in marriage.[6]

Where class differences do exist, the evidence seems to indicate that a higher-status husband can get along with a lower-status wife better than the lower-status husband can get along with a higher-status wife. The explanation most often given for this phenomenon is that the husband needs to feel superior and the wife wants him to feel so. A higher-status wife may make her husband feel less masculine, and so he may come to resent her. At the same time, the higher-status wife may resent her lower-status husband because he is dragging down her standing in the community. Consider the following case:

CASE 12 Social Class Distinction

"I met Jack when we were in college," Nancy told the counselor. "He was the captain of the football team. Every girl on the campus wanted him. On Saturday nights when our team had won, it was thrilling to be the one he chose. I got excited—yes, even sexually—when I got close to the 'hero.' I felt like the Roman women must have felt when they saw their victorious soldiers coming home from battle.

"In those days, I had never had any doubt that I wanted to marry him, even though I knew that he was from a background very different from mine. His mother and father were as poor as church mice. His father had been an alcoholic, and his mother never was able to earn very much. They lived in a slum, but I always used to think it was to Jack's credit that he pulled himself up enough to stay in high school and to get a football scholarship to college. It made me love him even more, because I felt sorry for him, I guess.

"My father is the vice-president of a large corporation in San Francisco. I know now that he was very much opposed to my marrying Jack, although he said very little about it before we were married. We had a big wedding, and then we went to live in a little town near our college, where he had a job as an assistant football coach. For two or three years we had a good marriage. Our first child was born there, and at first we were happy. But the friends he brought home were kind of rough, and we had almost nothing in common to talk about. I had majored in fine arts, and Jack knew almost nothing about painting or music. Moreover, we had a hard time of it financially. My folks tried to help out, but he resented the things they gave us. I think he was unhappy in that little town before I was, perhaps because it was such a conservative, family-centered town, or perhaps because he knew I was missing the kind of life I had lived before I went to college, and this made him feel more guilty than he had to be. Actually, I don't think he was any great shakes as a coach anyway. So our marriage got to be a little unhappy, and he took to either staying away or bringing his friends in to drink beer. I got pretty disillusioned. He was a nice dresser before we were married, but afterward he used to sit around the living room in his underwear and watch television. He never wanted to do the things that my father used to do (before Daddy got rich), like cutting the grass and painting the house. He just didn't seem to care what the yard looked like. I had to go out myself and cut the grass.

"Shortly after our first child was born, my father saw to it that Jack got an offer from the same industrial firm in San Francisco that employs Daddy. It was a good job as an expediter. I was delighted, of course. We moved away from the little town and back to San Francisco, where I had grown up and where my parents lived.

"But instead of making Jack happy, this only seemed to make him worse. He didn't like my friends there, and he didn't seem to want to make any new ones. He said

[6] Julius Roth and Robert F. Peck, "Social Class and Social Mobility Factors Related to Marital Adjustment," *American Sociological Review*, **16** (August, 1951), 480–483.

Expects Jack to be successfull

that my friends had grown up having everything and that they were snobbish and didn't like him. This wasn't so at all. They tried hard to make him a part of the group. They wanted him to try going sailing and skiing, which he had never done, but he said they just wanted to show him up.

"Before long, he got very depressed and sat around the house in his undershirt watching television even when there weren't any sports events on. By this time I didn't seem to love him anymore. I couldn't get the least bit excited about this despondent man who didn't seem to know where he was going. Sex relations became an unwelcome tolerance, and pretty soon I began to resent him altogether.

"He never wants to go anywhere with my friends or do anything culturally interesting. What am I going to do?"

When Jack came in to see the counselor, he started right out with the issue of her friends. "She and her snooty friends," he exploded. "When we were back in that small town where we started our marriage, she wouldn't have anything to do with my friends. Now she expects me to like hers. They're the country-club set, and all they can think about is sailing or golf. They're so smug I can't stand them.

"When we were in college, I thought Nancy and I had a lot in common. She used to want to come and watch me play football, and she knew a lot about the game. She liked the people I knew then, or at least she pretended to. They were all in college just like us. She didn't make any fuss about my wearing a T-shirt then. Now she hits the sky if I sit in the living room without my coat on. What's a man's home supposed to be, anyhow?

"She's scared to death of what the neighbors are going to think about us. The grass never gets a half-inch high before she's out there cutting it. She says that I never do it, but the truth of the matter is that she never gives me a chance. Her old man is the rigid type, too. He's so bad that he has to have the points of the pencils on his desk all pointing in the same direction or he throws a tantrum. She says that she wants to be happy, but she's never going to be happy until she relaxes a little and stops worrying about what other people think.

"The most important problem in our marriage right now is sex. She's completely frigid now. When we were first married, I thought she was one of the best sex partners I ever had. But now she doesn't want sex anymore. I can't understand what's come over her. She hit the ceiling when I told her about some of the girls down at the office, and yet she won't extend herself a bit to be sexy with me. Actually, I think she was all tied up about sex as a kid: You know, she was a goody-goody girl. Her parents made her that way. You would almost think that sex wasn't natural the way they didn't talk about it.

"Anyway, if she doesn't start coming around soon, I'm going to step out on her. I've told her that before, but this time I mean it."

What should be done for this marriage now? What could have been done earlier?

Religion and Marriage Success

Marriages in which the partners come from different religious backgrounds have received more research attention than the other forms of mixed marriage, probably because there are large, organized religious groups with a vested interest in protecting religious endogamy. Regardless of the happiness or stability of religiously mixed marriages, the very mixing ordinarily tends to dilute the denominational exclusiveness of one or both of the partners, so these religious

organizations are probably justified in their fears, whether or not they are justified in their reactions.

For the individuals concerned, however, the problem is much more
personal. What are the prospects of happiness and stability in a religiously
mixed marriage? The studies of religiously mixed marriages appear to indicate
that they are more fragile than marriages in which the partners have the same
religious background. Judson T. Landis, in his study of 4108 couples in Michigan,
found a divorce rate of 4.4 where the parents of both partners were Catholic,
5.2 where they were both Jewish, and 6.0 where they were both Protestant. In
religiously mixed marriages, these figures ranged from 6.7 where there was a
Protestant father and a Catholic mother to 20.6 where there was a Catholic
father and a Protestant mother.[7] See Table 9–1.

H. Ashley Weeks studied 6548 couples in Spokane, Washington, and
found a divorce rate of 3.8 among Catholics and 10.0 among Protestants, but
17.4 in mixed marriages.[8] Howard M. Bell analyzed the marital status of 13,528
families in Maryland and found divorce rates 6.4 among Catholics, 4.6 among
Jews, 6.8 among Protestants, and 15.2 in mixed marriages.[9] Carle Zimmerman
and Lucius Cervantes, studying 40,000 urban families, concluded that the divorce
rate was almost three times as high in mixed Protestant–Catholic marriages than
in unmixed marriages.[10] Lee Burchinal and Loren Chancellor, who studied all
the marriages licensed in Iowa in the early 1950s, concluded that religiously
mixed marriages tended to be of shorter duration than those where both
partners were of the same faith.[11] Although the weight of evidence from these

Table 9–1
Study of 4108 Religiously Mixed Couples

Condition	Percent Divorced
Both Catholic	4.4
Both Jewish	5.2
Both Protestant	6.0
Mixed Catholic–Protestant	14.1
Both none	17.9
Protestant changed to Catholic	10.7
Catholic changed to Protestant	10.6
Protestant father and Catholic mother	6.7
Catholic father and Protestant mother	20.6
Father none and mother Catholic	9.8
Father none and mother Protestant	19.0

Source: Judson T. Landis, "Marriages of Mixed and Nonmixed Religious Faiths," American Sociological Review, **14** (June,
1949), 401–407. Copyright 1949 by the American Sociological Association, Washington, D.C. Reprinted by permission.

[7] Judson T. Landis, "Marriages of Mixed and Nonmixed Religious Faiths," American
Sociological Review, **14** (June, 1949), 403.
[8] H. Ashley Weeks, "Differential Divorce Rates by Occupation," Social Forces, **21**
(March, 1943), 336.
[9] Howard M. Bell, "Youth Tell Their Story," Washington, D.C., American Youth Com-
mission, American Council on Education, 1938, p. 21.
[10] Carle C. Zimmerman and Lucius F. Cervantes, Successful American Families, New
York, Pageant, 1960, p. 76.
[11] Lee G. Burchinal and Loren Chancellor, "Survival Rates Among Religiously Homogamous and Inter-religious Marriages," Research Bulletin No. 512758, Ames, Iowa, Agriculture
and Home Economics Experiment Station, Iowa State University, December, 1962.

studies appears conclusive—mixed marriages are more fragile—other ways to interpret these research results will be discussed in the next chapter, when we will examine the case against endogamy.

The problems encountered in interfaith marriages are *not* usually the result of clashes over doctrine and religious argument. More frequently, they are the outcome of differences in childhood conditioning and general values in living. Religion has an influence over far more than the spiritual life of its adherents, for religious groups usually have some differing customs, attitudes, values, and expectations as well as differing religious beliefs. Young people are often more able to change their religious beliefs (or to abandon them altogether) than the accompanying style-of-life patterns.

Harold Feldman, in his illuminating study of the development of the husband–wife relationship, pointed to some of the important style-of-life differences resulting from the varying religious backgrounds of the 850 couples in his study. Feldman's sample consisted of 175 marriages in which both partners were Catholic, 301 in which both partners were Protestant, 232 in which both partners were Jewish, and 144 in which the partners were of mixed religions or in which one or both partners had no religion.[12] Feldman compared the both-Protestant, both-Catholic, and both-Jewish couples with each other and with the mixed- or no-religion couples on a long list of marital habits and behaviors. When the Protestant couples were compared with the Catholic couples in Feldman's study, the Protestants appeared to be more open in their relationship, interacted more often with each other, were more aggressive, were more achievement- and ego-oriented, and had more value differences between husband and wife. The Catholics were more serene and conventional, although they occasionally directed an outburst of aggression toward the spouse. Religion appeared to be a more significant factor in their marital relationship.

When the Catholic couples were compared with the Jewish couples, the Catholics appeared to be more satisfied with their marriages, which were more conventional, more placid, and less emotional. Jewish wives were more active and Jewish husbands more nurturant (doing things for the spouse and playing with the children), and husband and wife tended to interact more with each other. Their marriages were not as serene as the Catholic couples' marriages, but they were more exciting and gay, and the partners more easily expressed hostility toward each other.

In the Protestant–Jewish comparison, Feldman found the largest number of statistically significant differences. When compared with the Jewish couples, the Protestants had a higher level of marital satisfaction. The Protestant couples' conversations were generally about objective and interpersonal or emotional topics, and the results of these conversations were generally positive to the marriage. The relationship between the husband and wife appeared to be more traditional with familistic values seen as in the wife's sphere. The Protestants tended, in general, either to be more restricted in their emotional output when they were fighting, or sometimes to have a kind of cyclical behavior, in which they became aggressive from feeling guilty and then began feeling guilty because they had been aggressive.

The Jewish couples, in comparison with the Protestants, tended to be more emotional in general but less satisfied with their marriages. "It may be,"

[12] Harold Feldman, *The Development of Husband–Wife Relationships,* research report to the National Institute of Mental Health, Grant M-2931, Cornell University, Ithaca, N.Y., 1965, pp. 90–105.

Feldman speculated, "that the more open one is to a wide variety of feelings, the more likely one is to have discontent; while those with a more restricted range of emotional output are less open to injury to the ego but also less likely to reach the highest level for fulfillment."[13] The Jewish couples were more involved with marriage, had more gay times together, were more expressive in conflict, felt closer after communicating, and were more involved.

When compared with the mixed–no-religion group, the Protestants were more verbal, more likely to suppress their negative feelings, and generally more satisfied and positive toward each other. In the same comparison, the mixed-religion group had a lower level of marital satisfaction and more conflict and were more different from each other in their values, putting less emphasis on togetherness and more on their individualistic satisfactions. Religion often appeared to be a source of conflict.

In comparing the Jewish with the mixed–no-religion group, Feldman found that Jewish couples placed a higher value on marriage and sharing the nurturant values, whereas in the mixed-no-religion group, the nurturant values were perceived as belonging more properly to the wife's role. Individualistic values were more important to the mixed–no-religion group. In these same comparisons, the Jewish group appeared to be more outgoing, expressive, and communicative, more committed to marriage as a companionate rather than an individualistic venture, more kin-group-oriented, and more prone to positive interactions with each other. The mixed group was calmer, more controlled emotionally, and more committed to individuality and to the separate functioning of the marital partners.

In a comparison of the Catholics with the mixed–no-religion group, Feldman found that the Catholics were generally happier with their marriages, which were much more settled, sedentary, and lower in friction and excitement. They valued the kind of marriage they had: an orderly home, good cooking, and financial security, with husband and wife tending to agree with each other about their values. Religion played a large part in their lives and was a great source of unity.

In comparison to the Catholics, the mixed–no-religion group had more conflict, were more self-indulgent, and were searching for more self-fulfillment rather than cohesion in their marriages. Neither the children nor the home nor even their mate, was as important to them as their own personal growth. They gave evidence of more differences between the spouses and more conflict.

The importance of Feldman's study is that it documents and validates the style-of-life background differences associated with religious groups. It is the customs, attitudes, values, and expectations that Feldman has identified, rather than the religious doctrines or dogmas as such, that cause the problems in most interreligious marriages. Clearly, not all Protestants have the characteristics that Feldman associated with them. Nor do all Catholics. Nor do all Jews. Nor do all religion rejectors. But it is the strength of these tendencies that builds the "take-another-look; it's-better-to-be-safe-than-sorry" case for religious endogamy.

One of the many cases that Albert Gordon, a scholarly Boston rabbi, reported in his well-documented book on intermarriage is that of a man identified as "Irwin." A condensation follows:

[13] *Ibid.*, p. 103.

CASE 13

"After eight years of married life, our interfaith marriage ended in divorce. Neither Ann nor I ever imagined that this would happen, but it *has* happened and, unfortunate as it is for us, it is still worse for our young daughter.

"I am a Jew. Ann is a Protestant. Actually she had always been a church going liberal Protestant. When we married, she retained her religions affiliation and I retained mine. We were quite certain that no force or series of forces, family, friends, church, or synagogue, would ever break up our marriage. . . .

"I come from an orthodox Jewish family. At least my parents were orthodox even if my brothers and sisters were not. I have two brothers and two sisters. We are all deeply devoted to one another and since our early years have been close. My father was a learned Jew. He was a highly respected member of the community in which we lived, not only because of his knowledge of the Talmud and other Hebrew texts or even because of his active participation in the Jewish community, but also because he was a very successful businessman. My mother was as sweet and kind a person as one could ever meet. She was a devoted wife and mother and a genuinely religious soul. We, her children, loved her very much. We were close to her as she was to us. . . .

"I had gotten a legal position in the city with a good firm. Ann was a secretary. She came from a lower-middle class working family. Her father had died about ten years before, so through all of her teens Ann had been cared for by her mother. Ann had graduated from high school, and the pressing financial needs of the family had obliged her to go to a secretarial school and take a job thereafter. Both parents had regarded themselves as Protestant although her mother was now affiliated with a very liberal church that had no formal creed. Ann had always regarded herself as a religious Protestant.

"Ann and her mother had lived in Peoria for about five years. Prior to that, they had lived in a small town in Missouri. I can only guess that the opportunities for work were greater in the big city and Ann and her mother both needed to work in order to live, that the move to Peoria was prompted by this consideration. I am quite certain that during all the time I knew her, Ann's relationship with her mother was excellent and I remember Ann telling me that they had always been good.

"We met on a double date. One of my friends had a date and he asked his girl friend to bring along someone for me. This was not one of those "quickie" affairs. We actually went together off and on for about two and one-half years before the affair became serious. All this while I was at the law office and enjoying my work, but I was lonesome. I didn't go out very much. Of course, there was my own family for part of the time, but due to another change in fortune, my parents decided to move back to their first home town. So, really, I was pretty much alone. I didn't see the family very often. I wasn't earning too much and things were generally quite tight. My office associations did not bring me in contact with Jewish girls. I hardly knew any Jewish people socially. Then, too, one man in the office had intermarried and he was getting along fine. Ann and I were invited over to their home rather often and I saw that intermarried people could get on very well together. The few people I knew who saw us together all seemd to think of her as a sweet girl. The office in which she worked was just around the corner from my law office, and all of these factors sort of drew us together more and more.

"I knew, of course, that the members of my family would not approve of an intermarriage. I knew that they would try to dissuade me by every possible means, but I also knew that my mother would eventually accept whatever I did. I felt certain about that all the time. Yet it was a difficult decision to make because, even though I had drifted far from my parents' orthodoxy, I still had some strong feelings about

He has a big ego and thinks it will be
threatened by ann so he acts
ethnocentric. Also social class differing

being a Jew and I had no real intention of giving up that identification. I guess that the strongest point was the fact that I knew of at least one successful intermarriage and this helped to convince me that, regardless of what others in the family might say, I knew what I wanted to do.

"I shall never forget the way in which my mother pleaded with me not to marry Ann. She cried bitterly. She talked and pleaded with me, but somehow I didn't feel that she understood me or Ann. When the other members of the family, including my father, talked with me, they were just as anxious as my mother to dissuade me, but, even though I knew that it would hurt them, I felt that they would get over it. I thought that all they needed was to really get to know Ann. But it obviously required more than that.

"I cannot today look upon their pleadings, discussions, and arguments as improper or as wrong in any sense. They were, I think, wiser than I was at that time.

"I think that our marriage ended in divorce not because of my family or Ann's, but because of us. We were really very much different from each other and religion did play an important role in our break-up. But it wasn't the Church or the Synagogue that did it. It's the way we responded to our own religion after we were married.

"We were married by the liberal minister of the Community church Ann used to attend. Ann's mother had attended this church, too. In fact, she had worked hard for this particular church.

"But, however liberal I thought I was with respect to religion, I knew that I was a Jew, and I did not want to have my home become a Christian home. Of course, I felt this way much more after our marriage than I had ever realized I would.

"For example, at Christmas time, I would not permit a tree in the house, nor would I allow anything resembling a Yuletide celebration. To Ann and her mother, that was cruel and inhuman treatment, for it shattered the traditions of her childhood. (I forgot to mention that Ann's mother lived with us in our apartment.) Whatever Jewish symbols I tried to introduce into the home after my daughter was born, were made fun of by Ann. Now, lest you think that I was taking advantage of Ann by acting as I did, I want to make it clear that prior to our marriage, we had agreed that any children born to us would be reared in the Jewish religion. But Ann changed her mind about all that. She was disillusioned, I guess.

"I know that my family invited Ann and my daughter up to their home for vacation, etc. She came, mostly because I insisted, but it wasn't very successful for any of us. Ann was quite aloof from the family and I felt that she looked down upon their very Jewish way of life, the ritual observance, the Sabbath meal, with the candles kindled. Where, to me, this was lovely and warm, to Ann it was quite meaningless. Whether or not she thought the family were barbarians, I do not know.

"I spoke before about our differences, but they were not just religious differences. I think they were cultural, educational and social differences, as well. That came to the fore as time went on. When you marry, you actually bring your entire past—religious and cultural—with you and it remains with you.

"It was obvious after four difficult years that we could not remain together. We were separated for about three years, and it was my hope that somehow we would be able to reconcile our differences, but that was not to be. We finally got a divorce.

"Some people think that if things don't work out, you simply get a divorce, but I can tell you that there is much more to it than that. In our case, we had a daughter. Ann wanted the child to remain with her, and so I have been supporting her for the past ten years. But it isn't a question of dollars and cents that is important. It is rather what we have done to a child. I feel reasonably certain that my daughter, who is a very unhappy person, would not have been that way had we, her parents, remained together and had she known what she really was—Jew or Christian. She has been seeing a psychiatrist and has been quite ill for a time, but though neither Ann nor I feel entirely responsible, we cannot help but feel that our unsuccessful marriage was certainly a contributing cause to her unhappiness and illness. I am convinced today that interfaith intermirriage can work out only for people who either do not want or cannot have children. The arrival of a child into a mixed marriage changes the entire scope of the original intention, no matter how emotionally strong the professed love was before marriage.

"I do not believe that the unhappiness that came about in our marriage was the result of the fact that I came from an orthodox Jewish family while Ann came from a so-called liberal Christian family. Unfortunately the prejudice and deep-rooted intolerant attitudes that one finds in non-Jewish families must be considered, too. These attitudes are often such that nothing can overcome the outside pressure upon the non-Jewish girl. It may be argued that a highly intelligent girl, perhaps one who has a higher university degree or someone like that, can withstand all these pressures quite normally. But I would even challenge that postulate.

"I believe now that the only possible route for a Jewish man who marries a non-Jewish girl, and is determined to make his marriage last, is to gradually give up contact with his Jewish circle of friends. This happens sometimes and I know of such people. While I can recall a few mixed-marriage families who apparently seem happy and who have children, I feel quite certain that they are the exception to the rule.

"I would do everything within my power to convince a child of mine that he was violating every principle of his faith and every standard of his family and, more important, what was best for his own future welfare, if he considered getting married to a person belonging to a different religious group. I have discovered that, if one has any feelings at all about one's own faith and one's family, it is the height of folly to undertake such a marriage.

"In our case both Ann and I had strong feelings about our own religion, even though we did not realize it before we were married. But we found that out soon enough.

"I have remarried. My wife this time is a fine Jewish girl and we have two lovely daughters. I know now what it means to be happily married."[14]

Racial Endogamy
and Marriage Success

What about the other areas of marriage endogamy and their relationship to success in marriage? The studies of success in interracial marriages are meager and few. One old study seems to indicate that the average happiness rating for the total interracial group was very low—in fact lower than the total of all marriages of mixed nationality or mixed religion.[15] Racially mixed couples often encounter severe social pressures from their parents and the communities in which they live. They also face discrimination in the economic and business world, and they find desirable housing difficult to secure. Former friends and relatives sometimes break off relations, or at least introduce an element of strain into the relationship. More recent studies seem to indicate that there is less difficulty in Oriental–white marriages than in Negro–white marriages. At

[14] Albert I. Gordon, Intermarriage: Interfaith, Interracial, Interethnic, Boston, Beacon, 1964, pp. 342–347. Reprinted by permission of the Beacon Press, copyright © 1964 by Albert I. Gordon.
[15] Ray E. Baber, "A Study of 325 Mixed Marriages," American Sociological Review, 2 (October, 1937), 715.

least one recent study appeared to indicate that all interracial marriages among well-educated people are more successful now than they were in the past. However, the individual case reports cited in the study give small comfort to those who would like to believe that interracial marriages are something less than very difficult. As the report put it: "Over and over again the comments on the questionnaire drew a picture of sometimes hard times, rough sledding."[16]

Age

The studies of the relationship of the marriage partners' ages to their marital success are few and show no consistent agreement. Charles King, Robert Blood and Donald Wolfe, and Harvey Locke all found that it is somewhat favorable for the marriage partners to be the same age.[17]

Ernest Burgess and Paul Wallin found that no particular pattern of age differences was correlated with marital success, and Burgess and Cottrell found that it was unfavorable for the husband to be younger than the wife.[18]

Although there may not be enough consistency in the findings to indicate that age difference between the marriage partners is related to success or failure in marriage, there is considerable evidence to indicate that the age of *both* partners is related to it. Many studies have indicated that the probability of marriage unhappiness and disillusionment is much greater when the husband is under twenty and the wife under eighteen, and that, in general, divorce is more probable for couples who marry younger.

Many of these studies were made prior to or just after World War II, when the preponderance of youthful marriages was taking place among high-school dropouts and in social groups that had a lower marriage-stability rate to begin with. Moreover, many of the marriages were the result of premarital pregnancies, and the partners had little intention that the union should be permanent. It is still probably safe to generalize, however, that older, more mature partners whose decision to marry was not based on premarital pregnancy tend to contract happier marriages. Delaying too long can limit one's choice of marriage partners, but so can marrying too early. There is probably an optimum time somewhere in one's twenties when a person has lived long enough to know what he wants and is mature enough to undertake the close interpersonal relationship of marriage but has not lived so long that all of the most adequate partners have been chosen.

Education

As with age, the findings concerning differences in educational background as a factor in marriage happiness are somewhat inconsistent. Generally, it has been found that the more similar the husband and wife are in educational level, the greater is their marriage happiness. But Judson and Mary Landis, in studying

[16] "People Who Intermarry: Pioneers or Protestors?" Seattle Urban League Special Report, Seattle, Wash., April, 1967.

[17] Charles E. King, "The Burgess-Cottrell Method of Measuring Marital Adjustment as Applied to a Non-White Southern Urban Population," *Marriage and Family Living,* 14 (November, 1952), 280–285; Robert O. Blood, Jr., and Donald M. Wolfe, *Husbands and Wives,* Glencoe, Free Press, 1960, p. 163; and Harvey J. Locke, *Predicting Adjustment in Marriage,* New York, Holt, Rinehart and Winston, 1951.

[18] Ernest W. Burgess and Paul Wallin, *Engagement and Marriage,* Philadelphia, Lippincott, 1953, p. 521; and Burgess and Cottrell, *op. cit.,* pp. 161–164.

6166 marriages, found no reason to believe that marriage partners who were similar in education had a significantly lower divorce rate than those who had widely differing educational backgrounds.[19]

. One thing that almost all the studies agree on is that education is related to marital success in the sense that the more education a person has, the lower is his probability for divorce and the higher is his probability for a good marital adjustment. It may well be, of course, that education is not really a controlling variable. More likely, people who have the determination and ambition required in getting higher education also have the kind of background conditioning that makes them want to stay married and to make a success of marriage.

THE POSITIVE CASE
FOR ENDOGAMY

At the beginning of this chapter, it was pointed out that the case for endogamy was commonly supported by negative reasons, i.e., reasons why one should *not* marry someone with an unlike background. There are, however, positive reasons for endogamy, too, and Robert Coombs has summarized these in several of his papers on value theory in dating and mate selection.[20] Coombs starts with the premise that persons with similar backgrounds learn similar values (and, as we have seen, similar customs, attitudes, and expectations, too). He goes on from there to suggest that interpersonal attraction is enhanced when persons perceive themselves as sharing similar value systems, because then their relationship is mutually rewarding. One of these rewards is the ease of communication that results from a similarity of experience. He says:

> Similarity facilitates the expression of positive affect (favorable feeling, self-involving interest, acceptance, esteem), which enhances interpersonal attraction. Disagreement is more apt to arise between dissimilar persons and to be ego-threatening since it challenges one's values and sense of social reality. Consequently, communication between dissimilar persons is likely to be more restrained and to involve emotionally neutral topics. In short, it is less rewarding.[21]

The second benefit that those of like value systems receive is closely related: Coombs calls it *self-validation*. If a person's values are rejected, he feels rejected. When his values are accepted, he feels secure. Moreover, he feels that his feelings are both vindicated and validated, and that the person who made him feel that way likes him. As a final step in this progression, when he perceives them as liking him, he likes them in return, and communication becomes even easier.

But even these positive reasons for choosing a mate among those with similar backgrounds and values do not necessarily make the case for absolute in-group mate selection in present-day American society conclusive for everyone. The next chapter presents the case against endogamy.

[19] Judson T. Landis and Mary G. Landis, *Building a Successful Marriage*, 4th ed., Englewood Cliffs, N.J., Prentice-Hall, 1963, p. 216.
[20] Robert H. Coombs, "A Value Theory of Mate Selection," *Family Life Coordinator*, **10** (July, 1961), 54; "Reinforcement of Values in the Parental Home as a Factor in Mate Selection," *Marriage and Family Living*, **24** (May, 1962), 155–157; and "Value Consensus and Partner Satisfaction Among Dating Couples," *Journal of Marriage and the Family*, **28** (May, 1966), 166–173.
[21] Robert H. Coombs, "Value Consensus," *op. cit.*, 168.

10

THE CASE
AGAINST ENDOGAMY

With the secularization, deprovincialization, increased cross-cultural associations, urbanization, and rebellion against traditional mores that have occurred in the last half-century in the United States, there has been an increasing rejection of endogamy, both philosophically and in actual practice. In a society newly awakened to the implications of civil rights, social democracy, and religious ecumenicalism, it could hardly be otherwise.

To many of those who are concerned with the civil rights of minority groups, traditional American endogamy has often appeared as a kind of de facto nuptial segregation based on laws as outmoded as the poll tax. Laws against racial intermarriage were voided in California soon after World War II. The United States Supreme Court, in its historic 1967 decision *Loving vs. Virginia*, probably made all state laws against racial intermarriage unenforceable, even though they remain in the law books in some states.

The intellectualist urge for greater social democracy and the anti-establishment movement of the beatniks and hippies in the 1960s have also played a part in the philosophical rebellion against endogamy. The snobbishness of a class-conscious society, which was accepted as part of "the system" in most colleges and universities up to the time of the Great Depression, gave way to a new kind of social integration as the G.I. Bill brought veterans from all walks of life to the campuses of the large universities after World War II.

The old concept of "rating and dating" (ranking dates by social status), which Willard Waller found to be part and parcel of the campus life of the late 1920s, is almost unheard of at many universities today.[1] Not only is there more dating without regard to family background, there is also more international dating. Robert Blood and Samuel Nicholson found that almost everybody

---

[1] Willard Waller, "The Rating and Dating Complex," *American Sociological Review*, 2 (October, 1937), 727–734.

on the University of Michigan campus had some acquaintance with students from other nations and that almost half of the women students had dated foreign students. Even those women students who had not dated foreign students often said they would if they were asked.[2]

In another paper, Blood and Nicholson indicated that "international" dating did not appear to be related either to rebellion or to symbolic protest against prejudice. The women reported satisfaction with their experiences, their women friends were sympathetic, and their American boyfriends and parents were usually neutral.[3]

Although this particular group of students may have acted without reference to rebellion against established mores, many others are motivated by protest. There is considerable evidence from Freeman and others, as we saw in Chapter 9, that many young people do date and marry those from dissimilar backgrounds as a deliberate defiance of the traditional values of their families and society.[4]

The fact that endogamy is prescribed and promoted by conservative moralists and religionists whose very philosophy so many young people (and some social theorists) are in rebellion against often damns endogamy by association, regardless of what actual merits it might have. Even some of those who generally accept statistical validation as the measure of ultimate truth often find a reason for rejecting statistical evidence that seems favorable to the case for endogamy. Unhappily, in some cases, such across-the-board rejection appears to be another classic example of C. C. Bowman's suggestion, first cited in Chapter 2, that because the mores contained irrationalities, gross generalizations and other illogical elements, some have jumped to the unwarranted conclusion that diametrically opposed beliefs will be rational, logical and scientific.[5]

But there have been some more carefully considered criticisms of endogamy, too. Some object to the traditional pattern of urging people to make conventional, conforming, stable marriages by selecting their partners within their own race, nationality, religion, and social class on the grounds that any resulting "marital adjustment" does not really produce happiness. At best, the argument goes, this endogamy reinforces the antiindividualistic, antipersonal freedom bias of the American middle class, which, although it results in accommodation to the status quo, does not lead to the achievement of positive goals in marriage. To date, there has been very little definition of these new "positive goals" other than in terms such as "new experience" or "personality growth." But the proponents argue that these objectives, however vague, should be used as the test of a happy, really well-adjusted marriage rather than the absence of conflict or the degree of conformity to social conventions.

However, while new experience and full personality development are indeed laudable goals for marriage, there is presently little solid evidence that they are not available within an endogamous marriage system. Indeed, many present marriages offer fairly eloquent evidence that they are possible. If new experience and personality growth are inhibited within any particular marriage,

[2] Robert O. Blood, Jr., and Samuel O. Nicholson, "The Attitudes of American Men and Women Students Toward International Dating," *Marriage and Family Living,* **24** (February, 1962), 35–41.
[3] Robert O. Blood, Jr., and Samuel O. Nicholson, "International Dating Experiences of American Women Students," *Marriage and Family Living,* **24** (May, 1962), 129–136.
[4] Linton Freeman, "Homogamy in Interethnic Mate Selection," *Sociology and Social Research,* **39** (July–August, 1955), 369–377.
[5] Claude C. Bowman, "Hidden Valuations in the Interpretation of Sexual and Family Relationships," *American Sociological Review,* **11** (October, 1946), 543.

it may very well be that the inhibition is more related to the internal creativity of one or both partners than it is to the fact that traditional patterns of social endogamy were followed in mate selection.

A more readily demonstrable criticism of endogamy is that it embarrasses the modern ecumenical movement among religionists. As older doctrines and dogmas have fallen into disuse, there has been considerable pressure among professional theologians and churchmen to break down interdenominational barriers and so (intentionally or not) make interfaith marriage easier.

One major milestone in this ecumenical relaxation was the 1966 change in the Roman Catholic church easing the universal requirement that the non-Catholic partner in a mixed marriage must promise *in writing* that the children would be raised as Catholics. However, the non-Catholic partner is still expected to promise orally, the Catholic partner must still file a written promise, and the wedding must still be performed by a priest if the marriage is to be valid in the eyes of the Church.

Although the ecumenical movement is widespread, it is often more apparent on the university campus or in the intellectual community of a large city than it is in rural areas and among the more evangelical and fundamentalist church groups. Nonetheless, even among hard-shelled religionists in America old prejudices and patterns of doctrinal separation appear to be diminishing.

If more and more of the old divisions and differences between denominations and even between major religious groups disappear, it could become even more difficult to justify religious endogamy. The rate of religious amalgamation may accelerate as our iconoclastic age progresses. However, old traditions die hard in some subcultural groups, and it is doubtful that, in the foreseeable future, a modern urban agnostic will have much philosophical communality with an Amish farmer. Moreover, there are still clergymen of every faith who take strong and unyielding positions against interreligious marriage.

MANY MIXED
MARRIAGES SUCCEED

One of the major arguments used against endogamy is the fact that there is a vast—and increasing—number of people who are happily married to a partner of a different religion, nationality, social status, education, or race. In a society oriented to accepting success as reason enough for overturning tradition, and in a society oriented to accepting change as a value, this is a powerful argument indeed.

Statistics often cited by those promoting religious endogamy are used by Glenn M. Vernon to refute the implication that religiously endogamous marriages are vastly more successful than mixed marriages. Vernon points to the Landis study, reported on page 102, which showed that the divorce rate for those people in the sample who married people of like faith was only about 5 percent but the divorce rate for those who married outside their faith was almost 15 percent. He points out that it would appear from these figures that the rate of failure is three times higher for religiously mixed marriages. However, if you look at these figures another way, Vernon suggests, it might be correctly stated that 95 percent of religiously endogamous marriages survive, and that *85 percent of religiously mixed marriages also survive.* Thus, by marrying outside the faith, one reduces his chance of success by only 10 percent.[6]

Whether they read the statistics the Landis way or the Vernon way or whether they don't read them at all, an increasing number of young people are entering religiously mixed marriages. Although the rate of increase in interfaith marriages in the United States is difficult to assess because religious data for the country as a whole are not available prior to 1957, Canadian records do show a definite trend. In Canada there was an almost steady increase in interreligious marriages from 1927 to 1957.[7]

Many observers feel that the trend in the percentages in the United States has been about the same. In a 1967 report by Victor Sanua of Yeshiva University, there was a clear indication that interfaith marriages were on the increase. The study found that, in some parts of the country, as many as 50 percent of Catholics and Protestants married outside their faith. The figure was about 17 percent for Jews.[8]

College and university students appear to be about equally divided on whether or not they approve of interfaith marriage. Albert Gordon found that in his sample of 5407 university students throughout the country, 50 percent of the students did not favor marriage to a person of another religion. In contrast, only 13 percent did not favor marriage to a person of another nationality. Thirty-one percent of the students in Gordon's sample did not favor marriage to a person of another educational group, but 91 percent of the students did not favor marriage to a person of another color.[9] The strong negative attitude of the university students toward interracial marriage probably reflects the strength of the general population's continuing taboo against color mixing in marriage. It was pointed out in Chapter 9 that, in the past, interracial marriages have probably been less successful than endogamous marriages. If the number of interracial marriages increase, will they become more successful? There are some who believe so. Even Negro–white marriages, which, in the past, have been cited as the most difficult marriage mixtures of all, may become increasingly stable.

The writers of a 1967 Seattle Urban League Report thought they saw better days ahead for interracial marriage. "Someday," they said, "this report may be just a footnote to sociological history; nobody will notice or care whether the couple strolling down the street or living next door "match" racially. Those who have intermarried in our time may be seen as pioneers and not as protesters."[10] But, "someday" may be a long time away. As the nation moved into the 1970s, there were sociologists who were saying that the polarization of the ethnic groups was actually stronger than it had been twenty years before.[11]

[6] Glenn M. Vernon, "Bias in Professional Publications Concerning Interfaith Marriages," *Religious Education,* **55** (July–August, 1960), 261–264.
[7] David M. Heer, "The Trend of Interfaith Marriages in Canada: 1922–1957," *American Sociological Review,* **27** (April, 1962), 245–250.
[8] Victor D. Sanua, "Intermarriage and Psychological Adjustment," in Hirsch L. Silverman, ed. *Marital Counseling: Psychology, Ideology, Science,* Springfield, Ill., Charles C Thomas, 1967.
[9] Albert I. Gordon, *Intermarriage: Interfaith, Interracial, Interethnic,* Boston, Beacon, 1964, pp. 36–37.
[10] "People Who Intermarry: Pioneers or Protesters?" Seattle Urban League Special Report, Seattle, Wash., April, 1967.
[11] *The New York Times,* July 28, 1968, p. 35.

WHITE–ORIENTAL
MARRIAGES

Since World War II, the largest number of interracial marriages among the U.S. population has taken place between native-born white men and foreign-born Oriental women. Many of these marriages have undoubtedly been successful. One reason for this has been the cultural conditioning that makes the Oriental woman subservient, an ego-building and security-producing characteristic that the average American male often finds appealing. In James Michener's novel *Sayonara*, Airman Joe Kelly describes why he thinks Japanese–American marriages are so successful:

> In the bunks at night you never hear one man who married a Japanese wife complain. You hear a lot of other guys complain about their women. But not the ones who got hitched in Japan. . . . Men with wives in the states talk about Junior's braces and country club dances and what kind of a car their wife bought. But the men with Japanese wives tell you one thing only. What wonderful wives they have. They are in love—it's that simple.[12]

Actually, of course, it's *not* that simple. Being waited on hand and foot by a woman who enjoys this has a deep need-meeting novelty value for men of all social levels, but having a wife who is only a subservient slave will not meet the social expectations of most more highly educated men for very long. And when his social expectations are not met, sooner or later his needs will no longer be met either. Moreover, Joe Kelly was talking only about the satisfactions that Caucasian men derive from Oriental women. There is considerable evidence that women conditioned to the expectations of American society are not likely to accept easily the expectations of the Oriental male. As a matter of fact, during my practice on the West Coast, many marriage-counseling cases came to my attention involving Americanized, emancipated Japanese–American women who had been born and raised in the United States but who were married to tradition-oriented Japanese men. These women, Japanese ancestry or not, wanted to be treated in the American way.

Most foreign women find it easy to step up to the American female role, with its rights, privileges, and relative luxury. This is, as we saw in the previous chapter, in sharp contrast to the difficulty an American woman experiences in living as a native in many other cultures. Once freed from subservience, hardship, and an inferior role, women—in fact, all human beings—usually show great determination in avoiding a repeat performance of that role.

The following case describes an apparently successful international (but *not* interracial) marriage. Examine it carefully for clues to why nonendogamous marriages may be successful.

CASE 14

"Overseas I had a few blind dates which ended with the first date. I dated one girl regularly for about two or three months, but this ended platonically. After more than a year in Germany, I met my wife-to-be, who at the time was engaged to another man. At first ours was a restricted relationship until she broke off her engagement to become my girl. After twelve months of courtship, we were married. This was the best, smartest, most fortunate move I ever made.

"My wife and I both feel that our love affair was highly romantic and believe that

---

[12] James Michener, *Sayonara*, New York, *Random House*, 1954, pp. 16–17.

we based our marriage almost entirely on romantic love. Today when we think back we realize that we really did not give much mature thought to many important considerations in marriage. In spite of this, we consider ourselves very fortunate to be so well adjusted and share similar views on life and similar attitudes on things in general. We consider a happy home more important than anything else in this world. We have the same ideas on the roles of mother and father, husband and wife and children.

"In spite of our very different backgrounds we have the same interests and very similar values. When I was going to cowboy movies, she was going to the opera, and when I was worrying about getting a new pair of shoes because there were holes in my only pair, she was trying out her new birthday bicycle. But I have grown fond of music and opera and she lost much of her wealth as a result of the war. Today our needs, wants, and desires are the same.

"We had problems in the beginning. At first her family was unwilling to accept me because I was only an enlisted man. The first thing her father asked me was how much money I had. My parents were also reluctant to consent to our marriage, because Gretchen was not a Roman Catholic. But these things worked out without too much difficulty. We feel that our marriage is a stronger one because we overcame the difficulties in the face of opposition from both sides of the family.

"Financially, we have struggled successfully through four and a half years of married life with no serious problems or debts. Now that I am about to receive my engineering degree we look to the future for financial security. We have no religious problems. Gretchen became a Roman Catholic four months after we were married and is as enthusiastic about our religion as I am.

"Even when I try hard, I cannot even think of minor difficulties we have had because of cultural differences. I really feel that our cultural background differences have added a certain interest to our lives and have complemented our marriage instead of hindering it. Possibly the fact that my wife very rapidly became very much Americanized may have avoided many problems."[13]

What factors contributed to the success of this marriage? What stumbling blocks might these partners face in the future? Why?

The fact that many intermarriages, particularly religious intermarriages, are succeeding these days indicates that there are factors other than endogamy that affect the success or failure of marriage. One of these factors is personal flexibility, the personality attribute that permits those who have it to be accepting and pleasantly adaptable in almost any situation and compels those who don't have it to be rejecting and rigid.

Another factor is undoubtedly the strength of the conditioned attitudes and values held by one partner as compared to the strength of the opposing attitudes and values conditioned into his mate. A hard-shelled Methodist might not get along well with a staunch Catholic (or with a liberal Methodist either), but a liberal Methodist might easily get along well with a liberal Catholic.

Finally, the strength of the determination of two people to make a go of their marriage can make it successful for two people from almost any background, no matter how diverse. Although an endogamous marriage undoubtedly makes adjustments easier in most cases, perhaps there are some people who are successful because of the challenges implicit in intermarriage.

But since it is still true that the intermarrieds apparently have a higher divorce rate than those who marry endogamously, does this mean that those

[13] Jessie S. Bernard, Helen E. Buchanan, and William M. Smith, Jr., *Dating, Mating and Marriage*, Cleveland, Howard Allen, 1958, pp. 280–281.

who intermarry are less flexible, more compulsive and rigid, or less determined than their endogamously married friends? Or are they different in some other ways?

ARE THE INTERMARRIEDS DIFFERENT?

J. Richard Udry speculates that a factor in the higher divorce rate for intermarrieds may be that the people who tend to intermarry in the first place are unconventional people in other ways:

> Monogamous marriage, even in the United States in the twentieth century, is a very conservative and conventional institution and probably best designed to fit conservative and conventional people. Exogamy is only one form of non-conformity. Those who enter mixed marriages are in a way announcing to the world their disdain for its mundane rules. In many ways, marital adjustment is a measure of one's ability to make one's peace with the restrictions and conventions of proper society. To some extent, a low divorce rate in a group may indicate more happy marriages, but to a considerable degree it also indicates an unwillingness to upset apple carts, a willingness to compromise individual desires for the sake of upholding social obligations. It might be suspected that those who are willing to disdain the pressures for endogamy are not as willing to make these other compromises. In fact, it might be hypothesized that if half of those who were on the brink of exogamous marriages were persuaded to give up those relationships and contract marriages within their own social categories, the resulting marriages would not be noticeably less stable than the marriages of the half who went ahead and married across social lines.[14]

This notion that those who contract mixed marriages are somehow different from the rest of the population finds reinforcement in both popular and professional circles. However, the degree of nonconformity ascribed to the intermarried varies considerably from Udry's mild characterization to the statement attributed to psychiatrist Thomas Brayboy, that "deep-seated psychological sickness of various sorts underlie the 'vast majority' of marriages between white persons and Negroes." As reported in the *New York Times,* Dr. Brayboy went on to say that "the participants today in such marital unions often make use of the 'unique opportunity' that socially opposed or forbidden interracial sex offers for 'acting out' their personal problems." Thus, he observed, "these marriages often have little to do with love and tenderness; instead, they are arenas for hostility, control and revenge."[15]

Linton Freeman, who studied interracially married and interracially dating couples in Hawaii, reported that all of his respondents had early feelings of rejection stemming from their childhood relationships with their parents, and all reported poor social adjustment in grade school and high school.[16] But not every intermarriage involves partners who were openly rejected by their parents or who suffered apparent maladjustment in school. Consider the case of Jack, a white honor student from Wisconsin.

[14] J. Richard Udry, *The Social Context of Marriage,* Philadelphia, Lippincott, 1966, pp. 347–348.
[15] John A. Osmundsen, "Doctor Discusses 'Mixed' Marriage," *The New York Times,* November 7, 1965, p. 73.
[16] Freeman, *op. cit.,* 371.

CASE 15

"Jack has always been such a good boy," his mother told the counselor. "He always did what he was told, he went to Sunday School, and he was a good student. I don't know what's come over him all of a sudden, but his father and I are frantic. Ever since he has been at the university, and particularly since he got mixed up with this student civil-rights movement, he seems to have gone wild. He went down to Mississippi last summer to help in the voter-registration drive, and when he came back he was completely strange to us. He says he is going with a Negro girl, and he insists that he is going to marry her!

"It isn't as if we're prejudiced against Negroes. As a matter of fact, one of the reasons we were delighted when he took such an interest in church work was that we believe in Christian brotherliness. But marriage! Oh dear! Their children will never have a chance.

"If I could be convinced that he really loved this girl, I think I might be better able to accept it, although his father never would, I'm sure. But somehow Jack seems to just want to punish us by telling us that he's going to marry her. He knows how upset it makes us, and yet he persists. He says that we are dreadfully out of step with the times, and that we need to realize that we as white people should atone for the atrocious treatment that Negroes have had over the centuries. I declare, I don't know where he gets some of these ideas! His father is so disappointed. He expected so much of him, perhaps a little too much. He used to be very strict with Jack. I always tried to be very good to him. (To tell you the truth, he is my favorite.) I can't understand why he would want to do this to us.

"Jack is enjoying the publicity he's getting from talking about the civil-rights movement immensely. He's invited to all sorts of groups to speak, and he describes very forcefully some of the things that happened when he was on the registration drive. I know him pretty well, and I think that he's making up some of the things. Perhaps it would be better to say that he believes so strongly in what he is doing that he exaggerates. But I really don't know, since I wasn't there. Anyway, the more he talks about it, the more he builds himself up. Now he has announced that he intends to be married to the Negro girl next month. What are we going to do?"

Assuming that these facts are as the mother sees them, what can she do? A better question would be, what *should* she do?

SOCIETY'S DILEMMA

Up to now, we have been discussing the dilemma that modern young men and women face in choosing between endogamy and mixed marriage. Before moving on, we should point out that, in the elimination of endogamy, our democratic society is faced with a grave dilemma too. In the past, our parents and our politicians believed that it was possible to have a successful melting pot of cultural variation and at the same time marriage endogamy and subcultural-group loyalty. The United States became a great nation with cohesion, cooperation and national pride at the same time it was supporting internal competition (and often, unhappily, bigotry) among subcultural groups. There are many who believe that it was actually this competition among subcultural groups that made American society vigorous and progressive.

Now, however, there are some who feel that the one way to social progress and brotherhood is to diminish subcultural variations and promote intermarriage. There is also a large group that insists that marriage choice is strictly each individual's own business and that the state has no legal or moral right to be concerned in any way. Every American has—and should have—a constitutional right to stew in his own juice.

Clearly, however, the nation is vitally affected by the kinds of families that are created under its customs and its laws. The whole body politic must be concerned, if only because divorce, desertion, and illegitimacy create problems that affect everyone.

Society has a stake even greater than this, however, for there is evidence that intermarriage tends to reduce loyalty to particular value systems and thus insidiously to dilute belief in *all* values. Zimmerman and Cervantes found, for example, that six out of every ten children of a Catholic–Protestant marriage end up by rejecting all religious belief. Possibly more important to the nation as a whole is the finding that teenage arrest rates for children of mixed marriages are much higher than for children in families where both parents are of the same faith. Arrest rates for the children of Jewish husbands married to non-Jewish wives were as much as ten times higher in one city than for the children of all Jewish marriages.[17]

It is apparent that the association of two people holding different values —religious or secular—does not necessarily lead both or either of them to adopt the values of the other—especially if this involves self-denial. More often, it leads people either to emotional conflict or to abandon the values they brought with them to the association.

It used to be said that, if a Methodist boy who had been taught not to play cards and a Catholic boy who had been taught not to eat meat on Friday and a Baptist boy who had been taught not to drink alcoholic beverages and an orthodox Jewish boy who had been taught not to eat pork were placed together as dormitory roommates, before long they would be having beer with their ham sandwiches at the Friday night poker game.

Today most Methodists look upon card playing as something less than sin and the Roman Catholic prohibition against eating meat on Friday is gone. Perhaps these and some other doctrines of self-denial have lost their original purpose in modern living. But there are some deeper value commitments that, if they continue to be diluted by a similar process, can have tragic consequences for the family and for the nation.

For example, a man who cheats on his income tax should hardly be surprised if he finds his previously honest wife has taken to embezzling the grocery money. Nor should he be very surprised if one of his children is expelled from school for cheating. In the home, as in the dormitory, value dilution is contagious. On the other hand, marriage partners who *do* share the same ideals and values to begin with tend to reinforce those values within each other as they associate together. Family values and family rituals do more than provide security for the family members. They integrate the family and perpetuate standards of behavior for the nation as well. It seems increasingly clear to many people that, when and if any large majority of our families fail—perhaps as a result of value dilution though intermarriage—to teach and reinforce those ethical values that make democracy possible, we will no longer have social organization. And after that, we may not long have a free nation either.

It should be immediately apparent, however, that this is only one horn of the dilemma. The other is also potentially damaging. To urge that only those

[17] Carle C. Zimmerman and Lucius F. Cervantes, *Successful American Families*, New York, Pageant, 1960, p. 159.

with similar values marry each other eliminates freedom of choice, which is a primary value in itself. Worse, it could also perpetuate disvalues. If the man who cheats on his income tax were to marry a wife who *already* approved of embezzling, the dishonest result would be even more certain.

It seems reasonable to assume that, if our social structure is to continue, some new solution must be found to the problem of perpetuating values in the home. There is probably no greater challenge to those who see the current student unrest as a progressive force rather than a destructive one. As Charles Odegaard, president of the University of Washington, said in 1965,

> We have lived through a generation which has too often swept the difficult problems of analyzing values and their implications under the rug, presumably either to await definite scientific conclusions which will answer moral questions or to make these untidy questionings unnecessary. But meanwhile the pressure of events each day forces all of us to make value decisions now of titanic consequence, and youth increasingly will not be put off to a later day for moralizing.[18]

All right, what should be done now?

[18] Charles E. Odegaard, address to the National Academy of Sciences, Seattle, Wash., October 12, 1965.

11

PSYCHOLOGICAL
FACTORS
IN MATE SELECTION

E ndogamy is by no means all there is to mate selection. In fact, in most cases, all endogamy does is to establish the field of eligibles. The real choosing takes place for far more personal and much more emotionally related reasons.

The number one emotional reason for marriage is love. And love, as we saw in Chapter 7, usually results from mutual need-meeting. Therefore, some discussion of the details of need-meeting in specific relation to mate selection now becomes important. It is necessary, though, to point out right at the beginning that love is only one of the psychological reasons for selecting a mate. In many cases there are others: worry over waiting too long, an inadequate self-image, escape, adult identification, revenge, sexual attraction, desire for money and/or higher status. Any one of these or all of them can be controlling factors in who marries whom.

NEED-MEETING
IN MATE SELECTION

In selecting a mate, does an individual usually select someone whose needs are unlike his own but complementary, or does he more often find someone whose needs are very similar to his own? The answer is not as simple as it might seem at first. It is logical that one should choose a mate whose psychological strengths make up for any weaknesses he might have, whether or not he is conscious of them, but it is also logical that, to facilitate adjustment in marriage, like should marry like in psychological characteristics as in social endogamy. Which course do Americans follow in choosing marriage partners? Which might lead to better marriages?

Robert Winch, the leading exponent of the complementary-needs theory, started out with a hypothesis that complementariness of motivation (as, for example, dominance in one partner and submissiveness in the other partner) would maximize gratification. Thus, he reasoned, mate selection should follow a principle of complementariness.

As he developed his hypothesis, Winch decided that there was not one, but two, types of complementary-need satisfaction that led to mate selection. In one type, both partners have the same kind of need, but there is a difference in the intensity of the need, with one parner having a greater and the other a lesser need. For example, if one partner has a high domiance need, he will select someone with a low dominance need. In the second type that Winch identified, it was hypothesized that if one partner is high in a particular trait, the other partner will be high (or possibly low) in *another* trait. For example, if a man had a high need for recognition, he will select a wife with a high deference need.

Winch and his associates tested these propositions with elaborate research methodology but with a small sample. The results were inconclusive. Winch himself was disappointed but felt that the bulk of the evidence supported the general hypothesis of complementary needs in mate selection. "It appears," he concluded, "that not all of the variation in mate selection among our twenty-five couples is to be accounted for by complementariness, but it also appears that complementariness is probably *one* of the determinants."[1]

Later, Thomas Ktsanes, one of Winch's original associates, reworked the complementary-needs data. He concluded that the "tendency for an individual to select a spouse unlike himself in the total emotional makeup far exceeds the tendency for him to select a spouse like himself in that respect."[2] In his study, Ktsanes and his wife emphasized the idea that patterns or configurations of needs rather than single needs might be the more important in the marital choice.

A study by Robert M. Huntington of a sample of married couples and a study by Alan Kerckhoff and Keith Davis, who found the pattern of complementary differences in engaged couples, seemed to offer confirmation of the complementary-needs theory.[3]

But in at least seven studies made between 1956 and 1967, all of which had larger samples than Winch's, consistent patterns of complementary differences between partners were not found.[4] In fact, several of these studies showed

[1] Robert Winch, *Mate Selection: A Study of Complementary Needs*, New York, Harper & Row, 1958, p. 119.

[2] Thomas Ktsanes, "Mate Selection on the Basis of Personality Type: A Study Utilizing the Empirical Typology of Personality," *American Sociological Review*, **20** (October, 1955), 551.

[3] Robert M. Huntington, "The Personality-Interaction Approach to Study of the Marital Relationship," *Marriage and Family Living*, **20** (February, 1958), 43–46; and Alan C. Kerckhoff and Keith E. Davis, "Value Consensus and Need Complementarity in Mate Selection," *American Sociological Review*, **27** (June, 1962), 295–303.

[4] C. E. Bowerman and Barbara Day, "Test of the Theory of Complementary Needs," *American Sociological Review*, **21** (October, 1956), 602–605; Barbara Day, "A Comparison of Personality Needs of Courtship Couples and Some Sex Friendships," *Sociology and Social Research*, **45** (July, 1961), 435–440; Richard M. Lundy, "Self-Perceptions Regarding Masculinity–Femininity and Descriptions of Love, and Opposite Sex Sociometric Choices," *Sociometry*, **21** (September, 1958), 238–246; Bernard I. Murstein, "The Complementary Need Hypothesis in Newlyweds and Middle-aged Married Couples," *Journal of Abnormal and Social Psychology*, **63** (July, 1961), 194–197; Bernard I. Murstein, "Empirical Tests of Role, Complementary Needs, and Homogamy Theories of Marital Choice," *Journal of Marriage and the Family*, **29** (November, 1967), 689–696; J. A. Schellenberg and L. S. Bee, "A Re-examination of the Theory of Complementary Needs in Mate Selection," *Marriage and Family Living*, **22** (August 1960), 227–232; and Jan Trost, "Some Data on Mate-Selection: Complementarity," *Journal of Marriage and The Family*, **29** (November, 1967), 730–738.

patterns of *homogamy* (like chooses *like*) rather than complementariness.

There have been other criticisms of the theory of complementariness as it applied to mate selection, too. Charles Bolton suggested in 1961 that none of the studies which initially were cited to validate the complementary-needs hypothesis showed that the spouses themselves were aware of the complementary traits or that the existence of the traits had anything to do with their actual mate selection. Although this might in no way negate the importance of complementary needs (or any kind of needs) in falling in love, it is damaging to the validity of complementary needs as a process of mate selection.[5]

J. Richard Udry had another criticism. He pointed out the implausibility of the initial premise that, whichever sex has whichever trait, it will be equally satisfying to both partners. As an example, he suggested that, although a dominant male might choose a submissive female, it is not equally true that a dominant female would choose a submissive male. Rather, a dominant female might look for an even more dominant male, so that the usual sex-role expectation could be maintained.[6] Udry's comments conform to my experience in counseling people who are looking for mates. Time and time again the exceptionally dominant woman has only contempt for the mouselike male. What she more often appears to be seeking is a male who is dominant enough to dominate her, despite her effort to make it difficult for him to do so.

After examining all the studies pertinent to the matter of complementary needs versus need homogamy, Lee Burchinal concluded, "Homogamy studies provide greater predictive power for selection of mates than do studies based on complementary needs. Perhaps the chief value for the complementary-needs theory is to account for some of the residual variations in mate selection that are not first accounted for by the operation of endogamous norms, adherence to affectionate-companion norms, and other mate selection norms."[7]

In summary, some people *do* marry those with complimentary-need patterns and some don't. Unfortunately, some of the sociological studies of mate selection were designed to provide an orderly theory of mate selection, and their hypotheses could be validated only if a large proportion of the sample behaved in accordance with the theory of the researcher. A "some do, some don't" finding is unsatisfactory for theory-proving purposes. But for the purposes of the student of the empathetic approach, it is enough to recognize that people fall in love because of needs and that these love relationships often culminate in marriage, sometimes with people with complementary needs, sometimes with people of like needs.

This, however, begs the question, "But when *I* am trying to choose, which is better?" The answer: The mate for you is the one who will better meet your needs, complementary *or* like, in the long run. The qualification "in the long run" is very important, for needs do change. Sometimes a partner who meets your present needs may very well be inadequate in meeting future ones. We have already mentioned several cases in which women have married aggressive men only to find out later that aggressiveness was intolerable to them over a long period. But does this mean, then, that it is always safer to marry someone who has characteristics similar to your own? Not necessarily. Two very dominant and

[5] Charles D. Bolton, "Mate Selection as the Development of a Relationship," *Marriage and Family Living,* **23** (August, 1961), 234–240.
[6] J. Richard Udry, *The Social Context of Marriage,* Philadelphia, Lippincott, 1966, p. 235.
[7] Lee G. Burchinal, "The Premarital Dyad and Love Involvement," in Harold T. Christensen, ed., *Handbook of Marriage and the Family,* Chicago, Rand McNally, 1964, p. 669.

competitive people will probably spend an inordinate amount of their married life fighting. If they have the kind of personalities that enjoy fighting, this might be ideal, but for many people it would be devastating to marriage.

At the other end of the dominance scale, the situation can be even worse. Two very insecure people may be initially attracted to each other. But after marriage they often tend to cross-fertilize each other's anxieties. This kind of case is often seen by the marriage counselor, since insecure people, who had planned to lean on each other after marriage, usually find no support at all, and sometimes both partners seek support from the counselor. Moreover, whereas dominant people are usually so secure in their own self-conviction that they go ahead and get a divorce at the drop of a hat (often without proper consideration of other alternatives), less secure people sometimes vacillate anxiously, seeking advice from everybody, until whatever might have been saved of their relationship is lost.

Very many insecure people do marry each other. In the beginning, their mutual shyness binds them closer together, for each partner feels a real sense of understanding of the other's need for security in the social situation. Each feels he is lucky to have the other; each thinks he needs the other in order to survive and be complete, and each is flattered that the other needs him. Sometimes a person will partially recognize his prospective mate's insecurity but believes that he can live with it. After marriage, he has a great deal of difficulty when the full extent of his mate's need for help becomes apparent.

It is worse, though—far worse—when both partners completely deceive themselves and each other about their insecurities. This is fairly often the case, because insecure people tend to disguise their insecurity from others. One of the things they are most afraid of is what other people will think of them, so they act strong and self-confident on the outside, even while they are feeling insecure and frightened inside. When two such people get together, each believes that the other *is* a self-reliant, capable person who will be a tower of strength after marriage.

These people may think that they are getting married because of complementary needs, if they think about it at all. The old saying that love is blind probably results from the feeling that people tend to see in one another things that they wish to see or that they *need* to see. As Udry points out, "What *he* sees in *her* is very closely related to what *he* is, but not what *she* is."[8]

CASE 16

"When Carl and I were going together, I always thought he was socially able to get along with people," Irene said. "He appeared to make acquaintances easily and to talk smoothly in groups. I admired this very much, because I was all tied up inside when it came to meeting new people. He seemed so sure of himself, so able to make decisions. I guess that's what I wanted, because I knew how frightened I always was about everything.

"But now I know he is really a very insecure person. I blame myself for not seeing it much earlier. He had been an officer in the navy, but he resigned when he felt the navy was treating him unfairly. I should have been tipped off right then. He really doesn't get along well with people, because he's always worried that they're trying to do him out of something. But when he resigned from the navy, I just thought that he was even more wonderful because he had the courage to quit.

---

[8] Udry, *op. cit.*, p. 236.

"Then there was another tipoff that I didn't recognize, either. He showed me the letter of resignation that he was going to send in to the navy. I looked at it, and it was filled with hostility and recriminations. It could only have injured him in the long run. I told him that he couldn't send that letter in and I helped him reword one. He seemed sort of grateful for my help, and at the time I was very flattered to think that he needed me in some small way. Now I realize that he needed me in a big way. He needed my approval before he could really do anything.

"I am terrible for telling you this on him, but because he feels so inadequate himself, he tends to believe the worst about everybody else. Yet at the same time he wants other people to like him so much. I guess I know how this is, because I am very sensitive about what other people think, too. As a matter of fact, when I pass two people whispering, I am sure they are talking about me.

"Before we were married, Carl always seemed so optimistic. I am kind of a worrywart and pessimist myself. I always have been. But I didn't let it show then. Actually I tried to cover up a lot of things. I thought maybe Carl wouldn't love me if I allowed him to see how worthless I am.

"I am easily hurt by criticism. Carl seemed to know this and he seemed to be one of the few men that really understood me. Now I see that he knew it because he was the same way himself.

"I know you won't like me for saying this, and I guess I shouldn't say it, but he really is a very weak man. I think he wants me to mother him. I don't want to mother him. I already have two children to mother. I want him to 'father' me. He yells a lot at the children. I think he's reacting to all the frustrations he feels from the bosses at the office where he works. He isn't man enough to talk back to the bosses, but he comes home and takes it out on the children.

"I should have seen all this from the beginning. My mother always told me that men were self-centered and irresponsible, and I should have listened to her about that. Lord knows I used to listen to her about everything else. That is one reason why I was so fooled by Carl. He seemed to be interested in what I thought, even though he would still make the decisions. Now he not only doesn't make the decisions, he really isn't interested in what I think either. He says all my thoughts are negative, and that I just try to tear him down and spread gloom.

"I know I shouldn't say this, but he isn't much of a sex partner either. He complains that I'm not affectionate enough, but the truth is that he hasn't the courage to be aggressive himself. I don't want to be the one who decides when we have intercourse. He should make love to me and make me feel all warm and loving and then take me. But he expects me to give him some kind of permission. We never talk about sex, because I think he's as embarrassed about it as I am. Sometimes he literally cries when I tell him 'No,' and then he pouts for a week.

"I know you won't like me for saying this, but I have grown to hate him. He isn't the strong person I had hoped for."

When Carl came in to see the counselor, he started out by apologizing for saying anything bad about Irene. "Her big problem was that her mother dominated her so and kept telling her how worthless she was. When I met her she was so self-effacing it was painful, and she still can't make a decision.

"She is terribly negative. If I say, 'Wouldn't it be nice to go on a picnic Saturday?' then she is sure it's going to rain and that the children will fall in the river and that the car will break down, and so forth. She wasn't like that when we were going together. Everything pleased her then, so I didn't have to try and decide how I could make her happy. I know that that's a great part of my trouble. I want too much to make her happy. I try hard all the time to do little things that please her, but instead of pleasing her I seem to upset her. I think it contradicts what her mother kept telling her: men are brutes who will beat her. I often think she might love me more if I did beat her, because it would make her feel that she was right about men all the time.

"You wouldn't believe how insecure she is now. She goes downtown with lots of money and won't buy a dress that she badly needs. She always has some excuse. Either she thought I wouldn't like the dress that she picked out, or the clerk who waited on her looked at her as if she was a poor person who didn't belong in that ritzy store, or she couldn't decide between two dresses. It's maddening.

"The worst part about it all is that her anxiety is catching. I think I've made a final decision and then she says, 'Are you sure that's what you want to do?' and then I have to go through the whole agonizing process again, because usually I'm *not* sure.

"Sometimes she actually says things that increase my anxieties. We have a pony out in the backyard for the children. One morning I got up early and found that the pony had gotten out of the yard. I was so upset I could barely hold my breakfast down, because I was worried about losing that $500 pony. She could have made it easier for me by saying something like, 'Don't worry, I'm sure we'll find the pony.' Did she? No, indeed not! She said instead, 'Oh, dear, I'm sure the pony will get in the way of a school bus and cause an accident and all the children will be killed.' That shows you what kind of person she is.

"If only I could have seen these things before we were married! But I thought she was so sweet and trusting, and she made me feel so important. When she said, 'I'd be delighted to do anything you want to do,' I never realized it was because she was so insecure that she couldn't make up her own mind. I need somebody who will help *me* make decisions. I'm never going to get ahead unless she has some faith in me and tells me that I'm a great guy.

"I suppose she told you about sex; she would. Everything has to be just right, and I have to say all the right words or she won't let me get near her. Believe me, she wasn't like that when we were going together. She was scared then, but she was warm. I want her to love me and show me that she does. But now she seems to think that it's fun to make me keep chasing her and then refuse me at the end.

"I would have divorced her a long time ago except that I just can't make up my mind to do it. There has never been a divorce in my family, and my relatives would all condemn me if I were the first. Besides, I think of myself as being a good husband. I don't drink, and I don't chase after other women. A good husband shouldn't get a divorce. I just want her to love me more."

How did these people deceive each other about their needs? Why? Why didn't he see that she really wouldn't meet his needs before they were married? What kind of woman could meet his needs? What should these two people do about their marriage now?

The case of Irene and Carl points up the importance of individual emotional maturity and stability in marriage. Although love has its beginnings in mutual need-meeting, those people who are so needful as to be dependent and those who seek satisfaction for their needs so urgently that they cannot meet the needs of their partner sometimes actually extinguish love.

Jo Coudert makes a distinction between needing and wanting. In fact, she feels that wanting is a much better predictor of happy marriage than needing. She feels that in selecting a mate an individual should ask himself, "What would the other's life be without me?" Then she goes on to say,

If you have a sneaking suspicion that it would be a perfectly good life, go ahead and marry. If you have an equal suspicion that you, too, could manage reasonably well you can marry with double assurance, for you can assume then that you want each other more than you need each other, and wanting is a much better long-range basis for marriage than needing.[9]

The distinction between needing and wanting is thin and arbitrary at best. (W. I. Thomas called his list of needs "wishes." See Chapter 5.) It is possible to restate Coudert's basic proposition entirely in terms of needs this way. Two self-secure adult individuals who are not so needful themselves that they can't meet the other person's needs make good marriage partners. Unless a person is prepared to bring stability to the marriage instead of taking stability from it, he is not a very likely candidate for a successful marriage.

FEAR OF BEING LEFT

Need-meeting is only one of the many emotional factors in mate selection. Others include fear, escape, revenge, desire to appear grown up, sex, and ambition.

Probably one of the most potent fears is the fear of being left without a mate. Both men and women suffer from this fear, but in modern society we tend to think of it as primarily a woman's problem on the theory that men, because they do the asking, can always get some female to marry them whenever they want to.

For the young woman with a poor self-image, being "left" can be a gnawing source of anxiety that can and does lead to desperation. The problem can become self-enlarging, for, as the young woman becomes more and more anxious, she is apt to become less and less desirable.

Statistically, no American woman should have to go without a mate. But finding a suitable one, especially in later years, is something else again. Any woman's choice is limited not only by the number of potential candidates in her own social world and by her ability to interest any one of them to the point of proposing, *but also by her assessment of her chances of finding something better at the moment she is asked.*

It has been variously estimated that the average college woman has ten to twenty-five dating partners in her mate-selection years. She may superficially assess every one of them as a possible marriage mate, but actually she knows only a few of them well enough to determine the probability of marriage success with them. Several of these young men may propose at one time or another, but only rarely do two or more propose at the same time. If this were to happen, it is even more improbable that both or all of the candidates would be suitable. It seems reasonable to speculate that, in recent years, dating patterns have limited the typical young woman's realistic marital prospects to one at a time and to when that one is willing to propose.

Thus, hers is not the problem of *choosing* a mate but rather of accepting or declining what is presently offered to her. That decision is too frequently made not on the intensity of love or the degree of need-meeting but rather on the basis of the young woman's anxiety level about her future possibilities. The young woman who is sure of her desirableness can confidently turn down an offer, believing that she will have other chances. But the young

---

[9] Copyright © 1965 by Jo Coudert, from p. 206 of the book *Advice from a Failure.* Reprinted with permission of Stein and Day/Publishers, and Hodder and Stoughton.

woman who is insecure and inclined to be negative and pessimistic about the future may well "choose" (deliberately or half-consciously) her mate because of a fear of being left. Clearly this is not the best basis upon which to start a marriage.

It would be a great mistake to believe that it is only young women who are afraid of being left. Although it is generally thought that fewer men are affected by this fear, there are many men whose poor self-images inhibit them from proposing unless they find some young woman who makes it unusually easy for them. Consider the case of Shawn, as told to the counselor by his father.

CASE 17

"Shawn was the last of four children. He had two sisters and a brother who were considerably older than he was. They were all married when he was still in elementary school. Each of the older children was very popular, and each married before reaching age twenty. There was lots of love and affection around our house.

"Shawn was born with a strawberry mark covering the whole right side of his face. His mother and I were terribly shocked when we first saw him, but the doctor told us that there was nothing that could be done to improve his appearance. As a little kid he didn't seem to mind. He was a happy tyke and a very affectionate one. He was energetic and likable, and you had to be pretty perceptive to know that deep down he was very self-conscious. As he grew older, the mark seemed to fade some, but it surely must have troubled him inside. He never asked girls for dates, and he had very few social experiences with girls, although he was popular with the boys.

"Anyway, now he is a junior in college. He has met a woman graduate student who is eleven years older than he is. She is the teaching assistant in his history class. She has taken a great interest in him. I think she must be the first woman other than his mother who has ever made him *feel* that she cares. He thinks he is in love with her and wants to marry her. I'm sure she's a good woman; certainly she's a very intelligent one. She's not very attractive, though, and I don't think she has had many men friends. I wonder about her good judgment in agreeing to marry a twenty-year-old kid.

"As you can guess, I don't want him to marry her—at least not now. In the first place, he isn't ready to be married—no diploma, no job—and in the second place, he's never had any experience with other women to know what he really wants. But I honestly think that he's afraid that no other woman will ever love him again, so he'd better take this one while he can. I've tried to talk him out of it, but he's very determined. What am I going to do?"

What can this father do?

ESCAPE

Escape, usually from oppressive parents, is another common reason in mate selection. Throughout the history of the world, some young people have wanted to get away from seemingly repressive parents. But escape probably never was as possible as it is today. Now many young people, freed from any concern over starvation by their leaving their kinship group, can dash across the state line any time they want to. Often this appears to be an easy way of ending parental domination. Only later does the escaping pair discover that marriage does not diminish restrictions and responsibilities; it increases them.

ADULT IDENTIFICATION

It is possible that there is no stronger psychological drive in the typical young person than his desire to be—or at least appear to be—grown up, and some young people deliberately marry because they desire this adult identification. In order to prove to their parents or to the world that they are adults and should be treated as mature adults, they resort to a simple logic. Adults get married; since they want to be adults, they will get married, too. Interestingly, our whole legal structure supports this notion. Once a girl is married, regardless of her age, she has some legal prerogatives and responsibilities that are denied to a single woman of equal age.

This kind of adult identification is not necessarily related to what is often called the parental-image theory of mate selection. The belief that young people have an unconscious wish for a mate who has characteristics similar to those of his opposite-sex parent is classic in Freudian theory. That is, he has such a wish if the affectional relationship with that parent was satisfying to him when he was a child. Like so many of the other tenets of psychoanalysis, however, most of the efforts to validate this theory empirically have been futile. There is some reason to believe that parental images of *both* parents influence marital choice in some general ways. But it may not be because the parents are the child's fantasy lovers, as in the classic Freudian Oedipus family dramas. Rather, it may be because the parents establish the customs, attitudes, values, and expectations that guide and direct the child to look for someone similar to his parents.

REVENGE AND REBOUND

Revenge (or sometimes a milder rebellion expressed as "I'll show *you!*") is another psychological reason for selecting a particular mate and getting married now. Since this kind of mate selection indicates that the selector is relating to a third person and not to the individual he or she is about to marry, the results are usually unsatisfactory. Marriage is a relationship between the people involved, and, although others often have to be considered in making one's choice, allowing those others to be the controlling factor in that choice usually presages unhappiness. While this can be true when a girl marries a man because her parents thought she ought to, it is even more true when she lets her desire to "get even" take precedence over her real needs in choosing a mate. Consider the case of Ellen.

> CASE 18
> Ellen was thirty-two years old and very depressed when she came in to see the counselor. She was eager to be married, but she had recently learned that she had been deserted by Jay, a loose-living "swinger" who didn't have a dime of his own money. Ellen knew that he drank and gambled; he had told her that, but he had also told her that he loved her. Jay was tender and strong, and she felt both very safe and very desirable when he held her in his arms. Ellen had never known this kind of erotic excitement before.
>
> Long after she realized that he didn't mean any of it and that he never intended to return the money he had borrowed from her, she continued to want to marry him. And long after his touch meant nothing to her and she no longer wanted him, she

continued to act as though they were going to be married. "We would have been married if he had ever asked me," she said. "It wasn't that I was pregnant or obligated to him or anything like that, it was something else. . . ." Her voice trailed off, and she hesitated.

"It's harder to talk about this than anything else," she said when she spoke again. "You see," she said finally, "at the office where I operate the tabulating machine, I am only a clerk. There are two supervisors who don't like me very much because I catch them making mistakes. They can and do make my life miserable. I get all the dirtiest jobs and never a word of praise, but neither of them is married.

"When I thought I was going to be married, I could feel that I had something they didn't have. I could feel like a woman. I had the most important thing they wanted."

What would have been Ellen's chances for a happy marriage? Would she really have married Jay anyway? Would she have been better off if she had never met Jay?

Tangentially related to the revenge motive is the rebound phenomenon. This is so apparent in everyday life that it needs little explanation. A person who feels rejected by one love often rushes off to find another—sometimes to prove to himself that he is desirable, sometimes to prove it to the person who rejected him. In either case, he is not really relating to the new lover in any sound, permanent way. Rebound affairs sometimes culminate in disastrous marriages.

SEXUAL ATTRACTION

Sexual attraction is an obvious psychological factor in mate selection. Although the exact components of masculinity and femininity are hard to define, some people are just "sexy." They have an exceptional ability to stimulate the opposite sex merely by their appearance and manner. Sometimes two rather plain people seem to have a particular attraction for one another. They create images and fantasies within their partners that are beyond the objective understanding of most observers.

Sexual attraction is clearly necessary both to mate selection and to the perpetuation of the species. Problems arise, however, when sexual attraction is the *only* criterion by which a person selects a mate. If there is no greater cement to bond the two people together than sex interest, when the novelty wears off, and it inevitably will, the marriage partners are easily attracted to other sex partners. Someone who is even more sexy is bound to come along.

SUCCESS AND STATUS

Finally, still another psychological factor in mate selection is the individual's need for success—social or financial. Sometimes romantic and financial success are inextricably intertwined. Sociologist John Finley Scott has suggested that if a researcher were so blunt as to ask typical American young women if they would marry for money, the young women would probably feel highly insulted. They would be sure they would marry only for love. However, if the investigating sociologist were to follow up by asking what makes men lovable, he might arrive at a surprisingly different conclusion for his research. For the answers to his "What makes men lovable?" question might include such things as suave good manners, sophisticated good taste, and brilliant intellectual conversation. These characteristics usually depend on an expensive education and are generally associated with wealth. Said Scott: "Money, in short, tends to be despised only in the abstract; in concrete form, enjoyed by the unmarried scions of a rich family, it is highly admired."[10]

In another paper, Scott went so far as to suggest that Americans have a highly institutionalized process for achieving the devious, insidious purpose of young women in capturing upper-status males. The sorority house, he said, can be compared to the fatting houses of Nigeria, where women are sent to be specially fattened for marriage, or to the convents of the Canary Islands, where old women teach young women special skills and mysteries in order to be more attractive to potential marriage mates.[11]

If American women are so determined to find high-status husbands, many of them seem to be blissfully unaware of it. Most of them would deny not only that they intend to marry for money but also that they would choose status and prestige over companionship and easy marriage adjustment. It is true, however, that some lower- and middle-class members of both sexes *deliberately* choose marriage mates on the basis of an emotional hunger for the material satisfactions money can bring, just as some upper-class people of both sexes choose marriage mates on the basis of deeply conditioned anxieties about what would happen to their social position and, indeed, their own financial reserves if they were to marry beneath them. Moreover, some subcultural groups place a high value on their daughters' marrying high-prestige men. The intensity of this conditioned desire varies not only from subcultural group to subcultural group but also from family to family within the group. Some families, like some individuals, react to deprivation by struggling in every way (including marriage) to move up; others appear to accept their station resignedly.

CASE 19

"Mother made me promise that I would come and see you," Nancy Ann told the counselor. "When I was home on vacation from college last week, I told them I was going to be married in two weeks. Mother nearly flipped. It's true that I've only known Buzzy for two months, but what really got to her was when I told her who he was. She says that he's from such an obviously different background that the marriage can't possibly work. She's old-fashioned. She doesn't understand that today lots of people from different backgrounds marry each other and have very happy marriages. She insists that it's a terrible mistake, and that I'll be divorced within a year, but I know he loves me. If she doesn't agree to help us, we're going over to South Carolina and get married anyway."

As the counselor listened to Nancy Ann, he recalled having had her in one of his classes the previous quarter. He also remembered that she didn't get along very well with her classmates. She had to be right all the time, and she always had to have the last word. He remembered that Nancy Ann had bragged about having dates, although one of the other girls had told him that she rarely, if ever, dated at all. She was a little overweight (probably from compensating because of her lack of social success) and inclined to be argumentative and impertinent.

[10] John Finley Scott, "Marriage Is Not a Personal Matter," *The New York Times Magazine* (October 30, 1966), 72.

[11] John Finley Scott, "Sororities and the Husband Game," *Transaction*, St. Louis, Mo., Community Leadership Project of Washington University, September–October, 1965.

"Why do you think your mother wanted you to come and talk with me?" the counselor asked.

"She wants you to talk me out of it," Nancy Ann said. "The truth is that Mother doesn't like Buzzy because she's a snob. He grew up out by the milltown and never had any advantages. He's had a hard time, but what could you expect the way they treat those people? He hasn't found himself yet, but he will. I'll help him." Then she added, "He loves me."

"Is that Buzzy in the black jacket out by the motorcycle?" the counselor inquired.

"Yes," Nancy Ann responded.

"May I meet him?"

"No, you'll only make fun of him," she said. Then she thought for a minute. "Do you really want to meet him?" she asked after a while.

"Yes."

"All right, I'll bring him in."

Buzzy was a sallow-faced, stooped-shouldered young man who apparently had suffered some dietary deficiencies as a youngster. He was very defensive about meeting the counselor. He had grown up and still lived on a little patch of ground adjacent to a mill village in a dilapidated frame house with his father, mother, and three sisters. His father farmed a patch of butterbeans, but he was barely able to make enough to keep the family together on the marginal land. Buzzy himself had dropped out of high school and was expecting to be inducted into the army very soon. Meanwhile, he spent his time riding around town on his old motorcycle and occasionally doing odd jobs at the foundry. He wasn't sure what he was going to do after he got out of the army. He thought he might raise butterbeans too. "It ain't the way you think it is," Buzzy said. "It ain't because her daddy's rich and lives in that big house down in Florida. I really love her and she loves me and we're fixin' to get married next week."

After Buzzy had gone, the counselor talked again with Nancy Ann and gently pointed out that the differences in their background would make marriage adjustment difficult for them. "I know all that," Nancy Ann said. "But you don't understand; he loves me!" Then she was quiet for a while. "Besides, I don't have to tell him any stories; he really accepts me. He doesn't try to make me feel inferior. I know it isn't going to be any picnic at first, but I'll help him and someday he will be a really important man that I will be proud of. You'll see!"

What might Nancy Ann's mother do? There are several classic American approaches to this problem. One is to invite the boy to the girl's home. There, theoretically, he will see that her different value system would make their marriage difficult, if not impossible. Actually, however, this approach was all but unthinkable in Nancy Ann's case. She was a very perceptive young woman, and it was quite clear that she would believe, rightly or wrongly, that if Buzzy were invited to her home it would be for the purpose of embarrassing him. Almost immediately she would feel that he was being martyred, and she would be even more defensive and close-minded about the situation.

Another approach to this problem in the past was to remove the erring daughter from school and take her on an extended tour of Europe. In Nancy Ann's case, would this be a good solution? Would this have solved Nancy Ann's problems?[12]

[12] By this time, the student will be familiar enough with the empathetic approach so that many other questions will suggest themselves. Hereafter, questions following the cases will be omitted so that they will not interfere with individual thought and creative inquiry.

Motives for marriage such as escape, revenge, and social status are patently in conflict with predictable marriage success. Discussing them should serve to underline for the student who is interested in his own future happiness the importance of thoroughly understanding his own reasons for wanting to marry.

There are good, sound, psychological reasons for marrying. The most important one, antiromanticists and cynics notwithstanding, is a warm, close, genuine, and abiding love. This kind of love embraces not only the feeling of joyful exaltation in being together but also the feeling of tenderness that only two people who really care about one another can share. It is brought to its full fruition in a sexual longing to be one. Love like this is usually born of, and nurtured by, the ability to meet each other's deep emotional needs, whether those needs be complementary or similar. In turn, this need-meeting ability is usually enhanced by a similar value background, since similar value systems make an understanding of the other person's real needs more easily perceivable. Here Robert Coombs' value theory is again cogent: A similar value system leads not only to easier communication but also to a validation of self.[13] One mate is pleased, and so is the other, when his customs, attitudes, values, and expectations are confirmed as being "right."

In the end, the vast majority of present-day Americans, like their fathers and mothers before them, will probably turn out to be good marriage prospectors, with normal social and psychological reactions to mate selection. As we shall presently see, most American marriage partners insist that they are happily married.

WHAT ARE THE CRITERIA
FOR GOOD MATE SELECTION?

What conclusions can be drawn from this discussion for the person who is about to select his own mate? Three general guidelines suggest themselves. First, study yourself. Second, study the prospect. And third, study the possible effects of the relationship between the two of you.

Studying yourself is not easy, despite the amount of time you have in which to do it. We all tend to deceive ourselves—if only by holding our head at the most flattering angle when we look in a mirror and then assuming that we look that way all the time. To really know yourself, you have to ask yourself the hard questions, the ones that really hurt. What are your needs? Do you have a normal need to love and, more important, to give love? Do you have normal needs for security, recognition, response, and new experience? Are you dependent on someone else for emotional support? Can you accept some insecurity in other persons? If so, how much? Do you need a parent figure as your mate, someone who can tell you what to do?

Besides studying your needs, you also need to study your motives. Why do you want to get married? Panic? Escape? Adult identification? Revenge? Sexual attraction? A desire for higher social status? Will this particular marriage be a solution? Or will marriage only increase your problems?

You should also study your prospective marriage mate. There are several

[13] Robert H. Coombs, "A Value Theory of Mate Selection," *Family Life Coordinator*, **10** (July, 1961), 51–54.

ways of doing this. One is to listen carefully for the *real* meanings in what he says (there will be much more about this in the chapter on communication) and objectively observe the way he behaves. Could you live with him the way he is? Or do you think that he will change after you are married? The latter is very improbable. A girl who has many psychosomatic complaints before marriage is far more likely to turn into a full-blown hypochondriac than she is to get well after marriage. A man who drinks heavily before marriage is much more liable to become an alcoholic than he is to give up drinking after marriage. Listening to your prospective mate and observing him or her in action are probably your best guides to selecting a good mate.

There are other ways of judging, too. How well do other people like him? Does he get along well with other people of his own sex? This can be very important after marriage not only to your social life but also to his business career. What do your friends think of him?

Then there is another important criterion. What are his parents like? Your prospective mate was conditioned by them. Sometimes his behavior may seem very different from theirs, but often, under stress, he may revert to the patterns he learned as a child by direction or by example from his parents. Not all children of unhappy parents and broken homes are poor marriage mates, but children of happy and successful parents do have a better statistical probability of turning out to be successful marriage partners.

It is also wise to examine the prospective mate's relationship with his parents, for this may tell you something about why he wants to marry you (a question rarely even thought of when you think you are in love). Jo Coudert cites the case of a friend who looked closely at her fiancé's mother and thought her to be an unattractively positive woman inclined to demand that her husband and son cater to her:

> This was not the image my friend had of herself, of course, but in attempting to cope with the information honestly, she faced the fact that behavior of her own, which she previously defined as an inability to resist taking advantage of her fiancé's good nature, was, in truth, an inclination to manipulate him. At this point, she could say cynically that if that was what he wanted, why should she deny him his masochistic pleasures? Or she could take the long view and curb her own natural propensity in this direction so that, when the fever of love returned to normal, they could transit to steady love; she without contempt for his accommodating ways, he without a sense that he had been taken.[14]

Although it is probably going to make very little difference to two people who are really in love, looking at the prospective mate's parents can also be revealing as far as the future physical appearance of the mate is concerned. Most women are more likely than not to be shaped like their mothers when they arrive at their mothers' ages, and most men may look considerably like their fathers when time catches up with them, too.

Another major way to improve your mate-selection ability is to consider the possible effects of the relationship between your personality and that of your prospective mate. How able is he to meet your needs over the long run, and how able are you to meet his? Does he even now *really* provide what you want? Is he able to communicate with you? Does she talk so much you sometimes wish you weren't with her? Are you so flattered by his possessiveness or

[14] Copyright © 1965 by Jo Coudert, from pp. 203–204 of the book *Advice from a Failure*. Reprinted with permission of Stein and Day/Publishers, and Hodder and Stoughton.

her tendency to cling to you that you don't recognize that this really represents a pathological insecurity on his or her part? Can he provide the kind of decisiveness and leadership you want? Can she provide the kind of warm tenderness that you need when you both are faced by adversity? Does he or she have all the qualities of role appropriateness, personal integrity, and loyalty that will make for an enduring marriage? No one ever was perfect or ever will be. The person who keeps looking for perfection either may be left waiting or ultimately may have to settle for even less than he might have had in the first place. Yet, as Jo Coudert puts it, "Most men and women who truly want to marry, sooner or later find someone they truly want to marry, and it is infinitely preferable to come late to a good marriage than early to a bad one."[15]

[15] *Ibid.*, pp. 211–212.

12

PREMARITAL SEX:
PUBLIC AND PARENTAL
CONFUSION

It is singularly appropriate that the chapter on premarital sex follow a chapter on mate selection. These days, often the major reason why some people marry the mates they do is that premarital intercourse and pregnancy have already occurred. It is estimated that this kind of "mate selection" is involved in nearly 50 percent of all teenage marriages.[1] Moreover, it is probable that some other people do *not* marry a partner they might have married because guilt or panic resulting from sexual intercourse has cut short a potential romance.

Other ways in which premarital sex can affect mating and marriage relationships will be discussed later, but here it is important to point out that premarital sexual behavior is surrounded by confusion. There is public confusion, there is parental confusion, and, most important of all, there is personal confusion. These confusions, of course, cannot be wholly boxed off in such neat little categories. They are all inextricably interrelated, but to the extent that some of the elements can be separated out, let's take a closer look at these three great perplexities that surround premarital sex in America today.

PUBLIC CONFUSION

One of the most confusing aspects of premarital sex behavior is the general unsureness about the extent to which it exists. Nobody knows exactly what is going on. There is, first of all, relatively little valid, up-to-date research. Some of the authoritative books appearing in the late 1960s were based largely on the Kinsey reports, which then were almost a quarter of a century old and which reported the sex experiences of people born in the early 1900s. Even in those

[1] Lee G. Burchinal, "Research on Young Marriages: Implications for Family Life Education," *Family Life Coordinator*, **9** (September–October, 1960), 7, 11.

few cases where more recent data were cited, the reliability of the studies was open to serious question. One thing that sex researchers know is that, when it comes to premarital sex, people do not always behave the way they say they behave. It isn't that they always deny having sexual activity; some probably exaggerate their exploits. The Kinsey reports were widely criticized on this basis.

Even if the studies were both recent and reliable, there are such large regional, socioeconomic, educational, religious, and cultural differences in the extent of premarital sex activity that to talk about what American premarrieds as a whole are doing would be little more than nonsense. Even to talk about what college students are doing is almost completely speculative, despite the fact that most of the present research has been done with college students. The premarital sex situation on the campus of the University of California in Berkeley is probably far different from the situation at Columbia Bible College in South Carolina.

Today, just about enough is known about the extent and variety of premarital sex to be able to say confidently that anyone who says "*everyone* is doing it" really doesn't know what he is talking about.

Various behavioral scientists, after examining the research data, have concluded that there has not been any research evidence pointing to a significant increase in premarital coitus since the 1920s. Yet this conclusion appears to be in conflict with both popular and professional observations of the way young people are behaving. Therefore, some authorities, including both Robert Bell and Ira Reiss, have qualified their interpretations by pointing out that there has been a large change in young people's sexual *attitudes* and premarital petting behavior that probably will lead to increased premarital sexual intercourse unless there are sharp reversals of present trends.[2]

Since social research always lags behind actual performance, it is probable that no one will know in advance when premarital sexual behavior will catch up with the alleged new premarital sex attitudes, if it ever does. There are some professionals who believe that the gap has already closed. A psychiatrist in a student health service at a large Western university told me that all of the students on the campus were regularly engaging in multiple and diverse sexual affairs. When it was pointed out that the psychiatrist saw a select group of students whose sexual behavior might reflect their emotional problems, he stated that complete sexual promiscuity was as universal among his student friends as among his student patients. Later, however, a woman gynecologist from the same student health service indicated that among those students she saw for nonpsychiatric problems there were many students who were anatomically still virgins and some who dated so infrequently as to make the psychiatrist's description of a universally rich and uninhibited sex life highly improbable. The gynecologist believed that among the popular, well-adjusted women on the campus outright promiscuity was very infrequent. Sexual restraint, at least prior to engagement, was still a popular ideal, she thought, and extensive premarital coitus was probably far less general than most popular writers suggest.

Mervin Freedman reported in 1965 that,

All the studies on sexual activities of college students suggest that promiscuity, in the sense of frequent sex relations of an automatic kind, is probably confined to a very small percentage of college women. It is likely that promiscuity

[2] Robert R. Bell, *Premarital Sex in a Changing Society*, Englewood Cliffs, N.J., Prentice-Hall, 1966, pp. 58, 63–88, 169–172; and Ira L. Reiss, "The Sexual Renaissance: A Summary and Analysis," *Journal of Social Issues*, **22** (April, 1966), 123.

occurs more frequently among high school girls than among college women. The control and discipline required to prepare academically for college and to remain in college are inversely associated with the lack of inhibition and disposition to gratify desires without delay that characterize a sexually promiscuous woman.[3]

But what about men students? It has generally been supposed that there are more promiscuous men than promiscuous women and many fewer male "*virgins.*" Alfred Kinsey and his associates said at the time of their publication on the human male in 1948 that the amount of sexual activity that a male had varied inversely with his educational achievement. Many college men then, they said, were completely without sexual experience.[4]

In a 1969 comprehensive study of 1000 college seniors and 500 freshmen, the Roper Research Associates found that in their sample one-third of the seniors and half the freshmen said they had never had sexual intercourse, and of those who had had intercourse only about 10 percent of the seniors and 6 percent of the freshmen said it had been with "quite a few" different women.[5]

THE RESEARCH EVIDENCE

Most of the studies of premarital sex behavior in the United States are of historical rather than of present interest. Katherine Davis reported in 1929 that, in her sample of 2200 college women, 7 percent of the married women reported having had premarital coitus; in his study published the same year, G. V. Hamilton found that in his sample of 100 married couples, 54 percent of the men and 35 percent of the women reported premarital coitus; and Lewis Terman reported in 1938 that 60 percent of the men and 37 percent of the women in his study had had premarital sexual relationships.[6]

Burgess and Wallin interviewed 666 married couples and reported in 1953 that 68 percent of the men and 47 percent of the women said they had had premarital intercourse; the Kinsey group concluded that for the some 5000 males they interviewed, the over-all rate was 90 percent, but only about 50 percent of college men had had intercourse by the time they were twenty-one; and although about one-half of the 6000 females studied (including those marrying late in life) reported premarital intercourse, less than 20 percent of college women were not virgins at age twenty.[7]

In 1959, Winston Ehrmann reported that only 13 percent of the women in his sample at the University of Florida were not virgins.[8] Mervin Freedman in

[3] Mervin B. Freedman, "The Sexual Behavior of American College Woman: An Empirical Study and An Historical Survey," *Merrill-Palmer Quarterly,* **11** (January, 1965), 43.

[4] Alfred C. Kinsey, W. B. Pomeroy, and C. E. Martin, *Sexual Behavior in the Human Male,* Philadelphia, Saunders, 1948, pp. 335–337.

[5] Roper Research Associates, *A Study of the Beliefs and Attitudes of Male College Seniors, Freshmen and Alumni,* New York, Standard Oil Company (New Jersey), 1969.

[6] Katherine B. Davis, *Factors in the Sex Life of Twenty-Two Hundred Women,* New York, Harper & Row, 1929, p. 19; G. V. Hamilton, *A Research in Marriage,* New York, A & C Boni, 1929, p. 346; and Lewis M. Terman, *Psychological Factors in Marital Happiness,* New York, McGraw-Hill, 1938, p. 320.

[7] Ernest W. Burgess and Paul Wallin, *Engagement and Marriage,* Philadelphia, Lippincott, 1953, p. 330; Kinsey et al., *op. cit.,* p. 550; and Alfred C. Kinsey et al., *Sexual Behavior in the Human Female,* Philadelphia, Saunders, 1953, p. 296.

[8] Winston Ehrmann, *Premarital Dating Behavior,* New York, Holt, Rinehart and Winston, 1959, p. 10.

his 1965 study of 49 senior students at an Eastern woman's college found that 10 percent had not gone beyond kissing, 27 percent had not done more than petting above the waist, another 41 percent had been involved in genital petting, 16 percent had had intercourse in serious relationships, and only 6 percent were involved in "uninhibited behavior."[9]

Reiss summed up in 1967 what he called the "basic facts that seem to persist and that have been assumed to be accurate for America":

> There is widespread agreement that premarital coitus is more common for males than females and for Negroes than for whites. There is also widespread agreement that affection is a more important fact in motivating the female to perform sexually than it is in motivating the male. Further, it is generally assumed that different social and cultural factors produce different sexual behaviors and attitudes, although the literature is not unanimous as to just what these factors are or how they work. Several researchers have found that those relations wherein the male has higher social class than the female are much more likely to involve premarital coitus than the relations wherein the female has higher status than the male. Religiousness in several studies was found to be an inhibiting influence on sexual permissiveness; that is, religious persons are less likely to engage in sexual intimacies. There is also evidence that the consequences of coitus vary according to the standards an individual holds. Many studies support the contention that an increase in sexual behavior of several types occurred during the 1920's.[10]

Two studies published in 1968 did little to alter the general conclusions of the Reiss summary. Popular writer Vance Packard, whose data were given some added credence by the fact that they were analyzed by Eleanore Luckey and Gilbert Nass at the University of Connecticut, reported an increase of 6 percentage points in the number of twenty-one-year-old college males indicating that they had had premarital intercourse when his data were compared with the data from the college-educated males interviewed by the Kinsey group in the 1940s.

Packard also reported an increase of 16 percentage points in the number of twenty-one-year-old women in his college sample who indicated that they had had premarital sexual intercourse when compared with Kinsey's college female sample. Said Packard,

> We found no indication that copulation has become rampant among college women in general (or males either), which news accounts focusing upon extreme situations of promiscuous behavior might imply. A solid majority of our total sample of junior and senior women reported they were still virgins. (And more than 40 percent of the upperclass males did, too.)[11]

In examining attitudes—as distinct from behavior—Packard found that half his respondents from both sexes were not committed to the ideal that one partner in marriage should not have had previous intercourse experience with another person. Such previous experience by a partner would not "seriously" trouble a majority of either sex, Packard found, but it would trouble a majority of males, at least "some."

Landis and Landis in a study of 3189 students in eighteen colleges in

[9] Freedman, op. cit., p. 36.
[10] Ira L. Reiss, The Social Context of Premarital Sexual Permissiveness, New York, Holt, Rinehart and Winston, 1967, p. 7.
[11] Vance Packard, The Sexual Wilderness, New York, McKay, 1968, pp. 161–162.

1967 found that, of the women and men who had not in the past had a serious love relationship, over 90 percent of the women and over 60 percent of the men were virgins. When premarital sexual behavior was analyzed by the current dating status of the 2184 women in the study, it was found that 15 percent of those not now dating had at some time had premarital sexual relations, 20 percent of those who were dating had had premarital sexual relations, and 44 percent of those who were engaged were no longer virgins.[12]

Both the Packard study and the Landis and Landis study are subject to the "volunteer error," as were many of the previous sex studies. As Abraham Maslow and James Sakoda pointed out in a classic critique of the Kinsey studies, it may well be that those people who voluntarily tell about their sex lives, whether in person or on a blind questionnaire, have certain unconventional characteristics that make them unrepresentative of the total population.[13] More people reporting premarital sexual experience today may mean only that more people feel free today to admit such experience on a questionnaire.

CONFUSION ABOUT CONSEQUENCES

If the professionals who are trying to measure premarital sex have some difficulties, so do those professionals who must deal with its consequences. Many clergymen have become increasingly reluctant to preach about youthful sexual sin, because modern psychological concepts have raised serious questions about the wisdom of creating guilt. Social workers have faced much the same dilemma in dealing with illegitimately pregnant girls. Moral condemnation may be psychologically harmful and unfairly chastise the girl who just happened to get caught. On the other hand, complete acceptance of her behavior may lead to a casual repetition of it.

In recent years, medical doctors too have begun to agonize not only over what to tell the young people who come into their office for advice on premarital sex, but also over such ethical problems as whether or not to prescribe contraceptive pills for young single women. Many recent medical meetings have been devoted to just such troublesome dilemmas. Nor is the legal profession exempt from modern confusions over sexual ideas and behaviors. Such problems as the definition of pornography and the prosecution of homosexuals have become matters for legal anguish.

The causes of many of these professional confusions regarding premarital sex attitudes and behaviors have their roots in the basic social changes that have occurred since World War I. Many observers have offered differing explanations of how and why these changes came about. Nine such explanations are discussed below.

Changing Technology

The first of the factors pointed to as an explanation of altered attitudes is often the changing technology, which has brought the automobile, the "pill," and anti-

---

[12] Judson T. Landis and Mary G. Landis, *Building a Successful Marriage*, 5th ed., Englewood Cliffs, N.J., Prentice-Hall, 1968, p. 167.
[13] Abraham H. Maslow and James Sakoda, "Volunteer Error in the Kinsey Study," *Journal of Abnormal and Social Psychology*, **47** (April, 1952), 259–262.

biotics into general use. It is doubtful that any one invention has had a greater effect on premarital sexual behavior than the automobile, for it moved dating from the parlor out into the countryside and away from the prying, protective eyes of parents and relatives.

The availability of contraceptives and the many different forms in which they are sold has also affected attitudes and behavior. Contraceptives theoretically negate one of the oldest reasons for premarital abstinence. The word *theoretically* is important, for the statistics indicate that the rate of premarital pregnancies has gone up, despite the wide availability of contraceptives. Venereal disease has also increased drastically, despite, or perhaps even because of, the availability of antibiotics. The false security of believing that an easy cure was available may have had something to do with the increase in the V.D. rate, especially among teenagers.

Urbanization

A second reason offered for changing sex attitudes has been the urbanization of American culture. In rural America, primary-group associations tended to maintain traditional values. That is, there was constant association with relatives, friends, and neighbors, all of whom had approximately the same value systems. As people moved to the urban areas in large numbers after World War I, they found a far greater anonymity and a far greater freedom to behave as they wished. Today, fewer people in the big cities know or care what their neighbors are doing, even though apartment-house dwellers may live physically closer together than farm people ever did. The urban situation not only creates an opportunity for behavior disapproved of in the rural culture, it also creates the loneliness that motivates people to form transitory sexual liaisons.

Secularization

"Secularization" is another explanation for the new sex attitudes. Adherence to religious concepts and doctrines has been steadily declining. Luther Baker studied the changing religious norms and came to the conclusion that there is no correlation between present-day moral concepts and church participation. He concluded that the "values by which men live and which form the basis for their moral decision making have changed, even though lip service is paid to a set of norms deeply ingrained in the culture but long since forgotten."[14]

Commercialization of Sex

Another factor that has been pointed to as stimulating the new sexual climate has been the increased promotion and commercialization of sex by the mass media. Although there are those who would argue that this is an effect of changing popular attitudes rather than a cause of those attitudes, it is fairly evident that at times the movies and the magazines are leading public opinion rather than following it. Increasingly liberal court decisions about what constitutes pornography and increasing public acceptance of written material that

[14] Luther Baker, Jr., "Changing Religious Norms and Family Values," *Journal of Marriage and Family Living*, **27** (February, 1965), 6.

could formerly be classified only as salacious has played a part in changing attitudes toward premarital sex.

Affluence

Increased prosperity and the resulting "boom times" psychology of the 1950s and 1960s has also been suggested as a factor in changing sexual values. Some people have always defied sexual conventions, but prosperity and affluence make it easier for large numbers of middle-class citizens to make discreet visits to local motels or to have hideaway weekends at distant resorts. These people can get away from the sanctions of primary groups and still maintain a "respectable" social or business reputation.

Value Dilution

Still another suggested reason for changes in sex attitudes is the continuing increase in cross-cultural associations. America in the early twentieth century was a class- and group-divided society. The predominant middle class, who in general had relatively strict and somewhat Puritanical attitudes toward sex, had relatively little contact with people from lower socioeconomic groups, who generally had much more sexual freedom. (Reiss has pointed out, though, that there were—and are—some sexually conservative lower-class groups too. This is especially true of religiously conservative areas.[15])

During the crucial adolescent years, there was little social interchange between students from widely divergent backgrounds. The high school that the upper- and middle-class children attended had almost no students from lower socioeconomic levels. Besides, the lower classes couldn't afford for their children to continue in school much beyond the required minimum age. Those who did continue were made to feel uncomfortable about their clothes and manners, as August Hollingshead has made so clear.[16] Thus, middle-class values tended to be inbred and perpetuated in high schools.

But during World War I there was a large-scale exposure of middle-class American men not only to the greater sexual freedom of other American subcultural groups but also to that of some of the European cultures as well. The results were predictable. Middle-class men absorbed the freer sexual values and brought them home to the middle-class women. As a matter of fact, a popular song of the early 1920s was "How Ya Gonna Keep 'Em Down on the Farm (After They've Seen Paree)?"

The cross-cultural mixing was increased by the Great Depression of the 1930s, when, for the first time, large groups of lower socioeconomic-group boys and girls were forced by state law and economic necessity to remain in school until they were sixteen or eighteen. Again, it was far easier for the more strictly reared middle-class children to absorb the freer lower-class values than vice versa. World War II also contributed greatly to the decline of the old middle-class standards, as did the postwar upward social mobility that brought about large-scale subcultural group mixing in the housing tracts of the suburbs. The admission of large numbers of ex-G.I.'s, fresh from the wartime years of sexual freedom, to the colleges and universities completed the decline of some of the older sexual differentials.

[15] Reiss, "The Sexual Renaissance," op. cit., p. 125.
[16] August Hollingshead, Elmtown's Youth, New York, Wiley, 1949, pp. 329–360.

The first Kinsey report in the 1940s provided a wealth of empirical data supporting educational and social-class differences in premarital sexual behavior, but Reiss, in his well-financed and careful study in the early 1960s, found no such large over-all social-class differences, although he still found significant differences in a sample of 1515 adults who were not in college. And Reiss did find that when he divided his college groups into liberals (no religious affiliation, low on romantic-love beliefs, lived in the northeast United States, etc.), and conservatives (high church attendance, high on romantic-love beliefs, lived in the South, etc.), then there was an association of social class with sexual permissiveness among college students. Among the conservatives it was the higher the class, the lower the permissiveness; among the liberals, the higher the social class, the higher the permissiveness.[17] Reiss speculated that among the major reasons for the differences between his findings and Kinsey's were the difference in sampling technique, the fact that Kinsey studied sexual behavior whereas Reiss studied sexual attitudes, and the time that elapsed between the two studies. It is possible that the process of intercultural mixing, which was early in process when Kinsey made his study and was virtually complete at some colleges by the time Reiss made his, might account for the rapid wearing out of a difference that previously did exist.

Sexual Equality for Women

Another social change that has been suggested as contributing importantly to the new sexual attitudes has been the upsurge in sexual equality for women. It is doubtful that the women who gathered in the little chapel in Seneca Falls, New York, in 1848 to issue the manifesto for women's rights could possibly have foreseen that the accomplishment of political, legal, and social equality for women would also have a bearing on their sexual expectations and behavior. Women, many now believe, are entitled to as much sexual enjoyment (and possibly more, since they are capable of multiple orgasm), and as much opportunity for sexual variety as men have always had. There are, of course, wide regional and subcultural variations in the application of these attitudes, and, as we shall presently see, there are some reasons—both physiological and emotional—why female sexual response may never be exactly comparable to male. Nontheless, there has been a considerable movement toward sexual equality without restraint for women.

The concept that women are entitled to as much sexual pleasure as men has given rise to the notion that having premarital intercourse with a woman is no longer defined as exploiting her. Most societies have always sought to protect the unmarried female on the theory that intercourse was usually disadvantageous to her. Even our common folk language reflects this: for example, "He took advantage of her." Now, however, many men look upon having intercourse with a woman as a mutually pleasurable experience, if not actually a means of doing the woman a favor. Avoiding premarital intercourse for chivalrous reasons has become almost anachronistic, for most mature women seem to like being sexually emancipated. But there remains a problem of what to do about immature girls who can be impregnated or emotionally traumatized before they are old enough to recognize the consequences of their sexual behavior.

[17] Reiss, *The Social Context of Premarital Sexual Permissiveness*, op. cit., p. 67.

Crisis Philosophy

There is considerable agreement that the pressures of adversity and disaster can and do affect sexual attitudes and behaviors. Just how recent events and circumstances have influenced the move toward sexual freedom is, however, the subject of controversy. Theodore Ferdinand represents one point of view in suggesting that, in the early years of our society, severe adversity gave meaning to the ascetic ideal of severe self-discipline. But, Ferdinand points out, today's young Americans

> have never known a national disaster like the great depression or the strong likelihood that a world war would drastically interfere with their lives. Hence, many Americans today live in the present, confident that the future will take care of itself. For them an ethic of indulgence is more meaningful than one of self-discipline.[18]

Another, and almost diametrically opposed, view is that Americans have been living in a constant state of crisis ever since 1939. One international crisis has followed another in recent years, and war has been an ever-present threat. Three times in the past thirty years young men have been drafted and sent off to die on battlefields. Since 1945, there has been a Cold War and the threat of atomic destruction, and the consequent atmosphere of perpetual crisis has increased social instability. "Take what you want today, for there may be no tomorrow" seems to have become something of a national preoccupation.

It is possible that both of these views, polarized as they may seem, are applicable to the present times. Perhaps many people, now immune to *personal* anxiety reactions to crises, are using the higly publicized *national* anxiety as a good excuse to "eat, drink, and be merry," not really believing that there will be anything but many more bigger and better tomorrows.

Self-Fulfilling Prophecy

Finally, one very important factor in creating the more permissive attitudes may be that the so-called sexual revolution was touted as reality by the mass media writers and disseminated to homes throughout the United States via television, even though its original existence was—in the beginning, at least—doubtful. Many young people, hearing about this revolution, felt that they had a new norm to live up to. Because young people *want* to be normal, they helped to make real what otherwise might never have existed by exaggerating their sexual escapades to make themselves appear close to what they thought the sexual-conduct norms were, or by actively seeking actual sexual experience. In either case they gave credence to stories that originally had questionable validity and so tended to convince others that the stories were true in the first place.

Says Robert Coombs:

> Thus there is a self-fullfilling prophecy. Things defined as real (in this case "a sexual revolution," new morality, etc.) tend to become real in their consequences. In my judgment, many people, including some clergymen, have unwittingly been a major instrument in bringing about the very things they decry. By inveighing against the "new morality," they have anchored the norm into the fabric of the social structure.[19]

[18] Theodore Ferdinand, "Sex Behavior and the American Class Structure: A Mosaic," *Annals of the American Academy of Political and Social Science,* **376** (March, 1968), 77.
[19] Robert H. Coombs, personal communication to Richard H. Klemer, January 31, 1969.

To add to this self-enlarging confusion, no one is quite sure what "new morality" means these days. In the mid-1960s, the term *new morality* was sometimes used by thoughtful scholars to describe a situation in which premarital or extramarital sexual relations were not precluded by moral prohibition but became "good" or "bad" according to the intent or feelings of the partners. There will be more about this. In recent years, however, the term has been usurped by the uninhibited advocates of complete permissiveness. In this sense, "new morality" is a misnomer, for, although it may or may not be moral (some writers believe it is more moral because it is more honest), it is certainly not new. It's basic tenets, far from being really modern, go back to the hedonic philosophy, generally first credited in Western thought to Aristippus (circa 400 B.C.).

Any one or all of the nine major explanations for the new sexual permissiveness postulated in this chapter may be more or less relevant in the life of any particular person. Taken together they give some measure of the complexity of the factors that have brought us to the present state of public confusion over premarital sex.

PARENTAL CONFUSION

Public confusion is probably exceeded by the confusion among parents. Most parents have seen too many values changed in their lifetime to be able to give the kind of unequivocal answers to their adolescent children's questions that parents used to give their children. Two generations ago, Americans were surer about a lot of things. It was wrong to borrow money on the installment plan; it was wrong to get a divorce; it was wrong to bomb civilians; it was right to take care of your own aged relatives; it was right to avoid foreign entanglements; and it was right to believe that "free love" was a design of the devil. Today more and more parents have more and more difficulty being unequivocal about *any* answer they give to their children.

At least part of the parents' difficulty stems from the fact that, as we have pointed out before, change has become a value in itself. Tradition no longer seems to be an acceptable reason for any behavior. With this in mind, many parents are afraid of being called old-fashioned by their sons and daughters if they advocate sexual restraint. They have been told—perhaps correctly—that their "preaching" may have the effect of creating deliberate rebellion "acted out" in sexual experimentation. Hesitant to teach traditional values, some decline to teach any values at all. The resultant vacuum leaves it up to the child to decide what his or her sexual conduct will be.

Many parents, of course, have been taken in by their children's exaggerated protests that they don't need or want any direction. These parents have failed to recognize that the protests represent the child's eagerness to show how independent and mature he is. Most children can't ever bring themselves to destroy their self-images of themselves as "grown up" by admitting to their parents that they would like to have some guidance. These very same children are secretly disconcerted when their eager-to-please parents take them literally, refuse to supply criteria for good behavior, and thus burden the children with responsibility they are not ready to accept.

There have to be some limits by which people can evaluate their own behavior, or else they are completely insecure. In this connection, there is increasing criticism of the doctrine that bad things, like neuroses, always result from the inhibition of "sexual instincts." It now appears probable to some investigators that neurosis more often has its origin in anxiety over what is right and what is wrong in any culture than in the curbing of sexual drives in order to conform to clearly established sanctions. Thus, by not giving their children clear standards, parents have been creating the very pathology they had sought to avoid.

CASE 20

Sylvia, an eighteen-year-old college freshman, came in to talk with the counselor about her friend Melinda. "Melinda is absolutely wild," Sylvia told the counselor. She's a very intelligent girl and she could be doing straight A work in this college right now if she wanted to. But she's never even finished high school. She runs around all the time. I think she sleeps with a different man almost every night and sometimes two of them. Now she's pregnant for the third time.

"I've known her ever since we were little children. We've always lived close to each other. Her father is a very successful businessman, and when he still lived at home I thought they had a nice family. But her mother was a selfish person, filled with self-pity. Before long Melinda's father began staying away from home. Her parents were divorced about four years ago. Soon after that, Melinda started running around. Her mother was supposed to be caring for her but I really don't think her mother cared for anybody but herself.

"Melinda's mother never set any rules at all. Melinda could decide for herself when to come home and what to do. Up until the time I saw what happened to Melinda, I always thought it would be wonderful to be so independent, but now I think that one of the reasons why Melinda got herself into such a mess is that she was rebelling against her mother's lack of rules. She said as much to me one time. It was almost as if she was trying to do so much that she would force her mother to set some limits. It must have seemed to Melinda that her mother didn't love her because she never tried to stop Melinda from doing those things which both of them knew would sooner or later get Melinda into trouble."

Sylvia was silent for a minute absorbed in thought. Then she said, "Yes that's it, Melinda wasn't rebelling against rules; she was rebelling against no rules. Come to think of it, I've felt like that myself once or twice. It was about a year ago that I started smoking. My father just about flipped when he saw it for the first time. He lectured me up and down for a while, but then he seemed to become used to it. Every once in a while though, he let me know that he still didn't approve. I used to cry and carry on some when he talked to me. Last week he said to me, 'Would you rather I gave up and told you it was all right for you to go ahead and smoke?' I thought about that for a long while. All of a sudden it came to me very clearly that I didn't want him to do that at all. I never really wanted him to do that. I want him to stand up for what he believes. I want to be independent, sure. But I also want to make my own decisions stick because they are my decisions and they are right and not because somebody else gave in to me."

Perhaps one of the most insidious of all the confusions facing today's parents in their efforts to give more effective sexual guidance is the worrisome allegation that premarital sexual intercourse has become so general that there is no longer any hope for any real premarital sexual restraint on the part of young people. The implication is that no fair-minded parent should expect his child to buck the trend and stand up against the alleged majority in defiance of the supposedly steady march toward complete sexual freedom. Many parents, fearing the worst, seem to feel that about all they can do now is to help their children protect themselves from unwanted pregnancy by giving them contraceptive advice. Yet, as we have seen, no one knows for sure how far complete sexual permissiveness has gone in the mainstream of our society. It is quite possible that some of these parents are themselves enlarging the danger they are seeking to protect their children against.

Much of the perplexity of parents (and of the professionals and the public as well) has come as the result of the downgrading of premarital continence from the status of a first-class cultural value, which it had when the parents were young. It is alarming to some parents that some marriage-relations books include discussions of the "positive values of premarital intercourse." This, to them, is a measure of how far the downgrading of premarital sexual chastity has gone. By contrast, it is still almost unthinkable that any American book would discuss the positive values of blasphemy, burning the flag, or eating human flesh.

No widely acceptable modern standard of sexual behavior has been offered to replace premarital continence. "Permissiveness with affection," identified by Ira Reiss as a contemporary "standard," actually has very little that is standard about it.[20] There is no standard for the degree of permissiveness to be offered and no standard for the degree of affection to be required. The distinction between permissiveness with affection and outright sexual exploitation, moreover, is dependent upon a knowledge and perception of adult motivation and emotional reaction that is almost unteachable to inexperienced young people.

Most suggestions from professional counselors and educators, and even from popular writers, both moralist and antimoralist, have done little to help parents with their practical problems in sex education, regardless of the theoretical merits of those suggestions. Robert Harper has been insistent that parents, in dealing with children, "stop teaching them that premarital sexual intercourse is bad" and instead "teach them how to exercise their own critical faculties about deciding under what sorts of circumstances and with what sorts of partners it is likely to be functionally desirable for all parties concerned."[21] But even the parent who is emotionally able to adjust to the unconventionality of these directions and who is able to accept their implications for both child and society soon finds that the proponents have few practical suggestions to offer on how such teaching may be effectively accomplished with normal, sexually curious (but emotionally immature) children. Albert Ellis concedes that parents who try to carry out such directions

> not only have to explain their view to their own children (which is difficult to do when the children are quite young), but they also have to explain that other people think differently, and that there might be difficulties in presenting their view to these others. Raising children in a nonconformist manner, therefore, is much harder than raising them to conform to all the sexual prejudices of their community.[22]

Most parents are aware in a vague sort of way that almost all young people participate in some sexual activity from minor petting to premarital intercourse. But the idea of *their* children engaged in such activity is, as E. E.

---

[20] Ira L. Reiss, *Premarital Sexual Standards in America*, New York, Free Press, 1960, pp. 126–145.

[21] Robert Harper, "Marriage and Counseling Mores: A Critique," *Marriage and Family Living*, **21** (February, 1959), 17.

[22] Albert Ellis, *The American Sexual Tragedy*, New York, Twayne, 1954, p. 248.

LeMasters has pointed out, so traumatic and anxiety-producing to most of them that they emotionally "block."[23] Instead of giving much thought to better patterns of sex training, parents tend in their own anxiety either to shout and preach or to remain anxiously oversilent. Rarely does a parent stop to ask himself *why* he is so concerned, or what kind of sexual experience he ultimately wants for his children.

It seems reasonable to speculate that if they were to reflect on it logically, most middle-class parents would probably come to the conclusion that what they really hope for regarding their children's sexual experience is, first, to protect the children from exploitation and/or pregnancy until they are old enough to recognize the implications of their behavior. Second, most parents want to protect the family reputation and their own self-images as good parents by ensuring that their children do not get into sexual trouble. Third, parents want to ensure a successful marriage for their children. In the case of a female child, this may mean to the parent that she avoid getting a bad reputation. In the case of a boy, this may mean that he avoid getting entrapped by pregnancy and an early marriage. Fourth (and parents would less often add this), parents want to ensure that their children make positive creative use of their sexual capacities. Many parents would probably define the latter as having both sexual enjoyment *and* children, but only after marriage.

There are, of course, some parents who don't care what kind of sexual experiences their children have. There are some who deliberately promote their children into sex, and there are still others who, whether they recognize it or not, have unconscious wishes for their children not to marry, or neurotic wishes for their children to be sexually promiscuous so that they can vicariously enjoy their own repressed fantasies. But these would be exceptional parents—most have the more normal wishes stated above.

How can parents work through their own confusion in a socially turbulent and morally confused society to provide the environment and conditioning that will produce the desired sexual behavior in their children without completely alienating those children? Some possible answers to this question will be examined after we have taken a look at the problems of personal confusion about premarital sex.

[23] E. E. LeMasters, *Modern Courtship and Marriage*, New York, Macmillan, 1957, p. 205.

13

PREMARITAL SEX:
PERSONAL CONFUSION

One day, a young woman who was about to become an unwed mother sat in the marriage counselor's office and wept softly. She had just been told by the baby's father that he didn't want to marry her. "Before we started having intercourse," Marie said, "Roger said to me, 'You wouldn't want me to marry you for sex, would you? And if we don't have sex, how will you ever know I didn't marry you for sex?'" Then Marie added, "I was so confused, I didn't know what to do."

Roger's use of the psychologically sound implication that sex *in itself* doesn't constitute a complete basis for a marriage relationship illustrates the extent to which the sex–marriage association has been downgraded in our society. It is doubtful that anybody marries just for any one thing. However, had Roger said to Marie something like "You don't want me to marry you because you have great social poise, do you?" she might have had the courage to respond, "Yes I do, I would be good for you." But our society has gotten around to the point where Roger could make it appear that to be married for sex is ridiculous, if not almost immoral.

As late as fifty years ago, a college woman would not have faced Marie's dilemma. In the first place, most people believed that marriage had been created expressly for sex (and the protection of the children that sexual relations produced). Moreover, the double standard of the past clearly recognized "good" woman and "bad" women, and few educated men would have ventured to be so direct in attempting to seduce a woman of their own social level. Equally as important, the young woman would have been so deeply conditioned to the moral values of her society that she would have brushed him off with a frosty stare.

Today, things are different in some respects. "Good" men will make propositions, and "good" women have to make decisions. In almost all other cultures where there is a stated prohibition against premarital intercourse, there is an external pressure system, such as chaperones or duennas, to help the young woman's own conscience. But in modern America girls may be *told* by their parents that premarital intercourse is a moral violation and then those very same parents dress them up in their provocative best and send them off alone with a young man on dates that often end up in sexual experimentation. Usually only one shaky conscience—hers—stands between the cultural ideal and the fulfillment of two biologic urges.

To make the situation more difficult, there are, of course, the external pressures of the commercial sex establishment, including those movies, books, and magazines whose objective often appears to be to persuade the young woman that the very least she must have if she is to hold up her head as a real woman is a man who manifests an aggressive sexual desire for her. From there on, the progression is predictably simple: A woman wants a man, the man wants sexual experience, and frequently he wants it right now.

If the new morality really *had* brought about a complete metamorphosis in America's sexual attitudes and in the consequences of premarital sexual experimentation, the young woman might have no problem. But there is an increasingly widespread suspicion that the old French proverb, "The more things change, the more they remain the same," is particularly applicable to premarital sex in today's society. Even now, if a young woman too readily acquiesces, she may destroy the relationship she sought to enlarge. If a young couple have sexual intercourse early in their acquaintance, ordinarily they do so for very different reasons. Lester Kirkendall has suggested that young men who seek sexual intercourse soon after meeting a young woman do so primarily for physical pleasure and to demonstrate their manliness.[1] The young woman, on the other hand, often accepts premarital sexual intercourse primarily to please the man and to give herself the security of feeling she has a definite hold on him.

Mary Calderone has put it another way: "The girl plays at sex for which she is not ready because fundamentally what she wants is love; and the boy plays at love, for which he is not ready, because what he wants is sex."[2]

With such differing motivations, any premarital sexual experience that occurs early in a relationship tends to deteriorate rather than to advance the partners' feelings for each other. Embarrassment, guilt, and contempt are more likely consequences than are real tenderness or affection, often because the partners are unable to communicate meaningfully to each other what the sexual experience meant to them. Kirkendall cites the case of a young man who was asked in a research study whether or not the girl with whom he had had premarital intercourse had reached a climax. The young man appeared surprised at the question. "Why, I couldn't ask her anything like that," he said. "We weren't *that* close friends!"

Regardless of how new or how old the relationship may be, sexual intercourse is very often a chancy thing for the young woman involved. It isn't only the possibility of pregnancy that must concern her. It is also the very real danger that she may be triggering an unconscious emotional reaction in her male partner that could lead him ultimately to reject her. Some men who insist that they must have sex or they won't continue the relationship sometimes subconsciously wish that their female partners hadn't given in to them. Consequently, the

---

[1] Lester A. Kirkendall, "Premarital Sex Relations: The Problem and Its Implications," in Ruth S. Cavan, ed., *Marriage and Family in the Modern World,* New York, Thomas Y. Crowell, 1960, p. 227.
[2] Mary S. Calderone, "How Young Men Influence the Girls Who Love Them," *Redbook,* **125** (July, 1965), 45.

Table 13–1

Rate of Illegitimate Births in the United States for 1938 and 1965

(Per 1000 unmarried females by age of mother)

	Under 15	15–19	20–24	25–29	30–34	35–39	40 and Over
1938	0.3	7.5	9.2	6.8	4.8	3.4	1.1
1965	0.7	16.7	38.8	50.4	37.1	17.0	4.4
Percentage increase from 1938 to 1965	133	123	322	641	673	400	300

Source: Adapted from Joseph Schacter and Mary McCarthy, *Illegitimate Births: United States, 1938–57, Vital Statistics, Special Reports, Selected Studies,* **47** (no. 8), Washington, D.C., U.S. Government Printing Office, 1960; and U.S. Department of Health, Education and Welfare, *Vital Statistics of the United States, 1965,* vol. 1, Tables 1–26 and 1–27, Washington, D.C., 1967. From Vincent, Clark E., ed., *Human Sexuality in Medical Education and Practice,* 1968, p. 473. Courtesy of Charles C Thomas, Publisher, Springfield, Illinois.

girl who enters a premarital sexual relationship in order to avoid losing a partner often finds she loses him anyway. And if she does this with more than one or two men, she may find herself thought of as promiscuous. Although such a reputation may increase the number of times the telephone rings, even in present-day society it will probably make her a less-acceptable marriage prospect to the more-desirable males. Moreover, it usually considerably diminishes her self-respect.

There is another important way in which "the more things change, the more they remain the same" is demonstrated. Despite the accessibility of contraceptives, the illegitimacy rate is reaching a new high. New morality or not, pregnancy still occurs as a result of intercourse. The number of illegitimate children born annually in the United States has more than tripled since 1938, with the largest increases involving women over twenty years old. See Table 13–1. The rate of *reported* illegitimacy is generally higher for the nonwhite population, but between 1960 and 1966, the illegitimacy rate among nonwhite women declined slightly, whereas the rate among white women rose sharply.[3]

With all the confusion about premarital sex in today's society, alternative courses often present problems, too. What happens, for example, if a young woman does *not* acquiesce? A good deal depends upon her bargaining position in terms of her attractiveness, but often a young woman is surprised to find that, instead of being rewarded by her peer group for her virtue, she is regarded with suspicion as being a prude or a spoilsport, perhaps an unwelcome reminder of guilt to those girls who have already acquiesced. Thus, it sometimes appears to the less-permissive girl that those girls who *do* have sexual experience are rewarded not only biologically but socially as well. As Reiss has pointed out, in this period of confusion and transition almost any standard will lead to some personal conflict.[4]

MEN ARE CONFUSED, TOO

It isn't only the young women who are confused. Although most self-confident, self-sufficient middle-class males probably have less ambivalence about their

[3] *Vital Statistics of the United States,* 1966, Washington, D.C., U.S. Department of Health, Education and Welfare, 1968. Tables 1–26 and 1–27.

[4] Ira L. Reiss, "The Treatment of Premarital Coitus in Marriage and Family Texts," *Social Problems,* **36** (April, 1957), 335.

sexual behavior today than a generation ago, there are some young men who have even more problems. Living in a world that attaches status and prestige to evidence of sexual performance is not easy for less sexually aggressive males.

Rollo May pointed out in 1966 that this is the age of the sexual athlete.[5] "Masculine" men are supposed to have an innate ability to make females respond to them, and they are supposed to know so much about the mechanics of sex that they are more capable than other men in performing and delighting their partners. As a result, some men are confronted with a new kind of sex fear, the fear of faulty performance. They may also have a new kind of guilt. Relieved of their guilt over their sexual fantasies, masturbation, or the fact that they stole a young woman's virginity, some young men now feel guilty for not having sexual success.

Graham Blaine, Jr., Chief of Psychiatry at the Harvard University Health Service, cites the case of a male student who lived in a dorm that permitted women to visit without restrictions.

CASE 21

The story he told was pathetic. Although more dramatic and extreme than most, it was typical in character of many that are seen in college health clinics each year. He lived in a two-bedroom suite with a pair of classmates. Two afternoons a week one roommate had exclusive use of the rooms, and on the other three afternoons the second roommate took over by himself to make love with his girl of the moment. These young men were quite sure that they were entirely justified in asserting their rights to use the room for these sexual forays. Although there would have been some encroachment on their activities by further sharing, they also expressed both contempt and surprise about the fact that the third inhabitant of the rooms did not engage in similar pleasures. One day they taunted him until he agreed to be "fixed up," and a tryst was arranged by them for him with a girl who had been primed ahead of time to exert her seductive charms to the fullest and lure him into a sexual experience. As might be expected the student found himself impotent in this situation for which he was neither emotionally nor sexually ready. He brooded about his failure and became increasingly convinced that he was hopelessly perverted. His roommates eventually became concerned enough about his state of mind to take him to a psychiatrist. Treatment was successful in restoring this student to emotional health, but the problem would never have arisen at all had the pressure from the environment not forced him into a situation for which he was unprepared.[6]

The young man in case 21 is not as isolated as many people have been led to believe. Some young women who insist that all the men *they* date want sex all the time fail to recognize that there are millions of other young men who don't expect premarital sex and some who wouldn't have it if it were offered. There are widely differing attitudes among men about premarital sex, just as there are widely differing behaviors. The Roper Research Associates in their 1969 nationwide study found that 25 percent of 1000 male college seniors, 29 percent of 500 freshmen, and 38 percent of a special sample of 673 Class-of-1964 alumni believed that sex should be reserved solely for after marriage. Only 8 percent of the seniors, 7 percent of the freshmen, and 6 percent of alumni believed that sexual intercourse was appropriate with any woman who seemed

[5] Rollo May, "Antidotes for the New Puritanism," *Saturday Review*, **49** (March 26, 1966), 19–21.
[6] Graham B. Blaine, Jr., *Youth and the Hazards of Affluence*, New York, Harper & Row, 1966, p. 54.

Table 13-2
Attitudes of Male College Seniors, Freshman and Alumni Toward Premarital Sex

	Seniors %	Freshmen %	Alumni (Class of 1964) %
Sex should be reserved solely for your wife—after marriage	25	29	38
Sex is all right before marriage but only with someone you contemplate marrying	23	27	18
Sex should be confined to those *few* women you have very strong feelings for	23	19	17
Sex is appropriate with any woman you *like* who feels similarly inclined	20	18	20
Sex is all right with any woman who seems *attractive at the moment* and is willing	8	7	6
No answer	1	1	1

Source: Roper Research Associates, *A Study of the Beliefs and Attitudes of Male College Seniors, Freshmen and Alumni,* New York, Standard Oil Company (New Jersey), 1969, p. 23.

attractive and agreeable at the moment.[7] For the tabulation of this part of the Roper study, see Table 13-2.

THE NEW DIFFICULTIES

Far from solving young peoples' premarital sexual problems, the new permissiveness has, in many respects, complicated matters. Today, whichever choice he makes, a young person must do more than rationalize the conflicts born of his conditioned background. He must also buck the scorn of some of his peers and effectively counter—if only to himself—some of the persuasive arguments of the avant garde crowd. It may well be that the new morality, born of rebellion and supposedly dedicated to personal freedom, requires as much conformity as the old morality ever did. Conforming to nonconformity can be a vicious straightjacket, too.

Clearly there is a differential ability on the part of some young people to work through their confusion about premarital sex. Age has something to do with it: The younger and more inexperienced usually display greater insecurity and anxiety than those who have lived with the problem for a while. But in research and counseling, I discovered single adults who had built up a great anxiety over sexual behavior as they grew older. For some, increased awareness brought increased concern. "I was too young and too dumb to be worried about sex when I was a girl," said one troubled young woman. For others, long periods of repression and reaction-formation prudishness finally flowered into full-blown neuroses about sex. Some of these women behaved like the stereotype of the old maid who looked every night for the man under the bed.

[7] Roper Research Associates, *A Study of the Beliefs and Attitudes of Male College Seniors, Freshmen and Alumni,* New York, Standard Oil Company (New Jersey), 1969, p. 23.

Others were sure that every man who happened to glance at them on the street was intent upon raping them.

Even more pathetic, however, are people of both sexes who use sex to act out their confusions and conflicts. On almost every university campus there are students who seem literally driven to wander from sex relationship to sex relationship, never satisfied and never finding surcease for whatever compulsion is driving them. Many such promiscuous people don't even like sex. They merely use it to try to fulfill some need. Consider the following case.

CASE 22

"I think I know why I do it," Cecilia told the counselor. "I had a very pretty younger sister, and I always thought she got more of my father's love. I wanted him to love me very much. I think now he probably did love me in his own way, but I was so busy competing with my sister that I couldn't see it. Anyway, he was a strong, silent type of man who never did show much affection. He was a brilliant man, but he manipulated other people by any and every means he could. He made a lot of money, but that just made him busier, and it seemed to me that he had even less time for me.

"Now that I'm grown up, I just seem to be compelled to go from one man to another. They are all eager enough to go to bed with me. Before we have intercourse, I actually play that I love them very much and I want them to love me. I love to play act, in fantasy and for real. But usually after the intercourse is over, I have nothing but contempt for them. Sometimes I let them hang around for a while. The older married ones are pretty eager to have a young woman to sleep with, and they'll do almost anything for me. Sure, I exploit them; I make them buy me gifts. Somehow that seems to be a little bit satisfying—but the sex almost never is.

"I've had a lot of fellows my own age, and I think one or two of them really did love me. But usually they've let me push them around, and after a while I lost all feeling for them.

"I don't want to go on like this. I really would like to find someone I can love and who loves me, but somehow I just can't."

Promiscuous women are often labeled as nymphomaniacs. There are many people, including some professional psychotherapists, who believe that these women have a genetic or physiologic reason for their overactive sex appetites. There are others who believe that nymphomania is always the result of some deep emotional sickness. But Dr. Beverly Mead, Psychiatrist at Creighton University School of Medicine, notes that most of the so-called nymphomaniacs he has seen have been girls who either were physically unattractive, or who felt they were unattractive. They thought they were unable to compete with other girls in socially acceptable ways and usually felt very inadequate and unnoticed. As Dr. Mead puts it, "Everybody has to be somebody. Many of these girls feel it is better to be a bad somebody than a good nobody."[8]

It comes as a shock to many beginning social workers to find out that some, if not most, of the illegitimately pregnant girls whom they see had a desire, either conscious or unconscious, to get pregnant out of wedlock. Sometimes their aim was to blackmail their boyfriends, sometimes to feel womanly or to show how grown up they were or to punish their parents. But sometimes it was to punish themselves.

[8] Beverly Mead, M.D., address to the New York Academy of General Practice, New York, N.Y., September 17, 1967.

Not all unmarried women who get pregnant out of wedlock are so disturbed, and not all those who have premarital intercourse are emotionally unstable. Yet, counselors who have the opportunity to talk with college students are impressed by the fact that fewer mature, well-adjusted, popular students seem to need the multiple emotional involvements that promiscuity implies. Dana Farnsworth of the Student Health Service at Harvard has said that, "The experiences in our college psychiatric and counseling services lead us to believe that those who ignore the conventional standards are no more happy or effective than those who observe them. In fact, I believe that they have more depression, anxiety, agitation and other inhibiting emotional conflict than those who manage to adhere to their ideals."[9]

Proponents of sexual freedom often argue that, while it may be good to have restrictive "standards" for young children and for those who are emotionally unstable, no such prohibition should apply to normal young adults who have a strong affection for one another. They contend first of all that sexual intercourse between two people who are genuinely tender and understanding toward one another may enhance their love. Moreover, they argue that premarital experience often makes for better sex after marriage.

Let's ignore the problems implicit in deciding who is old enough and who is normal enough and deal with the major premises. It is undoubtedly true that sexual intercourse does strengthen the love between two people who have openly pledged themselves to each other in marriage. When there is tenderness and understanding in a genuinely secure and affectionate atmosphere, sexual intercourse can be a powerful love enhancer. The trouble is that most premarital and extramarital affairs fail to provide the oppor-

[9] Dana L. Farnsworth, "Sexual Morality and the Dilemma of the Colleges," *American Journal of Orthopsychiatry*, **35** (July, 1965), 680.

tunity or the setting for this kind of genuine and total expression. Many such affairs are, by necessity, carried on in sordid or unaesthetic surroundings. Some such affairs generate anxiety (over being discovered, or getting pregnant, or being inadequate) to the extent that sexual sensation is drowned in the adrenalin reaction to the fear. Moreover, there are problems in the opposite direction. Sometimes premarital intercourse actually becomes antimarital intercourse. Consider the following case:

> ### CASE 24
> "He made me feel as though it was very right for us to have intercourse even though we weren't married," Anne told the counselor. "Our sexual relations were perfect—he knew just how to hold me, just what to say.
>
> "I think he really intended to marry me at first, but his divorce took so long. And then there were all those debts. By the time we could have been married, we seemed like old married folks in some ways already.
>
> "But we had missed some of the important part of really being married. We never had the common interest of having children, a prideful joy of openly possessing each other, or a social expectation that we would stay together, to tide us over the rough spots. So every time we got even a little upset, we threatened each other with leaving or we separated for a while. Now the intercourse doesn't seem to mean so much to him anymore. We are drifting apart.
>
> "He hasn't cast me off like an old shoe or anything melodramatic like that. I just see now that nothing can come of this—nothing. I'm not sure I want to marry him now even if he begged, because our patterns of reacting to each other are already set and wouldn't change. It wouldn't be a happy marriage now.
>
> "What shall I do? Continue this for the rest of my life? Or shall I start out looking for someone else? I'm twenty-eight now and everyone thinks I'm Carl's. It's a bad situation."

What about the second part of the sexual-freedom argument—that premarital sex actually improves sex after marriage? If one is talking about the relationship of premarital sex to total marriage adjustment, the research evidence, old and statistically weak though it may be, points to premarital intercourse as being *inversely* related to marital adjustment. Terman, Locke, and Burgess and Wallin all found, in 1938, 1951, and 1953, respectively, that those who entered marriage with *no* premarital coital experience tended to have a high marital adjustment and tended to be least likely to be divorced.[10] However, here again the research was of the actuarial type, and no one can prove that any one particular couple will have a happier marriage because the partners avoided premarital intercourse.

There is some research evidence to indicate that premarital sexual relations are not detrimental to *sexual* adjustment after marriage. In fact, Eugene Kanin and David Howard found that wives with previous experience in intercourse were more satisfied with their coital experiences during the first two weeks of marriage than wives with no experience.[11] In commenting on this phenomenon, Robert Blood points out that, "Even though experienced men

[10] Lewis M. Terman, *Psychological Factors in Marital Happiness*, New York, McGraw-Hill, 1938, pp. 319–335; Harvey J. Locke, *Predicting Adjustment In Marriage*, New York, Holt, Rinehart and Winston, 1951, pp. 132–139; Ernest W. Burgess and Paul Wallin, *Engagement and Marriage*, Philadelphia, Lippincott, 1953, p. 518.

[11] Eugene J. Kanin and David H. Howard, "Post Marital Consequences of Premarital Sex Adjustments," *American Sociological Review*, **23** (October, 1958), 556–562.

and women have a head start on the sexual aspects of marriage, they are generally worse off in other respects. Perhaps, indeed, the wife's sexual responsiveness should be classified as a physical consequence of intimacy, rather than an interpersonal one."[12]

Other evidence seems to indicate that women who have a higher sex interest and responsiveness to begin with are the ones who are most likely to have engaged in premarital intercourse. Their interest and responsiveness would have been predictive of good sexual adjustment after marriage, even if they hadn't had premarital sexual relations.[13] Thus, any argument that sexual experience before marriage will improve a particular person's later performance appears somewhat specious at best.

But even if premarital sex were to improve the sexual adjustment of two people in the first weeks after marriage, that alone might not justify the later emotional cost. Some examples of these later costs are frequently seen in marriage counseling. Although a man may have argued insistently and used every trick in the book to obtain premarital acquiescence, the very fact that he prevailed may lead to festering suspicions after marriage. A husband may say to himself, "Well, after all, she did it with me, how many others were there?" This sometimes leads to such verbalized recriminations as "You were a tramp to go to bed with me." In the case of a premarital pregnancy, both partners may blame the other, even many years after marriage, for the fact that they had to get married.

Those who believe that premarital sexual intercourse is justified find plenty of nourishment for their view in some popular magazines whose circulations run into the millions. Whatever may be said for premarital sex, however, it is difficult to see how, in the light of the present research evidence, it can be maintained that such experience can provide any real "test" for successful marriage. As we have seen, what studies there are tend to indicate that *more* people with a history of premarital sex are divorced. Further, it is almost impossible to imagine a set of conditions under which a premarital experience could be compared with sex after marriage. Certainly a sordid episode marred by fear of discovery cannot be compared to the secure, socially approved sharing of marital intercourse. Neither can the excitement of an illicit weekend at a plush resort really be a criterion for judging whether or not two people can maintain sexual interest on an undistinguished evening after five years of marriage. Knowing your partner's nonsexual personality is probably far more predicative of long-term sexual compatibility than one premarital sexual experience or a hundred. Consider the case of Donna and Mitchell:

CASE 25
It was early May when Donna first came in to see the counselor. "Mitchell agreed he would come with me today and talk with you," Donna said. "We are both going to graduate from the university here in Los Angeles next month. We have grown up together in the same neighborhood, and we come from just about the same background. He has often told me he loves me. I know we are sexually compatible because we have been having sexual relations regularly. We have talked about getting married many times. Actually, we've been engaged at least three times. Every time, just when we're ready to set the date, he has changed his mind. There's

[12] Robert O. Blood, Jr., *Marriage*, Glencoe, Free Press, 1962, p. 143.
[13] Robert L. Hamblin and Robert O. Blood, Jr., "Premarital Experience and the Wife's Sexual Adjustment," *Social Problems*, 4 (October, 1956), 122–130.

no reason why we shouldn't be married. He has a good job waiting for him next month, and there is every reason why we should. Besides, I'm afraid that I might get pregnant."

Mitchell was quite frank about his indecisiveness. "I just can't seem to make up my mind to do it," he said. "I think maybe it's because I need some competition in order to want her. I break off with her, then she starts going with some other guy and I begin to want her again. I'm the kind of fellow for whom decisions are difficult. I didn't make up my mind about my major until I was a senior. At one time I was sure I was going to be a dentist, because the hours are good and so is the money. Then I was going to be a doctor, but it just seemed like too much effort. So finally I ended up in Business Administration. I knew I could get a good job, so what the heck.

"I'm kind of like that with Donna, too," he went on. "I just can't seem to make up my mind. I don't see any reason to be in a hurry about it, though. We have a good sexual relationship, and we can do all the things we want to do now. So why not wait until we're both absolutely sure. Either one of us might find someone we like better. Donna isn't the most perfect girl in the world. As a matter of fact, she'll tell you herself she has a small bust and too much hair on her body.

"I suppose, though, I would marry her if she were absolutely sure about it herself. But every time I seriously suggest getting married, she says 'Are you sure that's what you really want to do?' Then I begin to wonder again myself."

A week later the counselor saw Donna again. She said, "Mitchell told me that he told you that I always ask him if he's really sure he wants to marry me. It's true, I do. I want a man who really wants me. Is that wrong?" The counselor said, "In other words, you want a really decisive man who knows what he wants?"

Donna thought for a long while. "Now I'm a little confused," she said. "I know I want Mitchell. But I also know that I need somebody who is very secure, because I'm not secure myself. I guess that's why I've told Mitchell so often that I have a small bust and too much body hair. What I wanted him to do was to reassure me that it wasn't so. But I don't think he ever really did.

"Anyway, all of this is a little academic now. Mitchell has decided we're going to be married in July. You know how he proposed this time? He said, 'We might as well get married. What the heck!' "

In late June, Donna returned to see the counselor. "Mitchell's got cold feet again," she said. "For a while after we set the date we were very happy. Everybody approved, including both sets of parents. Now he has begun to wonder if maybe he should have waited. He keeps reminding me that we broke up several times before, and he says there isn't much glitter left in our romance anyway. All this couldn't have come at a worse time. In the first place, we've told all our friends. But worse than that, I think I'm pregnant. I haven't told him yet, but I'm three weeks late with my period."

Late in December, just before Christmas, Mitchell came in to see the counselor. "Well," he said, "I went and did it. When Donna was in to see you in June, she thought she was pregnant. At least she told *me* she thought she was pregnant. Before we were married in July she found out she wasn't, but I went ahead and married her anyway. I guess I got a little scared too, but I really think it was because I saw how frightened she was. Anyway, that's water over the dam now. We were very happy for the first few months. I guess everybody's happy when they first marry. But now she's beginning to get on my nerves. She wants me to tell her I love her all the time, and I'm getting fed up. I'm beginning to think I was sort of foolish to get tied down this way. After all, I had everything I wanted before we were married. You would think at least she could stop talking about whether we love each other or not and help me right now. I've got a tough decision to make.

THE LIVE-TOGETHERS

In these days of the new morality, there might be some who would suggest that Donna and Mitchell should have tried living together without getting married. News stories and case reports of students who have done just that are common on every large university campus today. It could be, though, that both Donna's and Mitchell's personalities preclude this, for reasons other than old-style sexual inhibitions. Arno Karlen, in his report "The Unmarried Marrieds on Campus," found fewer such relationships than rumor had led him to believe he would find, and the partners in those he did find belonged to the dissident youth subculture. More important, perhaps, is that several of the psychiatrists Karlen interviewed believe that the men in these relationships are generally dependent and passive, whereas the women are generally emotive and controlling, the kind of "mothers" the young men grew up with and still need. Karlen suggests that these youth desperately need a sense of family but lack a basic trust in families. With one hand they push fearfully away from ties, while with the other hand they cling to mutually protective mateship. Karlen reported the case of Ed and Louise, which is excerpted as follows:

> I [Karlen] ask why, after five years together, and three of domesticity, they haven't married. They answer in a light tone at first.
> *Louise:* But why should we?
> *Ed:* Oh, I guess being married has advantages—income tax, not having to con some little old lady at the place we stay when we go skiing."
> *Louise:* If something came up like my having a child or our getting a joint grant, I guess we'd do it.[14]
> *Ed:* Yes, there'd be penalties for the kid.
> *Louise:* If it lasts four years more, it'll be a common-law marriage. That's pretty ironic.[15]
> *Ed:* The contract [marriage] would create a mess if you had to get out of it. Besides, I can't see going to some bureaucratic hack for it, let alone (with slow sarcasm) *a man of the cloth.*

[14] Louise may be indulging in wishful thinking. Three weeks after the Karlen article, *The New York Times* published a letter from a woman who had also been an unmarried married. She cited her own sad experience as evidence that men won't always marry the women they have lived with and impregnated. Sometimes they won't even pay for the women's abortions, she thought. Often men use pregnancy as an excuse to break off a relationship that threatens to become too permanent and too demanding. The letter writer also imparted that because living together outside of marriage seemed to be something important that was "above the Establishment rules," she had been willing to toss aside conventions and security. But it was not like she thought. She was shattered to find that men living outside of marriage are not strong and bravely unconventional, and she now believes that they are indecisive and afraid of responsibility. February 16, 1969, p. 19.

[15] Louise could *already* be married by the common law if she and Ed had wished to be and were living in one of the 14 states in which it is recognized. Common-law marriage is based on the *intent* of the partners. Staying together for a certain number of years may be used to show the intent to be man and wife. But so can certain other overt acts, such as signing in together at the ski resort as Mr. and Mrs. There are no written rules about number of years in the common law; each case is decided on its merits by legal precedents.

Karlen: Is it just that you don't go to the trouble of observing a convention? Actually, it's less trouble spending a few dollars and a few minutes for a quick civil ceremony than years conning little old ladies and losing on income tax.

Ed: Buffoons run our country. I don't want any participation in a country that elects a . . . a well . . . , you name them!

Louise: But it isn't political, our not being married. What marriage fulfills for people, our relationship fulfills for us. You know, someone did a test of American wives, and it turned out that they saw their husbands as breadwinners, fathers, companions and lovers, in that order. It ought to be reversed! And the women saw themselves as mothers, first, then as housewives, and so on.[16] Just keeping house and taking kids around the suburbs! I'd be terrible! When you marry you have to be ready not to go to a movie without first hiring a baby sitter. We want to go to California next year. How could we do it with kids?

Karlen: Maybe you could. If you're strong enough to live as you do, mightn't you be strong enough to be married without falling into the conventional patterns you hate? You seem to think that being a wife and mother has an irresistible negative force.

Louise: No! That isn't so! I want kids very much, but I'd be happy to work four hours a day. I'd be a better mother, a better person to be around. You have to meet people outside your family. I'm afraid of the boredom I saw when I lived for nine years in the suburbs. I've actually met women who talk about their damned appliances all the time!

Ed: Louise, you're too angry. You're upset. He must have hit something.

Louise (pausing to think): Yes. I guess so. I should think about that.

Karlen: Do you have an agreement about sleeping with other people?

Ed: I made clear when I started living with her that a time would come when I'd want to sleep with other chicks. I can't imagine just making it with the same girl for 40 years. It's the same for her. The only real infidelity is living with someone you don't love.[17]

There are some readers who will ask, "Why don't these people get married?" or "What is the probable future of their relationship?" For many, though, Ed's statement about the "only real infidelity" may be as confusing as Roger's remark, "You wouldn't want me to marry you just for sex," at the beginning of the chapter. Perhaps this is where we came in.

[16] Louise was probably referring to a study by Helena Lopata of 299 suburban and 323 urban housewives in the Chicago area. Lopata found that 67 percent of her women respondents evaluated the role of mother and homemaker as higher in order of importance than the role of wife. (Helena Lopata, "The Secondary Features of a Primary Relationship," *Human Organization,* **24** (Summer, 1965), 116–123.

[17] Arno Karlen, "The Unmarried Marrieds on Campus," *The New York Times Magazine* (January 26, 1969), 28. © 1969 by The New York Times Company. Reprinted by permission.

14

PREMARITAL SEX: WHERE TO FROM HERE?

What should be done about premarital sex standards in our changing society? The problem has become one of increasing national concern.

Behavioral scientists, who often have a great deal to lose by entering sensational public controversy, have been reluctant to openly advocate any change in the established mores, even though their data may have convinced them of the need for change. On the other hand, publishers of popular magazines, who have a great deal to gain by entering sensational public controversy, have attracted widespread attention for their seductively beguiling notions about the advantages of uninhibited sex. Many young people, hungry for definitive guidance, have been impressed by the seemingly unequivocal honesty of the philosophy that "sex is fun for everybody; the more the better." Here, it often appeared, was a realistic, biologically satisfying philosophy that somebody genuinely believed in. For that reason alone, it seemed to be more appealing than the sometimes confused and hypocritical philosophy of self-discipline advocated by their parents and older folks in general, who often fail to practice what they preach.

Actually, there have been some courageous social philosophers quietly at work for years trying to redefine sexual mores so that they would be more acceptable in modern times. Their work, however, has had nowhere near the widespread publicity of the popular-magazine writers. Moreover, because most real students of human behavior recognize that considerable self-discipline is necessary in an ordered society, even the most liberal of them do not advocate the rapid abandonment of all sexual restraints.

The serious proposals of these philosophers regarding premarital sexual behavior range from advocating "permissiveness with affection" to an "absolutely not" position that would do justice to a mid-Victorian ascetic. When a statement concerning premarital intercourse made by David Mace, a former Methodist minister and a world leader in marriage education, is placed alongside a statement on the same subject by Albert Ellis, a New York psychotherapist and author of popular and professional sex literature, the wide differences of opinion among the professionals are glaringly evident.

David Mace

Since premarital intercourse is against the conventional code, few can seek it without subterfuge. Young people with religious associations (the majority of American youth today) suffer reactions varying from mild uneasiness to agonizing guilt. They may be consumed with remorse at having broken their code, let down their parents, and earned public disapproval. This results in misery to the individual and tension in the relationship. Where one feels guilty and the other does not, the former is likely to feel exploited. These guilt feelings can easily break up a potentially promising partnership.[1]

Albert Ellis

Since premarital sex relations are no longer viewed as morally reprehensible or sinful by most educated and informed individuals, there need be no intrinsic guilt attached to them.

People who are anxious and guilty because of their premarital affairs are usually emotionally disturbed individuals who are also anxious and guilty about many of their non-sexual participations. On the other hand, many people today are becoming anxious and disturbed because they are *not* copulating before marriage.[2]

Most of the social philosophers who appear to condone some premarital sex do so only as a concomitant of good intentions. Lester Kirkendall, for many years a professor of family relations at Oregon State University, has proposed that one's decision about premarital intercourse be made on the basis of whether or not it would improve the relationship between the partner's rather than "on the goodness of specified behavior or acts in terms of mores, taboos, commands or abstract logic." Since much premarital sexual intercourse tends to be exploitive to one of the partners, and thus damaging to the relationship, Kirkendall believes that in the long run, there would actually be less premarital intercourse if we could condition young people to put the emphasis on whether it would improve their relationship.[3] Kirkendall, who has interviewed large numbers of very realistic young men in research studies, concedes that there would be many difficulties in reorienting young people to a "good-interpersonal-relationships standard." But, he points out, the failure of the traditional system, based on rigid dictates that are all but unenforceable, is a good reason for trying something different.

When I asked a group of 113 university students about Kirkendall's proposals, I found almost universal interest in and appreciation of the good intent involved. But some 90 percent felt that his "positive goal" of more satisfying interpersonal relationships would not now be strong enough to maintain sexual restraint among young people. Many of these students indicated that they would *like* to live in a world where better interpersonal relationships were the bases for premarital sexual decisions, but they didn't really believe it could be that way now.[4]

[1] David R. Mace, "The Case for Chastity and Virginity," in Albert Ellis and Albert Abarbanel, eds. *The Encyclopedia of Sexual Behavior*, New York, Hawthorn Books, 1961, p. 248.

[2] Albert Ellis, *Sex Without Guilt*, New York, Lyle Stuart, 1958, pp. 34–41.

[3] Lester A. Kirkendall, "Values and Premarital Intercourse—Implications for Parent Education," *Marriage and Family Living*, **22** (November, 1960), 317–322.

[4] Richard H. Klemer, "Student Attitudes Toward Guidance in Sexual Morality," *Marriage and Family Living*, **24** (August, 1962), 260–264.

Said one twenty-year-old student, "I think it would be ideal if this important decision could be made on the basis of individual reasoning and beliefs, but I don't think it can be done at present. . . . Young people tend to rationalize to obtain the answers that allow them to yield to temptation." Then he added, "People today are too concerned with 'what they can get out of it' and 'what the other fellows will think' to be able to see the need for more uprightness and honesty."

Another male student said, "Premarital sex will be rampant if we use Kirkendall's approach. He is unrealistic. . . . I believe that more permissiveness as to the moral choices of youth will lead to greatly increased rates of premarital intercourse. . . . The interpersonal relationships of Kirkendall would be workable only for a minute percentage of the American adolescent and youthful population. My authority is my own youth and the knowledge of the lack of concern for moral issues in the majority of college students, especially males. The minority who would accept and practice the theory are those young people who already have high moral standards usually by virtue of their upbringing and parents who said 'no!' and meant it."

SITUATION ETHICS

Another scholar who has given considerable thought to the problem of premarital sex is the Reverend Joseph Fletcher, professor at the Episcopal Theological School in Cambridge, Massachusetts. In answer to his own questions "Should we prohibit and condemn premarital sex?" and "Should we approve of it?" he says, "To the first one I would promptly reply in the negative. To the second, I propose an equivocal answer, 'yes and no—depending on each particular situation.'" He qualifies his approval of premarital sex with the admonition that "charity is more important than chastity, but there is no such thing as free love. There must be some care and commitment in premarital sex acts or they are immoral."[5]

Fletcher has a second qualification. The decision concerning premarital sex, says Fletcher, must hang on the particular case. This is his "situation ethics" view, which, he says, implies the question

> How, here and now, can I act with the most concern for the happiness and welfare of those involved—myself and others? Legalistic moralism, with its absolutes and universals, always thou-shalt-nots, cuts out the middle ground between a virgin and a sexual profligate. This is an absurd failure to see that morality has to be acted out on a continuum of relativity, like life itself, from situation to situation.[6]

Situation ethics, however, sometimes appear incongruous with the realities of much modern premarital sex. Rarely, if ever, is a decision made in the back seat of a parked automobile on the basis of "how, here and now, can I act with the most concern for the happiness and welfare of those involved, myself and others?" Far more often, the decision is an emotional one, rather than a moral or even a rational one. Also, the "situation," which Fletcher contends is controlling, may not have a common definition between the partners. (He: "I will be doing her a favor to introduce her to intercourse"; She: "He

---

[5] Joseph Fletcher, "Ethics and Unmarried Sex: Morals Re-examined," in Daniel O. Price, ed., *The 99th Hour*, Chapel Hill, N.C., Univ. of North Carolina Press, 1967, p. 110.
[6] *Ibid.*, pp. 110–111.

wouldn't want to take my virginity unless he loved me.") Furthermore, neither partner may be able to make a realistic evaluation of the "situation" ("Neither one of us thought about getting pregnant at that minute; it just couldn't happen to us!").

Vance Packard, a popular writer on problems of social concern, postulated his own version of situation ethics for premarrieds in *The Sexual Wilderness*. Society should approve of premarital sexual intercourse, he said, only when three elements are present:

1. That a deep friendship based upon substantial acquaintance exists between the man and the girl.
2. That both are out of high school; and if college is planned, that they have completed the first year of college if they are still teenagers.
3. That they hope to marry, and that their best friends know of the hope.[7]

Even if these conditions are present, Packard added quickly, "such a code will be tolerable in the long run only if effective techniques of conception control are available to unmarried couples who have achieved this readiness to experiment."

Critics almost immediately pointed out that Packard's postulates raised almost as many questions as they answered. How "substantial" must the "acquaintance" be? By "acquaintance" does he imply "love"? What about sexual relations between a twenty-year-old high-school drop-out and a nineteen-year-old college freshman? Does academic achievement really make sexual behavior "right" or "wrong"? What if their best friends don't know of their hope to marry? What if the effective techniques of conception control are available but the couple doesn't choose to use them (as many don't)? Few reviewers seemed to believe that Packard had done much to clear up the monumental premarital sex confusion, although some gave him credit for trying.

THE MORE
TRADITIONAL VIEW

In this day and age, it isn't very popular to be a moralist. Relatively few definitive statements against premarital intercourse are now being made, even by churchmen. But in the early 1960s, Thomas Poffenberger, then a professor at the University of California at Davis, took a strong stand for chastity:

> The present preoccupation with sex in the culture needs to be replaced by other values. First, the survival of our highly technical society is dependent on inculcating in young people a drive for educational and intellectual achievement as well as occupational and professional productivity. Second, the stability of our democratic society depends on the effective functioning of the family unit. To facilitate these objectives, it seems necessary for the society to take the position that young people must hold chastity as a value at least until they have reached relative economic social and emotional maturity.[8]

In a book addressed to teenagers entitled *Why Wait Till Marriage?* Evelyn Duvall advocated sexual restraint, and often without the appearance of preaching. For example, she said,

[7] Vance Packard, *The Sexual Wilderness*, New York, McKay, 1968, p. 445.
[8] Thomas Poffenberger, "Individual Choices in Adolescent Premarital Sexual Behavior," *Marriage and Family Living*, **22** (November, 1960), 330.

What you do with your beloved is up to you. You may express your feelings in whatever ways make sense to you. Just do not kid yourself or each other, that you cannot really enjoy each other except through sexual intercourse. If that is the case, then what you have may be sexual attraction rather than real love for one another. What you do as sweethearts reflects the kinds of persons you are, your relationship with one another, and the life you see ahead for yourselves.[9]

In recent years, the notion that the inhibition of sexual impulses is a negative factor in mental health has been so emphasized that the positive value of sexual self-restraint in building self-confidence and self-respect have all but been ignored. This positive aspect was described by a twenty-two-year-old woman who was a respondent in a study of students' attitudes toward guidance. She said,

> Parents must teach their children in such a way that they will not want to go counter to what they believe to be right and just and good. Done this way, taboos become wilfull self-restraints. They are not set out as things that a child must not do or cannot do but rather they are things that under the prevailing circumstances the child himself wishes not to become part of him. This has worked for me; I would not want it otherwise.[10]

David Mace has put the same idea just a little differently:

> What we need is a new idea of chastity, as a discipline gladly accepted so that human love can be kept warm and tender and unsullied. The idea of chastity means refusing to use sex at sub-human levels and for selfish and anti-social ends. It is not the renunciation of sexual love as something evil. Rather it is the recognition that sexual love is something too good to be spoiled by misuse.[11]

Obviously, ideas such as these are not popular among those who advocate uninhibited sex. My suggestion in a professional journal that young people can be persuaded that premarital self-restraint need not be a negative inhibition but might be a positive value from which they could gain self-esteem drew heated responses from some magazine writers. Said James L. Collier in an article sandwiched among the foldout nudes in a magazine called *Cavalier:*

> What Klemer is describing is an approximate definition of the good old-fashioned Pavlovian brainwash. The use of words like "positive" and "negative" is the giveaway. Sociologists and psychologists like to think that they are not philosophers, but men of science. Value judgments, of course, have no place in science, so instead of saying behavior is good or bad, they call it either positive or negative, as if people were electrical systems which could be turned off and on at will. Klemer knows that simply telling the girls that sharing the goodies is evil is a "negative inhibition," and he knows that negative inhibitions give people rashes, migraine, and spastic colon. His trick, then, is to teach the girls to take pride in their ability to ward off the keenings of desire, so that when they crawl out of the stadium shrubbery with their maidenheads intact they can paste another gold star on their mirrors. Klemer's approach turns the relationship between the sexes into a state of perpetual warfare. What is likely to be more annoying is the encouragement it gives to the female tease. After all, if a girl can score points every time she parries a thrust, she is going to want

[9] Evelyn Duvall, *Why Wait Until Marriage?* New York, Association Press, 1965, p. 49.
[10] Klemer, *op. cit.*, p. 264.
[11] David R. Mace, "Is Chastity Outmoded?" *Woman's Home Companion*, **76** (September, 1949), 37–38.

a constant stream of men taking a stab at it. This is not my idea of decent "interpersonal relationships."[12]

One of the most idealistic arguments *for* premarital sexual restraint is made by Henry Bowman, a professor at the University of Texas, in his book *Marriage for Moderns:*

> Marriage is inextricably bound up as an integral part of the idealism of thoughtful people who want life to be meaningful. Such idealism is true realism because it rests upon a continual reaching out for the values that endure rather than for transient satisfaction. Hence, thoughtful persons of both sexes may make successful marriage one of their major goals in life. When they fail to achieve it, the whole structure of their lives may be profoundly shaken.
>
> In order to achieve the sort of marriage we are discussing, an individual must first decide that he wants it and then determine, with perseverance and courage, to get it. If the times are contributing factors that are inimical to such marriage, he must rise above the times. He cannot afford merely to stumble blindly along without ever raising questions about premarital behavior, without ever reexamining it to see whether it is contributing to the establishment of the kind of marriage he wants. He cannot afford to assume, as some do, that what is, is good, that all one needs to do is to conform to the pattern of the group or "get by" with the minimum required or the most tolerated, as the case may be.
>
> This new type of marriage rests upon a system of values involving love, trust, monogamy, family unity, the oneness of which husband and wife are parts, respect for human personality, the sharing, mutuality, and sexual exclusiveness mentioned above. Such a value system tends to be integrated. When one element is disturbed, the whole system is affected, like earthquake shock waves that radiate from a center of shift and may destroy buildings miles away from the place at which the quake originated, or like removing a stone from an arch. Therefore, disturbing one of the elements becomes of major importance—not only in and of itself but as part of the value system.
>
> If sexual exclusiveness is one of the expectations in this value system, it is clear that the kind of marriage we are discussing cannot be achieved if sexual intercourse is considered a casual experience of the moment, if it is disconnected from long-time goals and perspective. Sexual exclusiveness is not something that begins after the wedding. It is something that reflects an individual's point of view regarding the value system of marriage and the meaning of life. If marriage as we are discussing it involves the most profound sharing of which human beings are capable, that sharing is rendered incomplete to the degree that an individual has "shared" himself with another before the wedding.[13]

To many of the more cynical partisans of the new permissiveness and to many of those who write for the magazines and make the movies exploiting sex, Bowman's idealism might seem singularly out of step. But there is a real question, as we shall presently see, about whether Bowman is behind the times *or actually ahead of them.*

Bowman's statement reflects the kind of romantic idealism that motivated and directed generations of Americans in the past. In addition to providing a goal, it codified behavior so that people knew what was right and what was wrong and what was "good" and what was "bad." Those who followed Bowman's course avoided not only the difficulties of premarital pregnancy but also

---

[12] James L. Collier, "The New Puritans of the Sexual Establishment," *Cavalier,* **17** (January, 1967), 37.
[13] Henry A. Bowman, *Marriage for Moderns,* 5th ed., New York, McGraw-Hill, 1965, pp. 138–139.

the insecurities of confusion. By adhering to this idealistic code, they also made possible the social organization that enabled others to predict their behavior and so build a stable society.

The research evidence indicates that, in general, sexual exclusivity is still the ideal of most college-educated women. In this group, a large majority of the women who do have premarital intercourse have it only with the men to whom they are engaged.[14] Then, if everything goes as planned, they can rationalize that they didn't really spoil the exclusiveness.

Many college-educated women find great satisfaction in their belief in this kind of exclusiveness. If a young woman finds a supportive partner (and what better test is there of future congeniality and success?), their agreement to limit sexual activity may actually increase the tenderness between the two of them. And as every true lover knows, tenderness can sometimes be more passionate than passion itself.

There is an explanation for this increased tenderness that sounds plausible even to nonromantic social analysts. Romantic love was thought by Sigmund Freud to be "aim-inhibited sex."[15] Stopping short of sexual intercourse was seen to provide a heightened emotional feeling. Although no one has proved or disproved this, it is generally accepted as so by most behavioral scientists, as well as by lovers.

In any event, by the time most young people are old enough to read and understand Bowman's textbook, they are usually already committed to the patterns of behavior that permit or prohibit various kinds of premarital sexual experimentation. This is not to say that individual circumstances may not alter cases. During wartime, older women assigned to military outposts where there were large numbers of lonely men probably had many more sexual experiences than they might have had if they had remained in their civilian jobs. And some younger girls, thrown into a situation in which they think there will be no more dates for them if they don't consent to intercourse, acquiesce out of this mistaken fear. Yet these same girls might never have had to choose under other circumstances.

In our confused society with its many confused parents and confusing social circumstances, most young people muddle through as best they can. They make those compromises that seem to maximize their present security and that produce as little conflict as possible between their short-term satisfactions and the long-term values that have been conditioned into them. Few minds are changed by any amount of professional rhetoric.

In our present changing society, almost any choice or any compromise can lead to periods of self-doubt; consequently, the marriage counselor sometimes interviews people who bitterly regret a sexual decision once made. An occasional older woman may regret that her earlier prudish attitudes prevented her from having premarital intercourse: She now thinks that she would not have married her husband if she had not been so blinded by sexual attraction. Another woman may be convinced that if she had acquiesced to her boyfriend when she was younger, he might have married her and become a better husband than the man she ultimately did marry. In retrospect, it is easy for her to forget that the boyfriend to whom she refused sexual intercourse might *not*

---

[14] Winston Ehrmann, *Premarital Dating Behavior*, New York, Holt, Rinehart and Winston, 1959, p. 274.
[15] Sigmund Freud, *Collected Papers*, vol. V, London, Hogarth, 1950, p. 134.

Table 14–1
**Feeling of Having Gone Too Far in Sexual Intimacy, by Stage
in Courtship, for College Men and Women**

Level of Intimacy	Stage in Courtship	Men (%)	Women (%)
Petting	Casual dating	25	54
	Going steady	32	37
	Engagement	31	26
Intercourse	Casual dating	44	65
	Going steady	44	61
	Engagement	41	41

Source: Adapted from Robert Bell and Leonard Blumberg, "Courtship Stages and Intimacy Attitudes," *Family Life Coordinator,* **8** (March, 1960), p. 62.
Note: One hundred sixty men and 250 women students at Temple University at Philadelphia, Pa., took part. Reciprocal percentages of respondents never felt that they had gone too far.

have married her anyway. Rarely, if ever, is premarital intercourse the one deciding factor leading to a proposal of marriage.

Regret over *not* having had a premarital sexual experience is probably less frequent and less intense, however, than regret over having *had* such experience (see Table 14–1).

Since occasional petting is almost universal among young Americans today, students may be more interested in the petting report in Bell and Blumberg's table than in the intercourse report. "To pet or not to pet" is a decision that has to be made fairly frequently by young women today, and "to try or not to try to pet" is the reciprocal judgment thrust upon the young man. A surprisingly large number of young men have confessed to me that they did not want to start petting with a particular woman, especially since they ran some risk of rejection. However, they thought they ought to, both to maintain their masculine images and to fulfill what they assumed were the woman's expectations.

Perhaps because petting usually precedes intercourse, or perhaps because it is often a means of "testing" one's partner (with immediate rejection for the male, and ex post facto rejection for the female as real possibilities), it is sometimes a more difficult decision than the subsequent choice between intercourse and abstinence. Much depends on the partners and their conditioning, on the situation in which the decision must be made, and on the depth of the relationship between them.

Although it may involve a difficult decision, petting in general is clearly less often condemned by middle-class peers and parents than is premarital intercourse. Some still argue that petting invariably engenders intercourse, but there is considerable evidence that sometimes—perhaps most times—it is a subliminal release; it substitutes for intercourse rather than precedes it. Indeed, one of the current arguments against petting is that it may "fixate" sexual response at a less-than-intercourse level so that in later marriage, when intercourse is appropriate, petting is still preferred.

Intercourse, as can be clearly seen from Bell and Blumberg's table, is more often a cause for regret. Not everyone, of course, has any regrets, and not everyone who does have regrets really suffers. In fact, perhaps a little healthy regret—or at least the fear of it—may be a social good since it may act as a deterrent to promiscuity. But there are some people for whom regret becomes excruciating self-punishment. In extreme cases, depression and repression caused by regret can give rise to serious emotional difficulty, either immediately or in later life. By and large, though, the damage done by regret does not take the form of severe psychopathology. For many, it can cause nagging self-reproach that insidiously dampens sexual expression when the situation *is* right for genuine loving. For others, regret may just lightly tarnish self-respect and so inhibit, to some small degree, future social interaction.

Perhaps one of the few salutary results of the new morality is the widespread acceptance of the feeling that one sexual misjudgment does not portend the end of everything. Now, in addition to the older ways of discharging guilt by confession and by counseling, modern sexual frankness has added the new gentle way of talking it over with a trusted friend. I have pointed out to those who have come to my office with sexual regret that today most people find it easier to understand how a loving person could make a sexual misjudgment; but at the same time they would find it more difficult to be understanding about long periods of carried-over bitterness and self-recrimination. Anyone can learn from a sexual misjudgment, as he can from any other, but it is unwise to look back too often when there is so much opportunity for new self-respect and loving warmth ahead.

WHAT CAN BE DONE
FOR THE NEXT GENERATION?

Regardless of the basis for any person's decision to have or to avoid premarital intercourse—be it rebellious acting out, momentary excitement, genuine loving, or whatever—that person will find that he has something in common with almost every other sexual decision maker. Soon all are going to have their values about sexual experimentation up for question again. When their first child arrives, they are faced with the same old problem, now in a different dimension. What can they do to help the children they love to have an easier and better experience than they had with the sexual insecurities of a changing society? This brings us back full circle to the generalizations we made at the end of Chapter 12 about what parents want for their children: to protect them from exploitation, to protect the family reputation, to ensure successful marriage, and to help the children make creative use of their sexual capacities.

Basic to all these objectives is providing *security* for the child so that he *can* avoid exploitation, he *can* preserve the family reputation, and he *can* make a happy marriage. Providing this kind of security is often a matter of conviction, communication, and confidence.

It seems probable that the major reason for parents' failure to provide adequate attitude education for their children is that they have so few real convictions themselves. Parental confusion places the burden of decision on the child and builds into him a kind of insecurity and anxiety that can last a lifetime.

Those of us who have asked young people what kind of sexual guidance they would like to have have been impressed that they both need and want to know what the limits are, even though most make it clear that, for these limits to be really welcome, they must be based on a modern, practical, and at the same time idealistic basis, not on older metaphysical and theological concepts that may be out of step with present-day realities.

Perhaps in time our society will achieve enough cultural and religious integration so that there can again be some society-wide agreement on premarital sexual values. But in our present confusion, there seems to be more and more reluctance to teach any values because there are so many splinter ideas about which values should be taught. In this situation, it is up to the individual parent, to small groups of parents, or to subcultural organizations to work through their own doubts and arrive at some guidelines that they can pass along to their children. Once there is some acceptable standard, be it old or be it new, be it noble or be it normative, parents can feel secure enough themselves to start defining sexual values for their children.

Clearly, though, how parents present their convictions to the child is crucial. In an area as sensitive as premarital sex, it is as easy to overdo it as it is to default altogether. Some men and women have suffered all their lives because of the fear of sex that was built into them when they were children. Teaching can and should provide security rather than diminish it. It is possible to caution a child about sex in the same manner that cautions him about fire without frightening him away from it for the rest of his life.

Helping the child to maintain his values is probably as important as helping him to acquire them in the first place. The experiments of Solomon Asch and others have shown that most people who have made a correct judgment will change their minds if an overwhelming majority vehemently contends that their judgment is incorrect.[16] The greater the unanimity of opposing judgments, the more likely an individual is to abandon his judgmental conviction. In other words, if your child is to maintain your family values, he should not be put in situations where the overwhelming majority of his peers believe and behave differently. As Zimmerman and Cervantes have pointed out, if a family is to perpetuate its values, it must surround itself with families with similar values.[17] The child, like an adult, must be able to reinforce his attitudes. The greater the number of other children he meets with the same values, the greater is the probability of his maintaining those values.

Exceptionally good communication between parent and child is another requirement if sexual values are to be meaningful. First of all, the child needs to know the facts of human reproduction. More important, he needs to know the attitudes that make sex an expression of love instead of a routine, a duty, or an exploitative "feather in one's cap." The child also needs to know about the motivations, desires, and satisfactions of the opposite sex. This is important for all young people if they are to have good interpersonal relationships, but it is absolutely mandatory for those parents who teach their children that permissiveness with affection is the new standard.

Most crucial of all, parents need to establish the kind of communication with their children that permits an easy interchange of ideas. Regardless of what values he is teaching the child, the parent whose child can talk to him about his problems is probably doing a superior job. The very acceptance of the child's feelings provides him with some of the self-confidence that makes for a healthy sexual personality.

[16] Solomon E. Asch, "Effects of Group Pressure upon the Modifications and Distortion of Judgments," in H. Guetzkow, ed., Groups, Leadership and Men, Pittsburgh, Carnegie, 1951, pp. 177–190.
[17] Carle C. Zimmerman and Lucius F. Cervantes, Successful American Families, New York, Pageant, 1960, p. 76.

SELF-CONFIDENCE
AS A FACTOR IN SEX EDUCATION

Providing self-confidence is the most important factor in assuring healthy sexual attiudes for a young person. As we pointed out earlier, any youngster without social self-confidence, self-esteem, and self-worth has a very difficult time establishing any socially acceptable standard for sexual behavior. The insecure girl who doesn't make friends easily often finds that she must choose between being promiscuous or being a prude. Either she must have intercourse to win the male attention she craves, or she must rationalize away her normal affectional needs. The popular girl with an adequate feeling of self-worth has a much easier time deciding what she will do about sex.

The acne-scarred or nonathletic boy may also have serious emotional problems that he acts out through sexual promiscuity. On the other hand, the secure, athletic male who is openly admired by girls can more easily decide what his standards will be. Many other young men, neither remarkably desirable nor undesirable, feel that they must prove their masculinity by rushing from one sexual affair to another.

It is curious that, in this age of relative sexual freedom, there is sometimes less freedom now than in the past. The girl who fears that her popularity will wane if she refuses to experiment sexually is not really free, nor is the young man who belongs to a gang that insists he have intercourse or lose status. An individual's self-imposed bargaining position in an insensitive society is often a far sterner jailer than traditional sexual morality ever was. The only real freedom comes from enough self-confidence to maintain the integrity and self-respect to do what one believes is right. Perhaps the most important sex education that a parent can give a child is to help him to develop that kind of self-confidence, for, in the end, that is all that will protect him from exploitation—self-invited or otherwise.

Self-confidence is, as we have seen, also the key to the good first impression and ultimately to the relationships that lead to the good marriages parents want for their children. Moreover, self-confidence provides the security to enable a young man or a young woman to wait until the right partner comes along.

Finally, the individual's self-confidence permits him to make more creative use of his sexuality and to establish a deeper relationship with other human beings, both sexual and nonsexual. In many of the cases of sexually incompatible marriage partners cited in later chapters, the controlling role of self-confidence will be readily apparent. Here, however, it is enough to point out, as Erich Fromm has done so eloquently, that a man must love himself before he can really love anyone else.[18]

THE FUTURE OF PREMARITAL SEX

For the past half-century, observers of the American scene have been forecasting the demise of premarital sexual self-restraint. In 1938, psychologist Lewis Terman predicted that virginity at marriage would virtually vanish for males born after 1930 and females born after 1940, although he conceded that an "occasional virgin will come to the marriage bed for a few decades beyond the dates indi-

---

[18] Erich Fromm, *The Art of Loving*, New York, Harper & Row, 1956, pp. 57–63.

cated by the curves."[19] Terman's predictions have not been borne out, nor have others' predictions that all premarital continence would end when a reliable contraceptive appeared on the scene. Those who believed that fear, pregnancy, and venereal disease were the only reasons for young people exercising sexual restraint have had to revise their ideas in the light of recent statistics.[20]

Even the most ardent partisans of sexual permissiveness should be happy that the gloomy predictions did not come true. There is considerable reason to believe that any sudden end to sexual restraint may portend the end of the society in which it occurs. The last days of the Roman Empire, for instance, were characterized by pleasure-seeking and sexual gratification. Sexual release was so easily available and acceptable outside of marriage that many people decided not to marry at all. Arnold Nash describes it this way:

> Ancient family ideas no longer served to challenge the practices of a generation to whom a decline in moral standards was simply a matter of course. Marriage was no longer regarded as a matter upon which the dignity and honor of the state ultimately depended. Both men and women, following only the personal gratification of their own desires, chose illicit affairs rather than marriage with its legal and moral and civic responsibilities. In short, marriage tended to disappear to such an extent that Julius Caesar initiated a series of rewards as an incentive to the adoption of the marital state. But the canker had eaten too far into the fabric of Roman society. The sickness was too deep for financial inducement, direct or indirect, to have a profound effect. Augustus Caesar soon realized that Rome faced a crisis not only in her attitude towards marriage but also in her economic life and in her political ideals.[21]

But if we don't go the way of the Romans, what then? Marshall McLuhan and George B. Leonard suggest that sex may die before society does:

> In future generations it seems most likely that sex will merge with the rest of life, that it will settle down and take its place within a whole spectrum of experiences. You might not think so, what with the outpouring of sexed-up novels and plays since World War II. But these, like the slickly pictured playmates, bring to mind the death rattle of an era. When a novelist like Norman Mailer contends that man is boxed-in by civilized constraints, he is quite right. But when he goes on to say that the free human spirit can now assert itself mostly through sex and violence, he is being merely Victorian.
>
> The more that modern writers present sexual activity as a separate, highly defined, "hot" aspect of life, the more they hasten the death of SEX. Most "literary" novelists have not yet discovered the present, much less glimpsed the future; which is one reason why so many of the brighter college students turn to anti-novels and, in spite of its questionable literary reputation, science fiction. . . .[22]

Earl H. Brill, Episcopal chaplain at the American University in Washington, preceded McLuhan and Leonard in announcing the death of sex. Said he

---

[19] Lewis M. Terman, *Psychological Factors in Marital Happiness*, New York, McGraw-Hill, 1938, p. 323.

[20] J. Richard Udry, *The Social Context of Marriage*, Philadelphia, Lippincott, 1966, pp. 154–155.

[21] Arnold S. Nash, "Ancient Past and Living Present," in Howard Becker and Reuben Hill, eds., *Family, Marriage and Parenthood*, Boston, Heath, 1955, p. 99. There are, of course, many other theories about the proximate causes of the decline and fall of the Roman Empire. Some scholars subscribe to the notion that the elite leaders of Rome were poisoned by the lead pots in which their food was prepared.

[22] Marshall McLuhan and George B. Leonard, "The Future of Sex," *Look*, **31** (July 25, 1967), 59. Reprinted by permission of Harold Ober Associates Incorporated. Copyright © 1967 by Cowles Communications Inc.

in mid-1966, "Sex is dead. Nobody seems to have noticed its passing what with the distraction caused by recent reports of the death of God. . . ."[23]

In support of his premise, Brill made the following seven points: (1) Sex is no longer the most popular subject of campus discussion; it ranks a poor third after civil rights and the student freedom movement. (2) College males have become indifferent to the female body because miniskirts and bikinis have taken the mystery out of it. Modern college men don't give a second look at a well-turned thigh. (3) The fashion pages reflect the asexuality of our times; dresses are square, shapeless, and angular, and women's haircuts are ascetic and severe. (4) Popular music in the late 1960s, while primitive and loud, was not sexy. It aroused the adrenalin but not the libido. Popular dancing of the period tended to keep people apart rather than wrap them up together. (5) Sex has changed from being a deeply personal preoccupation to an impersonal art form. Brill appeared particularly jolted by the publication of William Masters' and Virginia Johnson's *Human Sexual Response,* which scientifically recorded the pulse, muscle changes, body temperature, and skin color during the sex act. "Perhaps," suggested Brill, "we will soon construct from these data the Perfect Sex Act and get it preserved for all time in silver, at the National Bureau of Standards." (6) The decline of sex is reflected in the way the subject is treated in current literature and entertainment. Said Brill, "if sex were alive and vital, wouldn't the portrayal of ordinary, normal, healthy sexuality be attractive enough to keep people coming back for more without the need to probe constantly into increasingly esoteric perversions?" (7) The existence of such sex-oriented magazines as *Playboy* is added evidence that sex is on its death bed. "*Playboy* is simply the house organ of the fundamentalists of sexiosity," said Brill. "It shouts, 'Sex is alive! It is! It is!' It shouts so loud that you wonder whether it believes itself."[24]

There are many present-day romanticists who refuse to believe that sex is dead. It seems more probable to them that the romantic tenderness once implicit in the sexual relationship between two human beings is only sleeping, encapsulated in the warm hearts of those who believe that life has richer meaning than it is presently being permitted to reveal.

Sexual behavior throughout the history of mankind has been subject to change without notice. Societies have moved from passive restraint to wild lasciviousness, and some of those that haven't collapsed have moved back again. It seems quite probable that, as we enter the 1970s, a new generation conditioned differently from any generation in the past, sexual behavior *will* change. Before long, the "New Morality" will become the Old Morality. Then, perhaps —just perhaps—it will be replaced by a new era of tenderness and romance in which sexual intercourse will once more be dignified as the ultimate expression of two people who love genuinely enough to make their commitment marriage.

---

[23] Earl H. Brill, "Sex Is Dead," *Christian Century,* **83** (August 3, 1966), 957–958.
[24] *Ibid.,* p. 959.

15

ADJUSTMENTS
IN MARRIAGE

Almost every American old enough to be concerned about marriage has heard that "adjustments" are necessary to make a marriage work. Marriage adjustments are the subject of countless magazine articles, soap operas, and advice columns in the newspapers. Despite this wide publicity, most young people enter into marriage convinced that they are already well adjusted and that they will not have the difficulties other people have had trying to get along with one another.

This blissful optimism may be a good thing, for some good marriage prospects would never marry if they were made apprehensive about all the adjustments that lie ahead. Everybody has to make adjustments not only in the beginning of his marriage but throughout his married life. For some, the adjustments are so easy that they don't even know they are adjusting. For others, adjusting is a conscious and deliberate process of learning to understand, to accept, and to change.

Most partners adjust well enough both to stay married and to be counted as happily married. In six research studies made between 1938 and 1962, almost 71 percent of all the respondents in all the studies were evaluated by themselves, by their friends, or by their children as being happily married (see Table 15-1).

There are, however, many young marrieds unable or unwilling to make even the initial adjustments to married life. Some who accept the idea that they have adjustments to make at the beginning of their marriage are often unaware that many of the most important and most difficult adjustments come many years after the honeymoon. These later adjustments are sometimes more difficult, for some of the romance may be gone, and partners have established change-resistant patterns of reacting to one another. They may also have developed painful individual problems that increase their criticalness and decrease

Table 15–1
Marital Happiness Studies

Researcher	Date Reported	Location	Number of Couples	Percent Happy	Who Rated
Terman	1938	California	792	85	Themselves
Burgess and Cottrell	1939	Illinois	526	63	Themselves
Lang	1939	Illinois	17,533	62	Friends
Popenoe	1939	California	2,080	58	Friends
Landis	1946	Michigan	409	83	Themselves
Landis	1962	California	2,640	74	Their children

Sources: Lewis M. Terman, *Psychological Factors in Marital Happiness,* New York, McGraw-Hill, 1938, p. 78; Ernest Burgess and Leonard S. Cottrell, *Predicting Success or Failure in Marriage,* Englewood Cliffs, N.J., Prentice-Hall, 1939, p. 34; Burgess and Cottrell, *op. cit.,* p. 139; Paul Popenoe and Donna Wicks, "Marital Happiness in Two Generations," *Marital Hygiene,* **21** (1937), 218–233; Judson T. Landis, "Length of Time Required to Achieve Adjustment in Marriage," *American Sociological Review,* **11** (December 1946) 674; Judson T. Landis," "A Re-examination of the Role of the Father as an Index of Family Integration," *Marriage and Family Living,* **24** (May, 1962), 122–128. Compiled by David Klein especially for this book.

their tolerance. Initial adjustments are hard enough; later ones can be devastating.

In this chapter, some of the typical adjustments that are required of marriage partners throughout their relationships will be discussed. First it is necessary, however, to answer two important questions: (1) Why don't partners realize their differences and either adjust to them before marriage or never get married? (2) Which of the partners does the adjusting?

WHY DON'T PROBLEMS REQUIRING ADJUSTMENT OCCUR BEFORE MARRIAGE?

A great many adjustments *are* made before the two partners get married. Some potential marriage mates are rejected during the dating process, because even the very first adjustments are too difficult for one or both partners to make. Others may be rejected during the engagement period, because, as the partners approach the actual reality of marriage, they recognize (or at least one of them recognizes) that they are not really able to adjust to each other.

Even after this selectivity has taken place, there are often many unforeseen difficulties in getting along with one's mate. Some of these difficulties occur because people tend to deliberately disguise their idiosyncracies before marriage, even though they are well aware that they have them. These can turn out to be "tremendous trifles" in a marriage. A young woman may know that she is usually cranky before she has had her breakfast. She is careful, however, not to let her fiancé find this out until after they are married. A young man may know that he doesn't like to make "small talk" and probably will like it even less after he is married. But before marriage he tries to keep up an entertaining stream of banter with his fiancée.

A second type of adjustment is necessitated by *unrealized* habits. He takes up three-quarters of the bed, but he doesn't know it since he sleeps alone. She hangs her nylons in the bathroom, but this never bothered anybody because she had her own bathroom before she was married. He is a compulsive towel-straightener; she tends to overlook such minor details of neatness.

More important than these unforeseen habits, though, are the partners' differences in marriage expectations. For example, what happens if a woman who emotionally needs and expects her husband to remember birthdays and anniversaries without being reminded (as her father always did) marries a forgetful man? Or what happens if a man with a conditioned need for an affectionate wife who talks sweetly (as his mother always did), even after a long day with the housework, marries a relatively unaffectionate girl who is easily fatigued?

Many difficulties occur because neither partner discovered beforehand the other's concept of husband or wife roles *after* marriage. Each assumed from his knowledge of the other's behavior during courtship that the other would naturally want to do the "right" things after marriage. These differing and undiscussed expectations can have a very serious effect on the stability of the marriage relationship, as the following case illustrates.

CASE 26

"John is ruining our marriage!" Eloise said. "I work hours preparing a nice dinner for him, and he's never on time to eat it. The worst part about it is that he doesn't even call me to let me know that he'll be late. He could be on time every night if he wanted to. He just doesn't want to. He doesn't love me enough. I know he'll tell you that he's a salesman and can't get up and run out of his prospect's office when suppertime comes, but 90 percent of the time that isn't so, and the other times he could at least call me. All he thinks about is himself. When he does get home and the dinner is cold or burned, he complains.

"He wasn't that way before we were married. He had the same job then, but he was almost always on time for our dinner dates. I'm just not going to put up with his selfishness any longer. I'm tired of begging him, and I'm tired of screaming at him; now I'm going to leave him."

John had a somewhat different version of the same story. "If Eloise told you that I can't get home for dinner every night right on the minute, she's right," John told the counselor. "She knew when I married her that I was a salesman. I have to be where the client is when he wants to buy, regardless of what time it is. She didn't make any fuss about it before we were married. She conveniently forgets about it now, but I was just about as late for our dates before as I am now. There were a couple of big differences then. In the first place, she wasn't cooking the meals. In the second place, it didn't seem to matter to her so much. She didn't give me the stuff she does now about her father always being on time! She and that perfect father of hers. He had a nine-to-five job and was never a minute late getting to the office and never a minute late getting home. Before we were married she seemed to understand how I couldn't always figure out my time to the second. She even used to smile about it a little and call me 'Johnny-come-lately.' But after we got married she changed. Now she never smiles; she just screams.

"I admit that I'm not the best one about telephoning. Sometimes there isn't a phone around. But there's more to it than that. I feel like such a baby when I have to report to her every five minutes. The other fellows don't have to go running to the phone to call their wives. When they're late, their wives understand. My mother used to understand, too. Before we were married and I was living at home, Mother didn't nag me all the time. If I was a little late coming, she would just serve supper to the rest of them and put mine in the oven. In some ways I think my mother loved me more than my wife does. She wasn't trying to make me out like a bad guy all the time.

"I don't want a divorce; I love my wife and kids. But sometimes I thing it would be better if she did get a divorce. She sure is making my life miserable the way it is."

There are other important reasons why people don't anticipate the necessity of adjusting in the courtship situation. For one thing, they are together only part of the time. He never gets tired of her talking, because he generally leaves when he has had enough. She doesn't get angry or upset over the number of towels he uses, because she doesn't have to wash the towels. Neither one of them gets hurt by their relative's cuts or slights, because they both tend to stay away from their relatives.

But after marriage all this changes. They are together sixteen hours out of every day, and on some days twenty-four. A repetitious behavior that once might have been endearing now becomes intolerable. Moreover, they find themselves drawn into prolonged contact with their relatives, and they have to deal with crucial conflicts that they once postponed or ignored. It is by perpetualness and enforced closeness that the adjustability of a partner is really tried—sometimes for the first time.

IT'S DIFFERENT
WHEN IT'S NEW

Novelty is another reason why adjustments aren't anticipated. In the beginning of any relationship, the partners are polite and eager to please. This is especially true of relationships between men and women. Good manners and consequently good feelings are especially important to a good first impression. The novelty of going steady and being engaged is a delightful adult adaptation of the child's game of playing family—"You be the father and I'll be the mother." Some people never get tired of this game. It is the source of enrichment for the rest of their adult lives, and it is actually an aid to unconscious adjusting. But for others, interest in the game fades soon after marriage. Then the long delayed real adjustments have to be made or the marriage fails.

Probably the most important reason why adjustability is inadequately tested before marriage is the *idealization* that is part and parcel of the romantic process. Idealization is, as the reader will recall from Chapter 11, the tendency for those in love to attribute glamorous characteristics and abilities to a prospective marriage partner that that marriage partner actually doesn't have. This often leads to one of two unreal assumptions. The first is that the prospective partner is such a noble knight in shining armor or such a delicate lady fair that it would be sheer ecstasy to spend one's life adjusting to this ideal person's whims. The second possible unreal assumption is that there will be no need for adjustment in living with this noble creature in the first place.

Idealization certainly isn't always bad. As we discussed earlier, positive trust is often rewarded by its own expectation. The man or woman who has faith in his or her partner may help that partner to grow toward greatness. With this kind of "good" idealization comes complete acceptance, the willingness not only to tolerate but actually to be enthusiastic about the partner with all possible emphasis on his good points. Complete acceptance is the stuff of which good adjustments are later made.

Complete acceptance was never better described than by a loquacious New York taxicab driver. "I see a lot of good-looking rich dames in the course of a day's work. I carry a lot of them in my cab. But I wouldn't trade any one of them for the wife I got up in the Bronx. You know what? The other Sunday afternoon when she thought I was asleep I heard her hanging out the window talking to the woman in the apartment across the court. She was telling her what a good guy I am. Imagine that! She was telling her how strong I am and what a good husband I am and how good I am to the kids. Most of it was a whole pack of lies, but I think my wife really believes them. I was a little ashamed that I can't really live up to all that stuff, but I felt good that she thought I could. She's a good mother; she works hard, and she gets tired. But she always tries to make the best of what we got, and most of all she tries to make the best of me. Way down deep I know what I am. But I also know I'm a lot better than I would be if I didn't have her. I think she's happy, too. At least she's a lot happier than those dames who get in the cab and don't know what to do with themselves except to spend their husband's money while they squawk about what a bum he is. My wife may not smell as good as them, and she may not have as many clothes, but she's got something a lot more important. And so do I."

There is "bad" idealization, too. It blinds a marriage partner to the real-life need for making constant relationship adjustments. In such cases, early hero images only tend to make later disillusionment that much greater.

CASE 27

"I didn't think it could happen to us," George told the counselor wistfully. "I can remember standing in the moonlight near a beautiful lake five years ago holding her in my arms. She was so eager to touch me and be close to me that I could feel her quiver in my arms. Nothing ever affected me like that. To know that she wanted to be near me so badly that she quivered was just about the most exciting thing that ever happened to me. In those days she wanted to do everything and anything for me; nothing was too much trouble. It wasn't that I needed all that much, it was just that nobody ever loved me like that before. Adjustments? What was there to adjust to? We never even gave it a thought!

"But now the quiver is gone. Yes, I think that's what characterizes our relationship now; the quiver is gone. One day last week I got thinking about that moonlit night and the lake five years ago and I got all slushy. So I went out and bought her a box of candy and some flowers. When I came in the front door at suppertime, I saw her standing in the middle of the living room surveying the carnage that the kids had wrought. So I just sneaked up behind her quietly and kissed her on the back of the neck. Do you know what she said? She said, 'I wonder if I turned out the fire under the peas.' How do you like that?

"Actually, it wasn't that she didn't turn around and want to be close to me that hurt. It's the fact that she no longer really accepts me. Now she is critical of things that I do, little things, like watching the ball game instead of cutting the grass. And she doesn't seem to want me to touch her anymore. I don't know what to do; I sure would like to have that acceptance back—and the quiver that goes along with it."

George's wife Lila was wistful about it, too. "It didn't start all at once. But one day a few weeks after we got home from the honeymoon, I began to see some things about George that I had never seen before. He wasn't strong and all-knowing like I had thought he was. He had a lot of anxieties and a lot of peculiar notions. And he wasn't as neat as he had always appeared. He left his dirty socks around, and he didn't hang up his clothes. I don't think I changed at all right then; at least, it didn't seem to me as if I did. But it must have seemed that way to George, because he changed a little in his way of behaving toward me. All of a sudden he got defensive. Then I guess I changed a little more in my way of behaving toward him, and then he changed again, and so I changed again, and the relationship went down, down, down, until it just seems now that I don't care very much.

"I certainly wish that I had had a better idea of what marriage was going to be like before we were married. I had heard you had to adjust, but I thought the adjustments would be kind of fun. I thought it would be nice to try to please him by changing my ways of doing things. Now I don't care. It doesn't seem important at all whether he's pleased or not. He doesn't go out of his way to please me, either. I don't know what we can do about it. I hate to think of spending the rest of my life this way."

WHO DOES THE ADJUSTING?

Which partner should do the adjusting is one of the basic problems of modern middle-class marriage. It probably always has been a problem, although in other times and in other cultures there were strict expectations of role behavior that, while they may have placed unfair adjustment burdens on women, tended to reduce controversy over what was "proper." In modern American society, with its fewer structured roles for men and women, deciding who defers to whom is more of a trial-and-error procedure. In the beginning, even before marriage, there is often a subtle and unconscious struggle between the two partners to see who will dominate. This struggle sometimes ends the relationship, and not always because one partner or the other loses. Some men and many women want to be dominated, and they become unhappy when their partner insists on *not* being the leader.

Once this initial jockeying for position has been satisfactorily resolved, the relationship often enters into a period of at least temporary stability. As the partners become more deeply love-related, they tend to be "syncratic" (sharing decisions equally). They talk over major decisions and arrive at mutually satisfactory solutions without the dominant one parading his dominance. As Robert Blood points out, even in this period, some aspects of the future relationship are controlled by one partner or the other. This is especially true for the minor routine decisions of early marriage that are linked to generally accepted sex-role behavior. For example the husband almost always makes a decision on what job to take or what auto to buy, while the wife more often makes most of the food purchases and the petty housekeeping decisions.[1]

The initial syncratic honeymoon, with its easy decision sharing, does not always persist as the marriage progresses. Blood believes that the longer a marriage exists, the greater the tendency is for decisions to be made unilaterally:

> This is one form of estrangement in marriage. Just as husbands and wives talk less about the day's events, so they talk less about decisions to be made, leaving more and more matters to the partner with the greater interest. Since family affairs are the wife's specialty, this means not only a shift from syncratic to autonomic decision making [equal number of separate decisions] but also to some extent to wife-dominance. Wives seldom seize power, but husbands often withdraw from decision making save in areas of special concern to them.[2]

[1] Robert O. Blood, Jr., *Marriage*, New York, Free Press, 1962, p. 242.
[2] *Ibid.*

Not all and perhaps not even the majority of marriages are readily taken over by the woman. In fact, in some marriages, the woman struggles *not* to accept the responsibility of leadership, insisting that her husband make the decisions. If the marriage is not to be equalitarian, the emergence of the partner dominant in decision making is controlled by a complex series of factors falling into two general categories: personality and the relative bargaining position of the partners.

PERSONALITY'S
EFFECT ON DOMINANCE

Although the democratic or equalitarian marriage has been held up as the ideal one by many of the professionals in marriage relationships education for years, many people do not have the emotional conditioning to accept a coequal marriage relationship. In the middle class at least, the male responsibility is still strong even though the male's authority has been considerably diminished in recent years. Moreover a large number of women still want men who can dominate them—at least to the extent of being resolutely decisive. Such women often test their men consciously or not, by giving them a little bit harder time than they need to so that the men will be forced to demonstrate their superiority. This need for dominance on the part of these women is believed by some to be culturally conditioned from the example of traditional male–female roles in their childhood homes. But there are others who believe that it is a characteristic inherent in all women. Helene Deutsch, a noted psychoanalyst, has referred to this phenomenon as the "natural masochism of women."[3]

Not all men are capable of consistently accepting a dominant position. Some, perhaps because of their conditioning by dominant mothers, have an emotional expectation (usually unconscious) that *they* will be dominated, and so they put themselves in a position of subserviency. Some other men have a self-concept of inadequacy in all relationships for reasons that are complex and obscure. They deliberately take a lower position in the "pecking order" in any group they enter.

The concept of "pecking order" is derived from observations of the hierarchy of status among barnyard hens. In a flock, one hen tends to be dominant and pecks all the others first. A second hen will peck all the hens but the top hen. The rest arrange themselves in descending order, leaving one poor hen that is pecked by all the others but that can peck no one. Among animals, size appears to be an important factor affecting pecking order, and since males are usually larger than females, they usually have the advantage. Male hormones apparently give the male some advantage, too. Hens low in the pecking order that are given injections of male hormones have been observed to fight their way up the pecking-order ladder.[4]

Among human beings, many psychological factors affect the pecking order. Size alone is not the controlling factor, nor are hormones. Such culturally conditioned factors as a willingness to fight or a readiness to compromise in order to avoid conflict are important. Then, too, conditioned self-images often dictate an individual's pecking order. If one thinks of himself as a dominant

---

[3] Helene Deutsch, *Psychology of Women*, vol. I, New York, Grune and Stratton, 1944, pp. 239–278.
[4] W. C. Allee, *The Social Life of Animals*, New York, Norton, 1939, p. 178.

leader, he may well become a "take-charge" type. Soon the rest of his group may defer to him, even though he may have no qualifications other than his own aggressiveness. On the other hand, the submissive individual who demonstrates a willingness to accept a lower status is often assigned a low position by the members of his group.

Much has been written about "castrating" females who presumably emasculate their men by dominating them. The result is classic—the "henpecked" husband. When this happens, however, it is often because the husband wants it to happen, either consciously or unconsciously. In such wife-dominated marriages, the husband does most of the adjusting. Some men try very hard to please their wives—perhaps too hard—and get emotional satisfaction from the fact that they *try* to be such good husbands. To the outsider it may look as if they are severely abused, but in reality they are getting contentment from playing the subservient role.

RELATIVE BARGAINING POSITION

Equally as important as personality in the control of who dominates whom is the relative bargaining position of the two partners. In 1921, E. A. Ross defined the law of personal exploitation: "The thing is common and its rule is simple. In any sentimental relation the one who cares less can exploit the one who cares more. In the man-woman relation and in the mother-child relation we see this plainly."[5] Subsequently, Willard Waller expanded on what he called the principle of least interest: The person who has the least interest in the continuation of a relationship is able to dictate the conditions of continued association.[6]

These postulates may sound cynical to those young people who are very much in love. And, indeed, in some marriages where neither partner is—or even feels—exploited, they may never have any valid application. But in some marriage relationships, they are all-controlling. The right to dominate is determined by such factors as physical beauty, amount of education, job status, achievement, and the presence or absence of children. The better bargaining position can fluctuate from one partner to the other at various times in the marriage.

There is very little specific research support for the effect of beauty on dominance, but it is common for a marriage counselor to find one partner or the other tyrannizing his mate by using his good looks as a bargaining weapon. The tacit threat "I can easily find another and you can't" is very often sufficient to control any relationship. A good job can raise one's bargaining position, too. Wives who are employed fulltime have more influence in family decision-making than those employed parttime, and the latter in turn have more influence than those who don't work at all.[7] The less the husband is employed, the less influence he has. In fact, as Robert Blood points out, when income is derived from both partners, the balance of power is correspondingly altered. The more the balance of participation in the economic system shifts in the wife's direction, the more the husband's power declines.[8]

---

[5] Edward A. Ross, *Principles of Sociology*, New York, Century, 1923, p. 136.
[6] Willard Waller, *The Family*, revised by Reuben Hill, New York, Dryden, 1951, p. 191.
[7] J. Richard Udry, *The Social Context of Marriage*, Philadelphia, Lippincott, 1966, p. 359.
[8] Blood, *op. cit.*, pp. 244–245.

CASE 28

"I'd been married to Marian for about seven years," Alex said. "She came from a home where she had a tremendously domineering father, and she was very much afraid of him. When he said she couldn't go out, that was that. For the first five or six years after we were married, she was pretty good about being a good wife. Whenever she went anywhere, she asked me if she could go. Sometimes it even seemed a little silly for me to tell a grown woman exactly what she could do.

"But then she got a job at a television studio. She is a very beautiful woman. At first I was all for it. I was pleased that my wife was so attractive. But pretty soon she began feeling very independent and staying out until all hours of the night. I began to scream and shout about her not coming in until two or three in the morning. Then she began to not tell me when she was going out. I'd get home and find that she'd left the kids at a babysitter's and gone off on some 'public relations' job. About the middle of the evening she'd call up and say she'd be home in half an hour. Then maybe at about two in the morning she'd finally get home. My yelling at her didn't seem to do any good, so I started trying to reason with her. That wasn't any better. She just told me that she'd do as she pleased.

"A couple of weeks ago I got so mad I moved out. I'd thought I'd show her. But now I'm wondering if I didn't make a bad mistake. She has shown no inclination to ask me to come back, and now she gets to go out anytime she wants to. Sure, I'm jealous. I don't know what she's doing out late at night. She says she's just either out with the girls or driving by herself. She says she wouldn't want any other man, and the way our sex life has been I don't think she would either. I think she hates men and sex too.

"What am I going to do? If I go back and tell her she can go out any time she wants to, I'll have lost face. Besides, I don't think that's what she really wants anyway."

When the counselor talked to Marian, she agreed that everything that Alex had said was right. "He used to carp at me and pick at me an awful lot. At first I tried to do better in every way he suggested. But I never could meet his expectations so finally I just stopped trying. Then I got my job. Everyone is nice to me down there, and I like the people and I have a sense of achievement. Besides, it is very flattering to be told how nice I look. I'm not going to stop working now no matter what Alex does.

"Yes, it's true that I lie to him. The thing that set him off three weeks ago was that I waited until the last minute to tell him I was going out for an evening show. I told him I'd be home by ten, but I knew that I couldn't possibly be home before midnight. I was afraid to tell him that, because he would have hit the ceiling and been mad before I left and mad when I got home. When I finally did get home at three A.M., he was only mad once.

"Sure, I understand he doesn't like me out until three in the morning. But he goes out with the boys until all hours, why shouldn't I? Actually, I really think I want him to stop me, but to tell you the truth I don't know how he's going to. I'll leave him if he tries to use force. He did hit me once, you know.

"I don't know whether I'm glad or sorry he walked out, but in many ways it's nice to be independent. Yet in some ways I think I still need him. I wish he could find some way to solve this thing."

THE EFFECT OF CHILDREN
ON BARGAINING POSITION

The absence or presence of children in a family can also affect the relative bargaining power of the marriage mate. Some infertile women feel inadequate because of their childlessness and are deliberately more patronizing to their husbands, sometimes fearing that he might seek a fertile woman. The coming of children may also affect the power structure of the family. James Bossard contends that the more children there are, the more complex and necessary the husband's role becomes.[9] This increases his relative power. But David Heer has offered another explanation for this phenomenon. He feels that each partner compares his present position in the marriage with the situation that might obtain if he were outside the marriage. The more children a woman has, the lower is her probable bargaining position for another husband or for a good job. Consequently, she accepts her husband's domination.[10]

Some husbands lose power when the children come. This is not only because they may be outvoted in the democratic process but also because they are afraid to get divorces, knowing that in most courts the woman will get the children. This raises the wives' relative bargaining positions and lowers the husbands'. It has also been suggested that, in some families, the father loses power after the children come because the wife can more easily manipulate the children's attitudes. If she has hostility toward her husband, either overt or latent, she can openly or subtly demean him to the point where he no longer has respect. He must then bargain with her in order to retain a semblance of control in his own household. Presumably, men are not so adept as women in turning their children against the spouse, even if they are so inclined.

THE EQUALITARIAN MARRIAGE

Are there no equalitarian marriages in which neither partner is noticeably dominant? Most assuredly there are. On an imaginary continuum that runs from male dominance to female dominance, there are couples at every point, so it is readily deducible that there must be some at midpoint. Moreover, since the equalitarian marriage has been a cultural ideal in recent times, there are, in fact, many marriages clustered close to that midpoint. Several studies have shown this to be true.[11]

Those who have achieved this ideal kind of marital arrangement believe that it gives a feeling of worth and dignity and an integrity of the spirit to both partners. Robert Blood interpreted his study of 909 couples as demonstrating that, in general, the greater the sharing of decisions, the healthier the marriage.[12]

In an equalitarian marriage, each partner is so satisfied with the joint decision-making process and with his separate areas of decision making that he never stops to question whether those assignments are exactly equal. This, the term *balanced marriage* might be more accurate than equalitarian. In fact, an overemphasis on equality can spoil what otherwise might be a perfectly satisfactory arrangement.

[9] James H. S. Bossard, *The Large Family System*, Philadelphia, Univ. of Pennsylvania Press, 1956.
[10] David M. Heer, "The Measurement and Bases of Family Power: An Overview," *Marriage and Family Living*, 25 (May, 1963), 133–139.
[11] Theodore Johannis, Jr., and James Rollins, "Teenager Perception of Family Decision-Making," *Family Life Coordinator*, 7 (June, 1959), 70–74; Robert O. Blood, Jr., and Donald M. Wolfe, *Husbands and Wives*, New York, Free Press, 1960; Russell Middleton and Snell Putney, "Dominance in Decisions in the Family: Race and Class Difference," *American Journal of Sociology*, 65 (May, 1960), 605–609.
[12] Blood, *op. cit.*, p. 242.

THE ADJUSTMENT PROCESS

Adjustment in marriage is a continuous process. As the complexion of the marriage changes, the two partners must resynchronize their ideas, values, desires, and goals if the marriage is to run smoothly. At the outset, newlyweds face a multitude of adjustments. Sexual relationships, spending the family income, keeping inlaws happy, relating to new friends and a new pattern of social life, and adjusting to the personal habits and hygiene of the new mate are all very important. In addition, each partner must learn how far he can push his mate in sensitive areas and which things and thoughts he must avoid. Some of the initial adjustments in marriage are so important that there will be complete chapters about them later. But the initial adjustments are only the beginning. Even after the interaction between the marriage partners has been successfully established, new and changing situations, together with the inevitable personality changes that result from aging and maturing, make further adjustments necessary and inevitable.

The arrival of the first child in the family signals the beginning of a whole new era in the relationship of the husband and wife. Some marriage partners who have made every other adjustment easily have trouble at this point as one partner or the other become jealous of the attention given to the baby. The need for disciplining the child and tending to his value education as he grows up necessitates another reevaluation of the partners' attitudes toward each other, toward the child, and toward the complete living experience. The arrival of the second child causes further adjustments not only for the marriage partners but also on the part of the first-born.

Another major adjustment occurs when the children go off to school, leaving the mother with time she had forgotten about. Shall she work outside the home? Still further adjustments must take place when the children leave home for good and the mother finds herself without a role. Perhaps the greatest adjustment of all occurs when the husband retires and suddenly faces the insults of old age without the crutch of feeling necessary or the motivation of competition with other men.

The variety of separate stages in marriage requiring new adjustments has led to the development of the concept of the family-life cycle. This formulation suggests that marriages proceed from their inception through a regular and predictable series of stages to which readjustments are necessary. Pitirim Sorokin, Carle Zimmerman, and Charles Galpin suggested a four-stage family-life cycle in their early conceptualization,[13] but Evelyn Duvall recently proposed an eight-stage family-life cycle:

1. beginning families (married couple without children)
2. childbearing families (oldest child, birth to thirty months)
3. families with preschool children (oldest child, two-and-a-half to six years)
4. families with school children (oldest child, six to thirteen years)
5. families with teenagers (oldest child, thirteen to twenty years)
6. families as launching centers (first child gone, last child leaving home)
7. families in the middle years (empty nest to retirement)
8. aging families (retirement to death of one or both spouses)[14]

In each of these stages, new adjustments have to be made and old ones

[13] P. Sorokin, C. C. Zimmerman, and C. J. Galpin, *A Systematic Source Book in Rural Sociology*, vol. II, Minneapolis, Univ. of Minnesota Press, 1931, p. 31.
[14] Evelyn Duvall, *Family Development*, 2nd ed., Philadelphia, Lippincott, 1962, p. 9.

reevaluated. For example, here is a summary of Duvall's "developmental tasks" (necessary adjustments) for the couple expecting a baby:

1. arranging for the physical care of the expected baby
2. developing new patterns for getting and spending income
3. reevaluating procedures for determining who does what and where authority rests
4. adapting patterns of sexual relationships to pregnancy
5. expanding communication systems for present and anticipated emotional needs
6. reorienting relationships with relatives
7. adapting relationships with friends, associates, and community activities to the realities of pregnancy
8. acquiring knowledge about and planning for the specifics of pregnancy, childbirth, and parenthood
9. maintaining morale and a workable philosophy of life.[15]

Duvall suggests that successful completion of family developmental tasks at any stage of the family-life cycle is necessary to satisfaction and achievement not only in that stage but also in all later stages. This developmental task concept has been useful in family study, but the direct application of its generalizations to specific family situations is limited by the widely varying structure, values, abilities, and circumstances of American families.

WHICH ADJUSTMENTS ARE MOST IMPORTANT?

Given the present state of unpredictability in human relationships in general and the almost universal practice of disguising one's real after-marriage expectations from one's friends, one's fiancé, and even oneself, there is probably no real way of predicting which partners will have to make which adjustments or how soon they will have to make them.

Social psychologists disagree among themselves about which of the initial adjustments cause the most difficulty for most people. In 1946, Judson Landis reported that, of 409 couples studied, the fewest number of partners agreed that they had had satisfaction from the beginning in their sex relations, the next fewest in spending the family income.[16] He did a similar study of 581 college-educated couples in 1967 and reported that "the problems couples face in marriage have changed little with the changing times. . . . 'New' problems listed by the present generation of married people are not the ones they ranked the highest. Their reports agreed with those of the earlier couples in giving highest ranking to problems in the area of sex, finances, in-laws and childbearing."[17]

John Thomas, on the other hand, in a study of a large group of Catholics, found in 1956 that most couples reported the biggest source of marriage breakdowns during the first year of marriage was inlaws; then adultery took the lead for the next five years or so; and after that, alcohol took over as the major problem the couple faced.[18]

[15] Ibid., p. 159.
[16] Judson T. Landis, "Length of Time Required to Achieve Adjustment In Marriage," American Sociological Review, 11 (December, 1946), 647.
[17] Judson T. Landis and Mary G. Landis, Building a Successful Marriage, 5th ed., Englewood Cliffs, N.J., Prentice-Hall, 1968, pp. 281–284.
[18] John L. Thomas, The American Catholic Family, Englewood Cliffs, N.J., Prentice-Hall, 1956, pp. 264–265.

Harvey Locke found that happily married couples reported few serious difficulties, but where they *did*, these concentrated around inlaws, amusements, and spending the family income. Among divorced couples, Locke found that reported difficulties covered a wide range, from sex to drinking, nonsupport, desertion, selfishness, and problems over relatives and amusements.[19] William Goode's study of divorced women revealed a similar pattern.[20] When asked what the main cause of their divorce was, these women mentioned the following:

Complaints	Percent
Nonsupport	33
Husband's attempt to dominate	32
"Drinking, gambling and helling around"	31
Drunkenness	30
Personality	29
Home life	25

Many marriage partners who seek marriage counseling report that sex is their problem. This is so often true that much of the literature in marriage counseling deals with handling sex-related difficulties. Sex, however, can be a convenient peg on which to hang other difficulties. Two marriage partners who have been fighting all day about spending money aren't likely to have a very good sexual relationship that night. Asked the next day what their difficulty is, sex would probably get the blame.

In any event, which adjustment is the more difficult for the largest number of people is not very important to most married partners who are not getting along. Their adjustments are their own special problems. Even after they know why they are having trouble, they still must perceive that they have only three possible ways of resolving it, regardless of what it is. These three ways are accommodation, alteration, or aggression.

ACCOMMODATION

"Accommodation" ranges from complete acceptance to the grumbling toleration of peaceful coexistence. The performance that leads most quickly to adjustment is the acceptance of one partner's attitudes and behaviors by the other. This does not necessarily mean that one should be required to subserve himself completely to the will of the other; to do so would damage feelings of personal integrity and so develop a need for even further adjustments. But when both partners can and do accept *most* of the attitudes and behaviors of the other without any loss of any personal worth and self-respect, adjustment is achieved relatively easily.

There are a few for whom a theoretically ideal marriage would be the one in which each partner completely accepts the attitudes and behaviors of the other *all* of the time. Usually this is impossible. Besides, most people expect at least some opposition and conflict, even from those who love them. They would be disconcerted by someone who always agreed with them and placidly

[19] Harvey J. Locke, *Predicting Adjustment in Marriage: A Comparison of a Divorced and a Happily Married Group*, New York, Holt, Rinehart and Winston, 1951, pp. 67–85.
[20] William J. Goode, *After Divorce*, New York, Free Press, 1956, p. 123.

permitted any behavior, no matter how outrageous. Such permissive acceptance would tend to destroy the recipient's ability to discriminate between adequate and inadequate performance. Thus, it would preclude the satisfaction that comes from earning the genuine approval of the other person. Greater satisfaction is obtained when one is accepted most of the time, rewarded by love for good performance, and rejected (in a manner the offender himself feels is appropiate) for obivously inadequate performance.

Many situations in the interrelationships between marriage partners require a "putting-up-with-it" kind of accommodation, which differs from pleased acceptance. The more happily such accommodation can be made, the more successful the marriage relationship. If, for example, either mate is forced by illness or accident to give up his traditional role, the other must learn to live with whatever new arrangements can be made. If the inevitable can be accepted gracefully, both partners will benefit.

There are less dramatic cases, too, in which accommodating oneself to the other person is possibly the most effective way of dealing with the problem. After a young husband has made his feelings clear about his wife's not screwing the top back on the toothpaste tube, he probably is better off not to keep nagging about it. Nagging usually just increases one's own resentment and the other person's hostility. Foolish though it may seem, some people ultimately get ulcers and/or divorces over matters that have no greater significance in the lives of either one of them than the top on the toothpaste tube.

The supercharged emotional feelings of love that most people bring to marriage have an important usefulness in making accommodations. Love-inspired desire plus personality flexibility allow some people to make all the initial adjustments without knowing they are doing so.

Moreover, given an understanding partner, such people can often establish, by their own example, patterns of interacting that will both ensure and increase both partners' ability to make future adjustments. These are the marriages that go on to a self-enlarging richness.

ALTERATION
AS A MEANS OF ADJUSTING

The second way to arrive at adjustment in a marriage relationship is through the alteration of attitudes and behaviors. Instead of one person either accepting or tolerating the other person's ideas, he seeks to persuade the other to adopt some new thought or course. Given a reasonable amount of openmindedness and good communicative ability, a couple can reach not only adequate but often a superior adjustment by compromise rather than by total accommodation on the part of one partner or the other.

Compromise has been the classic solution to disagreements throughout the history of the world. Unhappily, however, compromises are usually a solution in which neither partner gets all he wants. Thus, both partners wind up with a feeling of something less than complete satisfaction.

There is, however, almost always a possibility for "creative compromise" if the partners will seek for it long enough. Creative compromise is a solution in which both partners recognize that a certain compromise represents something better than either of them wanted in the first place. If she wanted to go dancing and he wanted to go to a ball game, they might find a movie that both eagerly want to see playing at a local theater. Such creative compromise is not always possible. But when it is, it maximizes satisfaction and is probably the best possible adjustment.

AGGRESSION

The third possible way of adjusting is through aggression. This might better be called a nonadjustment process, since most aggression, either active or passive, usually provokes more aggression in return and leads to conflict and hostility rather than to adjustment. Sometimes such conflict and hostility becomes a perpetual pattern of marriage interaction between two people. They may live out their lives in an atmosphere of constant fighting, or they may finally reach a saturation point at which they are so emotionally divorced from one another that legal divorce follows as an inevitable consequence.

Not all aggression is unproductive. Sometimes the aggressive behavior of one partner or the other can force his mate into accommodation. Indeed, sometimes aggressive behavior by one partner is really what is desired by the other. There are many men and women who deliberately goad their mates into aggression. Nor is all aggression violent. In many relationships there is "passive aggression," in which one partner is deliberately obstructionist or negative or tries to manipulate the other by tears and martyr-playing.

Many marriages combine all three types of adjustment: accommodation, alteration, and aggression. There are also other marriages in which the partners change their ways of relating as they mature and move through the family-life cycle. For example, some partners who at first accommodate wind up in aggression and hostility. But there are also some in which the partners learn and grow as they go along and move from immature aggressive patterns in early marriage to acceptance and alteration as they grow older.

ANTICIPATING ADJUSTMENTS

Just as it is important to anticipate the initial adjustments if a marriage is to get off to a smooth start, it is also necessary to anticipate the continuing changes in the relationship that will necessitate readjustment. Each new stage of the family-life cycle can best be adjusted to if the partners can anticipate its coming and the changes that will be required of them. Unhappily it is often easier to see in retrospect what should have been done than to look forward in one's own relationship to what might *be* done. Consider the following case:

> CASE 29
> "All Don thinks about is business and golf," Elsie told the counselor. "We've been married for twenty-six years now, and for the last twenty-five he hasn't paid much attention to me at all. He stays away from home many nights when I know that he could be here if he wanted to. He says his business needs him, but I think that they could get along without him. He spends every minute thinking about the business anyway, though, so he might as well be there. And when he isn't down at the plant he's out playing golf. Almost every weekend he's down on the golf course or in the clubhouse with the other men.

"I thought growing older together was going to be different. Now the children are all gone; the last boy went off to college last year. We have three sons, and he should be very proud of them. I think he is, although you'd never hear it from him. He hasn't paid much attention to them since the day the first one was born.

"I *need* more attention from him now. When the boys left home I suddenly felt deserted and very alone. I turned to him for some of the companionship we had when we were first married. But he doesn't seem to want to be bothered with me now. He only takes me some place when I force him to. He doesn't really fight with me about it; sometimes I wish he would. He just gets that resigned, hangdog look on his face.

"This isn't the way I thought it would be after the children were gone. When I thought about it at all, I just had a sort of nebulous picture of gay contentment, traveling to Europe and to the Orient, and doing all those things I've always wanted to do. Now I'm just terribly lonely and unhappy. I wish you would tell him that he should pay more attention to me."

Don did indeed seem to be resigned when he talked to the counselor. "Yes," he said, "I know that Elsie is my responsibility, that I have an obligation to take care of her. I always will. But we don't have anything in common any more. I don't enjoy talking with her, because we don't have anything to talk about. Not even the boys, now.

"I remember what happened, and it wasn't exactly the way Elsie said. When the first boy was born, she suddenly turned completely away from me. She gave all her attention to the child; at least that's the way it seemed to me. Sure I was jealous. I knew I was jealous even then. But what could I do about it? After all, he was my son and I wanted him to have his mother's love. So I just kind of pushed it down inside myself and tried to get more interested in my business. That wasn't hard, because I had a lot of problems and a great opportunity to make something out of it. Now my firm is one of the best in its field, and it's that way because I give it a lot of time. I handle every problem personally, and I know all the men and all their troubles. Sure, I like to play a little golf on the weekends. I'm one of the best they've got at the country club now.

"It isn't as if I didn't take Elsie out once in a while. Every time she asks me to go someplace I take her. And it isn't as if there were any other women. I know a lot of fellows play around but I'm proud of the fact that I've been faithful. After all, I've got enough trouble with the one woman I've got. Why should I want any more? I'll provide a home for Elsie for the rest of her life. What more should she want?"

The marriages that continue to grow richer are the ones in which both mates anticipate the changed needs of their partners. It isn't easy, but, with some advance planning, it can be done.

16

IMPEDIMENTS TO MARITAL ADJUSTMENT

If you could ask all the unhappy marriage partners in the world why they can't adjust to each other, you would probably get as many specific answers as there are marriages. But as you began to inquire more deeply, you might find certain basic patterns of maladjustment cropping up continuously. For example, the "who's right?" argument is one of the classic impediments to good adjustment. Quarreling and passive resistance are two others. There are more, including manipulation, blackmail, brainwashing, and the rest of the patterned behaviors that have been described as the "games people play." Since these behaviors can so drastically affect a marriage relationship, it is important to take a close look at them.

"WHO'S RIGHT?"

Of all the impediments to adjustment, no one is more insidious or more universal than the "who's right?" argument. The problem itself begins in the childhood family of the two marriage partners. In their early interactions with their brothers and sisters, most partners learned that if there was a dispute or disagreement of any kind, a weary, but usually impartial, parent would step in, decide who was right, reward the righteous one by giving him the object of dispute, and admonish the loser. In the typical American home, a girl wins these disputes as often as her brother, in fact, sometimes even more often.

With this pattern of settling differences deeply entrenched in the emotional system of both marriage partners, it is hardly surprising that they should perpetuate the "who's right?" habit after marriage, even though it is no longer effective problem-solving behavior. After marriage there is no impartial parent to step in and render judgment and so force the loser to do the bidding of the winner. Some partners don't give up trying, though. Either they undertake to act as judge and jury themselves, or they try to find a marriage counselor, either amateur or professional. Often, a marriage counselor will be asked by a husband or a wife to tell the other spouse that he is wrong and then to force that other spouse to change his way of behaving.

The fact that there is no impartial judge in a marriage is only a part of the futility of the "who's right?" argument. Even if each couple had its own private judge, he would find it impossible to render a decision about most questions. In an intimate relationship, many of the points of argument revolve around subjective evaluations. Stuart Chase cites an interesting technique used by Captain James Saunders, U.S.N., in teaching principles of agreement to a class of graduate students. Captain Saunders gives each class member a small piece of white paper and asks them to chew it and then report the taste—sweet, sour, bitter, or salty. A variety of opinions result, followed by much argument and confusion. Actually, the paper is the same for all, but the sensation of taste varies with the individual genetic differences of the students. Until this chemical reaction is explained, the students continue to argue about whose taste discrimination is right and whose is wrong.[1]

Given the differential conditioning of today's typical young husband and wife, it is no more surprising that there are unsolvable "who's right?" differences between them than that there were taste differencs among Captain Saunders' students.

There is an even bigger reason why the "who's right?" question is so futile: *It doesn't do any good to know the answer.* First of all, most marriage partners won't agree that they are wrong. A troubled wife once showed a marriage counselor a carefully typed list of reasons why she was right. "I am going to show this to my husband to prove that I am right," she said. Would this have solved her problem? Would her husband have accepted her logic? Probably not. More likely, it would only have stimulated him to think of more reasons why she was wrong. Moreover, it would have made him even more defensive and less willing to find a solution to the problem.

There is another reason why proving who's right is sometimes self-defeating. Suppose a wife were able to prove that her husband was wrong; would she really want to? Would it make her love him more because she had defeated him, or might she be a little distressed and unhappy because she had won? There are many situations in which wives or husbands cannot afford to lose, but there may be even more in which they cannot afford to win. Many husbands and wives haven't yet learned this. In most marriages, it is far better to protect the other partner's integrity by allowing him to save face and back off gracefully than it is to score an empty victory by proving you can win the "who's right?" argument.

Obviously, there are times when, if one partner has some special information, it does help to present the facts. For example, if a wife knows for sure that one should turn left instead of right in order to get to the Jones' house, she has an obligation to say so, even if a "who's right?" victory then becomes inevitable.

Usually, though, things are not so clear cut. A young woman complained to the counselor about her prospective mother-in-law. The mother-in-law, after inviting the young woman to her home for a weekend, demonstrated by making the situation socially impossible that she did not really want the girl to marry

---

[1] Stuart Chase, *Roads to Agreement*, New York, Harper & Row, 1951, pp. 8–9.

her son. She didn't introduce the prospective daughter-in-law to any of her friends, she embarrassed her by asking about complicated recipes, and she asked pointed questions about the girl's family and background. As the young woman recounted these things to the counselor, she said, "That just isn't right, is it?" after each one. Would it have done any good for the counselor to agree with her? Would this have helped her to solve her problem? No, indeed. Telling the young woman that she was right would only have aggravated the situation. Ultimately, the only solution to the problem lies in the young woman finding a way to relate to her prospective mother-in-law. A person can be completely right and still not get what he wants. Consider the following case:

CASE 30

"Tony just won't stand up to his mother, even when he knows that I'm right," Josephine said. "His mother is a foreigner, and she barely speaks English. She demands an awful lot of her son and I get sick of the way he waits on her. His father died when he was young, and ever since that time Tony's mother has made Tony her husband as well as her son. He has to run over there all the time. We have to spend every holiday with her. Never with *my* folks, always with her. It just isn't right.

"When we were first married, I tried very hard to be nice to her; ask Tony, he'll tell you. But she treated me like dirt. One time I bought paint for the kitchen floor and hired a man to put it on. I thought I had done a wonderful thing. But I didn't take the wax off first, and so the paint never dried. I felt bad about it when I found out and even worse when Tony had to spend hours scraping it off. But my feelings of being ashamed for having made the mistake turned to real anger when his mother told me how stupid I was in front of Tony. She went on and on about how I wasted Tony's money. The worst thing about it was that Tony didn't take my side. He just stood there and didn't say anything. That wasn't right.

"Tony's a good husband and father in almost every respect. He works hard and he's getting ahead. But he gives in to his mother all the time. What good is there in having a man if he won't stand up for you? My father shouted and hollered a lot, and I hated it. I was very glad when I got a man like Tony who was gentle and quiet. But now I see that my father yelled just as much when he was for you as when he was against you. I guess I want a man like that too.

"Last week I let Tony persuade me that maybe I was wrong after all and that I should be nicer to his mother. I have guilt feelings every once in a while because I really want to be a good daughter-in-law. So I invited his mother over to dinner. I worked all day long in the kitchen, and I had a beautiful dinner fixed. And then do you know what she did? At the last minute she called up and said that she had decided not to come. She was going to stay at Tony's brother's house for dinner. When Tony said, 'Yes, Mother, that'll be O.K.' I just blew up. I grabbed the phone and screamed at her. After all, right is right."

When the counselor asked Josephine what she expected to accomplish in counseling, her answer could almost have been predicted. "I want you to tell him that he should take my side when I'm right. When I'm wrong, that's something else again, but when I'm right I want him to admit it and to show it."

"And then after you've demonstrated that you are right, do you want your husband to give in to you?" asked the counselor. "Well," Josephine's voice trailed off. "I don't want him to give in *all* the time, but what is right is right and he should take my side."

Tony was the picture of dejection when he talked to the counselor. "I don't know what I'm going to do," he said. "I know that my mother isn't very reasonable about some things. She's from the old country and she expects a lot. Most of the time she's tried very hard to be nice to Josephine, but Josephine has a real chip on her shoulder. I know it's because Josephine thinks that I love my mother more than I love her. But that just isn't so. But Mother is all alone, and I've been responsible for her ever since I was a little kid. I can't just yell at her, like Josephine would like me to do.

"And besides, regardless of what Josephine says, Mother isn't always wrong. Take the other night, for example, when she didn't show up after Josephine had worked all day long trying to fix a dinner. It was because my brother's wife got sick at the last minute and Mother was trying to help take care of his kids. But do you suppose Josephine would listen to that? Oh, no, she just grabbed the phone and started screaming. Actually, I almost think Jo was delighted when my mother didn't show up for dinner the other night because it proved she was right in the first place.

"There are a lot of things that Josephine does that aren't right. She takes our boy over to her mother's house all the time, but when my mother wants to see him, Josephine tells her that she won't leave him there alone because she says my mother doesn't know anything about kids and is too excitable.

"If Jo would only stop worrying about being right all the time, especially with my mother, she could make my mother very happy, and then we'd all have some peace."

The ultimate goal of deciding who's right in marriage is to use the verdict to force the partner into changing his way of behaving. But even if it is possible to determine who's right, it is usually impossible to force the other partner to behave or conform. Curiously, another goal of deciding who is right is that of rewinning love. The marriage counselor frequently sees a spouse who says, in effect, "I am right, so you should tell him that he must love me." Sometimes it isn't as obvious as this; sometimes it is merely that the individual wants the other person to give him more affection because he is right. Yet being right is often the poorest way to redevelop a love relationship. Love is given as a reward for meeting needs, not as a reward for being right.

QUARRELING

Some level of quarreling, from placid discussion to violent shouting, is common in marriage. In fact, it is so common that a large number of marriage partners find it difficult to believe that there are some marriage partners who never quarrel at all and still others for whom even disagreement is a rare occurrence.

Most marriage partners who disagree frequently sooner or later settle into some pattern of resolving their differences. The posture that each chooses in this pattern is often either completely dictated by, or at least influenced by, the pattern of handling conflict that was present in the respective partner's childhood home.

People who never quarrel in marriage are usually from homes where quarreling was not acceptable. For them, settling a disagreement without hostility —and in some cases without even disagreeing—is an important value, both intellectually and emotionally. Often these people are repelled and frightened by any kind of deliberate aggressive hostility or even unintentionally aggressive behavior on the part of their mate. Such marriage partners were often the kind of children who hid behind the sofa when they saw any hostility displayed.

On the other hand, there are marriage partners who grew up in a rough-

and-tumble home where they learned how to quarrel magnificently and to make up joyously. Such people find it difficult to understand that there are others who get no enjoyment from quarreling. When a partner from a rough-and-tumble background marries someone like himself, they may get along swimmingly, fighting all the time. Neither one of them would be happy if it were any other way. If, however, a person from such a background marries one of the nonhostile people, there is liable to be trauma in both directions. The damage to the rough-and-tumble person, while it may be less evident at the time, is no less real than the damage to the quiet nondisagreer.

CASE 31

"He won't fight with me," Marion complained to the counselor. "He just withdraws and sulks, or sometimes he goes off by himself. He won't say what he really thinks, and it drives me wild. He is always trying to placate me, almost to the point of being patronizing. I need someone who will show me that he really loves me by expressing some emotion once a while. But I can do anything—including staying out all night—and all he does is try to smooth things over.

"There are times when I deliberately do such provoking things that he should take me over his his knee and spank me, but he won't. I know it must eat him up inside, but it isn't fair to me either. I need some reaction from him sometimes. If I'd done some of the things at my childhood home that I've done since we've been married, my father would have beaten me up. But at least I would have known that he cared. I don't understand this man I married at all."

"I don't know what do with Marion," Milton told the counselor. "I try to do everything I can to make her happy but she seems to want to pick fights. You're a marriage counselor; you know that fighting should be avoided. My mother and father didn't ever raise their voices to one another, and it makes me very uncomfortable to see a woman all excited and wrought up the way she gets. Sometimes I almost get the feeling that she actually wants me to hit her. But I'm not going to hit a woman, ever. I wasn't brought up that way. I don't want to fight, I want to be happy."

Present-day Americans have been told by many authorities that it is good to vent resentments and hostilities, lest they fester and cause even greater difficulty later on. This, together with the social changes that have brought more independence and social equality to women, has stimulated more and more open conflict between marriage partners.

Ventilation rather than suppression *is* a good thing in many cases, provided the ventilator (1) takes responsibility for his actions, and (2) receives emotional relief rather than emotional satisfaction from ventilation. Emotional relief tends to reduce tension and so lessens the possibility of a need for further ventilation. Emotional *satisfaction* derived from saying hostile things, however, leads to further hostile expression and ultimately perpetuates the difficulties between the partners rather than ameliorating them. This distinction is often overlooked by those who advocate the indiscriminate release of hostile thoughts.

Students of behavior have identified two types of quarreling: constructive quarreling and destuctive quarreling. As Duvall and Hill have suggested, constructive quarrels are those that leave the marriage stronger than it was before the quarrel started by redefining the situation that caused the conflict. Constructive quarreling is directed toward the issue and leads to a better understanding of the issue; it emphasizes problems and conditions rather than personalities as the object of constructive quarreling. Since these quarrels tend to reduce tension, they should become fewer and less violent as the marriage progresses and as patterns of adjusting are more firmly established. In constructive quarreling, people (1) spell out exactly what they don't like and how they want things changed, (2) stick to the point and avoid side issues, (3) stay with it until they thrash things out, (4) go on to some simple next step for improvement, (5) don't let the matter fester, (6) attack their problem rather than each other, (7) avoid dragging in relatives, and (8) give each other cues as the tension lets up.[2]

Destructive quarrels leave fewer assets in the relationship than were present before. Destructive quarrels are directed at the personality of the marriage partner and are intended to destroy the illusions and fictions by which he has lived. Destructive quarreling is belittling and punishing, and it leads to alienation and further quarreling.

Basically, most fights are a product of the individuals and not a product of the situation. People can fight about almost anything if they want to. They can avoid conflict, even in the face of severe provocation, if they have learned how to resolve their differences without fighting and if they have a mutual desire to do so.

It is, of course, easier to see how the one who is starting the fights can change the climate by holding his tongue than to see how the person who is constantly being attacked can avoid defending himself. Most marriage partners insist that they don't start quarrels but merely maintain their own integrity by defending themselves. But do they really have to be so defensive? Will they really lose their self-respect or the respect of their marriage partner if they let him get away with an insult made in a moment of petulance?

I have had some success in reducing hostility by suggesting to marriage partners who feel they are constantly being attacked by their mates that they treat their partners *clinically*. For example, if you were an attendant in the seriously disturbed ward at a mental hospital and a patient came up to you waving his arms and swearing violently, you would probably be able to accept his hostility, calm him down, turn him around, and steer him back to his room. This would be treating him clinically, and it would be possible because you didn't let yourself become emotionally upset by whatever he shouted at you. You understood that this represented *his* problem at the moment, and that you only happened to be the person who was closest at hand.

This approach is often a successful way of handling a specific hostility situation in marriage, even though the angry partner is only temporarily upset and in full contact with reality. However, since such clinical treatment is hardly conducive to the development of love, regardless of how successful it might be in specific therapeutic situations, it is not recommended as a permanent pattern of marriage interaction. But sometimes it does help people to help themselves over a rough spot in marriage. Occasionally it does more than that. Some of the help that can be given through marriage counseling when only one partner is available is based on the premise that, if one partner changes his way of behaving toward the other, the other cannot over the long run possibly maintain his way of behaving toward the first partner. A person who has been violent may change his way of behaving when his partner makes some change in his way of reacting. People do learn and people do change, even though guaranteeing such change is very risky.

[2] Evelyn Duvall and Reuben Hill, *Being Married*, Boston, Heath, 1960, pp. 285–286.

DISGUISED FEELINGS
AND PASSIVE RESISTANCE

There is another type of destructive behavior that is as damaging to marriage as destructive quarreling. This is described by the psychologist as passive-aggressive behavior. It is characterized by noncooperation, negativism, quiet hostility, "underenthusiasm," and other signs of subtle resistance. Since approval and acceptance are vitally important to any love relationship, withholding approval and acceptance can be as devastating as aggressive shouting and yelling—if not more so.

These various forms of passive resistance are often generated by unresolved resentments that have been allowed to fester quietly. As was pointed out earlier, it is now generally believed that it is better to "get things out" in most instances, even if some present hurt is involved, than to repress hostile feelings and risk greater hurt in the long run. Again, however, this is useful only when emotional release from tension rather than sadistic satisfaction is gained by expressing the hostile thoughts.

There are some people who have been so damaged by their childhood relationships that they are unable to express normal emotional feelings in normal ways. Some of these people develop devices and stratagems for obtaining the emotional satisfaction or release they need without ever having to admit to themselves that they were the ones who started the hostility. The least harmful of these devices is accusing the partner of "not loving me anymore," in the hope that the partner will have to change his behavior in order to prove that he does. The more harmful stratagems include playing the role of martyr and various forms of emotional blackmail and manipulation.

Martyrdom is also one means of seeking control in the marriage. Traditionally, the martyr role has been more often ascribed to the wife, but in recent times more husbands, deprived of the authority, have been seeking to control by overt or disguised martyrdom. This technique is based on the assumption that the other person will feel sorry for the martyr and, hopefully, change his way of behaving. Even if his partner doesn't change, the martyr gets the emotional satisfaction of feeling abused. Sometimes the martyr can win either or both ways. In fact, martyrdom (often initially learned from a parent) tends to be so effective and satisfying that it is one of the most easily conditioned patterns of marital manipulation. In its milder forms, it may be tolerated over a long period by a mate who is highly motivated to cater to the needs and desires of his partner. But because it is so satisfying to certain personality types, it tends to become self-enlarging, and ultimately it can reach a point at which it becomes intolerable, even to long-suffering mates.

> ### CASE 32
> "Dan spends all day Sunday either sleeping or watching television," Mona complained to the counselor. "He never takes us out anywhere. I work all week long waiting for him to come home, and then he just lies around like a lump. Why can't he be like other husbands who take their families out nice places over the weeknds?
>
> "I try to do everything I can to be a good wife. I spend every waking minute trying to keep the house cleaned up, watching over the children. I've even taken in dressmaking to help out. All I ask in return is that Dan love and be together with us like a family on Sundays. Is this too much to ask?"

Dan told a different story. "I could hardly believe what was happening at first," Dan told the counselor. "I'd offer to take her places, and she'd never want to go. She always had too much to do. She was a terrible perfectionist about the house. On top of that, she began to take in dressmaking—'to help out,' she said. We were getting by all right before she did that, but somehow she just seemed to be compelled to take on more, even though it meant staying up longer hours to do it. And then she would tell me how tired she was and how she couldn't go out.

"I got sick of asking her to go out on Sundays. She was always very sweet and self-sacrificing about just having too much to do, and she would urge me to either nap or amuse myself. So I got in the habit of watching television and snoozing. Mind you, she encouraged me to do it! Then she began to complain bitterly to the neighbors about what a bum I was and how I abused her. I tell you, I couldn't believe it the first time I heard her say it, but now she says it to me, too. She seems to get a lot of satisfaction out of feeling abused. Sure it makes me feel like a heel, but what can I do about it? She still won't go out, even if I ask her."

The case of Mona and Dan has some similarities to the "If It Weren't for You" game in *Games People Play*.[3] In this typical game, the wife complains that her husband has so restricted her social life that she has never learned to dance. Later on, when her husband permits her to take dancing classes, she discovers that she has a morbid fear of dance floors and abandons the project. Although she may not have been aware of it, she had picked a domineering husband so that she could complain that she could do all sorts of things "if it weren't for him." Actually, of course, her husband was helping her by forbidding her to do those things that she was afraid of and by preventing her from even becoming aware of her fears.

But there is more to it than that. His directiveness and prohibitions, along with her complaining, frequently led to quarrels that seriously impaired their sex life. These quarrels aroused his feelings of guilt, which he assuaged by bringing her gifts that might otherwise not have been forthcoming. Since they had little in common except their household worries and their children, these quarrels stood out as important events and were emotionally satisfying. Moreover, they allowed her to prove to herself one thing that she had always believed: that men were mean and tyrannical.

Berne insists that the solution to the "if it weren't for you" game is permissiveness. As long as the husband is prohibitive, Berne says, the game can proceed. If instead of saying "Don't you dare!" he says "Go ahead!" the underlying phobias of the wife are unmasked, and she can no longer castigate him.[4]

BLACKMAILING
AND BRAINWASHING

Not long after some marriages begin, one partner or the other finds that he can manipulate his mate by using subtle pressure techniques—very much like blackmail and brainwashing. All sorts of coercion, both subtle and obvious, both gentle and arm-twisting, are used in marriage. The wife who says, "If you want to have a nice party for your sister, dear, you'll have to help clean up the house," and the husband who says, "We could buy your mother a decent

[3] Eric Berne, *Games People Play*, New York, Grove, 1964, p. 50.
[4] *Ibid.*, p. 53.

Mother's Day gift if only you'd take back that silly-looking hat," are practicing fairly common forms of marital blackmail. But the wife who threatens to withhold sex and the husband who threatens to withhold money are practicing more crippling forms of legalized extortion. So are the wife who threatens divorce, knowing that she will be awarded the children, and the husband who reminds his wife that she had to marry him.

Like all threats, extended blackmail can lead to brainwashing, the technique of making certain behavior of the mate so painful that he foregoes it rather than accept the punishment that it provokes from his mate. Typical punishments are little unpleasantnesses rather than grandiose threats. Tears, sulking, and refusal to communicate can be enough, when repeated over and over again, to condition a mate to concede. As Jessie Bernard has pointed out, before long the anticipation of the punishment is enough to make the mate compliant.[5]

OTHER MANIPULATIVE TYPES AND TECHNIQUES

The forms of manipulating people are legion. Everett Shostrom, who believes that nearly all people some of the time, and some people nearly all of the time, manipulate other people with whom they have either business or personal transactions, has compiled a roster of "types of manipulatiors." His eight types are as follows:

1. The *Dictator* exaggerates his strength. He dominates, orders, quotes authorities, and does anything that will control his victims. Variations of the Dictator are the Mother Superiors, Father Superiors, the Rank Pullers, the Boss, the Junior Gods.
2. The *Weakling* is usually the Dictator's victim, the polar opposite. The Weakling develops great skill in coping with the Dictator. He exaggerates his sensitivity. He forgets, doesn't hear, is passively silent. Variations of the Weakling are the Worrier, the "Stupid-Like-a-Fox," the Giver-Upper, the Confused, the Withdrawer.
3. The *Calculator* exaggerates his control. He deceives, lies, and constantly tries to outwit and control other people. Variations of the Calculator are the High-Pressure Salesman, the Seducer, the Poker Player, the Con Artist, the Blackmailer, the Intellectualizer.
4. The *Clinging Vine* is the polar opposite of the Calculator. He exaggerates his dependency. He is the person who wants to be led, fooled, taken care of. He lets others do his work for him. Variations of the Clinging Vine are the Parasite, the Crier, the Perpetual Child, the Hypochondriac, the Attention Demander, the Helpless One.
5. The *Bully* exaggerates his aggression, cruelty, and unkindness. He controls by implied threats of some kind. He is the Humiliator, the Hater, the Tough Guy, the Threatener. The female variation is the Bitch or Nagger.
6. The *Nice Guy* exaggerates his caring, love, and kills with kindness. In one sense, he is much harder to cope with than the Bully. You can't fight a Nice Guy! Curiously, in any conflict with the Bully, Nice Guy almost always wins! Variations of the Nice Guy are the Pleaser, the Nonviolent One, the Nonoffender, the Noninvolved One, the Virtuous One, the Never-Ask-for-What-You-Want-One, the Organization Man.

[5] Jessie S. Bernard, "The Adjustment of Married Mates," in Harold T. Christensen, ed., *Handbook of Marriage and the Family*, Chicago, Rand McNally, 1964, p. 693.

7. The *Judge* exaggerates his criticalness. He distrusts everybody and is blameful, resentful, slow to forgive. Variations of the Judge are the Know-It-All, the Blamer, the Deacon, the Resentment Collector, the Shoulder, the Shamer, the Comparer, the Vindicator, the Convictor.
8. The *Protector* is the opposite of the Judge. He exaggerates his support and is nonjudgmental to a fault. He spoils others, is over-sympathetic, and refuses to allow those he protects to stand up and grow up for themselves. Instead of caring for his own needs, he cares only for others' needs. Variations of the Protector are the Mother Hen, the Defender, the Embarrassed-for-Others, the Fearful-for-Others, the Sufferer-for-Others, the Martyr, the Helper, the Unselfish One.[6]

It is often very difficult for new marriage partners (or any two young people in love) to believe that they would manipulate each other. They may remember that they manipulated their brothers and sisters and fathers and mothers, but the possibility that they would ever manipulate their mate or future mate is almost unthinkable, especially at the beginning.

The change from acceptor to manipulator in marriage does not happen all at once. As in the case of George and Lila in Chapter 15, most young people idealize and completely accept each other at the time of their marriage. They are filled with joy, the quiver of sex eagerness, and the anticipation of playing house together. But soon, one or the other begins to recognize that his mate is not without fault. No matter which partner gets the insight first, the other is bound to feel the subtle changes in his partner's attitude toward him. Then a reaction takes place.

Let's say it's the woman who first perceives that her new husband is neither omnipotent nor omniscient. He loses his temper, leaves his dirty socks on the floor, has an aversion for large family gatherings. She doesn't get hostile or begin to manipulate him at the moment of her realization, but her *attitude* toward him changes, and consequently her way of behaving toward him changes, perhaps unconsciously and perhaps only slightly. But he senses the change and so changes his way of behaving toward her in order to protect his ego. Then she has to change her way, he has to change his, and, in the end, they wind up in the marriage counselor's office, a hostile and manipulating couple.

Obviously, not all marriages follow this same pattern. John Cuber and Peggy Harroff, in their study of a sample of Americans who had been married ten years and who considered their marriages satisfactory and likely to continue, concluded that there were five distinct "configurations" of interaction: (1) *Conflict-habituated,* (2) *Devitalized,* (3) *Passive–Congenial,* (4) *Vital,* and (5) *Total.*[7]

The Conflict-habituated partners had almost continuous verbal conflict with each other. Efforts were often made to keep the conflict concealed from friends, relatives, and children, but this was seldom successful over long periods. In relationships with other people, many of these same partners were not hostile or argumentative; it was chiefly in the marriage that conflict had become habituated.

The Devitalized partners had marriages in which they had lost the close sharing identification and deep feeling that they had had at the outset. Cuber and Harroff noted that this devitalization often began to be felt when the

[6] From p. 36 of *Man, The Manipulator,* by Everett L. Shostrom. Copyright © 1967 by Abingdon Press.
[7] John F. Cuber and Peggy B. Harroff, *The Significant Americans,* New York, Appleton-Century-Crofts, 1965, p. 64.

partners became parents for the first time. Their interaction was characterized by resignation and apathy and rather dogged determination to accept whatever modest gratification they could obtain under the circumstances and to turn to other facets of their lives for their basic fulfillments.

The Passive–Congenial partners resembled the devitalized partners except that their relationship had never been really vital, even during the courtship, and therefore they did not have the feeling of disillusionment or regret that the devitalized couple had over the *loss* of closeness. Typically, these people asserted that they did not really want to be close, and they doubted that other "mature" people did either.

In the Vital marriages, the man and woman deeply invested their total personalities in one another. They empathized with each other. They spent a great deal of time together, but this was not necessarily what made their marriage vital. Cuber and Harroff felt it was more their desire and their need and the successful expression of acceptance that formed the vital bond between them. They were usually able to adjust easily and well to each other.

Those couples in the Total marriage configuration had all the strengths in their marriage that those in the Vital configuration did. In addition, the psychologic investment of each mate in the other more nearly encompassed the total needs and fulfillments of each of the mates. Cuber and Harroff believe that this kind of marriage is rare but that it does exist, despite the fact that such a relationship might be utterly incomprehensible to the people in the Passive–Congenial or Devitalized configurations.

Cuber has suggested in another paper that it is important to recognize that people in all five of these configurations are minimally satisfied with them. Once a relationship is established, it tends to endure in that form over a long period:

> Couples become adjusted rather early to some one of these patterns of gratification, defend it, and don't take readily to changes in it. There are, of course, exceptions; sometimes they are the "unequally yoked" and such people are the ones who may want a second chance or who are suffering one way or another. This minority suffers, however, not because the mode itself doesn't work, but only because it doesn't work for them. It manifestly works for many, many others.[8]

CHANGING THE
ADJUSTMENT PATTERNS

Is there no hope, then, that people who have difficulty in adjusting can improve their adjustment? Certainly over a long period people change. The personality of a twenty-year-old is not necessarily the personality that the same individual may have at forty. The problem is in controlling the direction of that change so that the individual's life becomes more successful and more self-enriching rather than less so.

It isn't easy to change or to help people change constructively. Cuber points out that to suggest that the Conflict-habituated couple "talk it over" is simply to continue an already pointless procedure. Moreover, the common sug-

[8] John F. Cuber, "Three Prerequisite Considerations to Diagnosis and Treatment in Marriage Counseling," in Richard H. Klemer, ed., *Counseling in Marital and Sexual Problems: A Physician's Handbook,* Baltimore, Williams & Wilkins, 1965, pp. 57–59.

gestion that the partners spend more time together and involve themselves more deeply with each other can actually worsen the situation for the Passive–Congenial and the Devitalized, who in their own intuitive way have already made the important discovery that the way for them to live with a minimum of inconvenience and frustration is to avoid the spouse as much as they possibly can while still carrying out their other life needs. Nor, says Cuber, is it necessary to tell the Devitalized to "act their age" or to "be mature"—they already have been pulling this off with remarkable adroitness. Sexual advice that might be appropriate for a Vital couple—who almost never need it anyway—would be almost impossible for the Passive–Congenial to understand, much less carry out. An attempt to do so would likely be seriously disruptive.[9]

In general, however, there are two ways of improving marriage relationships, and they are inextricably interrelated. One is to get the marriage partners who have been focusing on the negative aspects of their relationship to begin to reemphasize what is positive in their relationship. A wife who has been complaining that her husband is always late for dinner is looking at the negative side of the fact that her husband is working very hard for her and the children. By just switching her own emotional focus, the same behavior becomes a family strength rather than a family problem.

It is this kind of reevaluation that can help partners to move back toward the complete acceptance they had at the beginning of marriage. As one partner begins to recapture some of the enthusiastic joy he used to have in just being with the other, the other will gradually allow himself to let down his own built-up ego defenses and begin to be more positively appreciative himself. For some people, a step-by-step upward rebuilding of their relationship can make it even better than it was in the beginning. For others, the best that can be said is that it will be better than it is now.

The second thing that can be done to help those with adjustment problems is to help them to improve their communication. Communication is the *only* way to understanding. Although there is some controversy over whether understanding one's mate really improves a marriage relationship, there is every reason to believe that understanding is a necessary first step to acceptance, which *does* improve marriage relationships. In the communication-understanding-acceptance progression, it is necessary to start by improving the ability of the partners to communicate with each other. That is the subject of the next chapter.

[9] *Ibid.*, pp. 58, 59.

17

COMMUNICATION

Almost every bride thinks she can communicate beautifully with her new husband. Usually he thinks so, too. In their own little courting world, they have been talking easily about parties, friends, automobiles, and maybe even sex and Greek philosophy. Ordinarily, though, while they may not have been aware of it, they have been avoiding each other's tender spots. This has been easy to do, because so far they haven't faced any very deep relationships problems. The little difficulties they have had up till now were usually solved easily and seemed to increase the glowingly beautiful relationship between them.

Yet this same bride and groom may shortly find that they really cannot communicate with each other: that they really cannot talk about deep, intimate personal problems without resentment and hostilities.

Why not?

The answer to that question is presently not as easy to find as it might appear. Scholarly interest in communication dates back to Aristotle. This interest became intense among social psychologists, language pathologists, psychotherapists, and philosophers in the 1960s. But their promising abundance of individual theoretical formulations and research findings about the process of communication often lacked integration and synthesis, common definitions, or basic agreement of the fine points. As Dean Barnlund pointed out in 1968 in his comprehensive *Interpersonal Communication: Survey and Studies,* "The quantity and diversity of research combine to obscure what is known and what is not."[1]

However, by recombining selected parts of recent theoretical and re-

[1] Dean C. Barnlund, *Interpersonal Communication: Survey and Studies,* Boston, Houghton Mifflin, 1968, p. 12. For the interested student, Barnlund's book is an excellent survey of some of the important research literature in the several disciplines concerned with communication theory.

search conclusions with some very specific observations of marital interaction, it seems possible to postulate some tenable answers to such practical questions as that "why not" about husband–wife communication. It has been my persisting observation in marriage counseling that marital communication tends to fail because of a *lack of ability,* a *lack of desire,* a *lack of security,* a *lack of selectivity*—or sometimes because of all of these put together. Since adequate communication is so important to adjustment, it is appropriate to look at each of these factors individually.

ABILITY TO COMMUNICATE

In the past, there *may* have been some mates whose communication was less than perfect because they literally didn't know the meaning of some of the words their partners used. Today, however, denotative meanings of words cause very little—if any—communication trouble in marriage. Most people in our society are regularly exposed to the mass deprovincialization of modern television. If words are the problem, it is their *connotative* values rather than their denotative meanings that cause the difficulty. Connotation implies emotion and conditioned reaction. If, for example, the word "yellow" is mentioned in a mixed audience, almost all the women in the group will get a pleasant feeling. They will remember a party dress or a waving field of daffodils or something else that has delightful meaning for them. But what about the men? Most of the men in the group will probably get an unpleasant sensation and an association (either conscious or unconscious) with some earlier challenge to their masculinity. After hearing the same word, one person will be pleased and the other upset.

These connotation difficulties in communication are greatly magnified in such areas as sex and death, where most of the words are circumscribed by taboos. Some people have queasy feelings inside whenever *any* sex words are mentioned. Others react only to the words and symbols that they were taught were "bad." Many parents are unable to talk to their children about sex because their hands shake so badly at the mere mention of some of the words that all that they are able to communicate is nervous confusion rather than factual information and attitudes.

Failure to communicate because of different word connotations is not uncommon. But communication more often fails because of one's inability to communicate genuine attitudes and meanings—with or without words. In fact, words are sometimes unimportant. It is possible to say "I hate you" so lovingly that the person addressed recognizes almost at once that this is not an expression of hostility but rather one of tenderness. On the other hand, as many longtime husbands and wives know, it is possible to say "I love you" in such a flat monotone that it expresses nothing.

There are many other illustrations of the sometime superfluity of words. Young lovers make up their own words of endearment, especially in such emotionally sensitive areas as sex, where childhood inhibitions form barriers against using the scientifically correct terms. When this private language better permits the individuals to express their real feelings, it is an important aid to communication.

Some of the best communication takes place without the use of words at all. A gentle touch can be more meaningful than a thousand words. A look or a movement can communicate an indescribable feeling. Important ideas can be made explicit by a gesture. Emotions can be set on fire by a single glance.

But in all communication, whether by word, touch, gesture, or glance, there is a need not only for the communicator to project meaning and feeling; there is also a need for the receptor to perceive and accept that meaning and those feelings. Good communication depends upon the ability of the receptor to understand the *intent* of the communicator. It requires the skill to sense feelings by inference and to hear meanings rather than just words. Theodor Reik has called this "listening with the third ear."[2]

An example of the need for this kind of feeling inference is when the hostess, carrying a cake, comes in to her assembled guests and loudly exclaims, "This is the worst cake I ever baked!" Obviously, she doesn't want anyone to agree with her. She is deliberately using words directly contradictory to her meaning. Similarly, in many of the most significant relationships of marriage, people will say things they don't mean. "I guess we had better not make love tonight; it might disturb the children," may be a deliberate effort on the part of the wife to be assured by her husband that he *will* make love to her and it will *not* disturb the children.

Sensing what people mean from what they say can often be a very difficult task. Consider the following case.

CASE 33

"I see now what I should have seen last night," Myra told the counselor. "But it's too late. It's just three weeks ago since Tod was told by the doctor that he had Hodgkins disease and probably has less than a year to live. Last night he sat up crying in the bed. I was still half asleep when I asked him what was wrong. 'Oh, my darling,' he said, 'I'm so worried about what will happen to you and the children after I'm gone!' I just didn't think, I guess, because I said to him too quickly, 'Oh, we'll be all right, darling. I can take care of the children!' It didn't seem to help him a bit. Now that I have thought it over, I know why."

Sometimes people will go to extreme lengths to avoid saying what they really mean. In psychology, the concept of "reaction-formation" is used to describe a situation in which a person elaborately denies his own true feelings and openly disavows that which he really wants. For example, a young woman who has a deep desire for sexual activity might be a vociferous prude who crusades against sex in any form.

Other illustrations of disguised meanings are legion. Feelings of severe insecurity are commonly masked behind dogmatic assertions. Feelings of hostility sometimes appear as thoughtfulness and consideration. For example, a wife might say to her child, "Don't bother your father. He is too busy to play with you." To know whether this was a considerate wife or a deliberately hostile woman bent on downgrading the father in the child's eyes, one would have to know much more about the relationships involved.

There are times when communication can be expedited by ignoring the words that the communicator uses. The wife who says, "You always think you're perfect, don't you!" doesn't really want to talk about her husband's perfection.

[2] Theodor Reik, *Listening with the Third Ear*, New York, Farrar, Straus, 1954, p. 144.

Rather, she may wish to let him know that he is not really as good as he thinks he is, or she may want him to deny that he is perfect in order that she may win her point. In either event, the argument has nothing to do with whether he really is or is not perfect. The experienced husband will see this and not be trapped into a defensive rebuttal.

Another important aspect of the ability to communicate is sensitivity, the ability to anticipate reaction. This involves an empathetic ability to prejudge how the feeling that the communicator wishes to express will affect the receptor. Consider the following case.

CASE 34

Sally and Tom were a young couple struggling to complete their educations after marriage. They lived in a small apartment in a nice neighborhood largely populated by older, more established couples, all of whom had washing machines, which Sally and Tom couldn't afford. One day, Sally, an eager-to-please young bride who was intent upon showing that she could keep her husband's clothes clean just like any other wife in the community, washed clothes by hand all day long. When Tom came home that night she said to him, "Oh, darling, I'm so tired. I spent all day washing!" She was shocked and startled when Tom shouted, "Well, damn it, I'll buy you a washing machine in the morning." Sally dissolved in tears. "I can't understand what he got so upset about," she said later.

DESIRE TO COMMUNICATE

It is almost axiomatic that, in order for there to be good communication between two people, those two people must want to communicate. As we pointed out in the last section, this involves something more than just wanting to talk. (A man who came into my office for marriage counseling once said to me, "I don't know how you can say we aren't communicating, Doctor; people hear us all over the block.") Genuine communication involves not only the desire to project feelings but the desire to understand and accept feelings as well.

Not everyone has an equal desire to talk, let alone to listen. Mirra Komarovsky found in her study of working-class marriages that dialogue is frequently cut short by distinterest or grudging response. She said:

> If it is one of the functions of modern marriage to share one's hurts, worries and dreams with another person—a large number of couples fail to find such fulfillments. Moreover, breaks in the marriage dialogue are not a matter of preference. They result from abortive attempts at communication; attempts frustrated by what is felt to be the mate's lack of interest or an unsatisfactory response.[3]

Some people seem to be "naturally" quiet. Actually, though, the inclination to talk or to be silent is probably conditioned into the individual as the result of both his cultural and subcultural experiences. Men are said to be less talkative than women. Girls tend to talk more and to start talking earlier than boys.[4] (There are, of course, individual differences.) Many boys soon learn that

[3] Mirra Komarovsky, *Blue Collar Marriage*, New York, Random House, 1964, p. 140.
[4] Anne Anastasi, *Differential Psychology*, 3rd ed., New York, Macmillan, 1958, pp. 472–473.

they come out second best in a verbal contest with a girl. The stereotype of talkative woman is the subject of many jokes:

John: My father just died.
Joe: Did he have any last words?
John: No, Mother was with him right to the end.

Son: I just got a part in the school play.
Father: What part?
Son: I play the young husband.
Father: Too bad; maybe they'll give you a speaking part next time.

Not only do girls talk more than boys, they also talk about different things. Girls are encouraged to talk about people and relationships between people—including their own—and boys are encouraged to talk about mechanical and spatial things. This differential conditioning causes several problems in later life. For one, girls expect their companions—and later their husbands—to be interested in talking about the social relationships to the same degree they are. Men often aren't interested. Moreover, the differential conditioning often creates a situation in which the two sexes have little in common to talk about. It is said that when women are together, they talk about things that interest women, like men and clothes and other women. When men are together they talk about things that interest men, like sports and business and women. But when men and women are together, they talk about things that don't interest either one of them.

Modern urban adult men and women often work in different worlds, so they have very little knowledge of the people and procedures in the world in which their mates live. In rural America, a wife knew exactly what her husband's problems were and what steps had to be taken if the borers got into the corn, because she had grown up on a farm. Today many fewer wives have such a conversational understanding of their husband's business difficulties.

There is another problem created by the differing roles of men and women after marriage that tends to dampen the desire for communication. Men more often talk to other adults during their working hours. As a matter of fact, sometimes the men talk all day long for their living. By the very nature of things, they want to be quiet when they get home. On the other hand, their wives, who have been shut up in the house by themselves or with small children all day, are eager for talk and socializing in the evening.

CASE 35

"He never talks to me," Carolyn told the counselor. "I spend all day long doing routine things around the house and just waiting for him to come home so I will have someone to talk to. But all he wants to do is sit in that darn old easy chair of his and bury his nose in the paper. When he finishes the paper, he watches television, and then he goes to bed. Big deal! It isn't as if I didn't try to make conversation. I tell him about all the little things that happen around the house. I even try to read the newspapers and magazines so that I can keep up with him. I try to ask him about his work, but he just sighs and says nothing ever happens at his office. Sometimes I get so bored with him that I even try to start a fight for some excitement, but that's even worse. He won't fight at all. He just withdraws. Even when we have some real problem, he won't talk about it. He just sits there like a lump and lets me say anything I want to. Then he gets up and goes to bed. It's maddening! Believe me, it wasn't like that before we were married. He used to talk a lot about interesting things. But now he doesn't care anymore. I guess he has just stopped loving me."

Lester was indeed a quiet man. He even had very little to say to the counselor. At length he did say, "Yes, I guess I don't talk enough. People around my childhood home were very quiet when I was growing up. But it isn't altogether that. Sometimes when I come home she greets me at the door and says, 'What did you do all day?' I would like to tell her. But in the instant before I get it out, I think to myself, 'How am I going to tell her?' Take today, for example. Brown, the plant manager, had an argument in my office with Jones, the production manager, over the placement of the semiconductors in the flyback circuit. Actually, Brown was mad at Jones because Jones overestimated the production figures and made Brown look bad with the big boys back in the home office. That was really what the fight was about—not the design. Anyway, before we were through, we had Green, the foreman, and Kelly, the straw boss in the office, in on it, and it turned out that Kelly's daughter had beat out Jones' daughter in some beauty contest. You can imagine what that did to the discussion. Anyway, that was just the beginning of what happened at the plant today.

"My wife doesn't know anything about any of these things. She doesn't even know what a semiconductor is. When I thought of all the explanation it would take to even make any reasonable sense out of what had happened at the office today, I just said, 'Oh nothing, it was just sort of a routine day,' and let it go at that.

"Then she was mad. Heck, I work hard all day. I think I'm entitled to come home and sit down and have a chance to read the paper in peace. If she wants to talk, she can have the neighborhood ladies in for coffee in the morning. I just want to be let alone to make the money for this family so that I'll have something to leave her and the kids. She apparently doesn't understand that. She's always nagging me to talk, talk, talk.

"Sure, I may have talked more before we were married. I did my best to entertain her when we were courting. She did her best to catch me, too. She used to make me cherry tarts and bring them over to the dormitory when I was in college. She hasn't made a cherry tart in ten years. I don't yell about that. I know that she has enough to do being a good mother. But I want her to get off my back too."

Among those couples who do talk to each other, how much do they talk and about what? Feldman, in his study of 862 couples from all age groups, found that the average amount of time spent in conversation was about one-and-a-half hours a day. Their most frequently discussed topics were their work and current events (about once a day) and children and friends (several times a week). Sports, religion, and sex were talked about several times a month.[5] Curiously, most husbands claimed that these conversations were about topics such as homemaking and religion that were of more interest to their wives than to themselves, and most wives thought that more time was spent in talking about topics that interested the husbands, such as news and sports. Feldman found that the wife more often initiated conversations about most of the topics, including her work, the children's problems and accomplishments, her parents, and her personal feelings, whereas the husband's fewer initiations were primarily about his work, money management, and his parents. Interestingly, Feldman adds that the husband's parents are not his exclusive domain as much as the wife's parents are hers.

It is a fairly common observation that, as marriages continue over the

[5] Harold Feldman, *Development of the Husband-Wife Relationship*, Cornell University, research report to National Institute of Mental Health, Grant M-2931, 1965, p. 13.

years, some partners appear to talk less and less to each other. Komarovsky verified this in her study.[6] One suggested explanation is that "marital telepathy" sets in after a couple has been married a while. For example, a conversation between a husband and wife who have been married five years may go something like this:

"Did you get the ———?" asks the husband.

"Yes," replies the wife.

"Good," the husband says.

Only that husband and that wife understand that she picked up the shirts he will need for the trip to the branch office tomorrow.

If this kind of "telepathy" occurs, it is because people who live closely together learn to anticipate each other's thoughts through familiarity and "reduced cues" unintelligible to others. It has been suggested that marital telepathy gets worse as the marriage progresses. After fifteen years, a long dinner conversation may be:

"Did you ———?" begins the husband.

"Yes," replies the wife.

Statistical proof that marital telepathy is universal or even common does not exist. One sociologist has cited two studies involving a total of 340 couples (out of approximately 45,000,000 couples in the United States) as reason enough for labeling as "myth" such folk beliefs as marital telepathy and the notion that husbands and wives become more alike by living together. These studies, he says, have failed to demonstrate that couples either understand one another better the longer they are married, or anticipate one another's responses and communicate profound meanings to one another via glances, shrugs, and grunts. Such ideas as marital telepathy are, he suggests, "a part of the myth that marriages get better and better, that couples come to love one another 'more deeply' and that they 'mean more to one another' over the years."[7]

It is probably good that there are those with scientific skepticism to keep some of the older folklore in proper balance. It should be pointed out, however, that, although there is no proof that marital telepathy is a tendency in *all* marriages, it most certainly does exist in some. Again, this appears to be a case of "some do, some don't," which doesn't commend itself to the social theorist.

SECURITY IN COMMUNICATION

Security may well be the most important aspect of communication. One who is made anxious for any reason will not—and probably cannot—communicate as he should. Feelings and daydreams are fragile things. Once ridiculed or punished for them, their owner may never again reveal them. This is not to say that he will stop having feelings or daydreams; he will merely stop talking about them.

The tragedy about this is that spoiling communication by ridiculing or threatening often represents some basic insecurity on the part of the spoiler. It is almost axiomatic that a person who is disturbed because of what someone else has said is disturbed because he feels threatened. For example, a young

[6] Komarovsky, *op. cit.*, p. 145.
[7] J. Richard Udry, *The Social Context of Marriage*, Philadelphia, Lippincott, 1966, pp. 274–275.

husband might come home and tell his wife his idea for an invention. Because his wife's father was constantly spending the family savings on one harebrained scheme after another, the wife immediately jumps to the conclusion that her husband is about to raid their savings account. Before he is half through with his excited description of his idea, she is already planning how she can best talk him out of it. Often there is a very simple way: to laugh at him. So she laughs. Her ridicule has no relation to the merits of the idea. It is, rather, her reaction to a threat that, ironically, might never have come to fruition. She achieves her objective, for he never mentions his idea (or perhaps any other) again, but she loses something infinitely greater: his willingness and ability to talk with her about things that are important to him. Consider the following case.

CASE 36

"All he ever talks about is the women at his office," Gladys told the counselor. "He pays more attention to them than he does to me. A little secretary can have some trouble with her boyfriend and he listens for hours and then wants to come home and tell me all about it. He never listens to me; he just buries his nose in the television. Other husbands talk to their wives about their work and about politics and business, but not Harold."

"I try to talk to her," Harold said. "At least I used to. But she's so sensitive that everything I say she takes personally. It's especially bad since she got older and put on a little weight. Now everytime I mention something that concerns any other woman, she has a fit. I work in an insurance office, and we employ a lot of young women. Most of the things that happen to me during the day have something to do with the problems that the girls get into. I've found that it's easier to keep quiet at home and let her yell about my not talking than to talk to her and have a dramatic scene about the affairs she imagines I'm having with the office girls."

It is probable that fear—many kinds of fear—is the greatest inhibitor of communication. Some fears keep people from talking with their partners. Other fears cause them to reject that which their partners say to them. The fear of offending or of being offended is especially limiting for people who are new in a situation and who gingerly (perhaps too gingerly) limit their self-expression. The result, as we saw in Chapter 6 is often to make the other person believe that he is unwanted or distrusted. He, in turn, "clams up," and the relationship becomes stilted and mutually insecure.

Another fear that inhibits communication is the fear of starting an argument. Many people will not express their genuine feelings lest they provoke their partner. Then there is the fear that talking will give the other person license to talk also. Many husbands have told me quite candidly that they would rather not tell their wives their troubles because that would give their wives the right to talk on indefinitely about their troubles. Some people don't communicate for fear of getting an unfavorable reply. They have learned that it is better to assume they are right than to be told they are wrong. And there are still others who have a fear of saying something wrong or improper.

The greatest fear of all is probably the fear that a genuine expression of personal feeling will lose one's partner's love. Many children are conditioned early to remain silent by parents who punish them for expressing unconventional thoughts. A child, perhaps in all innocence, will come home and tell his mother something he has seen or done. The horrified mother may then punish the child either by physical means or by a withdrawal of her approval. The mother's reaction will not curtail or even forestall the child from seeing or doing such things again. It merely means that he will no longer communicate his experiences to his mother.

This provides a serious dilemma both for parents and for marriage mates. Can a parent or a marriage partner permit the errant child or spouse to tell what he has done and then let him "get away with it," simply because he told the truth or expressed an honest feeling? No one has ever found the ideal solution to this problem, but there are many who feel that permitting the expression of genuine feelings is more important in the long run to personality growth, to relationship improvement, and to learning than any hoped-for behavior change that punishment or withdrawal of approval might bring about.

Security in communication has two aspects. The first is, as we have seen, the responsibilty of the listener to provide the permissive acceptance that will encourage the speaker to express openly, and with as little fear as possible, his genuine thoughts and beliefs. But there is another aspect of security in communication. It is up to the listener to provide the secure climate in which the speaker can speak, but it is up to the speaker to provide security for the listener as well. A speaker has no license to alarm or ridicule or create anxiety in the listener under the pretext of permissive communication or freedom of expression. The problem of honesty of expression versus sensitivity to the feelings of the other is neatly illustrated by the case of Eunice and Larry.

CASE 37
Eunice had been living in a sorority house for four years before she married Larry. She loved hats, and, before her marriage, every time she bought a new hat she delightedly wore it back to the sorority house, whereupon all the girls would cluster around her and tell her how cute they thought it was and how it looked "just right" on her. Shortly after she married Larry, she bought a new hat and wore it home. At first, she was disappointed because her young husband didn't notice the hat. So she called his attention to it by asking, "How do you like my hat, dear?" He gave it a passing glance and replied candidly, "It stinks!" Eunice began to cry.

What should Larry have said? What should Eunice have done? Isn't marriage supposed to allow for the complete expression of one's feelings? How much absolute candor can there be in communication?

LACK OF SELECTIVITY

Good selectivity in communication involves selecting the right time, the right place, the right things to be talked about, and the right way of talking about them.

Almost every child who has grown up in a family learns that it is better not to approach fathers for favors until after they have had their dinners. Yet, it is amazing how often husbands and wives ignore this simple rule. Some wives (and some husbands of working wives) greet their tired mates as they arrive home with a recital of the day's problems and a long roster of complaints. "The furnace broke down, the television quit, your broker phoned to say he needed more margin to cover your stock losses, I told Junior you would punish him as

soon as you got home, and my mother is coming to spend a month with us."
is a classic greeting hardly calculated to get an evening's communication off to
a glowing start. Some spouses appear so eager to announce this kind of bad
news that it is hard to escape the conclusion that they may be obtaining a sort
of sadistic satisfaction from the relationship damage they are causing.

The person who wants to develop adequate communication must choose
the time wisely. He must also carefully pick the place. A crowded bus is no
place for a discussion of sexual-incompatibility problems.

But there are other aspects of selectivity, too. Choosing what to talk
about and how to talk about it are also vital to good communication.

Most people would be inclined to say that two people—especially husband and wife—should be able to talk about anything that suits the fancy of
either one of them. In practice, though, it really can't work out that way. There
are role responsibilities to be considered. A husband cannot talk constantly
about his anxieties if he is to be the leader that his wife and family expect him
to be, since the leader must be able to project calm, secure guidance. A wife
and mother cannot announce that she doesn't like one of her children or that
she likes one more than another every time such an idea enters her mind if
she is to be the loving wife and mother her family expects and needs.

As a matter of common decency, husbands and wives must occasionally
forego talking about something that would be aggravating to their mates. There
is no point in a wife mentioning how much her former boyfriend knew about
automobiles when her husband is sweating over a stalled car. Nor is there any
point in a husband going on about his mother's baked beans just when his
wife is about to serve her latest effort to their guests. Avoiding such sensitive
areas can hardly be called repression in any "bad" psychological sense. It is
more properly defined as good judgment.

J. Richard Udry, who wonders if a lack of communication leads to disturbed marriages or vice versa, believes that *selective* communication is a key
to the successful marriage. He says:

> There are some thoughts and desires and attitudes which are destructive when
> communicated. A wife who continues to communicate to her husband her dis-
> appointment that he is not more affectionate when she has seen he is incapable
> of changing, a husband who continues to communicate to his wife his desire
> that she get more pleasure out of her motherhood when he knows that this is
> not her nature—these are communicative acts which are not going to do any-
> thing but hurt the relationship.[8]

Jo Coudert cites the following interesting case involving selectivity. A
woman who had been happily married for some years didn't think that she and
her husband would ever have a problem about money. One turned up unex-
pectedly, though, when she mentioned that she was thinking of renting loft
space and moving her hobby of weaving out of the house. She would buy a
larger loom, she thought, and, if all went well, she might try to sell her fabrics.
"What are you going to use for money?" her husband asked. This question
surprised her, since he was a generous, easy-going man who was proud of her
accomplishment as a weaver and had never made the slightest objection to
giving her money for looms and materials. When she pointed this out, he said
that he considered a hobby one thing, a business another, and that he had no
intention of paying the rent on a loft. Over a period of several weeks both

[8] *Ibid.*, p. 280.

tried to make their points of view clear, but they got nowhere. Moreover, other minor hurts and disappointments each had experienced at one time or another began to creep into the argument, and soon the disagreement touched all areas of their married life. A sense of estrangement grew. They did not continue to quarrel, but their relationship was clouded. This so distressed them both that they finally agreed to accept each other's blind spot on the subject and abandon it forever.[9]

In commenting on this case the author said,

All writings I have seen on marriage have as a central piece of advice: Talk things over. Air your problems. Do not let grievances fester. Work out compromises. But the longer I live and the more I observe, the less sure am I that this is good advice. These two people had the luck and the wit to recognize an impasse and the generosity and mutual respect to be able, finally, to leave it alone, but much was said in the weeks before they let it lie there that, while not permanently damaging, would have been better left unsaid; and nothing was said in those weeks that had not essentially been said in the first five minutes when she stated her wish and he stated his opposition. This is almost invariably the case: the first five minutes are meaningful and necessary so that each knows the other's position, but everything after that is repetition and elaboration and, ultimately, the dragging in of irrelevancies. One person does not change another's mind with words; only the person himself can change his mind, and he is not likely to do so under the pressure of argument. He may give up or give in, but he honestly reverses his stand only when, in silence and within himself, he plays back the arguments on both sides and truly listens to them. The arguments have not been heard during the discussion designed to elucidate them, for this is when the person is expending all his brainpower on defending his own position; he hears what is said to him only as points to be rebutted; and the more he is compelled to buttress his position, the more he convinces himself that it is the right one.[10]

After further discussion, Coudert suggested a possible happy ending to the case of the loom in the loft: "You can count on the argument to continue turning over in the other's mind just as pervasively as it does in yours and to come up again. The husband of the weaver, if his wife had dropped the discussion, is certain to ask within the week: 'Have you given up your idea of a loft?' And the wife can easily reply, 'No, I'd like very much to do it, but I haven't come up with a way of managing it. What do you think?' The husband might restate his objections, but if he has had second thoughts, his wife has given him a graceful opening in which to offer his help.[11]

"HOW" IS AS IMPORTANT AS "WHAT"

The matter of what one talks about is inextricably intertwined with how one talks about it. Earlier it was pointed out that a person can talk about almost anything he wishes and still keep the other person interested, provided he is enthusiastic and confident. His own enthusiasm and confidence will ordinarily

[9] Jo Coudert, Advice from a Failure, New York, Stein and Day, 1965, p. 189.
[10] Copyright © 1965 by Jo Coudert. From pp. 189–190 of the book Advice from a Failure. Reprinted with permission of Stein and Day/Publishers, and Hodder and Stoughton.
[11] Ibid., p. 192.

be contagious to the point where the other person will not only become interested but will also feel secure in talking about it himself.

The qualification *enthusiastic* is important, for it implies a pleasantness of tone and manner. There are a great many people who talk about things that interest them (their physical ailments, for instance) but who talk about them in a complaining manner. This can be deadly and depressing both inside and outside of marriage. It is a number one communication destroyer.

Not long ago, *McCall's* magazine published a round-table discussion with eleven wives who felt that their communication with their husbands left something to be desired. Says the report of this seminar:

> The lives most women live, all seem to agree, are hardly fascinating, and they really don't blame their husbands for not taking an enthusiastic interest in how they spend their days. Said one woman, "Even *I* don't want to talk about babies, about cooking. But then, what else is new? What else do I have to tell him?"
>
> The women, therefore, tend to feel torn between a desire to spare their husbands women-talk and the need to assert the fact that they, too, are living a life, performing a needed, often difficult, function. Said the mother of four relatively young children, "If I didn't tell him, he'd think the house cleans itself and even though I do tell him, he can't understand what I do with all my time."[12]

If these women themselves can't be enthusiastic about what they do, how can they expect their husbands to be? A few of the women in the seminar seemed to resent the fact that their husbands expected attention to be paid to their dull recounting of workday routines. Said one: "He'll say, 'Well, we got an order from so-and-so today—we've got a big backlog, so we'll probably be busy for a month,' and I'm supposed to say, 'Isn't that swell? Tell me more.' "

Only one woman in the group claimed to be truly fascinated by the news that her husband brought home from the world outside. When someone asked what her husband did, she answered, "He's a private detective." Most of the women agreed that this was a different story. Who wouldn't listen enthralled to a private detective? But who, they asked, would want to listen to a dentist?

Actually, there are many interesting dentists and many boring detectives. The manner in which one tells his story is as important as what he tells—if not more so.

A common observation, backed up by validated psychological studies, is that men tend to report events differently from the way women do. Men more often tend to report on status and material relationships, whereas women tend to report on feelings and social relationships. This creates problems. The *McCall's* group of wives claimed that their husbands' descriptions of a neighborhood event are impersonal, unspeculative, and lacking prognosis and moral judgment—devoid, in fact, of life. The women complained that such stories were hardly worth hearing. One said, "I absolutely won't let him get on the phone anymore with any of our friends. Because anything they say to him is lost—gone for all of time. I never get to hear it. He may be on the phone for half an hour. Then when he gets off, and I want to know what it was all about, he gives me the essence of it in fifteen seconds. But I don't want the essence, I want the whole novel-length story."

On the other hand, many husbands are completely exasperated by the roundabout route that women take to get to the point of a story. Husbands

[12] Sam Blum, "Why Men Don't Listen or Talk to Their Wives," *McCall's*, **93** (February, 1966), 130.

sometimes concede that they long ago stopped listening to their wives (even though they recognize their obligation to do so) because their stories are so long and rambling. Men find it very difficult to follow or be interested in a tale that starts out with a promise of exploring specific problems and wanders on and on into all the ramifications and seemingly unrelated aspects.

The major complaint of many married women is that, as time goes on, their husbands no longer seem to be able to express their personal feelings. As a result, the wives are afflicted with the kind of nagging insecurity and resentfulness that comes from not being sure exactly where they stand.

As one woman in the *McCall's* panel put it, "During our courtship what we used to talk about—all the time—was our feelings. We'd talk about what was making us unhappy or was worrying us. We were both just masses of feelings. I saw marriage as an endless investigation of the way we felt about each other, toward everything. I was really that naive. And that, in my book, is what women are complaining about when they say that their husbands are silent. They don't express their feelings. You know, I'm convinced he still loves me but I can't tell you why I think it. I certainly don't hear it from him."

Many of the women I saw in marriage counseling also complained because their husbands wouldn't talk about feelings. And yet many of the husbands pointed out that they were tired of talking about feelings because this, in one way or another, only got them into trouble. Either their wives rejected their feelings as being inadequate, or else they accepted them and used them against the husbands later. ("Five years ago *you* were the one who thought my sister was so great.") Moreover, most men are conditioned by the business and social world in which they move to repress their feelings, not expose them. It is interesting to note, however, that despite these handicaps, there was a tendency of the husbands in Feldman's study to feel that they, *not* their wives, more often initiated conversations about personal feelings.[13]

In summary, it might be said that the essence of good selectivity and therefore good communication is a mutually satisfying way of expressing positive, love-enriching feelings. For some men—and some women—the richness of marriage comes from the quiet calm of the home that their mate provides for them. For these people, talking is not an essential ingredient of happiness. But for others, the pleasure of the marriage relationship comes from the partner's ability to transmit verbally the kind of ego reassurance that makes life worthwhile. This is the need-meeting that creates and nurtures love. In this, as in every other aspect of married life, the successful couples are those who can move toward each other until their needs for both communication and quiet reflection can synchronize.

It should be pointed out again that communication can lead to understanding and understanding to acceptance and acceptance to adjustment in marriage. It may not necessarily follow that those who communicate at any level and in any way have the best marriages. But certainly those who won't or can't communicate at all have little opportunity to either improve or even maintain their relationships.

There is considerable evidence that, in our American culture, most couples actually increase their communication and so their understanding by talking with one another. Feldman reports that the more time couples spend in talking with each other, the more likely they are to report a high level of marital satis-

[13] Feldman, *op. cit.*, p. 108.

faction. He adds that couples who spend more time in talking with each other receive reinforcement for even further conversations, for they feel closer to each other after the discussions.[14]

Those who would have good communication need to improve both their desire and ability to listen, to listen carefully and objectively, and to listen to their partner's meaning as well as to his words. In much of what ordinarily would pass for communication, one partner or the other is so busy rehearsing what he is going to say next, or so preoccupied with other problems, that he really can't listen to what his mate says—either in words or meaning.

Another thing that is needed for good communication is improved selectivity. It is important not only to choose carefully what one says but also to select carefully from the other person's verbalizations as well. In both of these ways, one can provide security: first, by not threatening the other person, and second, by understanding that usually not everything he says is intended just as it was said. Nor does it necessarily reflect his feelings for all time. No one has ever said this better than Dinah Maria Mulock Craik, an English novelist of the nineteenth century:

> Oh, the comfort, the inexpressible comfort of feeling safe with a person, having neither to weigh thoughts nor measure words, but pouring them all right out, just as they are, chaff and grain together; certain that a faithful hand will take and sift them, keep what is worth keeping, and then with the breath of kindness, blow the rest away.

[14] *Ibid.*, p. 29.

18

SEXUAL ADJUSTMENT IN MARRIAGE: MALE SEXUAL CONDITIONING

Many troubled married couples are convinced that sex is the one and only problem they have in marriage. Often, though, while these people have been blaming their sexual relationship, other problems have contributed to their difficulties. A good sexual adjustment usually, but not always, requires a fairly good total marriage relationship.

But there are some marriages in which sex is *the* cause of a marriage difficulty. Some partners have difficulty in synchronizing their sexual desires—or lack of them—with those of their partners. Sometimes it takes weeks, months, or even years to achieve sexual harmony. Some people never do. Some people start out well and then, as hostilities and resentments set in, lose their sexual empathy completely.

In sex, as in most other areas of male–female relationships today, things have changed. Formerly, when the marriage partners said they had a sexual problem, it was fairly predictable that the problem was the seemingly outrageous sexual appetite of the husband. Now, however, some women are disappointed that their husbands don't desire them as often as our current emphasis on sexuality has led them to expect. Moreover, although some men are—as in all ages past—disturbed because their wives aren't interested in meeting their sexual needs, there are many other men today who blame themselves because their wives don't achieve a climax at every intercourse experience, as some modern sexual authorities have led them to believe all women should. To understand sexual problems in modern marriage, it is necessary to go a long way back.

THE ROOTS OF THE PROBLEM

Unbelievable though it may seem today, throughout history there have been both religious and civil laws regulating sexual intercourse between married partners. Various authorities from Zoroaster (about 600 B.C.) to our colonial American forefathers sought to establish either the frequency or the appropriate times for sexual relations in marriage. In those periods when there were no religious taboos or strict laws, there were often inviolable customs that made one kind or frequency of lovemaking right and all others wrong.

Most contemporary Americans would undoubtedly view the enforced regulation of sexual activity (after marriage, at least) as intolerably restrictive. Yet many of these same Americans are confused about what are the appropriate expectations for postmarital sexual behavior. Although the laws and customs of the bygone eras robbed the individual of some freedom of choice, at least they provided him with some basis for knowing what the standard expectations of sexual responsibility in marriage should be.

Today, people with widely differing religious, national, educational, social, and cultural backgrounds are marrying each other, and their expectations and attitudes about what is "right" in sex behavior often differ considerably. Many partners cannot help but have their sexual expectations frustrated and their sexual sensibilities disturbed. In this confusion over expectations, many young husbands and wives have rushed off to the bookstore for so-called "sex manuals." Unhappily, not everyone finds real help in these guidebooks. Sex manuals usually place a heavy emphasis on the techniques of lovemaking. Moreover, the manuals are often contradictory, because each presents the expectations and the attitudes of its author, and these have resulted from *his* background and *his* conditioning. Some of the recipes for lovemaking in the sex manuals are so "far out" as to be emotionally unacceptable to conservative people, and some are so old-fashioned as to be laughable to the ultra-sophisticated. Anyway, sexual techniques are usually better discovered than learned from a book. The spontaneity and pleasure of mutual discovery is a part of the richness of lovemaking.

Even those sex manuals that give medical descriptions of the sexual organs and statistics about what other people are doing sexually provide only a minimum of help. A sexual relationship is an intimately personal thing. Success or failure often depends upon the complex feelings of warmth that are uniquely created deep within each individual and then lovingly interchanged with his partner. Diagrams and statistics may bolster the argument of the more aggressive partner, but they rarely add richness to the sexual feelings between two people.

In the final analysis, an understanding acceptance of the other person's expectations and attitudes (and sometimes his confusions, too), combined with an ability to communicate more meaningfully about sex, are the primary factors in good sexual adjustment. To achieve such an adjustment, you must start by understanding why your partner behaves the way he does.

WHY DOES A MATE
BEHAVE THAT WAY?

Sexual behavior results from sexual expectations and sexual attitudes, which in turn arise from an individual's physical capacities, his childhood environment, his later experiences, and the subtle dynamics of the relationship he has with his sex partner. In any particular person, any one of these factors may be more important than in others.

Just how much effect the basic physical functioning of the body has on an adult's sex interest and sexual capacity is still open to serious question. With rare exceptions, all individuals are born with all the potentially excitable sexual equipment they need. There can be, of course, individual differences in the neurological capability for that sexual equipment to respond exquisitely, just as there are individual differences in the capacity to perform any feat involving precise physical control. Moreover, some people have more active thyroid glands and so are more active in all bodily functions. But physical differences among individuals probably account for only a small part of the differences in their sexual responses.

In the past, some investigators believed that the body's production of sex hormones might be the key to an individual's sex interest or lack of it. It can be demonstrated that, within limits, sex response may be modified by increasing the level of the *male* hormone in some males and in most females. (Both males and females normally produce low levels of the other sex's hormones.)

But again, this in itself does not appear to be a wholly satisfactory answer to why some people are responsive and others are cold. For even if hormones can perceptibly affect the frequency and intensity of sexual response in some people, they probably do not wholly account for the differences in sexual desire. Nor do hormones have any effect upon an individual's interest in any particular kind of sex activity. Nor do they even control his interest in getting sexual release with a person of the opposite sex rather than a person of his own sex. There is something more than physiology involved.

That something more is the psychological and social conditioning that the individual receives as he is growing up. Almost all adult sexual behavior—or lack of it—is dictated by the way the child was molded in his family and in his peer groups. It is this psychosocial conditioning that causes most of the difference in sexual expectations and attitudes not only among men and among women but also *between* men and women.

To really understand sexual behavior, it is necessary to look into some of the differences in the sex conditioning that is given to males and females, respectively, in our modern society.

MALE SEXUAL
CONDITIONING

Men are different from each other in a lot of ways. Some men differ from other men more than they differ from women. This is true not only in muscular strength and mechanical ability, but also in what they like and what they like to talk about. Most women grow up knowing this. But there is one area of male variability—sexual desire and sexual responsiveness—about which many women know very little. This causes a great deal of marriage misunderstanding. For some women, some men appear to have too much sex appetite; for others, not enough.

The sex conditioning of the typical American male is a complex and paradoxical process that involves infant training, mother influences, group pressures, social-class customs, romantic rhapsodies, dilemmas, contradictions, winked-at behaviors, moral exhortation, experimentation, pornography, biologic information, and intellectual conviction. These can be categorized into four major nonphysical influences that shape and reshape the developing sex consciousness and behavior of the typical middle-class American man: (1) infant love-response patterns, (2) early sex training, (3) sex-role identification, and (4) gang and man-group influence. There are, of course, also those differences occasioned by temperament, physical structure, and glandular output.

Infant Conditioning

A boy's affectional conditioning (and so, to some extent, his sexual conditioning) begins at birth. If he is cuddled, fondled, and loved, if affection and the demonstration of affection are intimately connected on every occasion with the pleasurable sensations of warmth and the satisfaction of biologic tensions, his so-called affectionate nature is more likely to develop. He is probably started on the way to becoming a normal, marriageable man.

But what if he is emotionally deprived or neglected? Harry and Margaret Harlow demonstrated conclusively that monkeys, deprived of a mother's cuddling, were permanently impaired in their ability to form effective relations with other monkeys. At maturity, few showed normal sex interest or mating behavior. The Harlows reported that case studies of children reared with indifferent mothers or nurses "show a frightening comparability."[1] In her study of 2,000 college students, Alice Thompson reported that men who were not now in love and who never had been in love tended to have come from childhood homes in which they had been deprived of affection.[2]

Not every man who is denied affection turns into a celibate recluse, of course. The human capacity to adjust is enormous. Some deprived men will be able to experience very normal love relationships. And there are some others who, because they were denied genuine affection in infancy, may spend the rest of their lives seeking it without surcease. They may wander from sex adventure to sex adventure, trying to satisfy their desperate need for affection with one sexual partner after another.

Early Sex Training

There are other early influences as important as affection, and some of these directly affect the developing sexual nature of the boy. His first sexual lesson may come from a horrified mother who is upset by his natural sensory curiosity and his penis handling. She can—and sometimes does—punish him for this so severely that it markedly affects his later sex life. It is difficult to be specific about this one thing, though, for often there are so many other possible causes for any later abnormality that few authorities are willing to say for sure what caused what.

The Freudian interpretation of the results of this early genital play is, however, quite clear. During masturbatory activity, the three-, four-, or five-year-old boy fantasies that he has an incestuous craving to possess his mother and tries to seduce her by proudly showing her his penis. This brings him into conflict, either real or imagined, with his father. The boy develops an intense fear that the bigger and stronger father will punish him by cutting off his

[1] Harry and Margaret Harlow, "Social Deprivation of Monkeys," Scientific American, **207** (November, 1962), 143.
[2] Alice Thompson, "An Experimental Approach to the Problem of Infatuation," paper presented at the annual meeting of the American Psychological Association, Washington, D.C., August, 1958.

genitals. This so-called castration anxiety, it is said, will cause sexual repression and later neurotic behavior.

Whether or not penis handling is a middle-class boy's first introduction to sex repression, it certainly will not be his last. By the time he is three or four years old, he knows that sex, like death and excretory functions, is circumscribed by taboos in our culture. He is carefully taught what sexual things he may not do, may not say, and may not even think, without guilt. The punishment for violating any one of these taboos is liable to be more severe than for other misbehaviors. Most middle-class parents, who were carefully sex-inhibited themselves, have deep-rooted emotional anxieties about childhood sexuality, regardless of how glibly they may talk about sex or sex education in adult groups. In a classic study of how American mothers socialize their children regarding sex, Robert Sears, Eleanor Maccoby, and Harry Levin, found that, when exposing their children to other living experiences, the mothers explained carefully and offered alternatives, but when it came to childhood sexual behavior, they offered no alternatives and hurried off the subject.[3]

The sexual conditioning given a boy from a conservative middle- or upper-class family by his parents is only the beginning. The ridicule of playmates given for a taboo violation are often far more effective reprimands than the embarrassed silences or the blushes of his parent. It may take much group reassurance or biologic urging in later years before he again mentions sexual thoughts or indulges in sexual play. Thus, long before a middle-class boy ever learns the real significance of genital stimulation—much less sexual intercourse—social attitudes about sexual behavior have been absorbed into his personality.

As the typical boy grows up, he probably will learn from his middle-class mother to make a romantic association between sexual activity and love. This notion, too, will find reinforcement among his middle-class age mates, for their mothers also promote the notion that kissing, hugging, and other sexually tinged acts that their children are permitted to see are the special prerogatives of those who are married or, at least in love. By the time most middle-class boys from even moderatly conservative homes approach adolescence, the sex-love relationship is ingrained in their emotions. For some boys, the very idea of sex activity with a woman they do not love is as dishonorable an act as betraying a friend.

The sexual conditioning of a boy from a lower-social-level home is liable to be considerably different from the middle-class boy's. This was a major conclusion of the Kinsey report in 1948, although the more recent study by Ira Reiss seems to add the important qualifications of "liberal" or "conservative" to any generalization about sexual behavior and social class.[4] (See page 142.)

Kinsey found that most lower-social-level males (as measured by education, father's occupation, and later-attained occupation) were far less sexually inhibited and far more familiar with all kinds of sexual behavior at a much earlier age than the boys from less-disadvantaged homes. Unbelievable as it may seem to middle-class adults, most lower-class boys had observed their parents and other people engaged in sexual intercourse not just once, but often. They were well aware of the techniques, functions, and pleasures of sexual activity at an age when middle-class boys had only a vague idea that there was such a

---

[3] Robert Sears, Eleanor Maccoby, and Harry Levin, *Patterns of Child Rearing,* New York: Harper & Row, 1957, p. 185.
[4] Alfred C. Kinsey, W. B. Pomeroy, and C. E. Martin, *Sexual Behavior in the Human Male,* Philadelphia, Saunders, 1948, pp. 327–393; and Ira L. Reiss, *The Social Context of Premarital Sexual Permissiveness,* New York, Holt, Rinehart and Winston, 1967, pp. 56–75.

thing as sexual intercourse. They came to regard sexual intercourse, both inside and outside of marriage, as normal and usual. Any substitute, such as masturbation or petting, was looked upon as perversion. Moreover, many lower-social-level parents, while condemning masturbation, advised their male children how to get sexual outlet through intercourse before marriage and what dangers to avoid.

The outside play group has its effect on the lower-social-level boys, too. But in his gangs, sex is discussed far more freely and with far less restraint than in the middle-class groups. The lower-class boy may learn to want to marry a virgin, but he also learns to take premarital sexual intercourse wherever he can get it.

Few of lower-social-level men in Kinsey's sample looked upon their intercourse experience as anything more than pure physical gratification. Far from loving their casual sex partners, these men very often had only contempt for them. Most regarded preliminary lovemaking and petting as a waste of time, if not a little abnormal. In this light, Kinsey's report which indicated that some lower-class males had had intercourse with several hundred or even a thousand or more girls before marriage, comes close to being at least conceivable.

Today, there may well be much less class distinction in the sexual behavior of men than there used to be, for the reasons outlined in Chapter 12, urbanization, economic prosperity, cross-cultural associations, freedom of women, mass media, and the "new morality" among them. But there are still some wide subcultural differences—especially in the early conditioning experiences—that often set the later patterns of social responsibility as well as sexual behavior.

Sex-Role Identification

The relative sexual aggressiveness of any particular male may be attributable more to his sex-role-identification conditioning than to his direct sex training. The process of male sex identification that produces the aggressive or the non-aggressive male begins very early. Since the mother is the first model readily available, it is probable that in most cases the boy first establishes a feminine identification, as Talcott Parsons and many others have pointed out.[5] But the boy soon learns that it would be absurd, indeed shameful, for him to grow up like a woman. As he approaches puberty he rejects the company of girls, lest he be termed "sissy," and adopts an almost compulsive masculinity. He learns in his competitive play with other boys to be very jealous of his masculine image, and to be very anxious about any threat to it. Since boys are supposed to be tough, he guards against any expression of tender emotion.

This anxiety over maintaining a masculine image is carried on into later life and sometimes has a special relationship to a particular male's sexual experience. There is considerable psychiatric evidence that it is the male who has doubts about his masculine desirability or about the adequacy of his sexual performance who goes to elaborate lengths to reassure himself by ultraaggressiveness or ultrapromiscuity.

Even the "normal" male is under considerable pressure to demonstrate his masculinity by sexual achievement. As Winston Ehrmann has put it, "Our culture, in innumerable ways, many of which are unrecognized, instills in the

[5] Talcott Parsons, "The Social Structure of the Family," in Ruth N. Anshen, ed., The Family: Its Function and Destiny, rev. ed., New York, Harper & Row, 1959, pp. 257–258.

male the all-important idea that eroticism is essential to maleness, and that it is the mark of a man both to make sexual advances and to have some reasonable expectation of success. . . ."[6]

The Male's Concept
of the Female Role

Much of a young man's later sexual aggressiveness depends upon his childhood conditioning concerning the female role. If, while he is growing up, he internalizes the assumption that a man is the virtual owner of women, and his every whim, sexual or other, is immediately to be satisfied, he will be a far different boy in a parked automobile than if he had been brought up to believe that women are coequal human beings. It is only temporarily surprising to learn that the boy with selfish, sex-demanding attitudes is often rewarded both with sex opportunities and with adulation from the women he dates. After all, most often the young women are brought up in homes with the same cultural background as the young men and are subject to some of the same attitudes and ideas. Aggressiveness in men is admired in our competitive society. Many girls feel that a boy is acting in his appropriate role when he is sex-demanding, and they like him better for this appropriateness.

Being rewarded for aggressiveness may begin very early in the boy's life—long before he has had any sexual experience. Parsons suggests that there is a strong tendency for boys' behavior, in contrast to what is expected of girls, to run "in antisocial if not directly destructive directions." He speculates that

> the mother secretly—usually unconsciously—admires such behavior and, particularly when it is combined with winning qualities in other respects, rewards it with her love; the bad boy therefore is enabled to have the best of both worlds. She frequently treats a "bad" son as her favorite, instead of a "sissy" brother who fulfills all her overt expectations much better.[7]

Clearly this doesn't happen in every case. Some boys, faced with mothers who say, "If you are a good boy, mother will love you," or mothers who overtly withdraw their affection when the boys misbehave, are emotionally conditioned to believe that this is the way things really will be. In this situation, as Urie Bronfenbrenner has suggested, some boys are made overanxious and overpassive by this love-withdrawing technique.[8]

If the young man who is conditioned to believe that his aggressiveness will be punished by the withdrawing of a loved one's affection is taught also that women are delicate flowers to be cherished and idolized, it is easily understandable that he may turn out to be wholly supplicative and timid in his lovemaking. Such men are so afraid of offending the woman they are with that her slightest implication of displeasure or pain is enough to cause them to retreat. They are hypersensitive to rejection. They not only need the mate's permission to make a sexual advance, they actually need her enthusiastic cooperation before they can bring themselves to have intercourse with her.

[6] Winston Ehrmann, *Premarital Dating Behavior,* New York, Holt, Rinehart and Winston, 1959, pp. 286–287.
[7] Parsons, *op. cit.,* p. 258.
[8] Urie Bronfenbrenner, "The Changing American Child—A Speculative Analysis," *Journal of Social Issues,* **27** (1961), 6–18.

In marriage counseling, it is common to find unhappy and mortified women who blame themselves for their husbands' failures in sexual intercourse, feeling that impotence results from their own lack of charm. Usually this is not so. Although there are many causes of impotence, in some instances the difficulty can be traced to the attitudes mothers inculcate in their sons. Sometimes, childhood conditioning has established a "madonna" image that results in the husband's overromanticized tenderness for his wife, so that he is unable to "defile" her. In other cases, young men have had their future sex lives blighted by an overdose of conditioned anxiety about what their partners think —to the point where the slightest rejection from a woman sends them into emotional panic.

Since most women are conditioned to expect and want some male sexual aggressiveness, with varying degrees of socialized restraint, few have the desire or capacity to pamper the emotional system of the more timid male. Consciously or unconsciously, they become somewhat contemptuous, a fact that noticeably increases the male partner's feelings of rejection. Once this sense of failure becomes internalized, it often appears without any further stimulus just when the time is appropriate for sexual action. This sets up a kind of neurologic confusion within the male that precludes erection or adequate sexual performance.

It has been speculated that some of the very women who neuterize their sons by implanting exaggerated notions in them of female delicacy and virtue are sometimes the very ones who, in their own secret sex lives, are consumed with passionate desires. The conditioning of their sons is another reaction formation—an effort to atone for the guilt they feel as a result of their own desires.

Of course, no one suggests that every mother who distorts the reality of sex in teaching her young son is doing so because of guilty projections. Often there are other motivations—a desire to keep the boy with her, a desire to have him enter the ministry or priesthood, or even a calculated hope that he will not be quite so demanding as his father.

It should be remembered that, although the sexual aggressiveness continuum for young males runs from extremely aggressive to extremely passive, in this, as in almost all other human attributes, there is a normal central tendency. Most middle-class men acquire enough security about their masculinity to live easily in today's tolerant society, so they can afford to adjust their sexual behavior to the more love-enriching level of mutual desire that successful sexual relationship requires. At the same time, relatively few middle-class men are so emasculated by the emotional needs of their mothers that they cannot be adequate sexual partners.

Male Influence

In the traditional father-dominated homes of previous eras, and in homes where Father spent a good deal of time with his sons, the father's influence on a boy's sexual conditioning was considerable. Sometimes, especially in the lower social levels, this influence took the form of a sly wink from Father that said "Don't believe everything you hear," or "You're only young once," which nullified the effect of Mother's carefully planned program of indoctrination. Often, though, in middle-class homes, the father either initiated the stern moral teaching himself, or at least, added his weight to enforce the mother's teachings. But in many urban homes where Father was away much of the time, Mother answered most of the questions and instilled most of the values. Many of the fathers of today's men really didn't have much idea what their children thought about sex or anything else.

Perhaps it was because they received so little of their early sex conditioning from their fathers that many of yesterday's middle-class adolescent boys had large readjustments to make when the sexual realities of modern society began to filter through to them, which brings us to the fourth major conditioning influence—the outside man-group.

In recent years, an increasing amount of information about reproduction and human biology has been dispensed in formal sex-education classes for boys as well as girls. But it is still true that most of a young man's practical sexual training comes informally from the older boys and the men he associates with. A study by Paul Gebhard and associates in 1965 confirmed the findings of earlier studies that a vast majority of young men (about 90 percent) receive most of their early knowledge about sexual behavior from peers, friends, or their own experiences.[9] Some boys learn by eavesdropping at the bowling alley or by whispered snatches at the bicycle shop; others learn from the boastful exaggerations of other boys in the locker room. In this way, the middle-class boy learns the prevailing male attitudes about sexual activities and the techniques of petting and seduction that lower-class boys have grown up knowing. Spicy information is freely volunteered in an enticingly dramatic way. All he has to do is listen.

One of the first things he learns is that much of what his mother may have taught him concerning sexual continence before marriage is just not so. He finds that most other men do have premarital sexual experience. He is free, of course, to reject this shocking news if his home indoctrination has been strong enough, and some men do, completely. But most of the studies, including those of Kinsey, Burgess and Wallin, and Ehrmann, agree that most men go on to have premarital sexual intercourse before they are old enough to vote. Moreover, the frequently cited Burgess and Wallin study of 580 married men indicated that of the approximately two-thirds of the men in the sample group who had had intercourse, less than 20 percent had intercourse *only* with the girl they later married.[10]

Even if they don't have actual intercourse, Kinsey's figures suggest that over 90 percent of all men will have had some petting experience by the time they reach the usual marriage age.[11]

Some young men take this new understanding of the sexual world right in stride. It bothers them no more than when they learned there was no Santa Claus. In fact, it provides an easy rationalization for their increasingly strong biologic urges. Soon they adopt some of the freer patterns of behaving and occasionally act as if they were trying to make up for lost time.

But there is often one major difference between these late-blooming middle-class Don Juans and lower-class men. Most of the middle-class young men who change their behavior are aware that they are doing something their parents wouldn't approve of. Although they may appear to revel in such sexual rebellion, they usually never adopt the completely uninbited and ruthless

[9] Paul H. Gebhard et al., *Sex Offenders*, New York, Harper & Row, 1965, p. 469.
[10] Ernest W. Burgess and Paul Wallin, *Engagement and Marriage*, Philadelphia, Lippincott, 1953, p. 330.
[11] Kinsey, *op. cit.*, p. 345.

attitudes of the men who were brought up to believe that premarital intercourse is absolutely normal and completely right.

It seems reasonable to speculate that the majority of middle-class boys approaching manhood neither immediately reject the idea of sexual activity before marriage nor immediately run out to find an intercourse partner. As with the many other paradoxes and contradictions in our social and ethical concepts, they muddle along trying to find compromises that will let them remain at peace with their consciences, keep up with the rest of the men they know, and, most important of all, not miss anything.

There was a time in the not-too-distant past when a substantial number of educated middle-class men, because of an inner conviction, religious or otherwise, adopted a definite premarital sexual stance. (Contrary to those who advocate uninhibited intercourse, it is not biologically necessary for any man to have any particular amount or kind of sexual activity for good health. Nor is the tide of social pressure so strong that a resolute, think-for-himself middle-class man cannot adhere to any standard of conduct he genuinely believes in—even today.) These men were probably the most readily marriageable men in our society, for usually they were well-behaved, yet decisive, men who had had high standards of ethical behavior throughout life and still had a positiveness that might make them leaders. They had probably been mentally and emotionally conditioned to associate sex, love, and marriage in the same way that most women had. Their natural sex drive was channeled by their conditioning toward one approved outlet—marriage. They *wanted* to get married.

There were then, however, as there are today, good potential husbands among the large group of men who never place any conscious limit on their sexual activity, but just drift with circumstances. For the most part, these men play the classic "dating game." The young man sees how far he can go without being so offensive that he is disliked; the young woman is expected to yield as little as possible, yet still give the impression she is enjoying the game and still be seductive enough to keep him coming back for more.

In a very real sense, this puts the control of the sexual destiny of any one of these young men in the hands of the women with whom they associate. If they happen to meet more women who are either unskillful at saying "no" or who never intended to say "no" in the first place, these men will have greater sexual experience.

Some investigators, including the Kinsey group, appear to disagree, but I think there is every reason to believe that there are some middle-class men who would go into marriage with scant sexual experience, except for such circumstances as military service, in which sexual experiences are unusually significant and easy for them. For even in this day of easy sex, sexual knowledge and sexual desire are a long way from actual sexual experience for the average middle-class boy. Unless his initial experience is with a prostitute (not likely for a middle-class young man who lives at home these days), there is much for him to learn before he will be successful in any sexual approach to a "nice" girl. And that goes for petting as well as intercourse.

Scraps of information—and misinformation—concerning how to excite the female, what to say to overcome her objections, and what to do to avoid pregnancy must be fitted together and agonizingly reconciled with his early teaching before a boy starts experimenting. By a process of trial and error in his early dating, he furthers this learning. He discovers what happens when he touches a girl, what happens when he asks her permission to touch her, and how far he may go without encountering genuine resistance and hostility.

In this process, still another sorting-out takes place. The developing male learns what women think about him sexually. Much of his later behavior may well depend on the reflected impression of himself that he gets at this time. Any bumbling may be quickly punished by the girl partner's censure. This creates further inhibitions in the unskillful or unattractive young man. On the other hand, the attractive, "smooth," aggressive individual may be rewarded and encouraged to make further experiments.

Regardless of the ultimate limits to premarital sexual behavior that any young man accepts, his association with the outside man-group usually has an effect on his sex life. In many instances, his misunderstandings of what women really want have their origin in the sexually excited imaginations of his misinformed friends. For example, as a result of the exaggerations and misconceptions they acquired in the locker room, many men are convinced that all women have the same sex appetites as they do. These men are likely to approach women sexually the way they would like to be approached—with direct genital stimulation. Some, because such things are deliberately kept from them when they are boys, never really understand that women usually prefer emotional stimulation in the form of tender exchanges of love talk before any specific sexual contact. Kinsey, in pointing out why some women prefer homosexual relations, suggests that women are likely to understand the anatomy, psychology, and responses of their own sex better than they understand the direct approach of the male.[12]

This misunderstanding of the other sex's desires works both ways, of course. Some women find it difficult to believe that some men at times have an intense desire for a sex experience, without necessarily any desire for love play either before or after. But again, it should be remembered that there are many men for whom intercourse without tenderness would be impossible. There are some men who want no sex without love, just as there are some women who can take the sex experience as casually as some men—if not more so.

CASE 38

"I read somewhere a couple of weeks ago that a lot of women complain that their husbands don't give them enough love—just sex," Norman told the counselor. "But my problem is that my wife doesn't want sex or love. I like to make love, and I don't just mean to have intercourse. I like to hold her and touch her and tell her how much I love her. But she is some sort of cold fish, and she's always got some kind of excuse from being afraid I'll muss up her hair to worrying that the children might hear us. Maybe once a month or so she'll let me near her. Well, I'm an affectionate guy, and that isn't enough for me.

"I've always liked to hug and kiss and be close. She knew that a long time before she married me. But it was all right then; she even kissed back once in a while. I don't mean she was real sexy. I think maybe one of the reasons I finally proposed to her was that I couldn't get her to go to bed with me. I guess I must have figured she was some kind of angel, and for a romantic guy like myself, that just made it so much the better. But back in those days she did try to extend herself to be cuddly, and when we were driving down the road she would move over close. I never dreamed we'd have a sex problem.

"I've always needed a lot of sex. When I was in the navy I guess I had more than any man on my ship. But I was romantic about it even then. It's a funny thing, but I could go to bed with some woman who was initially very repulsive to me. But

[12] Alfred C. Kinsey et al., *Sexual Behavior in the Human Female*, Philadelphia, Saunders, 1953, p. 468.

while we were having intercourse—that is while I was actually touching her —I used to feel very tender toward her. For that period it was almost as if I really loved her. After it was over, though, I used to feel very badly about it. I used to be ashamed of myself, not for having intercourse, but because I let myself feel loving when I knew darn well that she didn't have any feeling for me.

"But that's all over now, and I'm trying to be a real straight husband. I haven't had another woman in years, but I tell you I'm going to unless she stops making excuses. A man has a right to some sexual happiness. He has a right to feel loved."

"Norman must be oversexed," Edith told the counselor. "Or else, he's crazy. We have two young children and frankly they wear me out. I just about fall into bed every night. All I want to do is sleep. But not that satyr I married. He comes storming in every night and wants intercourse. Sure I give him a lot of excuses. Sometimes I go to bed early deliberately, but it doesn't help very much. He's so inconsiderate he wakes me up sometimes and demands that I give myself to him. I suppose a wife has an obligation to let herself be used, but he certainly overworks his rights.

"I suppose he told you that I won't touch him or pat him or even get close to him. That's true. And for a very good reason. If I give him the slightest encouragement in the early evening, then for sure he's after me when we go to bed. Sometimes he doesn't wait that long. Sometimes he can't even wait until the children are asleep. That isn't right.

"A wife has a right to expect a considerate husband, but Norman just plain isn't considerate. Not only that, he isn't smooth and subtle about lovemaking. He thinks he's affectionate but actually he's corny. He gets all sentimental and overeager. I suppose I will have to put up with this for the rest of my life, but right now I don't see how I'm going to."

Human physical variability and conditioning being what it is, it is doubtful if any two men want the same amount of sex or want it in the same way. The range is from the abnormalities at the one end, impotence or complete lack of sex interest, to the abnormalities at the other end, the completely uninhibited Don Juan.

With sex, as with other marital adjustments, there are some men and women whose customs, attitudes, values, expectations, and, in this case, appetites fit together so perfectly that very little adjusting is necessary. There are others whose desires are so far apart that adjustment often seems impossible. For the great majority of young marrieds, though, the sex-adjustment process *itself* is both necessary and rewarding. After all, there is no other adjustment in which just trying can be so satisfying and so love enriching.

19

SEXUAL ADJUSTMENT
IN MARRIAGE:
FEMALE SEXUAL CONDITIONING

Since sexual adjustment requires mutual understanding, it is equally as important for the man to understand the woman's conditioned attitudes and expectations as for her to understand his. In fact, in some cases, it may be even more so, because, biologically speaking, sexual activity has a more permanent meaning for women than it does for men.

Margaret Mead makes this point very cogently:

> Where for men actual sex activity, however insistently it may intrude upon attention, is a matter of a few minutes, for women each of these few minutes is laden with commitment, commitment before and commitment afterwards. . . . A woman's life is punctuated by a series of specific events: the beginning of physical maturity at menarche, the end of virginity, pregnancy and birth, and finally, the menopause, when her productive period as a woman is definitely over, however zestful she may still be as an individual. Each of these events—because once past they can never be retraced—is momentous for a woman, whereas a man's ability to command an army or discover a new drug is less tied to the way his body functions sexually. So we can say—at least as far as human beings have thus far developed during the course of civilization—that sex in its whole meaning, courtship through parenthood, means more to a woman than it does to a man, although single sexual acts may have more urgency for men than for women.[1]

Not only is sexual behavior biologically more portentous for women, it is often quantitatively—if not emotionally—more possible for them to respond completely to it. Masters and Johnson are among the more recent researchers to point out that there is a large (and probably increasing) number of modern

---

[1] Margaret Mead, in the introduction to A. M. Krich, ed., *Women: The Variety and Meaning of Their Sexual Experience*, New York, Dell, 1953, pp. 9, 12. Copyright, 1953 Western Printing and Lithographing Co.

women who are capable of multiple orgasms in a brief period of time, a feat that few males can accomplish.[2]

Despite the greater meaning of sex for some women and the modern emphasis on the female orgasm in sophisticated circles, in the past in our culture not only have most young women been less interested in physical sex than men, many also have been conditioned to avoid sexual thoughts and sexual activity altogether. For them, Margaret Mead's statement has no real meaning. They couldn't care less.

This, in itself, is hardly surprising, for the sexual conditioning of young females in modern society, as well as in recent history, has been fraught with paradoxes and perplexities. Many of the sexual problems of today's female go back to the very earliest formulations of her psychosexual attitudes, which were influenced in large part by the emotional struggles of her carefully sex-inhibited mother. Such a parent, having read something of modern psychology, is thrown into disturbed ambivalence when she sees early evidences of her young daughter's sexuality—usually genital play. Frequently the mother's reaction to this entirely normal play makes a poor beginning for the development of sound sexual attitudes and feelings in the child. Later, the child's sexual insecurity increases when she begins to understand that traditional sex mores and actual sex behavior in our culture are not necessarily congruent. This confusion continues even into adulthood, when she is perplexed by a new need (if she wants to be sexually successful) to demonstrate an enthusiastic sexual response she may not feel. Sexual incompatibility in marriage grows from just such sexual histories.

This is not true, of course, of all women. Some young females accept their sexuality with a joyful enthusiasm. Some are as eager as their male marriage partners for sexual activity. In this case, very little "adjustment" is required. At the other extreme, there appears to be an increasingly large number of women whose sexual desire exceeds that of their male partners. This disparity also creates marriage difficulty.

No one knows for sure exactly what portion of the total married population is sexually incompatible or which direction that incompatibility takes. Many marriage counselors are still preoccupied with the older "sex-inhibited woman, sexually deprived man" problem, but some researchers see the opposite situation as the emerging predominant difficulty. In 1967, Robert Bell reported a study of 196 college-educated women in Philadelphia, all of whom were married ten years or less, with a median age of 26.2 and a religious composition of 51 percent Jewish, 38 percent Protestant, and 11 percent Catholic. In this study, only 6 percent of the women questioned thought they had intercourse too frequently. Twenty-five percent thought they had intercourse too infrequently. Unfortunately, their husbands were not interviewed, so there is no way of knowing whether or not these were genuine incompatibility problems. Perhaps 25 percent of the husbands also wanted more intercourse, but were prevented from having it by time limitations or other causes.[3] Moreover, it should be noted that Bell's sample was a group of highly educated women in a large metropolitan area. That his findings would be true in a rural or semirural area is doubtful.

[2] William H. Masters and Virginia E. Johnson, *Human Sexual Response*, Boston, Little, Brown, 1966, pp. 283–284.
[3] Robert R. Bell, "Some Emerging Sexual Expectations Among Women," *Medical Aspects of Human Sexuality* (October, 1967), 65–72.

In the same study, Bell found that some 14 percent of the women who had been married less than three years felt that their husbands were not happy in their sex lives. On the other hand, some 30 percent of the women who were married some seven to ten years thought that their husbands had problems of sexual adjustment. Bell suggested that these data might support the proposition that, as a marriage continues, the wife becomes more relaxed and more able to enjoy her sexual life, while her husband becomes more preoccupied with his work and less interested in sex. However, it also might be speculated that many women who are eager to accept their husband's sexual approach at the beginning of marriage become less responsive later on. It may well be that these women predispose their husband's loss of interest in sex rather than become victims of it.

In any event, it is clear that, in modern society, there are some women who want less sex than is demanded and some who want more than is offered. Since it is historically the more important (and still probably the more prevalent) problem, let us start by discussing the traditional female sexual conditioning that helped to create the woman who desires less sex than her husband.

THE IMPORTANCE
OF PSYCHOSEXUAL CONDITIONING

There is general agreement among those who have studied human physiology and behavior that, except in rare cases, all females are born with a potential capacity for sexual desire. But it is also very clear that, by the time they are adults, there are some women who never have any conscious desire for sexual activity and others who have only a very low desire at the age when most other women have maximum sexual interest—in their late twenties.

The causative factors for lack of sexual motivation are subject to dispute. Some investigators feel very strongly that inhibitions deliberately conditioned into the child as a means of assuring later moral purity and poor sex-role identification are the two major factors accounting for low sexual motivation. Both inhibitions and sex-role identification are psychological rather than physiological factors. Kinsey pointed out that more very religious women have lower sex interests than unreligious women, and were frequently less sexually active.[4] John and Joan Hampson concluded from their studies in the early 1960s that sex-role identification is a result of a learning process that is independent of such physical factors as chromosomes or hormones.[5]

But there are other very reputable investigators who believe that low sexuality has some physical component. In some cases, the relationship between low sex desire and physical abnormality can be demonstrated. Dr. Carney Landis reported during the 1940s that psychosexual immaturity in women is associated with immature body form and with a history of late onset of menstruation and irregular duration of the menstrual period.[6] However, those who believe in the

[4]Alfred C. Kinsey et al., Sexual Behavior in the Human Female, Philadelphia, Saunders, 1953, p. 529.
[5]John L. Hampson and Joan G. Hampson, "The Ontogenesis of Sexual Behavior in Man," W. C. Young, ed., Sex and Internal Secretions, vol. II, 3rd ed., Baltimore, Williams & Wilkins, 1961, p. 1413.
[6]Carney Landis, Agnes T. Landis, and M. M. Bolles, Sex in Development, New York, Hoeber-Harper, 1940, p. 78; and Carney Landis and M. M. Bolles, Personality and Sexuality of the Physically Handicapped Women, New York, Hoeber-Harper, 1942, p. 115.

primacy of conditioning factors could here point out that gonadal function—especially that concerned with menstruation—is sometimes susceptible to psychologic modification and that, therefore, any cause–effect relationship is obscure.

Moreover, even if a physical malfunction causes the delay of sexual interest, it is often a conditioning factor that makes that delay permanent. If a woman in her late teens or early twenties is not physically or emotionally mature enough to be interested in sex, she may later be prevented from accepting sexuality by autoinhibition, for, by the time she does become physically mature enough to have desire, she may have so organized her life around a particular cultural pattern of living, religious or secular, that she will be psychologically unable to recognize the desires she now could have. Recent research findings are adding new complexity to the controversy over the primacy of physiology versus conditioning in sexual behavior. These experiments seem to indicate that an excess or shortage of sex hormones during infancy and childhood may affect later sexual identification and/or behavior. David Hamburg and Donald Lunde summarize it this way:

> The traditional approach centered on *contemporary* correlations, e.g., concomitant fluctuations in the level of a hormone and the performance of a particular kind of behavior. These recent studies call attention to the possibility of developmental correlations, in which the presence of a hormone in adequate amounts during an early critical period may have consequences throughout the life span, even when the hormone is no longer present (or is present in much smaller quantity).[7]

But whether or not physiologic factors are present, it is clear that the socialization and conditioning that the female receives as a child plays a very large part in the development of her sexual desire and in the fulfillment—or lack of fulfillment—she receives from adult sexual activity.

FEMALE SEX-ROLE IDENTIFICATION

Sex-role identification for the female child as generally understood by modern social psychologists appears to be much simpler than for the male. The girl, like the boy, first identifies with her mother. But, unlike the boy, all she has to do is to continue this role identification until she becomes an adult. She carries no such heavy burden to demonstrate her femininity as the boy does to demonstrate his masculinity. Even so, however, as she approaches maturity, her own role problem may become more difficult than a boy's. Though no crisis of sex identity is involved, some young females experience great anxiety over such things as being chosen for dating and marriage and the confusion over the limits of sexual activity.

Psychoanalytic theory with regard to the psychosexual development of the female is much more complicated and controversial. According to the Freudians, at about the age of two, a girl, in the reverse situation of the Oedipus complex, sometimes called the Electra complex, displays a marked preference

[7] David A. Hamburg and Donald T. Lunde, "Sex Hormones in the Development of Sex Differences in Human Behavior," in Eleanor E. Maccoby, ed., *The Development of Sex Differences*, Stanford, Calif., Stanford University Press, 1966, p. 15.

for her father that remains dominant until about the age of six. Then she turns back toward her mother, realizing that she cannot replace her mother in her father's affection and that, if she were to continue to try, she would lose her mother's love. From then on, ideally, she tries to emulate her mother. Although incestuous wishes play a part in this "complex," in that the girl subconsciously desires to have a child by her father, it is said that there is no such anxiety-laden fear for girls as the boy child's dread of castration.

FEMALE SEXUAL CONDITIONING
IN A CHANGING SOCIETY

The beginning of sexual conditioning for the infant female, as for the infant male, is probably the warmth and cuddling that she gets while she receives the biologic satisfactions of nourishment. Learning to associate pleasure with intimate body contacts is a primary source of later acceptance of sexuality.

A girl's introduction to sex is liable to vary widely with the kind of home in which she grows up. Differences in toilet training, in opportunities for privacy, and even in the acceptance of talk about sexual activity make for a great diversity in sexual patterns. But despite these early differences, certain fairly definite and widespread expectations exist concerning the sexual attitudes and behavior of the American girl at every age level.

Most very young American females are expected to be almost completely nonsexual. Any indication of sexual knowledge or experience ordinarily earns a severe reaction from parents and the neighbors as well. As the girl child grows up, she usually is made painfully aware of society's expectations if only by its silence. She learns that nice girls don't talk about sexual things, even with each other. Although boys are rewarded by their peers for tales of sexual exploits to the point where it may make them exaggerate sexual experiences, girls are often punished by other girls as well as by their parents for admitting to sexual thoughts and behavior. Thus are created in the girl feelings that sexual activity is "wrong" and feelings of guilt about any form of sexual release, especially masturbation.

The female conspiracy of silence regarding sex not only prevents many growing girls from getting the emotional catharsis that group discussion might provide, it also makes inevitable a rude awakening when they come face to face with the realities of teenage sex expectations in our contemporary society.

At the beginning of puberty, expectations regarding female sexual behavior change. Now to be a successful American female adolescent, a girl is expected to know enough about sexual behavior to say no at the appropriate minute. At the same time, she is expected to be sufficiently provocative sexually to keep the boys coming back for more dates. Margaret Mead puts this in terms of the "positive sex response":

> In the United States, positive sex response has come to be defined as something women ought to have, like the ability to read. Just as men feel justified in judging a girl by whether or not she keeps her stocking seams straight, because this is a sign that she is the kind of girl who "pays attention," so they now feel justified in demanding that she know how to respond positively to sexual advances.
>
> To respond positively includes the ability to say no, to postpone, delay, repulse without offending, during the long years of dating. The whole pattern

places heavy demands upon both men and women, not the least of which lies in the contrast between the role of play without completion, appropriate to dating, and the shift to complete sex satisfaction in marriage.[8]

As she enters adulthood, the mature American woman is expected to reorient her sexual emotions a second time. Now she must be the responsive tigress with an invariable ability to achieve complete orgasm, despite whatever inhibitory process was built into her developing emotional system. In contemporary society, it often appears as if cataclysmic orgasm, perceived as taking place in the vagina (where, in fact, all orgasm does take place) is the ultimate test of feminine achievement.

Margaret Mead made a pertinent comment about this second change of expectation, too. She says,

> As experiencing a positive sex climax is probably no more congenial to the whole female sex than was the passive, unemotional role demanded of their great-grandmothers, these demands force some women to learn to simulate, as they have always had to learn to simulate through the ages, in order to conform to the current style of sex behavior.[9]

Obviously, these complex and sometimes contradictory goals of modern female sexual conditioning, requiring two major shifts in emphasis, would be difficult enough to achieve with any particular female, even if there were precise agreement on how it should be done. Unhappily, however, it is over just this point that the confusion among parents and educators is greatest. As a result of her elders' perplexity and consequent default, a typical young female gets very little more information about the realities of sexual behavior than is provided in whispered conversations at slumber parties or that she can infer from forbidden books, her mother's magazines, and the movies she is permitted to see.

True, some effort has been made in most large urban schools to provide a film about menstruation, and in some schools a section in a home economics or health course is devoted to human reproduction. But even in these few instances, those who are in charge of presenting the material ordinarily bend over backwards to assure themselves and the general public that only "scientific" facts are presented and that such practical problems as how to deal with the excitability of the male or the basics of family planning are not discussed. Often the most important aspects of sexual education—attitudes, values, and expectations—are totally ignored. With this kind of preparation, it is a remarkable tribute to human adaptability that as many females turn out to be as sexually well adjusted as they are.

Because of sex taboos, many young women of recent generations learned to sublimate their sex drives and to concentrate on the romantic aspects of man–woman relationships. It was quite all right for them to dream about tender love and to be made starry-eyed by romantic novels, provided they made no display of overt sexual activity. Young women were encouraged by their parents to develop romantic attachments, provided they did not involve *overt* sexual

---

[8] Margaret Mead, in the introduction to A. M. Krich, ed., *Women: The Variety and Meaning of Their Sexual Experience*, New York, Dell, 1953, p. 16. Copyright, 1953 Western Printing and Lithographing Co.

[9] Margaret Mead, in the introduction to A. M. Krich, ed., *Women: The Variety and Meaning of Their Sexual Experience*, New York, Dell, 1953, p. 17. Copyright, 1953 Western Printing and Lithographing Co.

response. Thus, whatever sexuality most young women felt became equated with—or at least indissolubly associated with—tenderness and affection.

As a result of their greater love-sex association, some females found out after marriage that the men they married had neither the same attitudes nor the same expectations about sexual behavior that they had. A woman might be appalled to find that her husband no longer felt obligated to woo her. He appeared ready—too ready—for instant sexual activity. Such a woman might also be distressed to find that he became sexually excited by viewing pictures of other women, or that he would go out of his way to look when the woman next door left her bedroom shades up.

In comparing the sexual response of males and females, Kinsey and his group pointed to many specific ways in which the females in their sample responded differently to psychological stimuli than the males did, even though they found no differences in the anatomy and physiology of the sexual response between the sexes that might account for the differences. For example, only half as many females as males were stimulated by observing members of the opposite sex. More than four times as many men as women were aroused by seeing portrayals of nude figures. Only a few of the females in the Kinsey sample were aroused by observing the male genitalia. This, said Kinsey, surprised many males. On the other hand, many females were surprised to learn that *anyone* found the observation of male genitalia erotically stimulating.[10]

Females and the males in the Kinsey sample responded erotically in about the same numbers to novels, essays, poetry, and other literary material, but females found romantic moving pictures erotically stimulating somewhat more often than males. Many fewer females could be aroused by their own sexual fantasies, though. Although 89 percent of all males had erotic fantasies during masturbation, only 64 percent of the females fantasied. Kinsey also found that those people who do fantasy while masturbating are often surprised that there is such a thing as masturbation without accompanying sexual fantasies.

Having examined some of the differences in the differential sex conditioning of men and women, let's take a look at a typical adjustment problem arising out of these differences.

CASE 39

"Yes, I am resentful and bitter," Nina told the counselor. "In fact, I have grown to hate Glen. Before we were married I thought he was one of the most romantic men I had ever been with, and he was *then.* But now he not only won't take the time to be romantic before sexual relations, he also has the nerve to suggest we have sex after he has been fighting with me all day long.

"I believe sex should come at the end of a beautiful day together. It doesn't begin at bedtime, and it doesn't begin in the bedroom. It should be a reward to each of us for our day-long companionship. If he fights with me, I can't turn around and give myself to him. He has to make love to me, or else the whole thing is just animal."

Sound reasonable? Yes, for most people, sex feelings are enhanced by love. But so are love feelings enhanced by sex. Listen to her husband's side of the story.

"There wouldn't be any fights or resentments if only she would let herself be loving," Glen told the counselor. "Sure I desire her sexually, and she should be glad that I do. But I don't want to live my life in constant fear that if I accidentally

[10] Kinsey, *op. cit.,* pp. 652–685.

say the wrong thing during the afternoon, she is going to deliberately cut me out of sex that night. I want her to love me 'naturally,' not because I begged her for it or earned it by making pretty speeches. I *want* her to want me so bad that she can't worry about all the little niceties. Is that wrong?"

No, that isn't wrong either. Until Nina and Glen understand that these are deeply conditioned feelings that each has and not silly little notions that can be cured by punishment or force, they will continue to be sexually incompatible. What do you think can be done if two people like Nina and Glen have such definite wants? Why hasn't the other person sought to help? Who should make the first move?

As was pointed out earlier, not all sexual-incompatibility problems involve women who want more love and men who want more sex. Increasingly, the difference in expectations is appearing in the opposite direction. Some modern, sexually emancipated young women are finding that their expectations and attitudes exceed the sexual ability or sexual aggressiveness of their male partners.

Actually, some of these women may have expectations and attitudes that exceed any realistic probability of satisfaction from *any* source. The cataclysmic potential and earth-shaking splendor of the female orgasm has been glorified to such an extent in novels and popular articles (usually written by males) that it is probably an unattainable fantasy for many women. The results of this deception are indeed tragic, for if, as Morton Hunt has pointed out, "a woman has been assured that she will, that she ought, that she *must* see colored lights, feel like a breaking wave, or helplessly utter inarticulate cries, she is apt to consider herself or her husband at fault when these promised wonders do not appear."[11]

Should a young wife, as a result of her disenchantment, start to believe that there is something wrong with her—that perhaps she is "frigid"—then she adds shame and fear to her other sexual problems. If, on the other hand, she blames her husband for her inability to achieve the ultimate in orgasmic response, and if her husband is already frustrated because he cannot give her the pleasure she desires, she further frustrates him and perhaps destroys whatever potential their relationship might have had in the first place.

There are, of course, some cases of sexual incompatibility where the wife is not just deceived by unreal expectations, but really *does* have a sexual capacity that exceeds the ability of her husband to satisfy. Sometimes this is a matter of quantity—a woman can have multiple orgasms during the same intercourse experience and continue to feel desirous long after her husband has been totally satisfied and gone to sleep. More often however, problems of sexual incompatibility that develop from the wife's greater desire have a qualitative dimension. For example, often the husband fails to provide the aggressiveness (or, as we have seen, the tenderness) that the wife has been conditioned to expect will bring her greater sexual happiness.

Curiously, a man's lack of sexual aggressiveness *before* marriage is often interpreted by an inexperienced female as a sign of his strength and love, to her later regret. Consider the following case.

[11] Morton M. Hunt, *Her Infinite Variety*, New York, Harper & Row, 1962, p. 114.

"I can't understand it now," Irene told the counselor, "but I think I married Harold because he didn't ever touch me. It was very refreshing. He wasn't like a lot of the other boys who are always after sex, sex, sex. Harold seemed strong and resolute, and I interpreted his self-control as respect for my moral sensibilities and as evidence of his love. I honestly thought that after marriage he would turn into a 'roaring tiger' and be the sexually aggressive strong man that I secretly wanted. Of course, I didn't even let myself believe that I wanted that kind before we were married.

"Anyway, after we were married, he didn't take any sexual leadership—at least, not much. He almost literally asked my permission to touch me. I didn't want that. I wanted him to know what to do and to do it, whether I thought I wanted to or not. I found out, though, that I had to reassure *him*. That wasn't the way it was supposed to be. I don't respond to him anymore, and I don't think I really want him anymore. I want a man."

Then Harold talked to the counselor. "I've always tried to be a nice guy; when a girl said, "Stop," I stopped. I wanted to be certain that she enjoyed it before I touched her. If she didn't enjoy it, it wasn't going to be any pleasure for me. But Irene sure wasn't any help after we got married. In the beginning she used to respond beautifully, but then she began to stop responding at all and just would lie there like a lump. After a while I began to figure it out. She was trying to goad me into being more aggressive and into doing it all. Then if she didn't enjoy it, she could blame me. Well, that just made it more difficult for me. Pretty soon when she didn't respond to my first touch, I'd get so mad that I couldn't sleep. I tried pleading with her; I tried begging her; I tried asking her nicely. But nothing helped. She just seemed to get more resentful and less cooperative. What can I do now?"

Although the overly sex-aggressive husband married to the underresponsive wife may still be the most prevalent problem brought to the attention of the marriage counselor, the underaggressive-husband syndrome often presents the greater difficulty. Does Irene really want Harold to turn into a "roaring tiger," ruthless and a little brutal? Would she continue to love him if he did? Sexual behavior is often an expression of an individual's total personality. If the counseling process were effective enough to alter the "nice guy's" personality, it might make him so much more self-oriented that he would turn away from Irene, perhaps even divorce her. Is Irene prepared for that?

The whole process of adjustment involves each partner moving toward the other while at the same time reducing his own needs for having everything completely his own way. This is the subject of the next chapter.

20

SEXUAL ADJUSTMENT
IN MARRIAGE:
THE ADJUSTMENT PROCESS

A djustment" implies progress toward some new and better level of interaction for each of the individual partners and for the total relationship. But when is the optimum level achieved? What is a reasonable goal for the process of sexual adjustment in marriage? In other words, what is "good" sexual adjustment?

Some of the most vocal present-day experts in sexology insist that only when the partners have arrived at a pattern of invariable simultaneous orgasm during frequent intercourse, have experimented with every conceivable kind of sexual activity, and have completely rid themselves of any thought of sexual restraint will they have achieved a good sexual adjustment. Some Freudian psychoanalysts go even further, insisting that only when the woman perceives all of her orgasmic response as taking place in the vagina (rather than the clitoris, which is on the outside of the body) can she be considered "maturely" adjusted.

If everyone had been given the conditioning (and consequently the attitudes, values, and expectations) of these "experts," these goals might be both desirable and attainable. It is certainly true that those people who have achieved this kind of mutual sexuality believe that they have a richer living experience. But it is probably also true that there are many people who have been conditioned in such a way that only long-term psychotherapy might permit them to attain such sexual ideals. Meanwhile, these people feel constant shame that they do not respond the way the "experts" tell them they should.

It seems reasonable to suggest that there might be a better criterion for good sexual adjustment. This would be the melding of both partners' expectations into a single pattern of sexuality that is acceptable to both of them, regardless of whether anyone else thinks it is a good pattern or not. If both partners are satisfied with intercourse once a month, that for them is good adjustment.

If a husband can accept the fact that his wife will not have orgasm during every intercourse and not punish himself for his failure to make her respond, that too is good adjustment. And perhaps it would be better for a woman who perceives her orgasm as taking place in the clitoris to rejoice in the fact that she does have orgasm at all, rather than to punish herself for the fact that she does not perceive it as taking place in the vagina. When some sort of mutually satisfactory pattern is achieved, then—and only then—the marriage partners together can move, little by little, toward a richer and more exquisite level of complete sexuality.

How long does good sexual adjustment take? There is no rigid time schedule. Some partners whose expectations and attitudes synchronize easily and who understand and accept each other's feelings are relatively well adjusted from the time of their first adventure in sexual activity. For others it can take weeks, months, or years. In a study of 409 married couples, Judson and Mary Landis reported that one-eighth of the couples needed many weeks or months but did reach an adjustment they considered satisfactory within a year. However, one-tenth of the couples required an average of six years to work out the sexual adjustment in marriage, and some of them required as long as twenty years.[1]

Usually, if the partners genuinely desire to make their sexual relationship better, they can. Determination, coupled with personal flexibility and some creative imagination, can improve an already successful sexual relationship as well as a failing one. In fact, because relations between people are never static, it is probably necessary that each partner continue to reinvigorate his sexual participation throughout the life of the marriage.

For people who have never known the stark realities of sexual incompatibility, sexual adjustment may sound very simple and hardly worth discussing. But for those with sexual problems, marriage can become a nightmare of disappointment and frustration that can lead to deep resentment and, ultimately, to divorce.

By the time both married partners realize that they have a serious sex-adjustment problem, three distinct sets of feelings usually have developed already in each partner. First, each partner has conditioned expectations of what is right and proper. Each also feels resentful because those expectations have been frustrated. And each, finally, fears what lies ahead, and such fears make the expectations and resentments seem much more important than they really are.

The initial step toward sexual adjustment in any marriage is greater understanding and acceptance of each partners' expectations and attitudes by the other partner. To do this, it is first necessary for each partner to understand that, however right or wrong his mate's feelings appear, they *are* his feelings. Ordinarily, these feelings were building up just as strongly and for just as long a period of time in one partner as in the other. Neither partner is able to change his feelings overnight.

The second step that both partners must take to improve their sexual relationship is explore each others' feelings by talking together.

[1] Judson T. Landis and Mary G. Landis, *Building a Successful Marriage*, 4th ed., Englewood Cliffs, N.J., Prentice-Hall, 1963, p. 311.

SEXUAL COMMUNICATION

Lack of experience in sexual communication because of taboos in childhood homes has serious consequences in many marriages. Not only are the partners inhibited about expressing their expectations, needs, and desires to each other; sometimes they actually can't speak the words. Some women, for example, cannot, even let the word penis enter their consciousness without getting emotionally upset. Sometimes the words one partner does use are distasteful to his mate. Inappropriate sex words can be devastating to a lovemaking mood. Most people know this, and it is one of the reasons why communication between inexperienced partners is often so inadequate. Given enough time and the right kind of security, though, most people can work through their emotional inhibitions about both hearing sexual words and even about using them.

Some marriage partners, with or without sexual-adjustment problems, find that communication security is better achieved by inventing their own words for sexual activity and sexual parts. As long as both partners understand the meaning of these terms, this is probably harmless and very often can be helpful. But it should alert both partners to the fact that they have deeply emotionalized conditioned feelings that make their own private language necessary. They need to be very sure that they are not perpetuating their inhibitions by using this sexual shorthand.

Sexual communication can and should be used for something more than problems. Some couples increase their sexual incompatibility by talking about sex only as a problem. Sexual communication can be, with practice, a deep source of marriage enrichment. As the partners explore each others' feelings and fantasies, they can come to have a depth of understanding that makes it seem as if their two very beings, as well as their bodies, can touch.

Talking about sex can be as stimulating as a caress—sometimes even more so. Often, one's own sexual fantasies not only excite the other partner but provide knowledge for him of how he can be even more successful in lovemaking. Only by communication can one partner learn what the other really desires. Yet this is a stumbling block in many marriages. Most wives have no difficulty at all in directing their husbands where to scratch their backs—a little to the left, a little to the right, a little up, a little down—to provide the greatest relief for the itchy spot. But many find it impossible to be so explicit in directing them in sexual activities. If you were to ask one of these women why she doesn't tell her husband what she wants, she would probably reply, "He's supposed to know that!" Just why he should be expected to know what feels good to her sexually is somewhat obscure, since he has never been a woman, and he has never been that particular woman.

ACTION BEYOND COMMUNICATION

Just being an expert in talking about sex isn't enough to assure good adjustment. The partners have to be able and willing to do something about it. Sometimes doing something about a sexual problem means going to see a psychotherapist for either individual or conjoint help with the sexual problem. In many cases of impotence and frigidity, this may be absolutely necessary, and the sooner the partners do it the better. There are other circumstances, such as partners with unconscious repressions and homosexual tendencies, where professional help is needed, too.

But often by evaluating their situation, marriage partners *can* help themselves. To begin with, they can deliberately work at being more like the sex partners their mates expect. In some cases, this may mean that a husband will try to be less demanding sexually or more aware of his wife's need for more quiet tenderness before intercourse. In other cases, it will mean that a wife will not deliberately stay up to watch the late show so that she can avoid fulfilling her husband's sexual needs.

For most sexually incompatible marriage partners, reversing their long-established patterns of behaving isn't easy. Although each may have been eager at the time of their marriage for the caresses of the other, now their resentment and hostility is so great—often *because* of a poor sexual relationship—that one will not permit the other the satisfaction of meeting his expectations, even temporarily.

At least a part of this problem results from the fact that both partners often had unrealistic expectations to begin with about the marriage relationship. Each had built up in his mind an idealized picture of what his mate could produce, both as a human being and as a sex partner. Soon after marriage, the process of disillusionment (so well described in the case of George and Lila in Chapter 15), sets in.

If this disillusionment begins with the wife, the husband soon senses her change of attitude, even though it may still be unconscious on her part. The realization that he is no longer her infallible hero hurts, so he begins to protect himself, perhaps also unconsciously. In turn, the wife has to adjust to the husband's slightly changed new attitude, the result of his defensive maneuver. Then he has to adjust again, then she does, and so forth. This goes on until both partners are totally hostile, or worse, apathetic, as a result of the constant need to protect their own egos from the insults of their mate's disillusionment.

In this process, no single rejection was important in itself, but ultimately there was one that represented the final denial of expectation, the ultimate disillusionment, the last straw. Not infrequently, it is the man who suffers disillusionment earlier than the woman, perhaps because his expectations are often more unreal. Which is the first to be disillusioned is unimportant, however, for sooner or later disillusionment affects the other partner, too.

The only way to reverse this process is for both mates to concentrate on each others' positive characteristics and so rebuild the acceptance that existed at the time of marriage. As one partner begins to recapture some of his original enthusiastic joy in just being with the other, the other will gradually allow himself to lessen his own built-up ego defenses and begin to be more positively appreciative himself. The beginning of this process of reenchantment is reselling oneself on what is good about his mate and his expectations. If he can concentrate on remembering the good times they have had together, especially the sexual good times, it is quite probable that he will begin to permit himself to believe that it can happen again. It is also important for him to remember that the more meaningful the emotional relationship between the partners becomes in *every* human activity, the more love-enhancing the sexual relationship will be. This, in turn, further enriches their nonsexual life together, which, in turn, re-enriches their sex life.

A common complaint, especially from women, is that, although they may *want* to please their husbands sexually, by the time they actually go to bed they are so physically tired or so emotionally unready for lovemaking that they reject their husbands either by active opposition—or even worse—by passive non-cooperation. The woman who really wants to do something to avoid this pattern can either budget her work in order not to be so fatigued or, if this proves impossible, find sometime during the week when she is relatively less over-worked that she can give to lovemaking.

It goes without saying that most men can do at least this much and even more. Most people know what they ought to do to improve their relationship. Sometimes fears and resentments are the reasons why they don't.

FEARS AND
RESENTMENTS

Regardless of the exact nature of the incompatibility problem, it is usually fears and/or resentments that prevent normal physical responses from taking place. What often happens to the married partner who cannot physically respond to a sexual approach is that his initial stimulation may have been extinguished by some fear or resentment. These may be big fears or little insecurities; they may be long-smoldering hatreds or passing annoyances. Nevertheless, they are ex-traneous to the lovemaking, and they sometimes are sufficient to cause the beginning stimulation to disappear. For example, a woman may suddenly be chilled by the fear of getting pregnant, or of being overheard by her children, or even her parents, if they happen to share the same house. An unaesthetic or coarse word or gesture on the part or her husband may repulse her. She may recall some unpleasant sexual incident. Any such distraction, if it occurs in the crucial early moments of sexual excitation, can prevent her from having an orgasm. She can continue on through intercourse, yes; but she will not reach a climax herself.

Similarly, a man can be so disturbed by the thought that his wife didn't respond to him the last time, or winced with discomfort when he entered that he too loses his ability to engage in intercourse. The unconscious (or sometimes conscious) feeling that he might be doing something wrong is a primary cause of both transitory impotence and premature ejaculation in the male. One failure to perform in intercourse creates a fear of further failures and so makes further failures almost inevitable. In some males, as in most females, there appears to be a crucial period early in the excitation process that controls the individual's ability to reach a successful climax.

Reassurance and familiarity are the specific antidotes for fear. The woman who has been inhibited by the fear of pregnancy may find a vastly improved ability to respond once she has some reliable assurance that she will not become pregnant. Similarly, the woman who has been fearful that she would be hurt by sexual intercourse often loses this fear when repeated intercourse experiences have been successful.

Providing real emotional security is a difficult task requiring careful thought. It isn't very reassuring for a husband to tell his wife that she "is bound to get over her fears." This may just make her feel that he doesn't understand the real depth of her problem. Nor is it always helpful for a wife to be sexually aggressive with a timid husband. She may just make him that much more afraid that he can't meet her desire for immediate intercourse. In this case, perhaps it is better to be warmly seductive without any overt demand for intercourse, and so build up both his stimulation and his security at the same time.

Resentments are equally as hard to work through as fears. Insights into their causes, achieved either by self-introspection or communication, are a helpful beginning. Once one has insight into the causes of his resentments, relief can often be obtained by ventilating the hostilities that have been suppressed. This should be done in a way that doesn't hurt the other partner, though. Professional psychotherapy is often the best answer.

There are some cases in which marriage partners were so traumatized by their childhood sexual conditioning or so deeply disturbed by later fears and resentments that they now have severe emotional damage that can be helped *only* by psychotherapy. Yet there are other cases in which fears and resentments can be resolved by the partners themselves if they can give enough security to each other. Actually, in the end the partners are the only ones who can really help each other. In these days, some professional therapists are basing their major treatment efforts in sexual incompatibility cases on that assumption. They see their role as aiding the partners in helping each other. Here is an illustration of the process:

Paul was a good-looking but rather shy chemical engineer. He was thirty-five years old, had been married for twelve years, and had two children. He started out by telling the counselor that his problem was his difficulty in getting stimulated enough to have intercourse. Until a year ago, he had had no problem. But at Christmas of that year he had had a fight with his wife in the presence of his father and mother. Things went from bad to worse, and for the past six months neither Paul nor Mildred had made any attempt to have sexual relationships. Paul said that at the beginning of their marriage their sexual relationship was excellent, but that his wife soon began to refuse him at times when he thought intercourse was appropriate. Paul's resentment had been festering for ten years. From what he said, it was apparent that Paul was a considerate husband. It was quite important to him that he please Mildred, and he did not want to risk offending her by forcing his attentions upon her. He believed Mildred to be a conscientious, kind, and publicly affectionate person. He also thought of her as strong willed, decisive, and sensitive to criticism. He said he had a nervous stomach and an ulcer.

When Mildred saw the counselor she confirmed these facts. After the big fight at Christmas, Paul had had a great deal of difficulty in trying to relate to her sexually, according to Mildred. She had not encouraged him to try sexual intercourse before they came for counseling, and she indicated her remorse at not having been more accepting when they could have had sexual relations in years past. She was very cooperative and very interested in trying to help now in any way she could. She said she had tried to become sexually aggressive but that this didn't seem to help her husband. In fact, it just seemed to make the situation worse.

Over the period of the next three weeks, the counselor saw Paul and Mildred several times each. Paul talked considerably about his relationship with his father, a Baptist minister, and a strict disciplinarian. At thirty-five, Paul has not been able to allow his father to know that he smokes and takes an occasional drink. Paul conceded that there were many taboos in his house when he was growing up and that his sexual inhibitions were many. He had had almost no sexual experience before marrying Mildred, other than masturbation.

Mildred talked about her own family life. Her parents were much more liberal than Paul's. She was more creative than her brother and two sisters, and she was the leader in her play group. She had been attracted to Paul because there was something "winsome" about him and because she thought she could help him to get ahead. She reported that Paul sometimes broke out in a cold sweat when sexual intercourse was mentioned.

In subsequent counseling sessions, some positive approaches to the problem were discussed. Paul began to get out more of his hostilities both toward his wife and toward his own father. At home he began to talk with Mildred about things they had never discussed before. He told her of his guilt over early masturbation and was very much relieved when he found out that Mildred had also masturbated and had also felt guilty about it. This appeared to be the opening of a new kind of communication about sex between the two of them. Before long, they were able to talk warmly and intimately about things that neither one of them had previously been able to discuss. Mildred was able to assure Paul that it wasn't necessary that they have intercourse every time they caressed each other. She was quite happy just to be close to him.

The marriage relationship improved in other ways. Mildred and Paul were able to talk about many of his feelings that he had previously felt he had to suppress. Mildred realized that in the past she had sometimes tried to provoke him into being hostile and forceful with her. She began to understand that this caused him to erect further defenses against her, since he was incapable of fighting with her.

Within the next month, Paul and Mildred found that, when there was no demand for intercourse, Paul frequently became very stimulated. They had several successful intercourse experiences. After the first success, Paul's optimism rose markedly. Before long, there was a more successful relationship between the partners than ever before in the past. Mildred told the counselor that it was the most wonderful time of their marriage. She felt as if they really knew each other for the first time.

After the emotionally satisfying experience of ventilating resentments, the person with a sexual-incompatibility problem faces the more difficult task of deliberate self re-education so that the problem doesn't occur again. For many people, this is a continuing adventure in self-discipline that may last a lifetime. Usually, once the initial pent-up resentments have been released, it is easier to dissipate new annoyances before they fester.

WHAT IS NORMAL?

Even for those married partners who have come to want to understand and accept each other's expectations, who have developed meaningful sexual communication, and who are motivated to want to try to do something about their sexual incompatibility, there often remains the question of what is normal in sexual behavior.

The simple answer that "what is normal for any particular marriage partner is what pleases him" is not very satisfactory in itself. Some marriage partners need the reassurance that other people do what he and his mate have been doing, since mankind has been conditioned from time immemorial to believe that something is right if most—or at least many—other people do it. It helps some marriage partners to feel more "normal" if they know, for example, that the married women in Kinsey's sample had intercourse 2.8 times per week when they were in their late teens. This dropped to 2.2 times per week by the time they were thirty and to 1.5 times per week by forty. By sixty, the women had intercourse once in about every twelve days.[2]

It sometimes helps some marriage partners to know that a man's sexual desire and/or ability reaches its peak at about age eighteen and thereafter gradually declines, while women's sexual interest and desire peaks when she is in her late twenties and remains relatively stable. It helps some partners to know that experimentation among married partners in positions and techniques for intercourse and other sexual activity is extremely common but that its acceptance varies with the backgrounds from which the partners came. It also may help some partners to know that sexual experimenting between married partners of all backgrounds has been increasing in recent times. Kinsey and his associates report that manual genital stimulation has become widespread, especially among highly educated couples, and that some other previously taboo sex practices are becoming more frequent.[3]

But even though there are tendencies in these directions, none of these activities is necessarily important to any one couple's sexual adjustment. Some marriage partners are satisfied with infrequent intercourse. Some men lose sex interest in their thirties. Others continue to be sexually active into their seventies. And it is interesting to note that in Kephart's study of Philadelphia divorces between 1937 and 1950, wife-initiated divorce suits involving sexual complaints frequently blamed the husband's desire for unusual sex practices.[4] Robert Blood, commenting on this, said: "In short, while marriage manuals may encourage variety for variety's sake, respect for the partner's scruples is still fundamental."[5]

Often therefore, the best possible conclusion to the what-is-right problem is "what is acceptable to *both* partners is right." This is something quite different from suggesting that everything either partner conceives of is right. In many cases, the value system or religious belief of either one or both of the partners may prohibit many forms of sexual behavior that might seem quite right or normal to the other.

Sexual behavior is—and should be—the expression of the individual personalities of the sex partners. There are marriages in which both partners agree that gentle tenderness is satisfactory to both of them. On the other hand, there are normal marriages where both partners are more pleased when the mate expresses himself with ferocious abandon. But in any case, the mutual acceptance of each partner by the other is the significant factor in adjustment. Although orgasm, and more particularly, simultaneous orgasm, may be important, the mutuality of satisfaction is probably even more important. Many men, and some psychiatrists as well, find it difficult to believe, but some women apparently get satisfaction without orgasm. In Terman's study of marriage adjustment among his gifted group and their wives, he found that almost half the wives

[2]Alfred C. Kinsey et al., *Sexual Behavior in the Human Female*, Philadelphia, Saunders, 1953, pp. 348–349.
[3] Kinsey, *op. cit.*, p. 399.
[4] William M. Kephart, "Some Variables in Cases of Reported Sexual Maladjustment," *Marriage and Family Living*, **16** (August, 1954), 241–242.
[5] Robert O. Blood, Jr., *Marriage*, New York, Free Press, 1962, p. 367.

who seldom or never experienced orgasm still claimed they derived either complete or fairly complete satisfaction from the sexual act.[6]

Again it is important to point out that sexual adjustment in marriage—like all other adjustments—is slowly achieved. One woman interviewed by the Kinsey researchers reported that she had finally achieved a sexual climax in her twenty-ninth year of marriage.[7] Moreover, sexual desires and expectations are in a constant state of change throughout married life and require new adjustments. There is ample evidence that these changes can be for the better if both partners want it that way. There are many people for whom sex is more exquisite at forty than it was at twenty. But the sexual relationship doesn't improve for everybody.

CASE 41

"Mike says I'm frigid," Elizabeth told the counselor, "and perhaps I am. I know that very often I don't want him to touch me, and I invent all kinds of excuses so he won't. I tell him I feel ill or else I stay up later than he does. Most of the time I just don't feel like it because I'm mad at him. He is a very intelligent, usually well-mannered man, but sometimes he says such stupid things at a party that I could just scream. Or maybe he won't telephone me when he said he would. Then I just get so angry that I can't make myself let him make love to me. My father was always kind, courteous, and considerate—too much so, I guess. He used to let Mother walk all over him. Finally, he became an alcoholic and she divorced him.

"Mike and I were married later than most people. I was a little shy in high school and in college too. I studied hard and got very good grades, but I didn't date very much. I wasn't very good-looking in high school, but by the time I got through college I was very pleased with my appearance. After college I had lots of dates, but the boys were rarely sexually aggressive. I guess I scared them off. They all seemed to try very hard to please me, but I guess I didn't really want that kind.

"Anyway, when Mike came along I was about thirty. He seemed so secure and positive. He appeared to be so at ease with people. Now I realize he really isn't very secure; as a matter of fact, inside he is shy, too. I think he is much more shy about sex than I am. He doesn't talk about it easily, and he says silly things. Every once in a while, though, he tries to be the strong possessive caveman type, and I have all I can do to keep from laughing. If he really would be genuinely aggressive, I think I would love it, but I'm afraid it's too late for that now.

"I remember when we were first married one time he wanted me to touch him. I said to him 'Oh no, Mike, I couldn't do that,' hoping that he would insist. But he didn't. Actually he started apologizing to me for having asked. I think that was the beginning of my loss of feeling for him right there.

"It isn't as if I didn't have sex feelings at all. Sometimes I wake up in the middle of the night with lots of desire. But he's sound asleep, and he's the one who's supposed to start things, so that's all there is to it. I just go back to sleep."

"I grew up in a very good home," Mike said. "My father was firm but loving. There were very few conflicts. He was a good churchman and there was no drinking or smoking in my house. I was slow with the girls, and I never went out on wild parties. Sure, I had sex desire like the rest of the fellows, but I used to pride myself in being a gentleman about it.

"When we were first married, she seemed to be almost as interested in sex as I was. She was warm and receptive, and we got along fine. But then somewhere along the way—it seems to me it was soon after Mike, Jr., was born—things began to get bad.

---

[6] Lewis M. Termen et al., "Correlates of Orgasm Adequacy in a Group of 556 Wives," *Journal of Psychology*, **32** (October, 1951), 128.
[7] Kinsey, *op. cit.*, p. 374.

All the time there were excuses, and even when we did have intercourse she stopped responding to me. I don't believe she's had a climax in the last two years, and she doesn't even care whether I know it or not.

"I don't want to force myself on her. As a matter of fact, I would like it if she were more aggressive, but it seems to be too late now. I've just about resigned myself to the fact that I'm never going to have the kind of sex relationship with Elizabeth that I would like to have. I've talked to a lot of the fellows down at the office and they don't seem to do much better than I do. Some of them step out on their wives. I could never do that, although it might help me if I did. Some of the guys say that you benefit two ways. First, you get sexual satisfaction outside. And then if your wife finds out about it and if she doesn't divorce you, things get better at home, too."

A good sexual adjustment involves patience and practice as well as passion. It derives its excellence from the complete emotional acceptance of each partner by the other and not from any standardized set of techniques or social norms. To arrive at a better sexual relationship, or to solve a sexual problem, the partners have to understand why their mates behave the way they do and then help each other to achieve greater perfection. Remember that only when *both partners* really want to help each other can there be any substantial improvement.

21
THE PROBLEM
OF INFIDELITY

One of the major sex-related problems in marriage is infidelity. Today's
society, with its new freedoms for women, now provides every wife
as well as every husband a relatively easy opportunity to try and solve
his real or fantasied problems, be they sexual, affectional, or social, by seeking
satisfaction elsewhere.

There is some evidence that adultery has been on the increase. Kinsey
and his associates found that more than half of the men in their sample and
over a quarter of the women had experienced sexual relationships outside of
marriage.[1] But the Kinsey data came from men and women who grew up in the
early part of the twentieth century and who were never exposed to modern
suburban living. In a 1966 survey of 154 Family Service Associates agencies,
64 percent of those agencies that answered a question about infidelity felt it
was more commonly admitted by their clients than it had been even five years
before.[2]

With extramarital sex, as with premarital sex, no one knows for sure
exactly what percentage of today's population is involved. It is certain that there
are some who have sex outside of marriage. Clark Vincent reports a study of
425 women seen for premarital and extramarital pregnancy in which 11 percent
were then married but they had been impregnated by someone other than their
husbands.[3] It is also certain that there are many women and men, even in
today's liberal society, who go through their entire marriages without having

[1] Alfred C. Kinsey, W. B. Pomeroy, and C. E. Martin, *Sexual Behavior in the Human
Male,* Philadelphia, Saunders, 1948, p. 585; Alfred C. Kinsey et al., *Sexual Behavior in the
Human Female,* Philadelphia, Saunders, 1953, p. 416.
[2] June Callwood, "Infidelity," *Ladies Home Journal,* **82** (April, 1965), 76.
[3] Clark E. Vincent, "Counseling in Cases Involving Premarital and Extramarital Pregnancies," in Richard H. Klemer, ed., *Counseling in Marital and Sexual Problems: A Physician's
Handbook,* Baltimore, Williams & Wilkins, 1965, p. 157.

sexual intercourse with anyone other than their mates. But there the certainty ends. We will be spending much of the rest of the chapter talking about the alleged increases in extramarital sex, but it should be remembered that these "increases" could be very small. In fact, they may not even be increases at all, since it is quite possible that the apparently greater rate of extramarital sex means only that more people are now willing to confess to having participated in it.

It should also be remembered that the self-fulfilling prophecy is as applicable to adultery and infidelity as it is to other modern sexual behavior. Because one hears in the mass media that "everybody is doing it," some get the feeling that they will be missing something if they don't. It is seldom pointed out that some people will be missing something if they *do*, since loyalty and trust are not only the foundations of the marriage relationship but also one of the "promises that men live by."

There appear to be three major suspected trends that are causing alarm among those who see infidelity as a threat to the stability of the family in our society.

MORE MIDDLE-CLASS
MALES INVOLVED

The first of these apparent trends is the larger number of middle-class males who are accepting sexual relationships outside of marriage as permissible and perhaps even as desirable. There has undoubtedly always been a great deal of extramarital sexual experience among men in most of the societies and cultures where the concept of monogamous marriages has been an ideal. But in the past, in America, extramarital sex has more often involved organized prostitutes patronized predominantly by males from the lower social levels.

Until recently, the public notion went relatively unchallenged in the United States that middle-and upper-class males upheld their status and their reputations by being faithful to their wives. Extramarital affairs were sometimes punished by the loss of job and standing in the community. Of course, this was never universally true. At the height of Victorianism in the late nineteenth century the Reverend Henry Ward Beecher, one of the most popular preachers of the times, was publicly accused of extramarital sexual activities. Elizabeth Tilton, a young married Sunday School teacher at Beecher's church, confessed that she and Beecher had been intimate. But, as Arthur Schlesinger, Jr., has pointed out, neither the size of Beecher's congregation nor his popularity and moral influence was perceptibly affected.[4] Still, the very fact that this affair was so newsworthy then, and is still remembered now, points up the general conclusion that it was counter to the public expectation. By and large, marital fidelity for both men and women was an American ideal of no small significance.

As recently as 1962, Harold Christensen reported that, in his sample of midwestern Americans, only 9 percent of the males and only 2 percent of the females approved of sexual infidelity involving a love relationship between one married person with an unmarried one. Only 7 percent of the males and, again,

---

[4] Arthur Schlesinger, Jr., "An Informal History of Love in the U.S.A." *Saturday Evening Post,* **239** (December 31, 1966), 34.

2 percent of the females, approved of extramarital sexual relations when both of those involved were married.[5]

In our modern urban culture, however, there is a very real question about the number of people who pay more than lip service to the ideal of marital fidelity. John Cuber and Peggy Harroff found in their study of 437 upper-middle-class "significant Americans" that many of their respondents were involved in extramarital relationships either for one night's thrill or for some deeper, longer lasting affectional reason.[6]

Cuber and Harroff point out that some business firms now use "total entertainment," including the services of a playgirl for the evening, as a form of sales promotion when customers come to town. Since most middle-class businessmen travel, invitations to "play a little" are said to be hard to avoid. As Cuber and Harroff put it, these practices have passed the stage of being naughty oddities that only a few people know about. They are standardized, understood, and almost institutional.

Such practices are, however, probably only a small part of the extramarital sex picture for the average American middle-class male. Equally as important are the many opportunities he has for affairs with the women who work in his office or whom he meets in his suburban neighborhood, perhaps while his own wife is working in somebody else's office. Sometimes these relationships blossom into full-scale love affairs fulfilling needs for both partners that are not met in their marriages.

MORE FEMALES INVOLVED

The second suspected trend in extramarital sexual relations is that there has apparently been an increase in extramarital sex among middle-class women, too. As with the males, much of the evidence for this increase is circumstantial. For example, in testifying before a Senate committee in 1966, a manufacturer of electronic eavesdropping equipment reported to the committee that in 1961 he sold more of his bugging devices to women who were checking up on errant husbands, but in 1966 some 80 percent of his domestic clients were husbands trying to find out what their wives were up to.[7]

Occasional newspaper and magazine stories about "wife-swapping" and suburban housewives caught in call-girl raids do nothing to diminish the popular notion that such behavior is fairly widespread. Again, however, the very fact that it is headlined in the newspapers indicates that it is still news and that the

---

[5] Harold T. Christensen, "A Cross-Cultural Comparison of Attitudes Toward Marital Infidelity," *International Journal of Comparative Sociology*, **3** (September, 1962), 130.

[6] John F. Cuber and Peggy B. Harroff, *The Significant Americans*, New York: Appleton-Century-Crofts, 1965, p. 152. Cuber later explained that they were interested in context, not number, and thus did not publish exact statistics in this study. They felt that a mere count would yield a useless and possibly spurious statistic, because any count of adultery would lump together behavior incidents of such diverse character as the action of a man who had had "one too many" at the office party, the tender "mismate" who found warmth wherever he could, the lecher who seeks every possible sexual variety, and the mate whose marriage is capable of destroying him but who is sustained by an extramarital relationship. John F. Cuber, "Adultery: Reality Versus Stereotype," unpublished paper read to the 1966 Groves Conference, Kansas City, Mo.

[7] "Do-It-Yourself Kits 'Bug' Erring Mates, Senators Are Told," *New York Times*, June 15, 1966, p. 25.

overwhelming majority of the population looks upon it as aberrant rather than typical behavior.

Robert Bell, among several others, has suggested that in present-day America, many men feel that a wife's adultery is an irreparable blow to their marriage, even though women are often less inclined to view male adultery in the same extreme way. Therefore, as Bell puts it, "Of greatest significance may be the indicated behavioral change in the sexual activity of many wives. The philandering husband has often had latent social acceptance in the United States but the philandering wife has not, either in the past or in the present."[8]

Bell's statement is not wholly congruent with the case histories that Cuber and Harroff report. At least some of the husbands interviewed knew that their wives were having extramarital affairs and continued to live with them anyway. Cuber reports the views of a lawyer who said, "A couple of years ago, when I thought my wife was sleeping around with our pediatrician, I was inclined to raise hell at first but the longer I thought about it—well, she wasn't doing any-thing I hadn't done, so maybe it would be just as well to try and be rational about it."[9]

It has been suggested that American women are not really very good at adultery. Morton Hunt puts it this way:

> The adulteress in America generally makes a rather poor mistress even when she is sexually responsive and suitably flattering to a man's ego, because she wants too much of her lover—she wants him to be her mainstay in life, her be-all and end-all, and, inevitably, her legal mate. It is enough to frighten any sensible philanderer away.[10]

On the other hand, Cuber cites evidence to suggest that there are some American women who can be as casual about their temporary sexual liaisons as their male partners.

CHANGING ATTITUDES

The third trend in extramarital sex is the attitude toward it. Until the early days of this century, adultery in our culture was defined as sin, an abominable evil, and a threat to the monogamous base of society. In the last few decades, as we have turned more away from the concept of sin and more toward psychological and psychiatric behavorial interpretations, some have been inclined to describe the adulterer as sick, immature, narcissistic, or neurotic, all designations imply-ing a psychopathologic state.

Robert Whitehurst has come to the conclusion that adultery is now so prevalent for middle-class males that it can be described only as normal be-havior in the social context in which many men live in today's United States. In a paper read to the 1966 meeting of the National Conference of Family Relations, he pointed out that an increasingly large proportion of adulteries can-not be considered the function of seriously neurotic personalities, as it would have been until recently. Said Whitehurst,

[8] Robert R. Bell, *Premarital Sex in a Changing Society*, Englewood Cliffs, N.J., Pren-tice-Hall, 1966, p. 151.
[9] Cuber and Harroff, *op. cit.*, p. 11.
[10] Morton M. Hunt *Her Infinite Variety*, New York, Harper & Row, 1962, p. 139.

By this is meant that many persons can and do commit adultery without strong guilt feelings, without underlying intrapsychic complications, or other commonly described neurotic symptoms. Adultery . . . involving extra-marital involvements of upper-middle class business and professional people, can be considered an extension of fairly normal (meaning non-pathological) behavior.[11]

This is also the conclusion reached by Cuber and Harroff, who feel that, because much of the evidence about adultery has come from those adulterous people who sought help for their neurotic problems, it has been too soon concluded that those who are adulterers are therefore neurotic. Cuber and Harroff point out that many people have had the same extramarital experiences as the clinical cases. These people are not ordinarily included in the conventional stereotype. Cuber and Harroff report that an overwhelming number of their "significant Americans" who had participated in extramarital sex expressed no guilt with respect to these affairs. The implication is that perhaps those who have extramarital affairs and are neurotic were either neurotic or potentially neurotic before they had the affairs.

In a subsample comparison of 45 of his "significant Americans" who had sought no help for marital or emotional problems with 45 who did seek help, Cuber found virtually no difference between the two groups. Thirty-seven of the 45 nonclinical respondents had had extramarital coitus either in a love relationship or for a thrill, whereas 40 of those who sought help had had similar experiences.[12]

Albert Ellis, the New York psychotherapist, feels that, in modern society, there are both "sane" and neurotic reasons for adultery as well as various other kinds of unconventional sex behavior. He cites the "freeing of the human spirit" as a "healthy" reason for extramarital sex (and even promiscuity). Ellis believes that many people "find that they are freer, more labile and more truly themselves (as distinct from well behaved conformists) when having promiscuous rather than conventional mating relationships." He also suggests that adulterous affairs not only provide sexual variation but also improve sexual techniques and helps relieve the boredom of living by the excitement of adventure.[13]

Ellis concedes that there are some unhealthy reasons for extramarital sex too, including the danger of becoming compulsively promiscuous and so destroying existing or potential involvements by hastening from one affair to another. He also includes a neurotic need for ego-bolstering and escapism among his unhealthy reasons for seeking sex outside of marriage. Further, he is not accepting of extramarital sex that involves hostility and rebelliousness, since this precludes some from getting the "real joy and personal growth they might experience from being healthfully promiscuous."[14]

In examining these speculations and opinions about extramarital sex, it should be borne in mind that marital fidelity is still the *ideal* for most people in the mainstream of American living today. Cuber and Ellis have sampled only an infinitesimal part of the 45 million American couples who, by-and-large,

[11] Robert Whitehurst, "Adultery as an Extension of Normal Behavior: The Case of the American Upper-Middle Class Male," paper presented at the meeting of the National Council of Family Relations, Minneapolis, Minn., October, 1966.

[12] John F. Cuber, "Three Prerequisite Considerations to Diagnosis and Treatment in Marriage Counseling," in Richard H. Klemer, ed., *Counseling in Marital and Sexual Problems: A Physician's Handbook*, Baltimore, Williams & Wilkins, 1965, p. 55.

[13] Albert Ellis, "Sexual Promiscuity in America," *Annals of the American Academy of Political and Social Science*, **378** (July, 1968), 66.

[14] *Ibid.*, p. 67.

maintain more traditional attitudes toward marital fidelity. It is probable that most Americans—even those who have had some extramarital sex experience—still think of such behavior as "cheating" and still respect the integrity of the husband and wife who really meant what they said in their marriage vows.

THE EFFECT
ON THE MARRIAGE RELATIONSHIP

What effect does extramarital sex have on marriage and the family? It is extremely difficult to tell how many marriages are destroyed in any one year by the infidelity of one spouse or another. In the past, adultery has been the third most often used of the legal grounds for divorce, but there is considerable evidence that cruelty and desertion, which are the first two most used legal grounds, were sometimes cover-ups for marriages that had dissipated as the result of infidelity. Even if it were possible to measure accurately the divorces resulting from broken pledges of faithfulness, it would probably be only a partial measure of the marital disruption caused. In many cases, the matter is quietly hushed up, but not before one partner or the other has suffered terrible mental anguish and self-doubt.

A deteriorating marriage is not a necessary concomitant of infidelity in every case. Nor is philandering always injurious to the mental and emotional health of those who participate in it. There are some marriage partners, especially some wives, who are pleased, either overtly or covertly, when their husbands engage in extramarital sex. Some, who didn't particularly care for sexual activity in the first place, are delighted to be rid of their wifely "duty" to satisfy their husband's "animal instincts." Other wives, relieved of some of their own guilt, feel justified in having extramarital affairs of their own. Still other wives receive masochistic emotional satisfaction in finding out that their mates are the reprobates they always suspected them to be.

Not all husbands are unhappy when they find out about their wives' infidelity, either. Cuber has asserted that he found cases in his study in which both wives and husbands knew of their mates' extramarital affairs but in which the marriage remained qualitatively at least as good as the average nonadulterous marriage.[15] Many happily married people who base their love on loyalty find these data hard to believe. It is still probably true that, in most marriages, evidences of the mate's infidelity is severely disruptive if not totally destructive. What should be done if adultery is discovered by a partner whe feels betrayed and outraged by the discovery?

WHAT CAN BE DONE
WHEN INFIDELITY IS DISCOVERED?

In the unknown number of marriages in which infidelity is occurring, there probably could be less trauma if the partners would recognize the *true* reasons for their mates' infidelity and then take some intelligent steps to do something about it.

[15] John F. Cuber, "Adultery: Reality Versus Stereotype," unpublished paper presented at the 1966 Groves Conference, Kansas City, Mo.

Doing something intelligent about infidelity usually requires some meaningful self-evaluation as well as some clear perception and decision making. To make those perceptions and decisions, one needs to know not only something of the nature of adultery but also something of the nature of the adulterer.

In order to understand the dynamics of infidelity, it is necessary to take a look at some of the different values and attitudes that motivate the adulterer. Later we shall see that the motivation of the unfaithful partner may control the type of reaction and decision that the aggrieved partner will want to make. No adulterer, either male or female, falls into a totally neat classification, but the following are some fairly general types:

The Libertine

People, particularly males, reared in a different national environment or even in a nonconventional subcultural group in our own society in which the prevailing value system views extramarital sexual relationships as both normal and desirable are not likely to make sexually faithful mates. Such people may argue quite candidly that, in the cultural group from which they came, "every man had sex outside of marriage, and what's wrong with that?" They may look upon monogamous marriage as a curious American custom, a mid-Victorian hangup, or a vestige of middle-class prudery. It is highly improbable that such individuals are going to change dramatically in order to conform with any of the notions the tradition-oriented middle-class mates may have about fidelity in marriage. Most marriage counselors would not go so far as to say that reorienting the cultural libertine is altogether hopeless, but most would certainly agree that it is difficult. Although it may be too long for their mates to wait, there is some evidence that, as the libertine grows older, he is inclined to become more faithful. It is also probably true that the young rebel who has "dropped out" of middle-class society in a show of nonconformity may have much less difficulty in returning to traditional conformity than the person who was never conditioned to a monogamous marriage expectation to begin with.

The Sexually Deprived

There are other large groups of adulterers who have strikingly different motivations. There are, for example, many people of both sexes who feel that they are sexually deprived in their present marriage. Such people often seek—deliberately or unconsciously—an extramarital relationship in order to show their spouses that somebody else desires them, or that somebody else can offer them the satisfactions they desire.

> CASE 42
> "I don't love my wife, Peggy, anymore," Ralph told the counselor, "and I'm not sure that I ever did." "Oh, I guess I did have some affection for her in the beginning: I'm a kind of a sentimental guy. Besides, she tried hard to please me then. But as time went by, she began to make it very clear that she didn't want me sexually. It got so that if I tried anything, she gave me all sorts of excuses, and if I persisted, she would just lie there like a lump.
> "About a year ago I met Claudia. She was unhappily married too, but in all of our

relationships she was all of the things that Peggy wasn't. Claudia was warm and eager to have sex. Moreover, she accepted me completely, and she listened to me. I didn't have to try to be something I wasn't with her. I could tell her all my troubles. I didn't have to hold back, as I did with Peggy, for fear that she would get upset. Instead of helping me get over my anxieties, Peggy would just add to them, and then there were two people twice as anxious.

"Some funny things happened after I began sneaking out with Claudia. I found that I wanted Peggy sexually more than I ever had before. As a matter of fact, I never really wanted Peggy until after I had been with Claudia. I don't think our poor married sex life was all Peggy's fault. She was brought up in a strict religious home. She wasn't ever allowed to believe that sex could be good. She was taught that it was something bad or dirty.

"Anyway, I told Peggy about Claudia almost two months ago. Peggy screamed and cried and carried on. But she didn't do anything to try to make our marriage better. I told her I wasn't going to leave her because of the children. And I won't either.

"I broke off with Claudia last month, though. I'm through with her. She wanted me to stop having sex with Peggy. Claudia thought she could tell me not to have sex with my wife. Imagine that! I was a little amused at first, but she started nagging me about it, and I began to realize why Claudia and *her* husband don't get along too well. Now I don't know what to do. I don't want Claudia, and Peggy doesn't want me."

"I have always been a little afraid of him," Peggy told the counselor. "He has such terribly black moods sometimes. I suppose I did try harder to please him when we were first married, but after a while I began to feel that some of his criticalness and moodiness and drinking too much at parties was the cause of our trouble. I guess I stopped trying to please him and started trying to punish him into being the pleasant, considerate, thoughtful man I had thought he was.

"My mother was very critical of me as a child. She was an absolute perfectionist, and I had to do everything just right or she told me about it. It's funny, I just traded a critical mother for a critical husband. I was resentful when she hurt my feelings, and I'm even more resentful when he does.

"Our sex life has never been very good for me. I used to like it when we were dating and he touched me, but I always thought that intercourse was a little dirty and disgusting. I'm not sure where I got those ideas. I don't think my mother ever said it exactly that way. She just made me timid about everything. I think I must have made up most of the inhibitions myself.

"Anyway, I need someone to help me about sex. Ralph was no help at all. He was very boyish about sex; he needed my approval all the time. He couldn't be happy when I just enjoyed it a little bit. I had to have some completely rapturous, earth-shaking response, or he thought I didn't care anymore and then he got in one of those black moods. I thought our sex life had improved recently. He started coming home more. And once in a while he was very aggressive about sex, and I loved it. He seemed happier, too, on these occasions. When I found out about Claudia I was terribly hurt and angry. I haven't yet decided what I'm going to do. But I'll tell you this: It's going to be a long time before I can respond to him again. Imagine his wanting to touch me after he has been with that other woman! When he tries to make love to me now, that's all I can think about. I get angry all over again just sitting here talking about it! I have a good mind to leave him."

It isn't always direct sexual deprivation that makes one mate or the other feel he is so abused that he has a right to seek solace elsewhere, nor is it always the male who feels abused.

"Larry was an absolute clod," Sylvia told the counselor. "All he wanted to do was to come home and sit and watch television or work on that stupid boat of his. He had no interest in art or in good music. We never went anywhere. He never wanted to take me out. I really don't know why I married him, since we had nothing in common. It must have been that he offered a kind of security. His family had lots of money, and we have a beautiful home now. He could provide all the things that I dreamed about having as a girl: fur coats, maids, the whole bit.

"About two years ago I met Roy at a cocktail party. He was handsome in a very masculine sort of way, and I was immediately attracted to him. But more than that, he could talk brilliantly and knew all about good books and music. He was vibrant and exciting, and I wanted to be near him. Roy was married, of course, but very unhappily. I invited him and his wife over to our house, and Larry even took them out on our boat. I would see Roy at the repertoire theater. (Larry wouldn't go with me, so I went alone.) Pretty soon it was obvious that Roy was attracted to me. One thing led to another, and before long we were having sexual relations. I just left my children with a maid; it was easy. Roy was a salesman, so it was easy for him too. Sometimes I convinced Larry that I needed to go away by myself for several days at a time.

"The sexual experiences Roy and I had were more exciting than anything I had ever known. He was self-confident and imaginative. I began to find out what real sensual pleasure was for the first time. Now I can't stand to have Larry touch me.

"I'm going to leave Larry and marry Roy as soon as he can divorce his wife. She won't give him a divorce easily. I can't understand that. Why should she want a man who doesn't love her anymore? He says he'll provide for his children.

"I can't make up my mind whether I want to keep my own children or not. They're a real problem to me sometimes. I couldn't stand them if it weren't for the maid and having Roy.

"I see it this way," Sylvia went on. "Human beings only have a short time on this earth, and they're entitled to all the pleasure they can get. They shouldn't be locked up for the rest of their lives with people they don't love. Sometimes I think I would let Larry have the children if that's what it takes to get a divorce. But not unless we settle everything the way I want. The judge will award me the children if I want them. They always give the children to the mother.

"Larry says he wants the children. But I think that's only because he is so conventional and thinks he should protect them. He never plays with them. He just sits there and watches that stupid television."

Larry looked at things very differently. "There is something terribly wrong with Sylvia," he told the counselor. "She is emotionally sick and should be seeing a psychiatrist. Both her sisters and even her parents have told me (and her too) that what she is doing with Roy is very wrong. I haven't done a thing to her. I have always tried to be a good husband. I don't drink, I don't run around with other women. As a matter of fact, Sylvia was about the only woman I ever dated. I guess I was kind of slow in that regard by modern standards.

"I've always tried to give Sylvia everything she wanted. I got her a maid because she thought taking care of three children by herself was too much. When I didn't enjoy something that she liked, I let her go ahead and do it anyway, and I'd make myself happy in other ways. That may have been a mistake. I let her go to the theater by herself, and she rewarded me by carrying on with that other fellow.

"There is another reason why I think she needs psychiatric help. She is very moody. She gets to feeling depressed, and then she says she has to go off by herself to 'think things over.' Sometimes she goes for several days at a time. She never tells me where she's going or where she's been. Usually when she comes back things are worse than when she left.

"I really don't know what to do about the situation. I threatened twice to put her out of the house if she saw that other man again. Then she went ahead and saw him again anyway. I don't know what to do now. I don't want to lose her. I still love her, and besides, the children need a mother. I talked with my lawyer about the situation, and he said to wait a while and do not do anything that would force her into the other man's arms. Maybe she will come to her senses or be willing to get some psychiatric help.

"Our sex life is down to absolutely nothing. When she permits me to touch her at all, she makes it very clear that I may have her body but under no circumstances will she respond to me. She seems to be trying to punish me for something. I can't understand it. She had a very forceful dominating father who always told her what to do. I always thought she would like being allowed to make her own decisions, but that isn't the way it appears to be at all. She doesn't even want to decide anything—even what color dress to wear. She seems to want me to tell her what to do. And I don't make decisions easily myself. I hate to make people angry with me.

"She has offered to stay on living with me at the house in a brother–sister relationship. I don't really want to do that, but I remember what my lawyer said about not driving her out. My cousin thinks I should throw her out, but I just can't do that. Tell me what I should do."

The Dangerous Age

Still another kind of adulterer is the man or woman who feels he is abused not so much by his mate as by increasing age. Much has been written about the so-called male climacteric, which often includes the notion that men, foreseeing the end of their sexual prowess, go out for one last fling. Many mature men do want the ego-building satisfaction of having a young woman sexually attracted to them. Ordinarily they get over it in time, since the difference in ages and interests usually makes such relationships either exploitative or unrewarding.

Age affects female adultery as well. Infidelity soon after the birth of a baby may indicate that a woman is seeking to reassure herself of her ability to attract men, despite her maternal role. If unfaithfulness occurs later in life, it may represent a desire on the part of the woman to compete with her daughter and so demonstrate to herself that she has not lost her femininity. Some women need even more reassurance of their continued desirability after their menopause. This need sometimes leads women to take part in adultery for the first time in their lives.

Since it is probable that more males than females are involved in middle-life adultery, let's first take a look at a fairly typical male case:

CASE 44
"I think he's just gone crazy," Della told the counselor. "Here he is, a respectable business man of 45 and he's gone off chasing after some twenty-three-year-old flibbety-gibbet. She works in his office—or at least she did—until I raised such a fuss. I threatened to go to the president of the company and then he would fire them both. There was no excuse for this! My daughters are eighteen and sixteen. When I told them about it, they were shocked, believe me. One of them told him what a terrible father she thought he was. The other, the younger one, just hung

her head and said nothing. But I know she thought it was terrible, too, the way he was acting.

"It isn't as if he were some real lover type who needed more than I could give him. Actually, he never was much at making love, and in the last few years there have been times when he wasn't even able to have intercourse at all.

"And of all the people to choose, that flighty little tramp at his office was the worst. I wonder what's the matter with him; he must be sick to take up with her. She's just a little mouse without any brains. Oh, she has a figure all right, but that's all she has.

"I really don't understand it. I tried all my life to make a good home for him. I''ve always had his dinner ready. I've helped him by scrimping and saving. I've raised the girls so he could be proud of them and he rewards me this way. I really should divorce him. He deserves to be punished for this."

George didn't deny any of his wife's accusations when he saw the counselor. In fact, he enlarged on many of them. "Yes, it's true. From the outside Della was everything a respectable wife should be. She did get my supper. She did scrimp and save. She did take care of the girls. But once they got old enough to talk with her, she never really talked with me again. This girl in the office, Caroline, would listen to me. She understood me in a way that I don't think Della ever did. And when she told me she loved me, I got a thrill I never had before. I felt young again —as if life wasn't really over for me. And when she let me know that she *wanted* me to touch her, I was happy for the first time in twenty years.

"In a way, it was like back when Della and I were first married. It was playing house all over again. Caroline was so neat and tidy, not only in the way she kept her apartment but also in the way she kept herself. She was immaculately clean about everything. I'll tell you, Della has gotten a little careless and dumpy lately. But Caroline was young and alive. She was graceful to watch. I still can't believe that she would really love me. But she did.

"It's over now," George added sadly. "I didn't end it; Caroline did. All of a sudden she seemed to turn cold and unresponsive. I guess it really wasn't any one thing that did it. An old boyfriend of hers came back and she started going with him again. I probably suffered in comparison with him. But I also think she was beginning to see that I wasn't the hero she thought I was. Part of the problem was that I really *wasn't* that hero, and *I* knew it better than she did. I couldn't keep up the pretense forever. I felt plenty guilty about what was going on, and I guess some of my guilt and anxiety was transmitted to her. She didn't want guilt and anxiety. She wanted courage and leadership, so she turned away from me.

"Now I guess I need Della more than I ever did. But she's mad at me now and she's turned the girls against me. I don't know what I'll do now. I sure need somebody to help me."

The Circumstantial Adulterer

Situational circumstances—some accidental—can often play a part in an adventure into infidelity and in creating a fourth type of adulterer.

The availability of a large number of young, sexually emancipated women in today's society who are eager to establish relationships with mature men has given the problem of adultery a new social dimension. Today's executive is more likely to meet more of these young women in more private situations in one day's time than his great-grandfather met in the course of his lifetime. Moreover, he often meets them at a period in his life when he has lost much of his youthful idealism and at a time in his life when his marriage relationship with his wife has begun to wear thin.

Even so, it is questionable how many married men deliberately set out with the conscious intent of committing adultery. Most have no intention of being unfaithful when they befriend the secretary who works in the office. Adultery is at the end of a long progression. The first step may be talking with the secretary about her desperate financial problems; the second step may be taking her to lunch so that they can talk at greater length about her problems; the third step may be offering to drive her home each night to save her carfare; and so forth. It is possible, of course, that this sweet, kind lovable fellow might have gotten into difficulty with some other girl if he had not with this one. But certainly *this* particular episode would not have occurred had he not met *this* particular girl at *this* particular time.

There are other situational circumstances that can play a part in adultery, as the following case illustrates:

CASE 45

"After she started working, Martha couldn't seem to leave the men alone," Ken told the counselor. "Oh, I knew there was a bunch of wolves at that big industrial plant, but she made it very easy for them. I should never have let her go there in the first place. I wouldn't have if I knew then what I know now. But she changed! When I married her she was a quiet, shy type of woman. She did everything I told her to do. As a matter of fact, sometimes I wished she would have had a little more spunk. I had to tell her what to do most of the time. Sometimes I even had to do the housework. She seemed afraid that she couldn't do it well enough to suit me. She will tell you I criticized her a lot, and she's probably right, but I knew she was capable of doing so much more than she did.

"It isn't as if there was just one man, now that she's working outside the home. She's had three or four. After the first one, I told her she had to quit playing around. But she wouldn't do it. She threatened to leave me. I put up with it as long as I could, and after the last one I walked out. Now I sort of wish I hadn't, because she didn't come to her senses like I thought she would. Now she keeps telling me she isn't sure she really wants me back. But I want her. And I sure want my kids."

Martha started out by telling the counselor that as a child she'd been shy and always felt a little inferior. "I had crooked teeth and I always thought of myself as rather homely," Martha said. "About three years ago, though, I got my teeth straightened. All of a sudden I began to feel differently about myself. The men began to look at *me*. Even so, none of this with the men would have happened if it hadn't been that Ken wanted me to go to work. We needed the money, but I sort of resented him pushing me out, and I think I sometimes justify what I have done by that resentment.

"Anyway, I soon found I liked it at the plant. There are a lot of men there, and they told me a lot of nice things. When somebody flatters me, I'm gone. I didn't think about the consequences, and I didn't care whether the men were married or not. I remember the first man. He really made me feel like something special. I had a kind of excitement inside of me that I had never known before. He made me feel important—not like Ken. Ken was always critical at home. Ken could do the housework better than I could, so sometimes I'd let him.

"When I got to work I felt very independent, especially after I got my first paycheck. Then I knew I could take care of myself and the children, too, if I had to. Up until then I had always been afraid that something might happen to me if I didn't do just what Ken said. I always thought I had to have somebody to take care of me, but now I don't, and I'm not going to put up with Ken's criticizing any more.

"I'm not sure I'll ever let Ken come home. He keeps begging me. But why should

I? I'm still having a good time at the plant. The kids are well taken care of. Ken sends me money in addition to what I make. I don't even think about Ken much anymore. And when I do, I feel a little sorry for him. The only time I even wanted to call him was a week or so ago, when I found out that he had gone out with another woman. It's a funny thing: That made me interested in him for the first time in months. I don't understand it, but that's the way it is."

Afraid of Missing Something

Not far removed from the people who wander into infidelity accidentally are the people who arrive there because they are afraid they might miss something. While I was collecting the data about single women, many reported to me that they regularly encountered married men who wanted to establish illicit relationships. Some of these men were perennial wolves, but there were also more timid men who made an approach, the single women thought, simply because they had heard that everybody else was "doing it," and they didn't want to miss out on what they had been led to believe was today's most popular thrill.

Several of the single women reported that it was fairly easy to send these men back home to their wives by using just a little amateur psychotherapy. There are, however, many men and women who enter an extramarital affair at least once, just so they can say they haven't missed anything.

The Emotionally Disturbed

Finally, there are some adulterers who are emotionally disturbed. No one knows exactly how large this group is or at what point to differentiate between those who are and those who are not disturbed. But it is obvious that there are some men and women who have deep-seated compulsions that drive them to seek sexual satisfaction in nonsocially approved ways. These people, like the other compulsively promiscuous people discussed earlier, are emotionally sick.

WHAT CAN THE PARTNERS DO?

Understanding that there are different kinds of philanderers as well as different kinds of philandering sometimes makes it easier for both partners to know what to do about infidelity. For if anything at all is to be accomplished in saving or improving a marriage relationship after infidelity has taken place, both partners must achieve some new insights into the dynamics of their own behavior and the weaknesses in the relationship itself. It is as important for the aggrieved partner to recognize the extent to which he has contributed to the infidelity as it is for the errant partner to come to understand why he behaved the way he did. As a matter of fact, it is frequently the aggrieved partner who must get the insights first, for if he or she doesn't take the right action, the marriage might be destroyed before anything constructive can be done.

Most aggrieved partners do the wrong thing when they initially find out about their spouses' infidelity. For example, some wives who find out that their husbands have been unfaithful may seek sympathy from a neighbor or a friend by telling her the whole story. Only later do they realize that revealing the sordid details hurt their pride as much as the infidelity itself did.

Another woman may order her husband out of the marriage bed, only to recognize later that this might perpetuate and enlarge the probability of his infidelity. Another woman may seek a quick divorce, later to realize that she didn't want to lose her husband but rather to regain him. She was only trying to threaten him into being faithful again.

Another woman may seek out her husband's sex partner—the "other woman"—and beg her to let her husband alone. Only later does this wife realize that she has added to the other woman's self-assurance and so possibly increased her influence over the husband.

Still another wife may take a moral, judgmental attitude, accusing her husband of "being bad." This undoubtedly will put him on the defensive, but it is very questionable that it will make him regret his infidelity. Another woman may punish her husband with silence, only to realize later that lack of communication was the problem in the first place. And yet another wife may play the role of martyr with a dramatic ability worthy of Sarah Bernhardt, only to convince her husband that he was right to seek the other woman who didn't openly seek to manipulate him.

While all these behaviors are unproductive or destructive in *some* cases, they are necessarily bad in *all* cases. Each situation has to be handled on its own merits. The aggrieved partner can best serve himself and his marriage by carefully examining his own role, discussing with his partner the basic backgrounds of the problem, and, with dignity and self-assurance, taking the action that seems most likely to lead to some sort of permanent solution. Consider the following case:

CASE 46

"As I look back on it now," Connie told the counselor, "I know I wanted Sam to find out that I had been unfaithful to him. Ever since we've been married I have been getting less emotional response from him than I wanted. He is the unemotional type who turns his back on feelings. It isn't only that he doesn't know how to enjoy the emotional qualities of music or of art, but I don't think he can even feel love or hate. Do you know what Sam did when he caught me in bed with Harold? He just turned around and walked out. Later on, he came around and wanted to discuss it like an adult. I thought the least he would do was to get a gun and shoot one or the other of us. Not Sam! Actually, I was a little disappointed the way Harold acted, too. After we were caught he stopped calling and didn't come around anymore.

"The man I want must have *feelings*. He must be happy, lively, and animated. He must laugh, and he must cry. I cry a lot, but I always feel even more frustrated after I have. Sam doesn't try to comfort me. He just withdraws. I don't think he has any feelings whatsoever.

"The funny thing is, he thinks he's a good husband because he stays home and doesn't chase after women and doesn't get drunk. I thing he is a poor husband because he allows me complete freedom. He even offers to keep the kids while I go out. I want a husband who cares.

"My mother felt sorry for herself most of the time," Connie continued, "and she controlled me by making me feel bad. She was a complete martyr. I used to hate it. But, would you believe it, I actually think that even though I hated it, I'm acting like my mother myself. Sometimes I catch myself being happier when I feel abused than I am when things work out well. I guess since he won't give me any emotion, I have to create it some way.

"As a matter of fact, that's why I'm continuing to call Harold every once in a while. It isn't really that I want Harold; I just want some excitement. I just want something to happen in my life other than washing dishes and changing diapers. Oh, I know I'm melodramatic. I play little scenes inside my head all the time. But what else am I going to do, married to this unimaginative jerk?"

Sam showed very little emotion when he talked to the counselor. "When I found Connie and Harold together, I was stunned," Sam said. "But I tried to be calm and logical about it. I've always tried to be calm and logical about things, but after a while I began to think that maybe a part of the problem was that I hadn't taken her out very much lately. She's always so busy with the kids, and she makes such a fuss about how bad things are for her when I got home, that I don't feel like taking her out. So anyway, I went to her, and I told her that I would forget all about the thing with Harold if she would, too. I thought she would be pleased that I was going to forgive her. She wasn't pleased at all. She screamed at the top of her voice until the police came. Sometimes I wonder why I married her. I don't think I ever really understood her. She apparently wants something that I can't give her. I don't know why she wants to make such a fuss. I've always thought it was good to be calm. I like to be objective about things, and anger is not using good judgment. There just isn't anything worth fighting about.

"When I was growing up, my father was very strict. He criticized me a great deal, so I try not to be overcritical with her. But she won't discuss things logically. If I try to tell her even very gently that there might be a better way to do something, she just begins to cry and scream, 'Oh I can never do anything right,' so then I have to apologize.

"She gets so excited about little things. I forgot our anniversary a week or so ago, and you should have heard her carry on. I think she got more emotional satisfaction out of my forgetting than she would have if I had brought her a gift. Sometimes I think she is pushing me to fight with her. I don't like to fight. But she keeps pushing and pushing and pushing until she stirs something up.

"She left home last week. She took the kids with her, and she rented an apartment. What shall I do now, let her have a divorce? Seek a divorce myself? Perhaps I would have a better chance of getting the children that way? Or should I try and make up with her? I think after she has had a little more of Harold she will have had enough. That fellow couldn't even get along with his own wife, and he isn't going to be able to get along with Connie for very long."

Obviously both partners—aggrieved and errant—have to help each other, through communication, to understand their emotional involvements and psychological needs. They may have to see and admit the satisfactions that the "other woman" or the "other man" has been providing for their mates before they can improve their own abilities in these directions.

It is revealing to examine the feelings of one wife who met the woman she knew to be her husband's mistress by chance. It gave the wife the opportunity to assess realistically the ability of the other woman to attract the unfaithful husband. The wife soon concluded that, under other circumstances, she herself would wind up liking the other woman, for she found her to be warm and accepting, easy to talk with, and nondemanding, calmly reassuring, and stimulatingly enthusiastic. Far from being a young sexpot, the other woman was in fact a gracious, mature human being who met deep emotional needs within people, regardless of their age or sex. Moreover, the other woman exuded quiet confidence about herself, about her environment, and especially about sexual activities.

As a result of her contact with the other woman, this wife said: "I have learned that I am a taking person. I have placed my needs first and under the guise of not being a nagging wife, I simply turned my back. Lucille—that's the other woman—gave my husband a mature love versus my taking, clinging variety. To be truly mature is to be able to give, and the immature take, cling, and refuse responsibility. I never realized before that this applies to sexual adjustment. Now I can see some of Don's effort to give me a mature relationship. Even living with me must be like living with a child in many ways—like a case of arrested development. You can't make love to a child. No wonder my husband chased girls and devoted so many hours to the adult world of business, and no wonder he spent those months with Lucille, who gave him the mature adult love and mature companionship and security that he so desperately needed and still needs."

This wife was well on the way to doing something constructive about her problem. If the aggrieved partner is willing to accept the realities of the situation and is motivated to some self-improvement, he cannot help but improve the marriage relationship. In the end, it is that relationship that is all-controlling to the faithfulness of the opposite mate, for, if the partners' deep emotional needs are satisfied within the marital relationship, the problem of adultery, although perhaps not altogether absent, is certainly far less significant. In short, the best way to avoid infidelity is through increasing the meaningfulness of the relationship between the two marriage mates.

22

THE SPENDING PROBLEM

U ntil the advent of our affluent society, this chapter might well have been headed "The Income Problem." Today, however, many Americans—and especially many college-educated Americans—have as much difficulty spending money as they do making it. As more and more income has become available, more and more decisions of ever-increasing complexity have had to be made within families concerning how it should be used. Robert Blood and Donald Wolfe found that financial disagreements in families are most common in the upper-middle-income brackets, where there is enough income to make a decision difficult, but not enough so that everybody can have everything he wants.[1]

Blood, along with many other sociologists and a great many home economists, believes that money is the most common source of conflict between husbands and wives.[2] If it is not the greatest source of friction, especially in the middle years of marriage, it is very close to it. A 1967 study by Judson and Mary Landis of three groups of couples—581 happily married couples, 155 couples receiving counseling help, and 164 divorced people—found that all three groups listed finances either in first or second place as a cause of their problems in marriage.[3]

Given modern society, with its enormous emphasis on the accumulation of material things, with its conspicuous consumption, with its keeping up with the Joneses, and with its mass-media-stimulated appetites, and given the urban society's increased potential for marrying a mate who has a value system different from one's own, it is almost inevitable that there will be trouble in many

[1] Robert O. Blood, Jr., and Donald M. Wolfe, *Husbands and Wives: The Dynamics of Married Living,* New York, Free Press, 1960, p. 245.
[2] Robert O. Blood, Jr., *Marriage,* New York, Free Press, 1962, p. 291.
[3] Judson T. Landis and Mary G. Landis, *Building a Successful Marriage,* 5th ed., Englewood Cliffs, N.J., Prentice Hall, 1968, p. 358.

marriages. Pointing up this inevitability are the research findings of the recent Landis study on engaged couples in which the partners were "almost completely unaware of potential differences over the use of money."[4]

In spending, as in sex and in every other sensitive area of marriage, two of the major sources of conflict are, first, the different value conditioning that each of the mates has had in his childhood, and second, the complex of anxieties, attitudes, and behaviors that make up each partner's personality. In addition, a particular family's financial and affectional circumstances at any given time have considerable influence on its spending problems. So too does the spending knowledge that each mate brings to the marriage or acquires as the marriage goes along. Each of these four factors, social conditioning, personality, circumstances, and knowledge, will be discussed in turn.

SOCIAL CONDITIONING FACTORS

Not everybody who lives "down east" in Maine is thrifty, and not everybody who lives in Las Vegas is a wheeler-dealer type. Nor is every Scotsman parsimonious or every foreign prince a wastrel. It is true, however, that there are subcultural group patterns of spending. Saving is more valued in some social circles and conspicuous consumption in others. A woman who expects that she will be able to show what a good provider her husband is by the number of mink coats she has is not going to be very happy married to a man who believes that money is to save and that any display of wealth is unseemly. A man who strongly believes in tithing had best not marry an atheist, for she may resent his giving 10 percent of his income to the church.

In marriage counseling practice, the differential childhood conditioning about money is one of the most common problems brought to the counselor.

CASE 47

"Curt drives me nutty with his constant penny pinching," Virginia told the counselor. "We have plenty of money now. Yes, it was difficult when he was in dental school and even after he was out starting his practice. But now he makes almost $50,000 a year, and we still fight all the time about spending a dime. He keeps all sorts of records on everything we spend. He grudgingly hands a few dollars to me and the children. The way he acts, you'd think he could take it with him. Whenever I try to talk with him about not being so stingy, he just says that he's trying to build up an investment income for me and the kids later on. And that's a very big laugh. We will have an investment income later on, but it will come from my inheritance. My parents are well-to-do; as a matter of fact, I think that's part of the problem. He's constantly trying to show my father that he can accumulate money, too. Actually, my father really didn't accumulate his; my great-grandfather did.

"Anyway, trying to show my father how good he is is only part of the problem. The real difficulty arises from the fact that Curt's father was always a record-keeper. That's what makes it so funny. Curt's father never really made any money, but he always kept track of everything down to the last penny. And he made his boys do it, too, or he wouldn't give them their allowances. It didn't take on his older son, Jack, but it sure took on Curt. Jack's been in and out of bankruptcy several times,

---

[4] Ibid.

but Curt, who doesn't ever need to think about his future income, keeps track of everything.

"I guess Curt's father got it from his father, too. They came from an old European family where pinching pennies was sort of their religion. I suppose they had to scrimp up until the time they came. But I think there was more to it than that. I once went to a neighborhood meeting where his father and mother lived. All the neighbors who came from the same background were exactly the same way about money.

"The worst part about all this is how confusing it is for the children. No, I take that back. That isn't the worst part. The worst part is the fights we have in front of the children, because I want to live a little now and because I believe you have to dress well and live well if your children are going to have the respect of their neighbors.

"If he had his way we would drive around in a beat-up old car and we would all wear rags. He can't seem to see that nobody would send their children to him for orthodontia then. Who wants to trust a professional man whose wife and children look dowdy?"

Curt told the story a little differently. "I know she told you I was a miser, and by her family's standards, I guess I am. She probably told you too that we don't have to worry because she's going to have a great inheritance. Well, let me tell you this. There isn't going to be very much inheritance, if any. Her father never had to work for anything in his life, and consequently he's gone through the family fortune. There's going to be darn little left. I'm sure Virginia must know this intellectually, but she can't believe it emotionally. She still acts and behaves as if she were rich.

"Sure I raise a row when I get a bill for $350 for one dress. I bet my mother didn't spend $350 for all the clothes she had in her life. But it isn't really the amount that upsets me. It's the fact that she doesn't even know how much some of her dresses cost. She just goes down and picks out one and waves her hand airily and says 'I'll take this.' She has absolutely no sense of responsibility. My mother helped my father to save money for what we needed. In fact, she sometimes made the decision that it was better to save the money than to spend it for something we really didn't need.

"I want to provide something for Virginia and the kids. I'm not a rich man. If serious illness kept me away from my practice for any extended period, it could cut heavily into our standard of living. I haven't been practicing long enough to build up complete security. But even that isn't the point. It just plain isn't right to spend hundreds and hundreds of dollars on silly little gee-gaws when there are other people who have so little. I wish to goodness my wife could know the problems that some of our patients have. I don't think she realizes that some of the dollars she just throws away may represent a great sacrifice to a patient who paid my bill.

"She feels we have to spend the money in order to keep up with her friends and my colleagues. Well, I don't think so. If the children are upset, it's because she's spoiled them, and I'll tell you I'm not going to have that much longer."

Specific Buying Habits

Both general attitudes toward spending (and earning) money and some specific habits of how and what to purchase are acquired in childhood. A child reared in a family where the acquisition of money and conspicuous consumption are primary values will usually form his attitudes and judge his own preformance by these values. Interestingly, both the child who grows up in a very well-to-do home where spending one dollar more or less has little meaning, and the child who grows up in a very deprived home where there is a desperate longing for a dollar to spend, may turn out to be unreasoning spenders. So, of course, may a middle-class child. Ordinarily though, he will have more of a middle-class value system of postponing present satisfaction in order to ensure future rewards. And if he has grown up in one of the more traditional homes, he may have absorbed something of the Puritan ethic that thrift is a virtue and ostentatious spending is not in good taste.

Along with these general values, the child often acquires specific buying habits. Even within the same socioeconomic group (and perhaps within the same subcultural group), two families will spend their money differently. One family believes in buying the best on the theory that it will wear longer. Another will buy the least expensive because of its low replacement cost. Each of these families would insist that their's was the more thrifty program. Both might get along exceedingly well with their own purchasing patterns. The only trouble might come when the daughter of one of these families marries the son of the other. Even though they share the common value of thrift, they might disagree violently over the ways to arrive at that objective. She might be outraged to think that he paid $3 for a pair of socks, but he might point out that they will last four times as long as a 75¢ pair of socks. She might then retort that, even if they did, she might have to darn them before they were completely worn out, but if he had bought the 75¢ socks, he could have afforded to throw them away. And so the argument would go on interminably.

PERSONALITY FACTORS

The line between family conditioning and personality factors is very blurred. But there is enough difference between the spending patterns of children from the same family to make it clear that spending is sometimes a very personal thing. Within the same household, one brother may grow up to be a compulsive gambler and another a tight-fisted saver.

The tendency to worry, which seems to be built into some youngsters very early, has an important effect on later spending patterns. Those who cannot tolerate the anxiety of any form of risk try to spend less and save more. In this, though, they may be self-defeating, if they turn down risk opportunities to make more money that would provide them in the long run with more security.

A chronic spending worrier may have a difficult time in life even if he never marries, but he is sure to aggravate his problems if he does marry. First, he will have the added responsibility of a wife and children. Worse yet, however, if he marries a woman who is as anxious as he is, they will probably increase each other's anxiety either deliberately or unconsciously by asking each other for reassurances of security. If, by the very seeking of this reassurance, each suggests to the other the possibility of failure, they will both wallow more deeply in anxiety.

CASE 48
"I think one of the reasons I married Kay was that she didn't expect me to spend a lot of money on her," Boyd told the counselor. "She came from a family that didn't have very much money, and instead of wanting to have everything she could get

because of that, she acted very sensibly about spending. That is, I *thought* she acted sensibly then.

"But after we got married I discovered that she was actually afraid to spend money. I had to take her by the hand down to the stores and make her buy a dress. Even after she got there she'd find some excuse. She'd say she didn't like the dress, or it didn't fit, or the clerk wasn't nice to her. If she did buy something by herself, she wouldn't tell me about it for a week or two. And then she would kind of sneak it into the conversation as if I was going to yell at her or beat her when she told me.

"At first I was sort of amused by all this, especially since it helped us save money. However, after a while her insecurity got to me. I'm not the best one about making a spending decision myself. Sometimes I needed her help to make a decision that involved spending, even if I was relatively sure it might make us a potfull. But she would always say either 'don't do it,' or else 'you must decide for yourself, dear.' I'm fed up with her insecurity, and I want someone who can really help me make some wise decisions."

"It's true what Boyd says," Kay told the counselor. "I just can't make up my mind to spend. I used to think it was all because my family had such a bad time when I was growing up and money was so important to us. I lost a nickel from the grocery change once when I was a little girl and I was afraid to go home.

"But it couldn't be all that. My brother isn't that way. He buys himself $200 suits that I know he can't afford and yet everything seems to turn out all right for him. Boyd gets so mad at me when I won't tell him about what I really think about buying something. There have been a lot of things I have really wanted but somehow I just didn't dare say so. Supposing it had turned out badly or I hadn't been right?

"I don't know why he gets so mad at me. I try to do everything else I can to please him, but I just can't bring myself to spend money. He's a man, and he should make the decisions and take the responsibility."

It is possible for a chronic spending worrier to marry a woman who is more secure than he. This may be good for him, but sooner or later she may get tired of his constant worrying and become contemptuous of his lack of spending courage. When her reservoir of reassurance gives out, she may start to berate him and thus confirm to him that his anxiety was justified in the first place.

Immaturity

Insecurity is a big problem in spending the family income, but immaturity, another personality factor, is even worse. The marriage counselor often sees a young married couple with a chronic pattern of immature spending.

CASE 49

"Lester takes money we need for the baby and spends it on his hobbies," Lydia told the counselor. "He buys all sorts of fancy chrome parts for his car, and he spends hundreds of dollars on flying lessons and shotguns. Why anybody needs more than one shotgun I don't know, but he has five or six of them. I plead with him and beg him to let me have a little money for the baby every once in a while. But he just doesn't seem to care. We're three months behind with the pediatrician's bill, and sometimes there literally isn't enough for the child to eat.

"All he says to me is 'I make the money, and I'll decide how it is spent.' We would have been kicked out of our apartment for back rent a long time ago if it weren't for my parents. When we get too far behind in the rent, my father can't stand it anymore, and he gives me the money to pay it. But it's so embarrassing. Sometimes my family gives me money for clothes, too.

"I knew I couldn't have everything I used to have after I got married. But I don't think Lester even tries to get ahead. He's happy the way he is. He's so busy with the car and the flying that sometimes he's late to work, and he never volunteers for overtime. But even at that, he makes enough money so that we could live fairly comfortably if only he didn't blow it all. My family is getting very tired of bailing us out, and they are beginning to suggest that I leave him. I don't know what to do."

But Lester told the counselor, "I was a freshman in college two years ago when she came to me and told me she was pregnant. I'll bet she didn't tell you about that. She put on a big act. I loved her, so I said, 'All right, we'll get married.' After we were married, it turned out she hadn't been pregnant at all. But she did get pregnant right away, and the baby came before we had been married a year.

"Before we were married she used to be as proud as I was of my car. But now all the spending has to be her way. We have to live in an apartment we can't afford because her father wouldn't want her in any average neighborhood. I'm supposed to give up everything—all the things I really enjoy—so she can spoil the baby.

"I don't know what she told you, but we always have plenty to eat and a good place to live, even though it is too expensive for us. But I work hard for the money and I want some fun with it. My father used to tell me, 'You're only young once; don't let any woman take all your youth.'

"Besides, what I spend on my hobbies is only a small part of my income. The real trouble is that she has no sense about spending money. She went downtown and paid $145 for a baby crib and $35 for a fancy blanket. She doesn't work, but she has to pay a maid $15 for one day to come in and clean the house so that she can take the baby over to see her mother. Then while she's there, her mother fills her full of a lot of trash like, 'What is that husband doing to you now?' Then she comes home and makes my life miserable about the car and flying. I don't care if she does leave. I used to have a lot more fun before we were married."

Obviously not all immature spenders are teenagers. Some older people don't know how to handle their money wisely, either.

There are some husbands and wives who try to use money to control the other person. Some men don't even let their wives know how much they make. They just dole out little dribbles of money so that she can pay the household bills as they come in. Often, even in these times, the male who behaves this way is unsure of his role and fears that sharing spending decisions with his wife will somehow diminish his male status. Some such males use money as a form of punishment, denying a wife who hasn't behaved the way he thinks she should some of the things she wants.

The man isn't the only one who uses money for control and for punishment. There are the few obvious cases in which women who come from higher income families buy or attempt to buy the affection or the adherence of their less well-to-do husbands. And there are many wives who punish their husbands for some insult, either real or imagined, by just going out and spending. In marriage counseling, this too, is often seen.

CASE 50
"Yes, I sure did close all the charge accounts at the department stores and everywhere else," Irving told the counselor. "Betty had us so far in debt I didn't know how I was ever going to get out.

"When we were first married, she was fairly reasonable about spending. But after a year or two, she began to go on shopping binges every once in a while. She'd run up several hundred dollars worth of charges at the department store in a few days' time. I couldn't figure it out at first. When I talked to her about it she just got nasty. Then a little later, she'd seem to be sorry about it and I'd forgive her. I figured maybe it had something to do with her menstrual cycle.

"But then I began to notice it was always after we had had some kind of disagreement that she did most spending. The longer we were married, the worse it got. Once after we had had a big row, she went down and bought over $500 worth of nothing. I'm not going to put up with that anymore. The charge accounts are closed, and they're going to stay closed, and I don't care what she does about it. We've been married ten years now. I can't understand it. She knows that when we get badly in debt we have a terrible time. The creditors keep calling her up, but apparently she just doesn't seem to care. How am I going to do a good job providing for my family if she carries on like this?"

Betty was equally indignant. "Can you imagine, Irving wrote the department stores and shut off the charge accounts and didn't even tell me!" she told the counselor. "I was so embarrassed I could almost have died when the clerk told me I didn't have credit at the store any more. There were a lot of other people standing around listening, too.

"I know that I spend more than I need to sometimes. But I'll bet in a year's time I don't spend as much on foolish things as he does on his golf and that silly boat. But he has to behave like Mr. Big Shot all the time. He sticks me on a budget, and if I go a few dollars over in any month, he gets blue in the face. It's then when I do most of the spending. I get so mad at his playing 'holier than thou.' You'd think he was some sanctimonious saver. Frankly, I resent his telling me how I should spend our money. After all, I work for part of it, too. I get mad thinking about it even now. Why should he be the one who is the boss? He thinks he's the lord almighty because he wears pants.

"It isn't as if he was some paragon of a husband, either. He thinks he's a ladies' man. He has a couple of drinks at a party and he makes eyes at all the young women around. I caught him a couple of weeks ago with his arm around some little blond who had a cute figure and was dressed to show it off. Oh, yes, he notices how other women look, but he never says anything nice to me. I'm just some old doormat to him. I went down and bought a new dress and a whole outfit of accessories the next day, and he didn't even notice them on me. He just blew his stack and closed all the charge accounts. I'm not going to put up with this much longer."

Closely related to the kind of punishment spending that we saw in the case of Betty and Irving is *compulsive* spending. This is a form of repetitive neurotic behavior in which the spender's motive is often unconscious. In some cases, it may represent a repressed desire to punish a parent or to punish oneself. In other cases, it may represent a form of sexual sublimation or signal deep feelings of inadequacy. In any case, when spending has become totally irrational and uncontrollably compelling, there is a clear indication of a psychological aberration requiring psychotherapy for treatment.

Before we leave the matter of personality factors in spending, there should be some mention of "his and her" money. It is surprising how often individuals bring these feelings to marriage. Sometimes the husband feels that his income is "his" because he earns it. Often a wife who works outside the home believes that the additional income should belong to her and that she should have absolute control over its expenditure, despite the fact that her husband is paying all the family bills out of his income. It is possible that the seeds for many of these "his and her" attitudes are planted in the childhood home. Parents deliberately give *each* child his own allowance and encourage him to spend it on himself. The idea of a brother and sister pooling allowances is almost unthinkable. With this pattern so well established, it is hardly surprising that in later life "his" and "her" money sometimes becomes a problem.

CIRCUMSTANCES

Some circumstances that are reasonably predictable, as well as some that are not predictable, have an influence on any family's spending problems. Many young couples, even well-educated ones, start out their marriage these days heavily in debt. Because of our affluent society's emphasis on instant gratification and the desire to begin marriages at the same level as one's parents now have, newly-weds often buy expensive appliances and automobiles. Sometimes they buy these costly items without figuring out the total monthly payments and the relationship of those payments to their income. Even some others who do manage to balance their budget are perilously close to insolvency. An unexpected pregnancy, an illness, the loss of a job, or any one of a hundred other emergencies can put them on the financial rocks.

If this happens, the damage to their credit rating is bad enough, but the damage to their marriage relationship may be even worse. Soon they may be blaming each other for their financial mess. Consider the case of the young divorcee who was explaining to the counselor how it happened:

> **CASE 51**
>
> "I can see it now, but I couldn't then," Vivian told the counselor. "We wanted everything to be nice when we first got married. We bought a larger house than we could afford, a lot of furniture, a new car, a color television, and we spent a lot of money on skiing weekends. We also had a boat and a trailer. I was working at the time, and it seemed like we could pay for everything easily.
>
> "But then I got pregnant. We still might have been all right except that there were complications with my pregnancy and I had to quit my job. I haven't been able to go back to work since, and that was two years ago.
>
> "Anyway, then we had doctor bills on top of everything else. At first it just seemed to increase our love for each other—the fact that we were facing difficulty together. But soon (it seemed like almost *too* soon) the creditors began to call. At first I didn't mind very much, but they began to get unpleasant and I got edgy. Sometimes I would tell Dan about them, and he would get angry. I can see now that he felt terribly guilty, but I couldn't understand it then. Then he began to get angry with me, and he seemed almost irrational. He would accuse me of being a bad manager, and sometimes he would say it was all my fault because *I* got pregnant. That would make me mad, and I would say some nasty things, too. They must have sounded much worse than I intended them to, because he went out and got a second job.
>
> "But even that didn't solve all our financial problems, and it made him much more tired and upset. Pretty soon he was yelling and screaming at me most of the time. Then we really said some ugly things to each other. I guess once or twice I told

him that if I had married somebody who was a better provider, this would never have happened. I didn't really mean it. Dan was a good husband.

"The thing that hurts worst is that after we were divorced he sold the house and most of our beautiful furniture and things. He apparently got himself out of debt and now he's doing very well. He's moving up in his company, and he seems brighter and happier than I've ever seen him. How do you think that makes *me* feel? I know—in fact I'm positively certain—that if we hadn't had all those debts we could have had a good marriage. But when we got started the way we did, I never had a chance to show Dan how really good a wife I could be."

Spending
and the Family-Life Cycle

As we saw in Chapter 15, there are some predictable phases that every family goes through in the family-life cycle that have an effect on spending the income. The first stage, the honeymoon period, often finds both partners working. The newlyweds are often relatively well off if they don't succumb to the temptation to load up on material things. They may even be able to save a little for the periods of heavier expenditures ahead.

The second stage in the family-life cycle often comes very quickly. The first child is born and expenses shoot up. And, since the wife ordinarily stops working, income goes down. A second child is born, and the economic pinch is increased. This period is sometimes the most difficult of all financially. Most young husbands' earning power increases very slowly and usually does not keep up with the increase in expenses. This is the stage in which careful money management is most needed.

As the children grow and move on into the upper elementary-school grades and even into high school, the expenses increase further. However, after all the children are in school, many mothers are able to to go back to at least part-time work (and by this time many want to). Consequently, in many families, the strain is eased somewhat. Moreover, a college-educated father's earnings will be probably increasing as the years go by.

But there may come another crisis period when the children are in college. Fortunately, by this time, the father's income is approaching its maximum level in many families, and often children themselves can help out. Moreover, some wives are by then able to work fulltime, and total family income may reach its highest level.

The next stage in the financial cycle of the family occurs when the children have left home. At this point, income is usually the highest. Often a college-educated wife is holding a full-time job. Investments are beginning to mature, and surplus income can be plowed back into investments, further increasing them. Hopefully this will be the time in which income for retirement can be built up.

The final stage in the cycle is retirement. Retirement income varies widely. Social Security will provide a bare minimum for some. For others who have had an opportunity to save and invest, retirement is a relatively easy time. Government subsidies in the form of income-tax exemptions and medical programs also help to improve the level of living for older folk. Although there are still many elderly people who live at and below the poverty level, especially those who have no savings and those whose fixed incomes cannot take into account the decline in the value of money, generally speaking the older American is financially better off now than he ever has been before.

It is probably good that many young marrieds believe that they are going to conquer all financial adversity and wind up with security and personal riches. If there were no such dreams, there would be no dreams to come true. On the other hand, this same bubbling optimism often prevents some young couples from realistically assessing the expenses and needs of the next stage in the family-life cycle.

SPENDING KNOWLEDGE

The fourth major factor that influences spending decisions is the financial and management knowledge that both of the partners bring to the marriage. Clearly, those people who have some realistic expectation concerning the values and limitations of money have a great advantage over those who don't.

Most families that are financially successful have some common characteristics. First of all, such families have goals, both long-range and short-range goals. Next, they are able to plan ahead because they are motivated to set aside present desires in deference to long-range satisfactions. If the family provides satisfaction as well as success, its members will have a genuine ability to communicate with each other and enough "give-and-take" adaptability to compromise.

On top of these things, however, the financially successful family usually works out for itself some system of spending that is acceptable to its members. The system can be formal or informal. Evelyn Duvall and Reuben Hill suggest that there are five common systems that families use for the allocation of the money.[5]

First, there is the "dole" system, in which one family member hands out the money a little bit at a time to the other family members. Duvall and Hill feel that if it is not fully accepted by the partners, it can make for constant conflict—either open or concealed behind trickery.

Second is the "family treasurer" system. Although this may often appear to be similar to the "dole" system, it differs in the spirit and nature of the relationship. Family members get a personal allowance. The rest is turned over to the treasurer, who pays all the bills and does most of the buying.

The third system is the "division of expenses" system. Certain spending is assigned to the husband (perhaps for rent, car, or insurance), and the other spending is the responsibility of the wife (perhaps food, utility, or clothing). Additional spending is done by cooperative decision.

The fourth system is called the "joint account" system. Earnings of both husband and wife are put in a joint checking account from which either may draw to pay common or personal expenses. Often one partner or the other writes the monthly checks for the household bills. Duvall and Hill note that this system works well when both members are responsible and cooperative individuals and when the income consistently runs above the expenses.

The fifth is the "budget" system, which Duvall and Hill believe is the best for most families. Expenses are budgeted in advance by common agree-

[5] Evelyn Duvall and Reuben Hill, *Being Married*, New York, Association Press, 1960, p. 251.

ment. Any excess goes into a common fund that is saved or spent only by common agreement.

Although many people think of the budget as a device for saving, in reality it is a plan for *spending*. Basically it enables people to decide in advance what they want to spend their money for and then to be sure there is enough left to purchase those satisfactions previously agreed upon. The budget helps families to look at the whole spending picture and weigh short-range satisfactions against long-range goals.

It is probable that only a small portion of American families regularly and consistently attempt to live within a strict budget. There are, though, many marriages in which the partners have turned to the budget in order to get them out of some immediate difficulty at some time during the family-life cycle.

Many people at all educational levels prefer not to budget, even though they know this may be the wise thing to do. Some argue that it takes all the fun out of spending. They would rather live impulsively, even though they know that in the long run this can only lead to periods of difficulty.

For those who *do* want to undertake a budget, all sorts of information about how to go about it is readily available. Self-help books and pamphlets exist in profusion.[6] But in other areas of family finance, knowledge is not so easy to obtain. Moreover, many college-educated people are so busy acquiring knowledge to *make* money that they fail to acquire any that will help them to spend it wisely. Almost all girls have some introduction to buying food and clothing in a high-school home-economics course, and many boys have some idea of how to buy an automobile from the school of practical experience, but college men and women ordinarily have very little functional knowledge about the really major purchases they will soon be making—houses, insurance, and investments. Often, less well-educated people have a greater understanding of the practical workings of the commercial market place than do new college graduates. This is regrettable, for most colleges and almost all universities offer courses in family finance that could be useful.

Excellent books, ranging from scholarly texts on consumer economics and well-written volumes on money management to current magazines with helpful practical hints on buymanship, are available at almost every library.[7]

Unfortunately, in our rapidly changing economy, books based on research data and census reports are usually somewhat out of date before they can be published in hard cover. The information in Table 22–1 is from a 1966 Bureau of Labor Statistics report. Although it shows some interesting relationships that might be useful to those who find security in knowing how other people spend their money, some of the data have already changed.

Current consumer magazines, although they have some shortcomings, often provide information that is timely and readily applicable to the practical realities of family spending. For example, take the matter of buying a house, the largest single purchase most families usually make. Proper choice of a home can have a very great positive or negative effect on future family relationships.

[6] Some of the best are: U.S. Department of Agriculture, Home and Garden Bulletin #98, *A Guide to Budgeting for the Young Couple*, Government Printing Office, 1964; Education Division, Institute of Life Insurance, *Money Management for the Young Adult*, 1966; and Household Finance Company, *Money Management: Your Budget*, Chicago, 1966.

[7] Often suggested are Arch W. Troelstrup, *Consumer Problems and Personal Finances*, 3rd ed., New York, McGraw-Hill, 1965; Leland J. Gordon and Stewart M. Lee, *Economics for Consumers*, New York, American Book, 1967; and Irma H. Gross and Elizabeth W. Crandall, *Management for Modern Families*, 2nd ed., New York, Appleton-Century-Crofts, 1963.

Table 22-1
Family Expenditure as a Percentage of Total After Tax Income

| | Husband's Age and Income After Taxes | | | | | | | | | | | | | | |
| | Under 25 | | | 25-34 | | | 35-44 | | | 45-54 | | | 55-64 | | |
Income	7,500–9,999	10,000–14,999	15,000+	7,500–9,999	10,000–14,999	15,000+	7,500–9,999	10,000–14,999	15,000+	7,500–9,999	10,000–14,999	15,000+	7,500–9,999	10,000–14,999	15,000+
Food	19.9	—	—	22.8	19.8	27.5	23.1	23.1	23.5	23.8	24.2	20.6	23.8	23.3	17.4
Tobacco	2.5	—	—	1.4	.8	.3	1.5	1.1	1.4	1.6	1.0	.8	1.8	1.1	1.5
Housing (total)	25.8	—	—	27.9	29.6	19.4	28.1	26.5	31.0	25.9	14.5	24.5	24.4	22.4	24.9
Utilities	2.4	—	—	3.6	3.7	3.4	3.8	3.7	3.0	4.1	3.3	3.0	3.8	3.3	3.8
Household operations	7.5	—	—	6.2	8.2	6.4	5.2	5.5	7.6	4.7	5.7	6.9	4.8	4.4	4.8
Furnishings	3.3	—	—	5.1	5.2	4.7	6.0	4.7	7.1	4.6	5.4	3.5	4.8	5.9	6.3
Clothing	10.5	—	—	10.7	10.4	14.7	11.2	10.4	12.8	10.5	10.7	12.1	10.3	9.4	9.2
Personal care	2.2	—	—	2.6	2.1	2.0	2.8	2.6	2.6	2.9	2.5	2.3	3.1	2.7	2.1
Medical care	7.9	—	—	6.5	6.3	8.6	7.1	6.6	6.0	7.3	6.3	5.0	7.4	8.9	6.9
Recreation	4.2	—	—	4.2	5.4	11.2	5.6	5.0	4.7	4.3	7.1	6.1	4.9	4.3	3.6
Transportation	23.3	—	—	17.4	19.6	14.0	15.2	16.5	11.4	17.0	15.8	18.1	17.8	22.2	11.5
Other	3.7	—	—	6.5	6.0	2.3	5.4	8.2	6.6	6.7	7.9	10.5	6.5	5.7	22.9
Total	100.0	0	0	100.0	100.0	100.0	100.0	100.0	100.0	100.0	100.0	100.0	100.0	100.0	100.0

Source: U.S. Department of Labor, Bureau of Statistics, 1960–1961, "Consumer Expenditures and Income: Cross-Classification of Family Characteristics," supplement 2 to BLS Report 237–92, June, 1966, pp. 23–27

It may interest the prospective home buyer to know what percentage of the family income other people have apportioned to housing (usually between 19 and 30 percent), the kinds of mortgage and credit plans available to the home buyer (you pay back more than $55,000 on a $25,000, twenty-five-year mortgage at 7½ percent), and the philosophical advantages and disadvantages of buying a home versus renting one (advantages each way). But usually these matters are only tangential to the real buying problem when a couple is faced with actually finding a house in a new community. Often the realities of the market and the individual tastes of those who are buying are far more crucial factors. Specific information about current real-estate values in the local communities and practical tips about the best kind of heating and the closest shopping center is more important to home buyers at the moment of purchase than all the statistical tables and philosophical arguments.

Very practical guidelines are also available for newlyweds who are about to buy the family's two other major purchases—insurance and investments—if they will take the time to look for them and study the alternatives. The more eager the partners are to learn (and to learn together), the more successful the family spending patterns are going to be.

Because each family has its individual preferences, individual desires, and individual needs, it is probable that some learning has to come the hard way, through experience rather than through books. Spending mistakes can often hurt for years, but if the mistakes aren't repeated, the lessons can be worth almost any cost.

Sidney Margolius has suggested a checklist of ten common spending errors:

1. Constant payment of large finance charges on installment purchases, often resulting in a habitual loss of five per cent of a family's entire income.
2. Overspending for food, with some families feeding themselves nutritiously for as little as a dollar a day per person, and others in the same neighborhood and income bracket spending as much as $1.75.
3. High housing and household-operating costs, including surprisingly heavy outlays for utility bills, fuel and household supplies and failing to take advantage of potential home insurance savers.
4. Heavy car and car-operating expenses, with many families now spending noticeably more than the 12 per cent of after-tax income, which is a safe limit for all car expenses, including depreciation.
5. Larger-than-necessary expenditures for insurance, because of monthly payments instead of annual, or buying many small policies instead of combining.
6. Heavy spending for commercial recreation.
7. Overpayment of income taxes—about a third of the families interviewed [in Margolius' study] paid more taxes than they need to, because they don't understand all the tax rules.
8. Failure to time shopping to take advantage of opportunities such as annual sales and clearances, either because of lack of planning or family capital to finance advance buying.
9. Random spending for toiletries, cosmetics, and household drugs, by various family members, including teen-agers, in an era of high prices and increasing use of such products.
10. Failure to make savings produce maximum yield. For example, some families who shop most economically for food and other needs do not know what interest rates local savings institutions pay, or the best uses of E bonds. Thus

they forfeit the contribution even modest earnings on savings can make to an overall money-management program.[8]

Checklists such as these can be helpful, but the most important knowledge that a marriage partner can have is his awareness of his mate's personal spending idiosyncracies. Given such an understanding plus a great deal of motivation, a lot of planning, and some intelligent use of readily available information, young marrieds can make up spending-knowledge deficiencies as they go along.

Those partners who can remember that spending patterns and anxieties— one's own as well as one's partner's—were conditioned a long time ago will have an easier time making the spending adjustment. For they are the partners who can, with patience and understanding, gently teach each other new ways and patiently reassure old insecurities. At the same time, they can be flexible enough to learn some different ways themselves and steady enough to stay cool when the mole hills seem like mountains.

Trying new things—such as letting the other partner handle all the money for a change—can often help to reduce tensions. But in the end, only when both partners *really* want to find a better way will it be found.

[8] From *How to Make the Most of Your Money* by Sidney Margolius, by permission of Meredith Press. © 1966 by Sidney Margolius.

23

THE IN-LAW
PROBLEM

Mothers-in-law are very much joked about and very little studied. It is said, for example, that the classic case of mixed emotions is that of the man who sees his mother-in-law about to back his brand new automobile over a cliff.

Some sociologists believe that the jokes themselves have created part of the self-perpetuating stereotype that makes young people fear in-laws and thus creates trouble that might otherwise not have occurred. But the jokes aren't all the blame. There are other factors that can make friction between a husband or a wife and his in-laws almost inevitable. Dependency, for instance, is one of these factors. So is rebellion against one's own parents that is projected toward the partner's parents. So, too, is real interference by often well-meaning in-laws.

We will take a look at these and other factors in some of the cases in this chapter. First, however, we will look at the extent of the problem.

HOW MUCH
TROUBLE?

Because of the differing designs of presently existing research studies, it is difficult to generalize about the extent of in-law difficulty. Evelyn Duvall, who questioned 1337 men and women from newlyweds to those married more than forty years, found that almost 75 percent of them reported difficulties with one or more in-laws.[1] John L. Thomas, in a survey of some 7000 broken Catholic

[1] Evelyn Duvall, *In-Laws: Pro and Con*, New York, Association Press, 1954, p. 188.

marriages, concluded that in-laws were the greatest single cause of breakup during the first year of marriage.[2]

On the other hand, Robert Blood used data from a Landis study to suggest that only about 23 percent of wives and 16 percent of husbands experience friction with their in-laws, and that "most couples get along well with their relatives. . . ."[3]

Getting along with one's in-laws appears to be another case of "some do and some don't." As a matter of fact, some partners work out a better relationship with their in-laws than they had with their own parents.

THE MOTHER-IN-LAW PROBLEM

There is one thing about the in-law problem on which the experts agree: The mother-in-law is involved more often in whatever in-law difficulty there is than is any other in-law.[4]

The reason why the mother so often turns out to be the most difficult in-law seems apparent. As Gerald Leslie suggests, mothers' lives, more than fathers', are likely to be organized around their children.[5] When those children marry, the mothers, reluctant to give up the satisfactions of their role, often try to hold onto their former responsibilities and privileges. It also often happens that the children's leaving is coincident with other dissatisfying events in the woman's life, such as menopause and the advent of wrinkles and gray hair. This unhappy series of events has led David Mace to suggest that,

> Most difficult mothers-in-law are really middle-aged women unadjusted to life. They are lonely, frustrated, craving attention. Their plight is sometimes pitiful. They need, above all, warm affection and understanding. Yet by their irrational, critical behavior they cut themselves off more and more from the very things they most need.[6]

Apparently, wives have much more trouble with their in-laws than husbands do with their's, although the jokes have it the other way. Duvall found that women are involved in in-law problems six times as often as men. There are probably many reasons for this. For one thing, as Leslie points out, there is greater emphasis placed upon "being a good wife" than upon "being a good husband" in our society.[7] The wife who is in direct competition with the husband's mother fears she will be judged in terms of her ability to keep house, cook, and otherwise cater to her husband's needs. On the other hand, the husband more often feels he is judged in terms of his success in the occupational world. Although he may sometimes compete with his father-in-law for occupational success, usually he is not acutely aware of this competition.

It has also been suggested that the strength of a mother's attachment to her sons may create some of the antagonism between the daughter-in-law and

[2] John L. Thomas, *The American Catholic Family*, Englewood Cliffs, N.J., Prentice-Hall, 1956, p. 264.

[3] Robert O. Blood, Jr., *Marriage*, New York, Free Press, 1962, p. 318

[4] Duvall, *op. cit.*; and Judson T. Landis and Mary G. Landis, *Building a Successful Marriage*, 5th ed., Englewood Cliffs, N.J., Prentice-Hall, 1968, p. 331.

[5] Gerald R. Leslie, *The Family in Social Context*, New York, Oxford University Press, 1967, p. 321.

[6] David Mace, *Success in Marriage*, Nashville, Tenn., Abingdon, 1958, p. 67.

[7] Leslie, *op. cit.*, p. 320.

her husband's mother. Less commonly is a father-in-law's close relationship to his daughter so threatening to a son-in-law. Here is a case in the classic pattern.

CASE 52

"Arthur's mother is our major problem," Lucille told the counselor. "He is tied to her apron strings—but tight. I tried to be very nice to his mother when we were first married. But she never did like me. In fact, one time she came right out and told me that she didn't believe that I was the right woman for him and I never would be.

"The truth of it is that his mother spoiled him badly. She waited on him hand and foot. She was from an old-fashioned family, and she got all of her satisfaction from cooking and housekeeping. I don't keep house very well, and I admit it. But she didn't have to come over and pick things up after me like she did. It made me so mad I screamed at her and told her to get out. And do you know what, Arthur didn't even take my side!

"As a matter of fact, I think that's what hurts the worst. I can sometimes abide his running over there all the time, but I can't stand the fact that he doesn't stand up for me. He never says anything to his mother in my defense. He never talks back to his mother at all.

"His mother keeps working on his emotional system, even more so now that his father has died. She makes him feel like he ought to come and see her every day. He goes over there at least seven or eight times a week. If I try to make him promise not to, he just lies to me and goes anyway. I've caught him at it.

"I want to move away from his mother. He went and bought a house about a block from her place last year. I almost left him then.

"One time when we were first married, he took a good job down in Atlanta. Do you know how long we stayed down there? Two months! He just couldn't stay away from Mama. He'll tell you all sorts of reasons why we came back: It was a poor job, we didn't like the area, his boss was impossible to work with, but those aren't the real reasons at all.

"Actually, I don't get along any too well with my own mother. At least, though, I always know where I stand with my own mother. When I do something she doesn't like, she tells me about it right there and we can fight it out. But his mother—she just looks hurt and tries to do even more things around *my* house. It's infuriating. Last month I forbade Arthur to let her come around any more. And I made him promise again that he wouldn't go down there. I want you to tell him, too, that he has to stay away. If he doesn't, I'm going to get a divorce. And I mean it."

Arthur said, "Lucille is frantically jealous of my mother. She doesn't even want the children to have gifts from Mother. Lucille is younger than Mother, and she could at least try to understand how Mother feels now that her only son and her husband are both gone. Lucille could end this marriage problem anytime she wanted to by just acting decently to my mother. But she won't.

"Lucille is a terrible housekeeper. I think she'll tell you that herself. And really, that's part of the problem. Lucille knows she should pick things up, but when Mother came over here and did it, she began to boil. That's really what started all the trouble.

"I know Lucille says she wants me to take her side, but what it amounts to is that she wants me to punish my mother as a demonstration of my love for her. She has said it almost that way. What am I supposed to do, castigate my mother because she's trying to help? I can't do that. I've tried to make things as easy as I can for Lucille. I used to ask her to go with me to Mother's, especially on the holidays. But now I don't even ask anymore. Every once in a while I take the children by myself. And then does Lucille scream! She says my mother tries to condition the children against her. Actually, all Mother does is give them a little loving care that they rarely get at home.

"Anyway, I don't go down to Mother's so much myself any more. Actually, Mother has been a big problem for me all my life. Since I was the only child and her only real interest, she expected a lot of attention from me. I know I feel obligated to help her, especially since my father died. Who else is there? You just can't tell her to curl up and die. But Lucille doesn't understand this. Her own mother is an independent type who can take care of herself. She tells Lucille off regularly, and Lucille seems to respect her for it.

"I don't know what I'm going to do. My life is miserable this way. Lucille wants me to move way across town, and in some ways it might be a good thing, although I would never admit that to her. On the other hand, it might just increase the time I had to be away from home, because I know I can't ever abandon Mother altogether."

OTHER IN-LAWS

In Duvall's study of 1337 persons, sisters-in-law were named a source of friction by 20.3 percent of the sample as opposed to 36.8 percent who named mothers-in-law. Since brothers-in-law and fathers-in-law accounted for only slightly over 10 percent of all the problems, it is strikingly clear that in-law difficulty more often has a feminine angle in both directions. Not *always*, however. Consider the following case:

CASE 53

"We moved in with Georgia's father about two years ago," Craig told the counselor. "At the time it seemed like the only thing to do. Georgia's mother had just died, and there was no one to care for her father, who is a partial invalid. You wouldn't know there's anything wrong with him to hear him talk, though. He's fiercely independent. But I guess he does need someone near in case of an emergency. Besides, we needed to save money, and he had a very big house. It was just about the time I had realized that the only way I was going to move up at the research laboratory was to go back and get a Master's degree. All in all, moving in with her dad looked like a real good thing—then.

"But as soon as we got in the house, trouble started. Something seemed to come over Georgia. She stopped doing the housework when her father wasn't around. Now she never does anything around the house unless she's absolutely forced to. I'd like to help with the dishes and the housework, but if I do, she lets me take over completely. If I try to talk calmly with her about it, she flies into a rage.

"Sometimes she trys to compete with me like a little child. If I point out to her that we don't have enough money for some of the things she's bought in the last few weeks, she'll say, 'Well you spent money on yourself last month; now it's my turn to spend some on me.' She doesn't want me to give in to her. Apparently what she wants is a kind of a forceful dominating man like her father used to be. He told her what to do and she loved it. She talks to me about how everything should be fifty-fifty, but she really doesn't mean it. She wants the security of having a husband who is sometimes authoritarian and who is always self-confident. I'm not that way and I admit it.

"But her father is, or was. She still looks to him for leadership. Whenever there is a decision to be made, if I try to talk it over with her she says, 'We'll ask Daddy.' If I try to tell her what to do, then she sulks and I know she runs to Daddy after I'm gone. It isn't that the old man doesn't try to stay out of it. He knows there's a problem, too. But she nags and digs him until he tells her off, and then he tells her exactly what she should have done in the first place. Almost always it's just what I said, but she takes it from him and won't take it from me.

"Georgia is quick to criticize me, but she gets petulant and stubborn when I correct her. I don't mind her pointing out my goofs to me in a good-natured way when we're alone, but it sure fries me when she mentions some mistake I made in front of her dad. That's what most of the fights have been about in the last few months.

"I told her a week ago that we're going to move out of that house. But now she insists that the old man needs us more than ever. He doesn't need Georgia; she needs him. She apparently won't leave, and I guess I'm not forceful enough to make her. She says if I go, I'll have to go by myself and she'll keep the child. What can I do?"

Georgia agreed to almost everything Craig had said. "Yes, it's true," Georgia said. "I do trust Daddy more than I trust Craig. But that's because Craig takes such stupid positions sometimes. I can see now that it's often because he wants to make me feel like he's a leader like Daddy was. But somehow he just hasn't got the personality for it. I want him to be the leader—desperately I want him to be the leader —but I want him to show me that he's the leader by accomplishing things. And he needs to prove himself not only for me but for himself, too. He always feels as if I'm comparing him, and I guess often I am.

"I think sometimes I don't do the housework just because I unconsciously want him to punish me for not doing it. But he doesn't. He just does it himself. Daddy would never have done that. He would have spanked me, and I would have felt better about it.

"Now that Daddy is old and not so forceful anymore, I feel sort of lost. I guess really I'm looking for something I had a long time ago. This is a bad situation. I know we should get out of the house now, but I just can't bring myself to go. My father really does need me. But there's more to it than that. I have always felt completely accepted by him even when he was punishing me. When Craig criticizes me, I just get mad. Sometimes I get mad enough so that I wish Craig would leave."

The case of Craig and Georgia may be unusual in several ways. Sheldon Stryker found that, among his 104 couples studied, the husband's adjustment to his mother-in-law tended to be less adequate when his wife was dependent upon her mother, but his adjustment to his father-in-law tended to be more adequate when his wife was dependent upon her father.[8] Research findings, while demonstrating group tendencies, don't—as we pointed out in Chapter 2— always apply to individual cases such as Craig and Georgia.

DEPENDENCY

Running through many in-law problems is the recurrent theme of dependency. Some studies have shown that marriage at an early age is highly correlated with in-law difficulties, possibly because some young people aren't ready to leave home, even if they think they are.

[8] Sheldon Stryker, "The Adjustment of Married Offspring to Their Parents," *American Sociological Review*, **20** (April, 1955), 149–154.

Judson and Mary Landis found in their study of 544 wives that 63 percent of those who married at twenty-four or older reported excellent adjustments with their in-laws, while only 45 percent of those who married between the ages of seventeen and nineteen reported excellent adjustments. Only 7 percent of the older group reported only fair or poor adjustments, but 21 percent of those married at the younger ages indicated only fair or poor adjustments.[9]

A very common complaint of the husbands of teenage brides is that their wives spend half their lives on the telephone talking to their mothers. Some young husbands who have moved their wives a long way away from their mothers complain that the expense of long-distance calls can be staggering. Often, though, the psychological aspects of this mother-dependency are more detrimental than the financial aspects. Although not all men take an active pride in being good husbands, a surprisingly large number of them do. Such men resent the implication that other people—especially in-laws—can meet their young wives' dependency needs and solve her problems better than they can. Clearly, in such cases, the wife's dependency is only part of the problem. The husband's need for self-esteem is also a part.

Exaggerated independence on the part of one or both of the young partners is as common a cause of in-law difficulty in marriage as is overdependence. Many of the young people who have the most friction with their parents-in-law are rebelling against the influence of older people, symbolized until recently by their *own* parents, and against their own needs to remain in a childlike state of dependence.

Since this kind of exaggerated independence is more characteristic of the young and more characteristic of those who are newly married and still a little defensive about their prerogatives, it is one of the major reasons why age and duration of marriage are correlated to in-law problems.

CASE 54

"If Tony would only try, he could get along with my mother," Lisa told the counselor. "But all he does is carry on about how 'that mother of yours isn't going to tell me what to do.' The funny thing is, she really doesn't try to tell him what to do. But he's gotten so used to fighting with his own mother about whether he's old enough to do this or that that he thinks he has to do it with mine. The slightest thing she does to help us seems to offend him. She bought some cute new clothes for the baby last week. But as soon as Tony found out who they came from, he took them back to the store. He said he could provide for his family and didn't have to be beholden to anybody.

"I don't mean to say that Mother is always right and Tony is always wrong. She gets in a little dig at him every once in a while about how he ought to grow up. That just makes matters worse. Then there's no living with him for a week.

"But Tony's so sensitive that sometimes Mother doesn't have to do anything and there's trouble. He never has gotten over something that happened the first week we were married. I became seriously ill, and Tony took me to the same hospital where I had been a student nurse. When my mother heard about my being so sick she rushed over to the hospital, too.

"While I was being diagnosed, they wouldn't let either Tony or Mother see me. After they figured out that I had peritonitis, the director of the nursing school, who knows me well and who had been in the emergency room with me, went out to the lobby where Tony and Mother were. He was looking out the window and

---

Mother was on the other side of the room. The director knew my mother, but she didn't know Tony, so she went up and told Mother about my condition. Tony got all upset and told them both off right there. He said he was the one who was supposed to take care of me.

"That incident should be almost ancient history now, but it isn't. Tony still carries on about it. Now my mother has gotten angry, and she won't come to see us anymore. I don't know what I'm going to do. I'm caught right in the middle."

But Tony had a different story. "Lisa is so dependent on her mother that she can't see what's going on," Tony told the counselor. "Her mother influences her in a lot of subtle ways that I don't even think she realizes. She goes over to see her mother, and her mother tells her what we ought to have or how I ought to behave. Then Lisa comes home and tells me we need so-and-so or you ought to do such-and-such. I know what we need, and I know what I ought to do. Her mother is worse than my own ever was about trying to manipulate me.

"The worst part about it is that it's so insidious that Lisa doesn't see it. Her mother says to her something like, 'I don't want to tell you how you should do it, Lisa, but I know that when your father tried to take advantage of me sexually, I just got my doctor to tell him that I wasn't strong enough to have sex more than once a week.' I actually overheard her tell Lisa that. Now what do you think of that, Mr. Counselor?

"It's getting so I'm not the boss in my own home. Last week she and her mother went shopping, and when they came home she showed me a new coat she had bought. I didn't like it, and I told her so. But her mother said to her, 'It's beautiful and it fits you so well.' I made such a fuss that she finally took the coat back. But she didn't want to.

"I'm not going to put up with this much longer. Either we move away from her mother or else out I go."

REAL INTERFERENCE

Not always, but usually, there is something to be said for both sides in any in-law problem. It is true that some young marrieds overreact in an effort to emancipate themselves from in-law domination, but it is also true that there are many in-laws who really do interfere.

Possessive mothers—or fathers—are not likely to stop being possessive just because their children get married, nor are dominating parents likely to stop being dominating. When children have been the parents' primary concern and primary interest over a long period of years, it is probably unreasonable to expect them to divorce themselves completely from that feeling of responsibility or from that interest overnight.

But well-adjusted parents who have lived full, well-rounded lives themselves and who aren't overeager to run their children's lives can sit back and wait contentedly in the knowledge that soon they will have grandchildren to be interested in. This ideal type of in-law can find ways to help the newlyweds without increasing their dependency or threatening their independence. When there is reasonably good accommodation on the part of both the in-laws and the newlyweds, both of them can afford to relax a little, secure in the knowledge that whenever problems do arise they will ultimately be resolved, for, as the young people grow older, they will feel less threatened by advice and help. In fact, sometimes they wish they could get more of both when they themselves become parents and begin to experience all the problems and frustrations that they so recently looked at from the opposite direction. Stryker found that, in general, married offspring who had children of their own had better adjustments with their parents than those who did not have children. He speculated that this might be because they were more likely to appreciate the problems and difficulties their own parents went through.[10]

There are, though, some compulsively manipulating parents who just can't stay out of their married children's lives. Consider the following case:

CASE 55

"My mother is doing everything she can to break up our marriage," Rebecca told the counselor. "David has put up with an awful lot, but I don't know how much more he's going to take.

"My mother was against David from the time we started going together. At first she forbade me to see him. She found all sorts of reasons for not liking him. She said he was a jerk and a vulgar lowbrow because he got a little tight one night. Then she caught him in a little fib about where we were going one night, and from then on she wailed about his being a pathological liar. So we ran off and got married secretly. She didn't find out about it until I was pregnant. At first she wanted me to have an abortion. When David refused even to consider it, she screamed at him. But there was nothing she could do about it. She threatened all sorts of vile things. Among other things, she was going to cut me and our baby out of her will. She thinks David is just after my family's money.

"When she saw we weren't going to get an abortion, she tried to work on me to divorce David. She promised she would take care of the baby while I went back to school. All of a sudden she began to make noises like a grandmother—but only if I'd divorce David.

"The thing about it that makes it so difficult is that David has been having a hard time finding himself. He lost several jobs, and we've had a difficult time financially. His mother has been helping us a little bit. My mother could actually help us a great deal if only she would. She says I can come back and live with the baby in the big house anytime I want to, but that she's not going to have David around.

"Last week David gave a bad check in order to get his car out of the garage. Now the garage owner is threatening to have him arrested. Mother could help us out, but she swears she'll see him in jail first. What are we going to do?"

The counselor talked to David. "Rebecca's mother is responsible for all our trouble," David said. "She hates me because I took Rebecca away from a situation that was almost intolerable. When I first met Rebecca, she jumped every time her mother came near her. All she could say was, 'Yes, Mother.' I've gotten her to see that she should lead her own life and not be a puppet on a string. But the old lady sure has made it tough for us.

"I've had some bad breaks in the jobs I've had. At one place I had an accident with the truck the first day I was working, and that finished that. At another place they had an old jerk for the boss who tried to tell me what I should do every minute, so I quit the second day. Then I got a really good job where they had a training program. I might have moved on up, except that it turned out that Rebecca's old lady knew the vice-president, and she began filling him full of a lot of lies about what a bad guy I was—I'm sure that's what happened—and pretty soon the other guys got moved up and I didn't. So I quit.

"Rebecca's mother is forever trying to bribe Rebecca to leave me. She doesn't come right out and say I'll give you a hundred thousand dollars if you'll leave David.

[10] Stryker, op. cit., pp. 153–154.

Instead she just points out the advantages the baby could have if she'd only divorce me and come home.

"She won't help us when we need it. Last week I had a line on a new job, but I had to have a car to get it. My car was in the shop, and I owed about $150 for repairs. So I called Rebecca's mother and asked if she'd advance the $150. Do you know what she said? 'You're always saying how you can take care of Rebecca. Now let's see you do it!'

"I had to have the car so I wrote a check that I knew we didn't have the money for. It would have been all right if I had gotten the job, because then the garage man probably would have given me time until I got my first paycheck before he called the cops."

The counselor also talked to Rebecca's mother. "David is impossible," she said. "He met Rebecca at a drive-in restaurant when his car pulled up beside hers. He picked her up, to put it bluntly. But Rebecca was just a child. The fact that David was a juvenile delinquent—or at least he behaved like one—didn't make any difference to her. Certainly I tried to stop her from going with him. I would have done everything I could to prevent their being married. Yes, I am trying to do everything I can to get her to leave him. Some day she may come to her senses and thank me for it.

"In the first place, he's a liar. I tried to help him three or four times by giving him money when he told me he needed it for job expenses. I always gave the money to Rebecca so he would be sure to remember how he got it. Anyway, he didn't spend it for what he said he needed it for. Sometimes they bought something they didn't need; one time they even took a trip with the money.

"I'd think he would be smarter than that. After all, all he wants is my money. If he were really as clever as he thinks he is, he would try to do something right for a change, and then maybe I could accept him. But he never seems to learn.

"That's why I won't have him back to live in my house. As soon as I started taking care of both of them, he would quit even trying to find a job. Then first thing you know, she'd be pregnant again, and I'd have both of them for the rest of my life.

"Now he's really done it. He gave a bad check the other day, and the man is going to have him arrested. I want to let it happen; maybe it will teach him a lesson. But if I do, my family will have bad publicity. Imagine my daughter being married to a jailbird. Then if she ever does get a divorce, no one will want to marry her again. This is a terrible mess. In the end I may have to bail him out, but I'm certainly going to let him sweat a while before I do."

In agricultural America, when the husband's father often provided the land or the implements with which his son began his married life, it was understood that there was a certain obligation on the part of the son—and daughter-in-law—to conform to the father-in-law's wishes. Presumably the father-in-law knew best, having had more experience in farming. In those days, when people lived close to the edge of starvation or bankruptcy all the time, inexperience or experimentation could lead to disaster.

Today, many parents look for opportunities to give money and gifts to the children *without* placing them under any obligation, having learned that even the implication of lost independence might produce resentment. But there are still some groups and some situations in which generations clash over expectations of filial obligation. This often happens when the in-laws have come from a different cultural background than the young husband or wife. Consider the following case:

"I thought I was marrying someone with a similar background when I married Keiya," Carolyn told the counselor. "We went to the same school in San Francisco, and he seemed just like all the other kids at school. He was always very nice and polite to me. He was an Oriental, as I am.

"I grew up in a well-to-do home in San Francisco. I never did live in the Oriental section. My father was a college professor, and we always lived out near the university. We had many friends among Caucasians and I was brought up as a typically American girl. I wasn't taught to reject or hate Oriental things or anything like that. It's just that my family tried to make me as normal to the community as they possibly could. However, they did want me to marry an Oriental boy; they made that quite clear. They said I would be happier that way. Well, it hasn't turned out the way they thought.

"Keiya was the oldest son of older parents. They were both born in Japan, but they came over here before World War II. As a matter of fact, Keiya was born in an internment center during the war. They always spoke Japanese around his house; neither one of his parents spoke English very well.

"Even while he was in school, Keiya had to spend a lot of time helping his father in the nursery business. I don't know how he ever got his studying done. He worked morning, noon, and night, seven days a week. He always said that, because he was the oldest son, he would inherit the business some day.

"When we were married, I thought that would be wonderful, since it gave us financial security. But it turned out to be terribly wrong. For a while after we were married, we lived in his father's house, and that was absolutely intolerable. His parents criticized me all the time. Besides, they made him work fourteen hours a day, and we never had any time to spend together. Whenever I protested, he would always remind me that, after all, it was to be his business. His father never put anything in writing, though. He just expected Keiya to work with him. He never gave him any overtime pay, either.

"The worst part about it was that they expected me to behave like a Japanese woman. I wasn't supposed to talk when the father was talking, and I wasn't even supposed to eat with the men when they had guests. The absolute end came when they suggested to me that I should be working in the nursery, too. After all, his mother did. I put my foot down then and just about moved out by myself. But Keiya promised that, if I would stay, we would build a house of our own. So I stayed. By the time the house was built, I had a child and then I couldn't leave. I thought moving away from his parents' house might mean that they would leave Keiya alone for a little bit, but it seemed worse than ever. When he wasn't down in the nursery gardens, they would call him up all the time. And then they would come up to the house and criticize the way I was taking care of the baby. It wasn't the Japanese way. I don't know what I am going to do. I've reached the end of my rope."

Keiya told just about the same story, adding, "If only she would be nice to my parents! They aren't going to live forever. As a matter of fact, my father should have retired a long time ago. Then I will have the business, and we can live as we please.

"She insists that she doesn't want to live like a Japanese wife. But then she overdoes it in the other direction. She won't do anything! She thinks she ought to go out and play bridge or do club work like other women in the neighborhood. I want her to do this. I want her to be one of them. But she has to be a little bit discreet about it. She could help a little in the nursery and still have lots of time for bridge.

"She keeps telling me that I don't really know how it is. Heck, I know far better than she does. I've been living with it all my life. How do you suppose it was for me when I had to come home and work in the gardens when the other kids were out playing football? And there's a part of this problem that she doesn't see at all. She doesn't know how my parents give it to me for not being able to be master in my own house. They just absolutely don't understand why I don't just tell her what she has to do and make her do it. But if I try to do that, she'll leave me. She really will, too. She'll take the kids with her, and then we've got an even worse mess."

IN-LAWS CAN
HELP, TOO

As we said in the beginning, some in-law relationships are a great advantage to everybody. There are many cases in which in-laws have provided needed economic assistance. Marvin Sussman studied 195 cases and found that, in 154 of them, parents were giving either direct financial support or help and service to their married children.[11] Moreover, in the majority of cases, today's in-laws also provide large quantities of affectional support that the young marrieds need to work through their own early adjustment process.

Peggy Marcus did a study of seventy-nine marriages and found that nine factors were significantly related to good in-law adjustment for both husband and wife. They were: (1) approval of the couple's marriage by the parents; (2) meeting the prospective partner's family before marriage; (3) friendliness of parental families toward each other when they met; (4) a separate household for each couple and their children, free from the presence of other relatives; (5) happy marriage of the parents of the couple; (6) marriage between persons of the same religion; (7) wife's education for marriage; (8) happy relationship between the parents and the grandchildren; and (9) similarity in the pattern of social activity.[12]

But what happens when two people fall in love and get married without having all or any of these factors working for them? What can be done when there is trouble? Other than platitudes about doing one's best to understand other people's needs and the importance of cooperative understanding, there probably are very few generalizations that have specific meaning in any in-law situation. In modern America, there are as many millions of complex in-law relationships as there are marriages. An old rule-of-thumb—that the blood relative is the best one to deal with an in-law problem—may be the worst possible advice in a particular situation, since he may be emotionally incapable of solving his own problems. On the other hand, the newcomer to the established family group is often at a great disadvantage in trying to change established relationship patterns.

About the best that can be done is to counsel patience and determination. In some situations, this means inestimable patience and unshakable determination. For many people, the problem does get better. In their study of 909 Michigan families, Robert Blood and Donald Wolfe found that the percentage of in-law difficulties tended to decline as the couples grew older.[13]

[11] Marvin B. Sussman, "The Help Pattern in the Middle Class Family," *American Sociological Review*, **18** (February, 1953), 23.
[12] Peggy Marcus, "In-Law Relationship Adjustments of Couples Married Two and Eleven Years," *Journal of Home Economics*, **43** (January, 1951), 35–37.
[13] Robert O. Blood, Jr., and Donald M. Wolfe, *Husbands and Wives*, Glencoe, Free Press, 1960, pp. 247–248.

A final note to our in-law discussion is provided by Peggy Marcus. She points to one of the "feeling tones" in her study that seemed to stand out most clearly between those with good adjustment and poor adjustment: "Those young couples with a good adjustment seemed to be working as a unit, accepting both families as their own and regarding all problems as a common task. Those with a poor adjustment, on the other hand, showed a tendency to blame the spouse's family for friction in all areas."[14]

[14] Marcus, *op. cit.*, p. 37.

24

AFTER THE
CHILDREN COME

In almost every society throughout history, the arrival of children in a family has been culturally valued as a great blessing and as an integrating factor that enlarges the closeness between marriage partners. Most young Americans think of it that way, too, even though several research studies have shown that birth often creates a family crisis for which the partners are woefully unprepared.[1]

Whether having a child produces a crisis or not, it will surely bring some change to the marriage. Relationships will never be the same again. Moreover, the changes in the family brought about by the coming of the first child are the prelude to many more. With the coming of the second child, the triangular relationship of the family becomes quadrangular. Then in addition to husband–wife relationships and parent–child relationships, there are child–child relationships to be considered.

HUSBAND–WIFE RELATIONSHIPS
DURING PREGNANCY

Changes in the husband–wife relationship often start the minute the wife suspects she is pregnant. Individual reaction to impending parenthood varies widely. For some partners, the realization that conception has occurred is a

---

[1] E. E. LeMasters, "Parenthood as Crisis," *Marriage and Family Living,* **19** (November, 1957), 352–355; and E. D. Dyer, "Parenthood as Crisis: A Re-Study," *Marriage and Family Living,* **25** (May, 1963), 196–201. A third study, by Daniel Hobbs, found no such evidence of family birth crisis as LeMasters and Dyer reported earlier. Hobbs urged further study with larger and more representative samples. Daniel F. Hobbs, "Parenthood as Crisis: A Third Study," *Journal of Marriage and The Family,* **27** (August, 1965), 367–372.

source of anxiety, hostility, or regret. Such initial feelings are often followed by feelings of guilt, since there is a strong cultural belief that rejecting pregnancy is morally reprehensible. Whether the rejection is by the husband or the wife makes little difference. The marriage relationship is liable to deteriorate either way, particularly if one partner blames the other for not having taken greater precautions against the unwelcome event.

Ordinarily, though, especially with the first child, confirmation of conception brings pleasant satisfaction to both partners. Yet the pregnancy itself will almost inevitably change the interpersonal relationships of even the most delighted marriage mates, for although modern attitudes have drastically reduced some pregnancy problems, some complications of modern living create difficulties that Great-grandmother never faced when she was pregnant. For example, many contemporary American women are left alone for the first time in their lives in the latter months of pregnancy. Up until that time, they had either been in school or working—always with other people. When it becomes necessary for them to stay at home by themselves, sometimes in small apartments far from their childhood homes, many women need and demand more affection and social interaction with their husbands. Nagging fears and insecurities about the birth process and the normalcy of the developing baby add to this need for closeness.

Physiologic changes in pregnancy can create relationship changes, too. Sometimes a wife's altered hormonal balance can bring about unpleasant changes in her disposition, causing a placid, easy-going woman to become argumentative and moody, which doesn't improve marriage relationships. Moreover, some women are tempted to take advantage of their "delicate condition" to enjoy the opportunity to get a little more attention and perhaps a little more service from a doting husband than they know they deserve. In the long run, this is no help to the marital relationship either.

CASE 57

"Phillip takes no interest in my pregnancy," Sarah told the counselor. "He wasn't even excited when he found out I was going to have a baby. I didn't call his attention to the fact that I missed a period, and I don't think he even knew it. That's part of our problem. He never notices the little things about me. I could dye my hair green, and he wouldn't know it for six months. Anyway, I didn't even tell him I was going to the doctor. I thought it would be a very big surprise. When I was sure, I could hardly wait to tell him. But I wanted to do it big, so I planned a special dinner and had it by candlelight. And when I told him, do you know what he said? He said, 'Oh, is that so?' I thought he would come and tenderly take me into his arms and hold me very close. All he did was give me a routine little peck on the cheek and take his insurance book and go out and make some calls.

"I could have forgiven that if he would at least show some interest now. But he doesn't seem to care whether I feel well or not. I've had a miserable time with morning sickness, and I've had to stay in bed a great deal. I'm sure he doesn't care, and I'm not sure that he even knows how bad it's been.

"Now that I've felt life, I want him to take an interest in the pregnancy. Not him. The only time he's interested in looking at me is when he wants sex. You'd think he could control himself for just a little while. When he found out we couldn't have intercourse at all during the last three months, you would have thought he had been personally wounded. It was almost as if he thought the doctor had selected him out of all the men in the world to be deprived. He couldn't see that it was to protect my baby. All he thought about was himself.

"There's nothing I can do about it now, of course. I can't divorce him with my baby on the way. But I am thinking about going home to Mother's to stay until after the baby comes. She's very interested in my pregnancy, and I like to talk with her about it."

Phillip told the counselor: "If I had known that Sarah was going to carry on like this after she got pregnant, we never would have had a baby, believe me. She cried every day for three weeks because I didn't make a big enough fuss when she told me. I was real pleased then, and I tried to make that clear to her. Sure, I was surprised at first. But when I got used to the idea, I tried to tell her how happy I was. But by that time all she could say was, 'Oh, you spoiled it all!'

"I suppose she told you I don't care how she feels. That isn't so. Since she's been having such a bad time in the morning, I've been trying not to wake her when I go out. I get my own breakfast every morning. But I can't stay home from my job to take care of her every day. And even if I could, I wouldn't be much of a nurse. There have been a couple of Sunday mornings when she's gotten up to go to the bathroom and throw up. She leaves the door open, and I've gotten sick myself. I really feel bad about her being uncomfortable, but there isn't that much I can do about it.

"Besides, I'm beginning to wonder a little about this morning sickness bit anyway. She had it every morning until last Saturday. Then early in the morning—before we were awake—the telephone rang. It was some old friends of hers who were just passing through town. Actually, it was one of her old boyfriends who married another girl. She got on the telephone, and they invited us out to lunch. I couldn't go, because I had some insurance calls to make. But I was around the house until almost noon. You should have seen her rushing around. She washed and dried her hair, pressed a dress, and did a thousand other things, and she never got sick once. But Sunday morning—oh, that was different—she carried on all over the place again.

"The worst part about all this is that she says I'm not interested in the pregnancy. What she means is that I'm not as interested in it every minute, twenty-four hours a day, as she is. The first time she took my hand and put it on her abdomen so that I could feel the baby move, I was as thrilled as she was. But, believe me, by the 493rd time it began to get a little old, and I ran out of things to say.

"She wants me to know every detail, and I'm not sure that I want to know that much. I married a beautiful, romantic woman. Now she's turning herself into a biological exhibition. When I'm out making my insurance calls, sometimes I think of her with tenderness and I think of her with passion. But I don't think of her as some medical side show. I don't want to think of her that way. I don't want her to make me think of her that way. There are some things she just shouldn't make me know.

"She threatens me all the time that she'll go home to be with her mother until the baby is born. I'm beginning to wish she would. Maybe it would be better for all of us."

As the pregnancy progresses, many women become less interested in having sexual relations. Although they may not decline intercourse outright, their husbands sense their feelings and feel very rejected. Other women, especially those who are basically insecure about their ability to maintain their husband's sex interest, become ultrasensitive when they begin to feel less physically attractive during pregnancy. Because of their own insecurity, they accuse their husbands of interest in other women—accusations that may or may not have any basis in fact. Some husbands *do* use their feelings of sexual deprivation to seek sexual satisfaction elsewhere, especially in the long months at the end of the pregnancy. This, of course, can dramatically alter the husband–wife relationship.

By and large, though, in most middle-class marriages, the initial pregnancy—despite the transient difficulties and inconvenience that go with it—is a time of drawing closer. Some women never feel better than when they are pregnant, and some men enjoy nine pleasant months. In many cases, troubles— if there were any—are forgotten on the birth day. Divorce suits filed by women who are pregnant are often withdrawn after the baby is born.

HUSBAND–WIFE RELATIONSHIPS
AFTER THE CHILDREN ARE BORN

There are marriages, though, in which resentments created during pregnancy carry over after the baby is born. There are other marriages in which the pregnancy was a beautiful period of bliss but in which the happy world falls apart when the baby comes. The birth of a baby does not in itself necessarily improve a marriage; in fact, the new arrival brings with it a few new tensions to all marriages and a great many destructive tensions to some marriages.

For one thing, the new baby creates a triangle. In all triangular relationships, there are bound to be some jealousies. In most marriages, it is the young husband who suffers the most from jealous feelings. Used to enjoying his wife's full attention, he often finds it difficult to share. His frustration is compounded by the fact that he has nowhere to ventilate his hostility, since it is not socially acceptable to admit to feelings of animosity toward a tiny baby. His relationship with his wife tends to deteriorate as conflict festers within him.

Jealousy on the part of the mother is not uncommon either. Some women are extremely jealous of their husband's relationships with their daughters, especially when those daughters near womanhood. And, of course, it is very common for the child to be jealous of the attention that one adult partner receives from his mate.

Some young husbands *do* suffer from a loss of marital attention and satisfaction that is very real and more than just jealous fantasy. The coming of a child enormously complicates the wife's role. The amount of physical energy as well as the amount of nervous energy she must spend on her increased duties is usually fatiguing. This is especially true in our American culture where the young mother frequently has no help from another mother, mother-in-law, visiting aunt, or paid helper to make it even a little easier. One of the problems of today's society is that so many emancipated young women who have been raised in relative freedom and luxury find themselves trapped in a chrome-and-porcelain prison with no other adult to talk with when their first child is born. And it goes on 365 days a year from dawn to bedtime. The dispositions that result from this way of life are not always the kind that tend to enlarge loving relationships.

Children bring other problems, too. They interfere with not only casual conversations but the warm moments of mutual need-meeting between the partners. The child is imperious in his demands for immediate attention, regardless of how important the communication between the partners is at that minute. A young father who is excitingly telling his wife about the most meaningful experience of his day is quite likely to be interrupted by a child's screams for nothing more than a toy deliberately thrown from the highchair. Sometimes the one word that could improve the relationship between the partners has to be postponed because something has to be done for the children. And thus the right moment is forever lost.

It is not only conversation that suffers, either. After the children arrive, spontaneous lovemaking usually comes to an abrupt halt. Sexual relationships have to wait until the children are asleep, and by that time the wife is ordinarily so tired that she wants only to go to sleep herself. Even if she can manage to achieve some kind of stimulation, her sexual excitement may be limited by her apprehension that the children might wake up.

In marriage counseling, it is common for a husband to complain that his wife's sexual responsiveness came to an end when the first child was born. Sometimes the wives admit this and are as baffled for an explanation as the husbands are. Some blame the traumatization of the birth canal for their loss of sexual appetite. Others contend that it was just about the time of the baby's arrival that the novelty of sex wore off. There are other women for whom some deeper emotional reason, related to a latent fear of sex that became activated during the maternal experience, is a more probable explanation. Whatever the cause, though, the result of the new mother's sexual disinterest is another way of making her young husband feel rejected, and so another burden to their relationship.

Changes in husband–wife feelings toward one another can also result from arguments over how the child should be reared. This is especially true when the partners have come from homes with differing value systems. Traditionally, the male has more often been the authoritarian who tries to maintain stricter discipline by stern punishment if necessary. This isn't always true, of course. Many wives complain of husbands who will not take any responsibility for punishing the children or who tend to be too lenient with them.

Incidentally, Elizabeth Hurlock refers to studies of mothers' treatment of babies revealing that the way they treat them during infancy is significantly related to the way they treat them as they grow older. Changes are likely to occur in quantity rather than quality of treatment. That is, indulgent parents tend to become more indulgent and rejecting parents more rejecting. Consequently, small frictions in early childhood may well become major disruptions in late childhood.[2]

Arguments over child rearing become especially bitter in the "sensitive" areas of the marriage partners' relationship. Some husbands and wives can manage to compromise on how much allowance the child should have or whether he should be permitted to play football in junior high school, but they may literally come to blows over whether Grandmother has a right to buy the child fancy clothes, whether one partner has the right to insist on the child going to his church, or whether or not the adolescent daughter in the family may have a cocktail with adult guests.

Despite all the difficulties that children can create in a marriage, they also can be an integrating factor in the relationship between some marriage partners. Ninety-one percent of the respondents in Daniel Hobbs' study indicated that their marriages were more happy and satisfying since their first child was born.[3]

[2] Elizabeth B. Hurlock, *Child Development*, 4th ed., New York, McGraw-Hill, 1964, p. 656.

[3] Hobbs, *op. cit.*, p. 371.

At the very least, children can provide those partners who have managed to maintain an adequate relationship to that point with a common sense of achievement and pride, in the later stages of marriage. When Harold Feldman asked his 852 couples which stage of the family living experience they thought was most satisfying, he was surprised to find the two most-preferred stages were, first, when the children were infants and, second, when the partners became grandparents. The third preferred stage was the period before the children were born, the fourth was when the children were preschoolers, the fifth when the children were all in school, and the sixth when the children were teenagers. The least-preferred stage of all was when the children had left home but had not yet had children of their own. Said Feldman, "It is interesting that the most highly valued periods were those involving a relationship with a young child (infancy and being grandparents). The expectation that the honeymoon period would be clearly preferred to other stages was not borne out even though ours is supposed to be a youth-valuing culture."[4]

It is possible, of course, that Feldman's data were a little contaminated not only by the cultural idea of having children in the home on the one hand, but also by the same kind of nostalgia for facing difficulties shoulder-to-shoulder that led British air-raid wardens to speak of the "good old days" twenty years after the bombing had stopped.

In fact, it might be the very challenge of working together for a common goal that makes the early child-rearing period so significant in the lives of the married pair. Once there are children, there are reasons—and rationalizations—for sticking to it and trying to get ahead. There is a new basis on which decisions can be made: what is best for the children. There is a new kind of camaraderie with other young couples who are suffering through the same agonies of rearing children in a changing culture. Most important of all, there is a new feeling of responsibility and adultness that is magnified by the dependence of tiny children. The need to be needed is an important human drive. There is no greater fulfillment for adults than to provide happiness for a child. Many ultrasophisticates who formerly laughed at suburbanites become eager proponents of middle-class values, once their own children are born. Why shouldn't they? Some of them find real meaning and real purpose in their lives for the first time.

PARENT–CHILD RELATIONSHIPS

The notion that children were conceived in wickedness and sin, and therefore had badness born in them, died slowly. It was not until the early days of the twentieth century and the scientific study of culture and personality that the emphasis changed. When the shift came, however, it was a dramatic one. From placing blame on the child for his actions the pendulum swung to placing blame on the parents. Many experts insisted that there really weren't any bad children, only bad parents. "To meet Johnnie's mother is to understand his problem" reflected the preoccupation of midcentury psychologists and psychiatrists with

[4] Harold Feldman, "The Development of the Husband-Wife Relationship," research report to the National Institute of Mental Health, Grant M-2931, 1965, p. 21.

Table 24–1
Summary Chart of Faulty Parent–Child Relationships

Undesirable Condition	Typical Personality Development of child
Rejection	Feelings of insecurity and isolation. Attention-seeking, negativistic, hostile behavior. Unable to give and receive affection.
Overprotection—domination	Submission, inadequate, lack of initiative, tendency to passive dependency in relations with others.
Overindulgence	Selfish, demanding, with inability to tolerate frustration. Rebellious to authority, excessive need of attention, lack of responsibility.
Perfectionism—unrealistic ambitions for child	Child internalizes parents' unrealistic standards, Inevitable failure leads to continual frustration, guilt, and self-devaluation.
Rigid, unrealistic moral standards	Extreme conscience development. Tendency to rigidity, severe conflicts, guilt, self-condemnation, and self-devaluation.
Faulty discipline	Overpermissiveness associated with insecurity, antisocial aggressiveness. Severe discipline typically leads to excessive condemnation of self for socially disapproved behavior, anxiety over aggressive behavior. Inconsistent discipline commonly results in lack of stable values for guiding behavior with tendency to inconsistency and vacillation in meeting problems.
Sibling rivalry	Direct or indirect hostility, insecurity, lack of self-confidence, regression.
Marital discord and broken homes	Anxiety, tension, insecurity, lack of secure home base, tendency to evaluate world as a dangerous and insecure place. Conflicting loyalties, lack of adequate models for proper ego development.
Faulty parental models	Internalization of unethical and socially undesirable value attitudes which frequently lead to difficulties with the law.
Contradictory demands ("double-bind")	Lack of integrated frame of references; confusion and self-devaluation.

The exact effects of faulty parent–child relationships on later behavior depend on many factors, including the age of the child, the constitutional and personality make-up of the child at the time, the duration and degree of the unhealthy relationship, his perception of the relationship, and the total family setting and life context, including the presence of absence of alleviating conditions and whether or not subsequent experiences tend to reinforce or correct early damage. There is no uniform pattern of pathogenic family relationship underlying the development of later psychopathology, but the conditions we have discussed often act as predisposing factors.

Source: *Abnormal Psychology and Modern Life,* 3rd Edition by James C. Coleman Copyright © 1964 by Scott, Foresman and Company.

the so-called *Mal de Mere* syndrome. Adjectives such as "anxious" and "rejecting" were freely used by child-guidance specialists. Many parents accused themselves—or each other—of being responsible for their child's disturbed behavior.

A good case was often made—and still can be made—for the detrimental effects that some parents have on the conditioning and development of their children. James Coleman has summarized the parent-control conditions that are conducive to faulty parent–child relationships and the possible effects of those conditions on the child's personality. (See Table 24-1.) Not only can these conditions affect the personality and behavior of the developing child, they can also affect his later behavior in marriage, thus creating a new round of marriage problems and another generation of disturbed parent–child relationships.

Parental overambition (which Coleman identified as *perfectionism*) is a particularly difficult and disturbing problem. Here is a case that illustrates some of the problems created in an upwardly mobile, perfectionist home:

CASE 58

"I don't know what to do with Leroy," the father told the counselor. "He's twenty-four years old now. By the time I was his age, back down in Oklahoma, I was through college and out working for three years. I already had several thousand dollars in the bank, even though it was the Depression. But not Leroy. He's been in and out of three colleges already. He makes just enough C's and D's to balance his F's, and then he talks somebody into letting him stay on for another semester. I don't think it says much for the university that lets him stay on, but I want him to get a degree so badly that I'm not going to complain. He takes only a few courses each semester. He's pretty good at tennis, though. He gets on the tennis team whenever he's eligible. As a matter of fact, that's all he wants to do: play tennis. It's practically the only thing he does well. He even used to beat me.

"I've tried to cut him off financially a dozen times, but that doesn't do any good. The first time I decided to do it, I didn't send him any money for three months or so. He dropped out of school and got a job in a bar. But pretty soon he began to pile up debts, and I got letters from his creditors. He wrote some bad checks, and they were going to send him to jail. I bailed him out. What else could I do? Having a jail sentence would just ensure his turning into a bum.

"The tragedy is, the boy's got the ability. I know he has. When he was in elementary school, the teachers used to tell us he was bright. I had big hopes for Leroy. Somehow, though, he never seemed to measure up. I think most of the problem was that his mother spoiled him. If Leroy didn't do the work I assigned for him, she would try to wheedle me out of being upset about it. She'd excuse him and let him go off and play instead of sticking to what I'd told him to do. If he didn't do it well, she would say I had criticized him too severely. Maybe I was a little harsh, but no kid should be allowed to do sloppy work when he's capable of doing better.

"One reason why cutting off his financial support never worked was that she used to send him money on the side. I think she tried to buy his affection. I love him as much as she does—more even. I love him so much that I want him to make something of himself. She thinks loving him means doing everything for him. That will only ensure his unhappiness in this competitive world.

"I know what I'm talking about. I came up the hard way. I was a poor kid, and everything I got I had to work for. I sold papers after school, and I worked my way through college. I didn't get to be vice-president of my company by sitting on my hands, either. I went back and worked in the evenings when I didn't have to. Sometimes the other guys thought I was ruthless, and sometimes my wife had a fit, but I got there by using all the brains I had all the time. I want that for him, too. Is that wrong?"

The counselor talked with the mother. "It isn't Leroy's fault," she said. "You wouldn't believe how critical my husband was of our son. Leroy couldn't do anything right, or even well enough to please his father. When he was young, if he got four A's and a B in school, his father raised the devil because he didn't get straight A's. If my husband told the boy to have our enormous lawn mowed by 3:00

and the boy didn't finish until 3:30, he got criticized again. I had to stand by and watch the boy suffer. Finally, Leroy just gave up. It seemed to happen all of a sudden, as if he realized he was going to get criticized whatever he did. As a matter of fact, pretty soon my husband's hollering and criticalness wasn't even a punishment anymore. The boy became almost immune to it. And then something even worse happened. Leroy himself began to believe that he couldn't do the things that other children could do. When his father told him he was "dumb in arithmetic" because he missed two or three problems, Leroy accepted what his father said to an extent my husband never intended. He *believed* he was dumb in arithmetic. And so he never tried anymore.

"I don't know what we can do about him now. He *feels* inadequate, so he *is* inadequate. I think his father is just going to have to face up to the facts and take care of Leroy until Leroy can find himself again. Leroy is very good at tennis. He can beat his father once in a while, and that's why I think he likes tennis so much. I've sent him money from time to time so he could play. Maybe he will get to be a great professional some day. I hate to see him drop out of school, though, because it's probably his last chance to redeem himself.

"Leroy threatens his father all the time. He says that if he doesn't send him more money, he will just quit school and go to work. If he really would do that, it might the best thing in the world for him, but he won't. He'll just get into trouble, and we'll just have to bail him out again. That's the problem now: He owes money to almost everybody in the university town. I hope you can help him when you talk with him."

The counselor talked with Leroy, who was inclined to be both belligerent and resigned. "All right," Leroy said, "let's get it over with. You're about the twenty-first do-gooder they've made me come to see. Let's see what you can do.

"I know what they both have told you, because they've told it to me often enough. As a matter of fact, they might have been a lot better off if they had never even tried to analyze me. I might have turned out better if Mother had never felt so sorry for me and continually told me what a brute my father was. I might have been better, too, if he hadn't yelled at her all the time about coddling me. If they had gotten along together, the whole thing might never have happened. But you can't tell them that. Both of them still think that they were doing the right thing and that if only the other one hadn't messed me up I would have turned out to be a great success.

"Actually, I may turn out pretty well anyway. I have a lot more fun than many of the eager-beaver bookworm types at the university who will spend the rest of their lives in competition and hostility. And I'm a lot better off than the far-out protester types, who have masochistic compulsions to beat on themselves for humanity's wrongs. I don't polish and I don't protest. I just live, and my old man can afford to keep it that way."

THE NEW FAMILY
INTERACTION CONCEPT

As America moved into the space age, the parent–child emphasis shifted again. More and more experts came to believe that the parents weren't altogether to blame. The child, they postulated, was not a passive victim of his environment but rather an active participant in his family group. Considerable evidence was developed for the notion that, while the parents might affect the child, the child also affected the parents. Each family member was, according to this whole-family concept, an important actor whose presence codetermined the total performance of the family group. Thus, while parents could and did affect both the feelings and behavior of the child, the child also affected the feelings and behavior of his parents and his siblings in very significant ways.

Herbert Wimberger has given a very concise illustration of this interaction:

> An anxious and insecure young mother gives birth to her first child. She has prepared herself well for the job and looks forward to the experience of taking care of her infant. The baby turns out to be tense and fussy, however, and makes it difficult for the mother to cuddle him because he tends to stretch in her arms when she holds him. Mother, who had dreamed of a cuddly infant, becomes insecure, feeling that she has failed in her job. As a result, she withdraws from her role as much as circumstances will permit, thus giving less comfort to the baby who becomes even more fussy. Father, annoyed by her withdrawal and the baby's consequent fussiness, becomes angry, completely overlooking his wife's need for support. This example could be spun out almost ad infinitum, in all its cause and effect relationships, but by this time it should have illustrated the involvement of all members of the famiy.[5]

In order to accept the concept that the child is in part responsible for the total family-relationships pattern, it is necessary to believe—and this has been shown by recent research—that the child himself has a temperament that affects his parents. Thus, "difficult" babies set up more stress patterns in the same parents than "easy" babies do.

Child psychiatrists Stella Chess and Alexander Thomas and pediatrician Herbert Birch, in the report of an important study of behavior problems, validated the significant concept that behavior disturbance is a result of the interaction of the child's temperament with his family environment. They defined temperament as the behavioral style of the individual, his characteristic tempo, energy expenditure, focus, mood, and rhythmicity. Temperament, they said, refers to the "how" of behavior rather than to its "what" or "why."[6]

Chess, Thomas, and Birch believe that one specific temperamental pattern produces the greatest risk of behavior-problem development. This pattern is characterized by irregularity of biological functions, withdrawal responses to new stimuli, nonadaptability to change, frequent negative mood, and predominantly intense reactions. Mothers find that infants with irregular sleep and feeding patterns, slow acceptance of new foods, prolonged adjustment periods to new routines, and frequent loud periods of crying and laughter are hard to care for. Pediatricians frequently refer to them as "difficult" infants. The investigators

> found no evidence that parents of the difficult infants are essentially different from other parents. Nor do our studies suggest that the temperamental characteristics of children are caused by the parents. The issue is rather that the care of these infants makes special requirements on the part of their parents for unusually firm, patient, consistent and tolerant handling.[7]

But what happens if the parents aren't up to it? Then, said the investigators,

[5] Herbert C. Wimberger, "Counseling in Parent–Child Problems," in Richard H. Klemer, ed., Counseling in Marital and Sexual Problems: A Physician's Handbook, Baltimore, Williams & Wilkins, 1965, p. 187.
[6] Stella Chess, Alexander Thomas, and Herbert G. Birch, "Behavior Problems Revisited: Findings of an Antrospective Study," paper presented to the joint session on Child Development at the American Academy of Pediatrics and the Academy of Child Psychiatry, Chicago, October 24, 1965.
[7] Ibid., p. 5.

The same parents who are relaxed and consistent with the easy child may become resentful, guilty or helpless with a difficult child, depending upon their own personality structures. Other parents by contrast, who do not feel guilty or put upon by the child's behavior, may learn to enjoy the vigor, lustiness and stubbornness of a difficult infant.[8]

Does this mean that only difficult babies cause problems for their parents? No, indeed. While "easy" babies are a joy to their parents, pediatricians, and teachers, their very ease of adaptability may be the basis for later problem behavior. The child who first adapts easily to the standards and behavior expectations of his parents may have a difficult time when he moves to functional situations outside the home. In school, stress and malfunction may develop if the demands of the teachers or of the other children conflict sharply with the patterns he has learned at home. For instance, the child who has been urged to be creative and self-expressive at home may have a problem if his creativity or self-expression is not expected or desired by those he meets outside the home.

Chess, Thomas, and Birch described other temperament patterns of the child that affect the members of his family. One other such example was the "slow to warm up" child. These children differ from the difficult infants in that their withdrawal from new situations is quiet rather than loud. For instance, on first being bathed, the child lies relatively still and fusses only mildly. With new foods, he turns his head away and lets the food dribble out of his mouth. With the stranger who greets him loudly, he clings to his mother. If given an opportunity to reexperience these new situations without pressure, such a child gradually comes to show quiet and positive interest in them. The key issue on whether he becomes a problem or a joy in his interaction with his parents and teachers is whether other people allow him to make an adaptation to the new situations at his own tempo or insist on an immediate positive involvement.

Chess, Thomas, and Birch strongly rejected the concept that parents are completely to blame for all their children's problems. "The harm done by this preoccupation has been enormous," they said.

> Enumerable mothers have been unjustly burdened with deep feelings of inadequacy as a result of being incorrectly held either exclusively or primarily responsible for their children's problems. . . . Our data on the origin and development of behavior problems in children emphasize the necessity to study the child—his temperamental characteristic, neurological status, intellectual capacities and physical handicaps. The parents should also be studied rather than given a global label such as rejecting, over-protective, anxious, etc. Parental attitudes and practices are usually selective and not global, with differentiated characteristics in different areas of the child's life and with marked variability from child to child. Parent–child interaction should be analyzed not only for parental influences on the child but just as much for the influence of the child's individual characteristics on the parent.[9]

PARENT–CHILD COMMUNICATION

If, in fact, parent–child interaction is a two-way street, then the communication of ideas and attitudes becomes even more important. Although much of the

[8] Ibid.
[9] Ibid., p. 10.

communication is verbal, much of it is not verbal and is expressed through behavior and projected feelings. This is especially true in the case of the infant who has not yet learned to talk. But it is also true of the unconscious wishes and desires of the parent in his relationship to the child.

As we saw in Chapter 17, one of the bases for good communication is listening to the meaning behind the words. Children often become experts at this, sometimes to the point where they can detect attitudes on the part of their parents that the parents themselves did not realize they had. If the attitude that the children "feel" is different from the attitude that the parent verbally expresses, only confusion and misunderstanding can result, for the inability of the parents to give clear direction will make the child uncertain about himself and the limits of the expectations that are set for him.

Most parents don't recognize that they are sending out confused messages. For example, the mother who tells her young child to go to school and at the same time holds him tightly, tells the child verbally that he should go while she simultaneously conveys to him by her actions that she does not want him to leave her. The unspoken message "stay with me" may be the one the child obeys, to the displeasure of his mother. In the same manner, a mother who unconsciously hates men can transmit the idea that it would be acceptable for her daughter to act out hostility toward her father, even though the mother puts on an outward appearance of perpetual sweetness toward her husband. This kind of confused message may also be readily apparent in the attitudes of a mother who eagerly says to her daughter, "You shouldn't do those naughty things with boys, but tell me more." Confused communication among family members is not always so obvious, however.

CASE 59

"I don't know what I'm going to do with Agnes," the mother said to the counselor. "She won't go to school most of the time because she says she feels sick. I know she really should go to school, because I've had her to the doctor dozens of times, and he says he can't find anything the matter with the poor child. But I know how it is. I have headaches all the time, and sometimes I just absolutely can't get out of bed myself. And I remember when I was her age. I was just like her. I didn't have the strength to go to school some days.

"I don't think my husband understands about this, though. Sometimes he has to do all the housework after he gets home from the office. He seems to do it willingly, but I feel very badly about it.

"I certainly don't want a sickly child in the family. It's bad enough that I'm not able to do all that I should. The whole thing has made me so depressed that I can scarcely bear to live with myself sometimes. As a matter of fact, three weeks ago, I got so upset thinking about Agnes that I tried to take my own life. I just couldn't take it any more. You must try to help us."

The counselor talked with Agnes's father. "My wife has always been sickly," the husband said. "My mother was that way, too. I can remember as a little boy taking hot soup up to Mother. She would pat me and call me her little doctor. Actually, it was one of the few times I can remember Mother smiling. Most of the time she yelled at me. I had an older brother who did all sorts of bad things and hollered back at her. Somehow she seemed to like that from him. But it was rare that I found a way to please her.

"I don't know what's the matter with Agnes. But it certainly worries her mother. She frets over the poor child all the time. A month ago I came into the room and found my wife taking sleeping pills. I grabbed them away from her just in time.

I'm almost afraid to leave her alone now. I've asked Agnes a hundred times to help me do things for her mother, but every time I ask, Agnes complains about some pain she has, so in the end I wind up doing it.

"Sometimes Agnes says some very impertinent and nasty things to her mother. But we can't punish Agnes when she doesn't feel well. I'm hoping you can find some way to help her.

"Actually, Agnes has always been a difficult child. I guess we were spoiled because our son was born first, and he was so gentle and easygoing. But Agnes has been very demanding. As an infant she cried all the time. She nearly drove her poor mother out of her mind before she was a year old. My wife doesn't know how to cope with her. Really, I guess I should say that neither one of us knows how to cope with her now. I don't understand why Agnes doesn't want to be more like her brother. He's a good boy. He does well in school and never gives his mother any trouble at all.

"Agnes does very badly in school, that is, when she's there. Much of the time she tells us she doesn't feel well enough to go."

Agnes canceled two appointments in a row with the counselor. Each time she didn't feel well enough to come. The third time her mother brought her, but Agnes sat in stony silence, giving the counselor one-word replies to questions. Toward the end of the hour, however, Agnes asked the counselor if he really believed she was sick. He replied that he was not a medical doctor but that he would certainly like to work with her *and* a medical doctor until they could find out what was wrong.

At the next session, Agnes was considerably more voluble. "I don't think my father and mother really like each other," Agnes said. "To hear Mother tell it at the bridge club, she has the most wonderful man in the world, but if she really loved him she wouldn't impose on him the way she does.

"And he doesn't really like her, despite what he says. But he just can't seem to bring himself to tell her to get up off the bed and get her work done. He keeps trying to please her all the time. The more difficult she is to please, the harder he tries.

"I suppose you've heard that Mother tried to kill herself. That's a laugh. Father came in and found her stretched across the bed with an empty bottle of sleeping pills in her hand. She was mumbling about having taken them all. But they took her to the hospital and pumped out her stomach—she hadn't counted on that—and they found only a slight trace of the barbiturates. I guess she dumped the rest down the toilet. Do you think my father got angry when he found out that he had been tricked? Oh no, not him. He just said something about how much more terrible it was that she felt she had to deceive him.

"My mother doesn't love anybody, really. She'll gush all over you and tell you how sorry she is. I suppose she told you how sorry she was that I'm sick. Well, she isn't really. She doesn't care about much of anything except her precious son. She slobbers over him all the time. He can manipulate her into doing anything. She's always either giving in to him or backing him up in some fib he's telling my father.

"I think Mother wants to feel badly. She wouldn't be happy if she didn't. And my father wants to feel abused, too. No, that isn't right, he wants to feel helpful, too helpful. If you want to help me, you're going to have to help my 'kookie' family."

CHILD–PARENT COMMUNICATION

In addition to inadequate communication from parent to child, there is often inadequate communication from child to parent. Perhaps it is even more important with children than with other adults to listen to their meaning instead of their words. Children need the security of someone who not only accepts their thoughts and feelings as expressed but who also can interpret what they would like to have said. Haim Ginott gives the following illustration:

> Carol, age twelve was tense and tearful. Her favorite cousin was going home after staying with her during the summer.
>
> Carol (with tears in her eyes): Susie is going away. I'll be all alone again.
> Mother: You'll find another friend.
> Carol: I'll be so lonely.
> Mother: You'll get over it.
> Carol: Oh, mother! (Sobs.)
> Mother: You are twelve years old and still such a crybaby.
>
> Carol gave mother a deadly look and escaped to her room, closing the door behind her.
>
> This episode should have had a happier ending. A child's feeling must be taken seriously, even though the situation itself is not very serious. In mother's eyes a summer separation may be too minor a crisis for tears, but her response need not have lacked sympathy. Mother might have said to herself, "Carol is distressed. I can help her best by showing that I understand what pains her." To her daughter she might have said any or all of the following: "It will be lonely without Susie." "You miss her already." "It is hard to be apart when you are so used to being together." "The house must seem kind of empty to you without Susie around." Such responses create intimacy between parent and child. When the child feels understood, his loneliness and hurt diminish, because they are understood, and his love for mother is deepened because she understands. Mother's sympathy serves as an emotional bandaid for the bruised ego.[10]

Strong feelings do not vanish because they are banished, but they do diminish in intensity when they are accepted with sympathy and understanding by a listener. Ginott illustrated how empathetic communication can alter relationships both between children and adults and between two adults by citing an excerpt from a parents' discussion group:

> Leader: Suppose it is one of those mornings when everything seems to go wrong. The telephone rings, the baby cries, and before you know it, the toast is burnt. Your husband looks over the toaster and says: "My God! When will you learn to make toast?!" What is your reaction?
> Mrs. A: I would throw the toast in his face!
> Mrs. B: I would say, "Fix your own damn toast!"
> Mrs. C: I would be so hurt I could only cry.
> Leader: What would your husband's words make you feel toward him?
> Parents: Anger, hate, resentment.
> Leader: Would it be easy for you to fix another batch of toast?
> Mrs. A: Only if I could put some poison in it!
> Leader: And when he left for work, would it be easy to clean up the house?
> Mrs. A: No, the whole day would be ruined.
> Leader: Suppose that the situation is the same: the toast is burnt but your husband, looking over the situation, says, "Gee, honey, it's a rough morning for you—the baby, the phone, and now the toast."
> Mrs. A: I would drop dead if my husband said that to me!
> Mrs. B: I would feel wonderful!
> Mrs. C: I would feel so good I would hug him and kiss him.

[10] Haim Ginott, *Between Parent and Child*, New York, Macmillan, 1965, pp. 19–20.

Leader: Why?—that baby is still crying and the toast is still burnt.

Parents: That wouldn't matter.

Leader: What would make the difference?

Mrs. B: You feel kind of grateful that he didn't criticize you, that he was with you, not against you.

Leader: And when your husband left for work, would it be difficult to clean up the house?

Mrs. C: No! I'd do it with a song.

Leader: Let me now tell you about a third kind of husband. He looks over the burnt toast and says to you calmly, "Let me show you honey, how to make toast."

Mrs. A: Oh, no. He is even worse than the first one. He makes you feel stupid.

Leader: Let's see how these three different approaches to the toast incident apply to our handling of children.

Mrs. A: I see what you're driving at. I always say to my child, "You are old enough to know this, you are old enough to know that." It must make him furious. It usually does.

Mrs. B: I always say to my son, "Let me show you, dear, how to do this or that."

Mrs. C: I'm so used to being criticized that it comes natural to me. I use exactly the same words my mother used against me when I was a child. And I hated her for it. I never did anything right, and she always made me do things over.

Leader: And you now find yourself using the same words with your daughter?

Mrs. C: Yes. I don't like it all—I don't like myself when I do it.

Leader: You are looking for better ways of talking with your children.

Mrs. C: Yes, I sure am!

Leader: Let's see what we can learn from the burnt toast story. What is it that helped change the mean feelings to loving ones?

Mrs. B: The fact that somebody understood you.

Mrs. C: Without blaming you.

Mrs. A: And without telling you how to improve.[11]

CHILD–CHILD RELATIONSHIPS

When a discussion focuses on child–child interaction, the first kind of relationship usually mentioned is sibling rivalry. Because it is often conspicuous and dramatic—indeed, in many modern families, it is the predominant and controlling factor in the relationships among the children—sibling rivalry has received much professional attention.

Sibling rivalry results when a child feels replaced by another. But it may also result from the comparisons parents often make in front of the children. As Allison Davis and Robert Havighurst have suggested,

> Whether a child is a first child who has been replaced by a new baby, or whether he finds older and therefore more privileged brothers on the scene when he arrives, he will certainly have to come to grips with jealousy and rivalry. To make the situation worse, his parents unconsciously will train him in contradictory

[11] Haim Ginott, *Group Psychotherapy with Children*, New York, McGraw-Hill, 1961, pp. 180–182.

fashion concerning this rivalry. For they will urge him both to compete with his brothers and sisters in some ways, and not to compete with them in other ways.[12]

In early childhood, the result of a sibling rivalry frequently is clearly evident. Sometimes it takes the form of overt hostility on the part of the older child as he all but pokes the baby's eyes out. In other cases, it presages a psychological retreat. The three-year-old may revert to wetting or soiling, infantile speech, or sucking on a bottle in an attempt to be a baby again with the unconscious hope that the mother once more will lavish time and affection on him.

Some writers feel that some jealousy and rivalry are inevitable in American culture, since every child wants to be best loved by his parents. The first child usually wants it more than the others, since he was once the only child and knew what it was like to have all the attention. Davis and Havighurst, in studying two-child families, reported that most mothers thought that their first-born were more jealous and selfish, no matter what type of training they had received or whether or not they were treated more indulgently than the second child.[13] They concluded that no type of training whatever, whether severe, moderate, or indulgent, was likely to eliminate the first child's sense of having been replaced by the second and having lost some of his parents' love. It is possible, of course, that the mother could control to some degree the development of sibling rivalry by overcompensating with her attention for the child who is experiencing severe jealousy. Most authorities recommend that a mother be constantly alert to minimize the effects of sibling competition.

Sibling rivalry and child–child competition are by no means the only problems of child interaction, as any harried young mother can testify. Children are subject to most of the same conflicts and hostilities as adults. But children's overt reactions to conflict situations are usually more direct and more honest than their elders' reactions. Sometimes, though, even a child is caught in a dilemma in which he cannot express his true feelings. I recall vividly Judith, a woman who had deep feelings of guilt and hostility because her mother was unwilling to admit that Judith's retarded sister was abnormal and insisted that she go to school with Judith. Since Judith had been emotionally indoctrinated to be absolutely loyal to her retarded sister, she was tortured every day by the other students' taunts. She knew of no way to tell her mother what the children were saying, nor was she able to handle the emotional trauma that resulted from her own ambivalent feelings of embarrassment, shame, anger, and guilt. Soon she grew to hate her sister as the cause of her own emotional discomfort. This brought her into conflict with her conscience again. Later, long after her retarded sister had died, considerable psychotherapy was needed to help Judith.

Child–child relationships are not always unhappy. Sibling rivalry notwithstanding, the advantages of having brothers and sisters are numerous. The first and primary advantage is that a sibling—especially an older sibling of the same sex—can serve as a role model. Some authorities believe that, in the long run, the positive significance of siblings in teaching social roles to their brothers and sisters far outweighs the negative aspects of sibling rivalry.[14] In some cases, older

---

[12] Allison Davis and Robert J. Havighurst, *Father of the Man*, Boston, Houghton-Mifflin, 1947, p. 120.

[13] *Ibid.*, pp. 119–131.

[14] Donald P. Irish, "Sibling Interactions: A Neglected Aspect of Family Life Research," *Social Forces*, **42** (March, 1964), 279–288.

siblings are literally heroes or heroines to their younger brothers and sisters, and this hero worship often benefits both the older and the younger child.

Another advantage of multiple-child families is that the older siblings can serve as parent substitutes in the care and training of the other youngsters. Although they may not appreciate this role while they are involved in it, the older children receive considerable experience and grow toward adulthood faster as a result.

A third advantage is that siblings learn to share rights and privileges. Often they find it easier to accept life's greatest lesson that some wishes cannot always be satisfied because other people have needs, too. Still another advantage is that brothers and sisters in the same general age group can be playmates and lead each other to other playmates. Finally, siblings tend to reduce the ego-centrism and oversensitivity that are often identified with the only child.

Child–child relationships affect not only the children involved but parent–child relationships as well. Moreover, child–child relationships can affect the relationships between the parents. It is not uncommon for one parent to take one child's side against his siblings and against the opposite-sex parent. This can be one of the most divisive forces in the family. Such a situation usually signals an imperative need for professional help in establishing new patterns of family intereaction. To improve family living it is usually necessary to improve *all* the relationships between *all* the family members.

IMPROVING FAMILY RELATIONSHIPS

The literature on parent–child relationships fills thousands of volumes, and every student who looks forward to being a parent would be well advised to take coursework in this infinitely complex field. It is difficult even to cover the basic essentials in any brief condensation.

Asked in 1965 to summarize the most frequent sources of parent–child conflicts and childhood emotional disturbances, Herbert Wimberger, Director of the Child Psychiatric Clinic at the University of Washington, suggested three:

1. lack of emotional contact between parents and the child
2. devaluating attitudes of the parents
3. lack of defined limits by which the child can guide his behavior[15]

Each of these problems has already been touched on. The lack of emotional contact has been pointed out throughout the book; the case of Leroy earlier in this chapter is a dramatic example of what devaluating attitudes can do to a child. Although the lack of limits has also been a frequently seen problem (as in the case in Chapter 12 of Sylvia's friend Melinda, who was rebelling against *no* rules), perhaps it most of all warrants further discussion here. There is no more confused and controversial area of family difficulty in contemporary society than that of the parents' responsibility for, and methods of, providing guidance, direction, and discipline for the child.

Ever since the influence of parents on the development of the child became a popular field for critical examination in the early 1900s, parents, edu-

---

[15] Herbert Wimberger, "Counseling in Parent–Child Problems," in Richard H. Klemer, ed., *Counseling in Marital and Sexual Problems: A Physician's Handbook*, Baltimore, Williams & Wilkins, 1965, p. 186.

cators, and child-guidance specialists have been agonizing over what pattern of parental control is best. The pendulum has swung from strictness to permissiveness and appears to be swinging back again. Benjamin Spock, one of the most widely read journalistic pediatricians in the 1940s and 1950s advocated lenient disciplinary practices in his 1946 edition of *Baby and Child Care*. This was published at a time when accepting the child's current needs for gratification, rather than his preparation for adult life, was looked upon as the ideal goal for the "good" parent.

However, subsequent research in child development did not support the supposedly harmful effects of such restraints as strict feeding schedules, early weaning, and early toilet training. By the time of his 1957 edition, Dr. Spock conceded that a great change in emphasis had taken place, and that there might be more chance of the conscientious parents getting into trouble with permissiveness than with strictness.

But the matter was by no means settled. There were many who continued to argue that firm control inhibits the child's creativity, decreases normal self-assertiveness, and generates passivity and dependence. To some child-development experts in the midtwentieth century, it appeared that more democracy and permissiveness in family relationships was still the way to family improvement. As late as 1964, Edward Dager summarized research studies that seemed to point to this: "Permissive (not extreme) and democratic parent–child interaction," he said, "appear to be associated with children who demonstrate self-confidence, initiative, independence, creativity, and cooperation. Restrictive or overprotective parent–child interaction is associated with children who are withdrawn, permissive, and dependent."[16]

On the other hand, Urie Bronfenbrenner, after a major research study, concluded in 1961 that the "democratic family which for so many years has been held up and aspired to as a model by professionals and enlightened laymen, tends to produce young people who do not take initiative, look to others for direction and decision and cannot be counted on to fulfill obligations."[17]

There is considerable hope that we are now moving into an era in parent–child understanding in which empirical research will be used as basis for valid syntheses that can lead to improved family relationships. It may well be, for example, that, in parent–child interaction, *neither* permissiveness nor authoritarianism maximize child creativity and parental satisfaction. In her paper on the effects of parental control on child behavior, Diana Baumrind suggests a middle position, in which the parent is not authoritarian but authoritative.

> The authoritarian and permissive parent may both create, in different ways, a climate in which the child is not desensitized to the anxiety associated with non-conformity. Both models minimize dissent, the former by suppression and the latter by diversion or indulgence. To learn how to dissent, the child may need a strongly held position from which to diverge and then be allowed under some circumstances to pay the price for non-conformity by being punished. Spirited give and take within the home, if accompanied by respect and warmth, may teach the child how to express aggression in self-serving and prosocial causes and to accept the partially unpleasant consequences of such action.

[16] Edward Z. Dager, "Socialization and Personality Development In the Child," in Harold T. Christensen, ed., *Handbook of Marriage and the Family*, Chicago, Rand McNally, 1964, p. 766.
[17] Urie Bronfenbrenner, "Some Familial Antecedents of Responsibility and Leadership in Adolescents," in L. Petrullo and B. Bass, eds., *Leadership and Interpersonal Behavior*, New York, Holt, Rinehart and Winston, 1961, p. 267.

The body of findings on the effects of disciplinary practice as reviewed and interpreted here give provisional support to the position that authoritative control can achieve responsible conformity with group standards without loss of individual autonomy or self-assertiveness.[18]

On the face of it, there would also seem to be many common-sense reasons for believing that the authoritative parent, in contrast to the demandingly authoritarian parent and the ultrapermissive parent, might provide more of the security and healthy opposition that allow a child to realize his maximum potential. After all, the child learns by imitation. Leadership is best learned by observing a leader, *not* by having to submit to a tyrant or by manipulating a nonopposer. In learning both to respect and to oppose the authority of the authoritative parent, the child can gain the self-confidence that, as we saw in Chapter 14, will later let him be free to be self-directed in the face of group pressure. In the end, it is probably this child, conditioned to be neither reticently submissive nor uninhibitively aggressive, who will provide his parents with emotional security and satisfaction and so improve family living.

Again, however, it should be remembered that good family relationships are a matter of *total* family interaction. Only in cases where *both* parents are satisfied with the method of control is there liable to be family harmony. Complete agreement on details is often difficult to achieve, even when all the family members concede the wisdom and appropriateness of a certain philosophical approach to child rearing. So again, as in every other facet of family relationships, improvement depends on the understanding and communication that exists—or can be created—between husband and wife.

The future of parent–child relationships is no more or less assured than the future of marital relationships or premarital sex. But as with marital relationships and premarital sex, there is a perennial hope that, once we get adjusted to living in a rapidly changing technological society, things may settle down into a new and better pattern.

Most American married couples still have children—or grandchildren—as their major interest and major value. It could not be otherwise. In the final analysis, the most creative thing that mankind can do is child bearing; the most evident purpose for living is child nurturing; and the most comprehensible immortality comes through the children we have nourished, loved, and guided.

[18] Diana Baumrind, "Effects of Authoritative Parental Control on Child Behavior," *Child Development*, **37** (December, 1966), 904–905.

25

MEETING CRISES
AND SOLVING PROBLEMS

"A nd they lived happily ever after" is the most unbelievable part of any
fairy story, even more unbelievable than all the magic wands, en-
chanted slippers, and flying carpets put together. Every marriage faces
some unhappiness as the years go by. It's a good thing, too, for a perpetual
state of euphoria would become tiresome after a while. The joy, exaltation, and
warmth of happiness are more appreciated when they are compared with a
recent state of despair.

But if all families, like all people, face difficulties and crises, why is it
that some families survive whereas others disintegrate? And why do some families actually grow stronger as a result of crises? These questions have interested
sociologists for many years. Few definitive generalizations have resulted from
their studies, but a good many hypotheses have been suggested. There is general
agreement that the ability of a marriage or a family to meet the inevitable crises
that will affect it depends on such factors as (1) the *kind* of trouble the family
faces and whether that trouble came suddenly or slowly; (2) the *preparation* the
family had made in advance for meeting just such emergencies; (3) the previous
experience of a family in dealing with whatever the trouble is; (4) the family's
own definition of the trouble, that is, whether they regard it as a crisis; (5) the
number of supportive relatives, neighbors, and friends; (6) the social expectations of peers and customs; (7) the family strengths and resources; and finally,
and possibly of greatest importance, (8) the personal maturity of the individual
partners. As we shall presently come to see, nothing can substitute for the decisiveness, competence, and leadership ability of the marriage partners themselves.

WHAT KIND OF CRISIS?

Problems differ not only in their intensity and in their finality but also in the
way in which they start. In some ways, sudden disasters are easier for the typical

middle-class family to deal with. In fact, there is considerable evidence both in research and observation that a sudden crisis can often be a unifying factor in family relations. It isn't only in the movies that the husband and wife, having separated with apparently irreconcilable differences, are reunited by an accident that befalls their child. It may not always happen just that way in real life, but working together to overcome some obstacle does lead to family unity in many cases.

Sudden disasters are not always unifying, of course. If all the basic emotional ties between the partners have been cut prior to the crisis, or if the disaster is so overwhelming that solution seems impossible and hope turns to despair, or if the partners were not very self-reliant to begin with, the family can be shattered by an unexpected catastrophe. Many families are literally torn to pieces or thrown into depression states from which they never recover by the death, unemployment, or illness of the breadwinner.

The varieties of sudden disaster that can strike a family are infinite. They range from such natural catastrophes as floods, tornadoes, and earthquakes to such man-caused problems as bankruptcy, automobile accidents, and social disgrace. Even when they may be unifying in the long run, the immediate effect of such disasters creates profound shock and temporary demoralization.

One often overlooked sudden family disaster is the rapid rise of one partner to fame or wealth. This may constitute a crisis quite as disruptive as economic loss or social disgrace. Every movie fan has read of actors who achieve stardom and then divorce their mates. Many people believe that, because actors are notoriously unconventional and temperamental, the fragility of their marriages is to be expected. But family dissolution occurs in other professions, too, when there is a swift change from poverty to riches or from obscurity to fame. No one is quite sure of the extent of this kind of family crisis in our affluent society, but it seems reasonable to speculate that a great many families have been at least partially disorganized by some of the same dynamics of upward mobility. Consider the following case:

CASE 60

"Five years ago, before Chuck made all that money contracting, we were very happy," Stella told the counselor. "He was a good father and used to take a lot of interest in the children. Back then he was only a carpenter, but he worked hard and had some time off on Saturdays and Sundays. We'd all go out walking in the country and sometimes take a picnic with us.

"Now, all that seems like a dream. Somehow he was able to borrow enough money and get a little political help, and he landed a big contract to build low-income homes. He made a lot of money on the first job, but it was nothing to what he made on the second contract. Now I guess you'd say we're wealthy. Sure, I like the $300 dresses and all the jewelry, and I like having a car of my own and a summer place. And I like the things that money will buy the children. But I would give it all up to have Chuck back again the way he used to be.

"Now we hardly see him at all. He's always away on business. I don't even let myself wonder what kind of 'business' it is anymore. But I know it involves a lot of drinking and a lot of staying out all night. I think the drinking is the worst part about it. All those big-shot contractors get together and drink. They drink at lunch, and they drink before they have dinner. On a few occasions when he's come home recently, he's been high as a kite. I hate drinking. My father was an alcoholic, and I can remember how embarrassed I was. My father kept our family poor as church mice because he was forever drinking himself out of a job. And now I can see it happening to Chuck.

"I try to talk with him about it, but he doesn't pay any attention to me any more. Oh yes, once in a while, if he gets drunk enough, he'll want to have sex. But ordinarily he doesn't even talk to me. It's just as if we lived in two different worlds now. He says, 'You have all the money you ever wanted, don't you?' He doesn't understand that I really don't want the money. I want him the way he was.

"He won't go out with any of our old friends now. He says they're stupid country bumpkins. It isn't as if he wasn't raised in the country himself. But now he wants to be with all those fancy people at the country club, and he doesn't ever want to play cribbage or go out on a family picnic anymore.

"The money hasn't made me happy, and I don't think it's made him happy, either. He thought he was doing me a big favor because he built me this enormous house. Actually, it's increased my work four times over. When I told him about it, he made me get a maid. But that isn't what I wanted. I haven't found a maid I can get along with. I think the problem is mostly with me. I never learned how to tell other people what to do. I'm much happier doing my own work. I think the people who come to work for me sense this, and they know they can take advantage of me. I don't like it, and I never will.

"I want him to stop drinking and to come back to me. I want to move back to a nice little cottage like we had when the children were young, when we were happy. I don't know why he won't do this. I try to be a good wife to him. I work hard in the house. Please tell him that he ought to try to act more like a husband and father should act."

The counselor saw Chuck after he had made and broken four appointments. He had obviously been drinking. "The trouble with Stella is she can't accept the good things," Chuck said. "She was just a little farm girl, and that's all she'll ever be. She's compulsive about working herself to death around the house. We've got all the money we'll ever need, and she's acting stupid. It isn't only that she's wearing herself out; it doesn't look good for me down at the country club. All the other women come down and play bridge, and some of them even make business contacts for their husbands in their social activities. Not Stella. She just hangs around the house. Well, believe me, I want something more out of life than that.

"I suppose she told you that I drink too much. I don't drink any more than the rest of the fellows I know. We have one or two at lunch and then after we finish work in the evening we always have a couple of rounds. Sometimes I do get a little high, but so what? The other fellows don't catch hell like I do. The real trouble is that Stella is afraid I'm going to turn into an alcoholic like her old man. She isn't really angry about the little bit of drinking I do; she's upset because it reminds her of all the problems she had when she was a kid. I get blamed for what her father did. If she could ever get over being anxious about it, she'd probably realize my drinking isn't so bad. Everybody has a social drink or two these days, so what's wrong with that? She'd be a lot better off if she'd do it, too.

"Since I've been down at the country club, I've found out there's a lot more to living, and there's a lot more to man–woman relationships than I ever knew with Stella. Sure, I've met other women. I've learned a lot from some of them. They don't nag me about the drinking. They just listen to me and try to understand me. I'm no worse than any other guy, but I'm no angel, either. When the cookies are passed, I have some. That's normal, isn't it?

"If Stella would go down there to the country club, maybe she'd learn something. Maybe if she was there, I wouldn't get to meet so many other women. But don't tell her I said that, because she might go and then she'd be there nagging me about drinking.

"I suppose she told you I wouldn't go out with her and our old friends anymore. Well, that's true, but not for the reason she thinks. It's just that we have nothing in common anymore. I don't like to do the things they want to do, and they can't afford to do the things that I like to do. I've told her a hundred times that I would go out with her and any new friends she wants to make, provided they've got the income to go where I like to go and chip in for a round of drinks once in a while. How much more fair can I be than that?"

The Insidious Problems

The slowly building crises that result from small degenerative changes are often more demoralizing and devastating to family relationships than sudden disasters. One of the worst of these is the disenchantment that seems to take place in many marriages. Peter Pineo analyzed the disenchantment process and postulated three indices of impending romantic crisis. The first of these, he said, was a drop in marital satisfaction. The second was a decline in such behaviors as confiding, kissing, and reciprocal settlement of disagreements. The third was a diminution of certain forms of marital interaction, such as sexual intercourse. Pineo argued that disenchantment is an inevitable process, since the partners have maximum "fit" and maximum satisfaction at the beginning of marriage and thus have only one direction to go: down. He said it this way:

> In any situation, such as marriage, in which individuals have made a major, irreversible decision to accept a long-term commitment and where the data upon which they decide on are not or cannot be perfect, some process of disenchantment is to be expected. When fit and satisfaction are maximized at the point of accepting the commitment, they must, on the average, subsequently reduce.[1]

Pineo's view is somewhat cynical, but the statistical data back him up, just as he says, *on the average*. Here again, though, this is actuarial data and has nothing to do with any particular individual's marriage. There are many marriages that continue to grow, and to grow richer as the years go by. Nonetheless, disenchantment does reach the crisis point for many people. This is how divorces happen. Yet, if we accept Pineo's proposition that marriage represents a high point from which the only direction is down, it might also be said that somewhere in the process there is a bottom from which the only direction is up. The idea that partners can be helped to find an earlier "bottoming out" for their conflicts is basic to marriage counseling.

Alcoholism is another of the insidious disasters that affects family relationships. Here there has been a great deal of research. Joan Jackson has identified seven stages in the progress of the alcoholic from the start of the problem to an adjustment to it: (1) attempts to deny the problem; (2) attempts to eliminate the problem; (3) family disorganization; (4) attempts to reorganize in spite of the problem; (5) efforts to escape the problem: the decision to separate from the alcoholic spouse; (6) reorganization of the family without the spouse; and (7) reorganization of the entire family.[2]

As Donald Hansen and Reuben Hill point out, this progression of the alcoholic family is a refinement of the typical pattern that most families adopt

---

[1] Peter C. Pineo, "Disenchantment in the Later Years of Marriage," *Marriage and Family Living,* **23** (February, 1961), 3, 11.

[2] Joan Jackson "Adjustment of the Family to Alcoholism," *Marriage and Family Living,* **18** (November, 1956), 361–369.

in adjusting to all crisis situations. In the beginning, the family is numbed by the blow. They continue to act at first as if the blow had not fallen; then, as the facts are assimilated, the family members tend to become disorganized and to show their resentments. Soon, conflicts develop and are converted into tensions that strain relations. Ultimately, however, the crisis bottoms out, and things begin to improve with new routines being introduced that were arrived at either by chance or by thoughtful planning. Hope for the future continues the upward process of adjustment.[3]

The Aging Problem

Of all the degenerative changes that affect the family, none is more insidious than the physical and emotional effects of the aging process. The physical effects of growing older (not necessarily growing *old*, just older) are bad enough, but the emotional aspects are often devastating. The attractive young woman who has mirror-given self-confidence usually has enough ego strength to laugh and play with her husband and thus enhance their happy relationship. But when she begins to lose her physical beauty, she often begins to lose her self-confidence, too, and her interpersonal behavior then frequently reflects an anxious and serious quality that leads to unhappiness and conflict rather than harmony. Men are also victims of the psychological insults of aging, but they are not usually so anxious as women because the penalties for losing their figures are not ordinarily so severe.

There are other reasons why women have a more difficult time during the middle years. As they move into their late thirties, premenstrual tension often increases and a few years later some other physical and emotional changes preceding the menopause begin to take place. At this time, women are described as premenopausal and, sometimes, perhaps *because* of this labeling, develop many dispositional symptoms that create or exacerbate tensions among the family members.

But it is really the coincidence of a great many unhappy experiences that makes this period so difficult. As pointed out previously, it is just about this time that the children begin to leave home and the women begin to be dissatisfied with their diminished roles. This is the time of identity crisis when many women begin looking for something more than they have. For most middle-life women, the one helpful prescription is to busy themselves with new interests and activities. For some, this is a very satisfying solution. Others reject the activities that are open to them yet find themselves unqualified for the type of work they would like to do. This suggests that avoiding middle-life crisis for a woman probably involves two things: one is the motivation and the ambition to get out and do something once the children have left home; and the other is vocational preparation before marriage. The typical woman will spend at least twenty-five years of her life working outside the home. Yet it is surprising how many women come face-to-face with the middle-life role problem without having adequately anticipated it.

Usually the man's role-identity problem comes later in life. Some men don't get the "it's all over" feeling until they are forced to retire from active

[3] Donald A. Hansen and Reuben Hill, "Families Under Stress," in Harold T. Christensen, ed., *Handbook of Marriage and the Family*, Chicago, Rand McNally, 1964, pp. 809–810.

employment. Here, too, anticipation and preparation are the only true preventives.

BEING PREPARED

Preparation involves some intelligence, because one has to be able to foresee what his problem most likely will be, but it is also closely associated with value conditioning. For example, on the island of Yap in the Philippine Sea, there is little preparation for the typhoons that regularly devastate the unprotected villages, in spite of the fact that the natives know from experience that the typhoons will be coming, if not this year then the next. D. M. Schneider has suggested that they fail to prepare for the typhoons because they believe that supernatural powers send the storms as punishment. Their best hope, they believe, lies in rituals and magic.[4]

Lest anyone think that cultural beliefs that preclude practical action are limited to uneducated island peoples, it should be noted that few modern American women really prepare for the role of homemaker, even though they know from early childhood that this is basically what they want. One women's college announced a new program in "creative homemaking and family living," expecting many students to sign up as majors. It didn't turn out that way at all. Upon investigation, it was quickly discovered that none of the young women wanted to announce publicly that she was that eager for practical preparation. Somehow, that was unseemly. Romance was supposed to come like a bolt out of the blue. After the ring was on the appropriate finger, then and only then was it acceptable to rush to the homemaking teacher for a few cramming courses.

In general, advanced preparation for anticipated crises has been more characteristic of middle-class family patterns than those of lower-social-level families in the past. Middle-class boys learned in their childhood homes that it was right for the father to buy insurance to protect his family. Girls learned that it was right to save pennies by careful home management. Lower-class family members, on the other hand, were often prevented by economic scarcity from protecting themselves against future problems. Moreover, they had less of the "socialized anxiety" that made such behaviors "right." In many lower-class homes, there was more inclination, because of deprivation, to use whatever was available today for today's needs and hope that something would turn up for tomorrow. Harold Hodges, Jr., after reviewing studies of class-related behavior, points out that living for the moment is not frowned on in a group where opportunities for "living it up" are rare.[5]

There are, of course, *individual* differences in defining preparation as a value as well as social-class differences. Sometimes, as we have seen, two young people from the same family develop entirely different attitudes: One may gamble; the other may fear any form of risk. Although this may cause little inconvenience in their childhood family, it may be absolute disaster if they marry unlike mates. In such a marriage, one partner feels constantly inhibited and the other constantly anxious.

[4] D. M. Schneider, "Typhoons on Yap," *Human Organization*, **16** (Summer, 1957), 10–15.

[5] Harold Hodges, Jr., *Social Stratification: Class in America*, Cambridge, Mass., Schenkman, 1964, ch. 10, pp. 195–220.

Adequate preparation for family living means more than buying insurance or learning home management. It also involves preparing psychologically to face the crisis of an empty house when the children are gone and the crisis of an empty heart when a loved one dies. No one is ever fully prepared for any crisis, but the more successful families are generally the more prepared.

EXPERIENCE
WITH PROBLEMS

Experience can be the best and also the most costly part of preparation. Theoretically, little mistakes early in the marriage can prevent big ones later on. This probably happens more often than is recorded. Yet there are some "crisis prone" families that appear to be unable to learn from previous mistakes. Often these problem families have marriage partners with personality, motivational, and educational inadequacies that prevent them from solving their own problems.

College-educated people have a greater-than-average ability to succeed in family groups, both because of their larger income and because of their status-conferred self-confidence, but even among college graduates there are some people who seem to be chronically incapable of anticipating or solving their own practical and emotional problems. Many such individuals eventually seek psychiatric treatment. Most people and most families, however, profit from past errors and become better at avoiding crises as time goes by. In fact, some who have faced many early emergencies are more successful in the long run because of their early learning experiences.

DEFINING IT
AS A CRISIS

The definition of a crisis depends not only on the nature of the experience itself but also on the values and beliefs of the family members. What is defined as a crisis in some families is not even recognized as a problem in others.

The sudden loss of employment in a middle-class family might be defined as a total disaster, yet in some lower-class homes, where the breadwinner is laid off every few months, it might be just another period of belt-tightening. Discovering that one's husband has been unfaithful, finding out that one's daughter is pregnant out of wedlock, or learning that one's son has killed a man depend for their crisis effect on the cultural definition of the behavior involved, as well as on the particular circumstances surrounding the event.

In recent years, there has been considerable study of the "why" and "when" of family definitions of crises. For example, parents who define a child's mental illness as their fault are more adversely affected by it than parents who consider the illness independent of them.[6] Mothers with younger children tend to be able to accept mental retardation better, and this acceptance is encouraged by religious beliefs.[7]

[6] B. Farber, "Effects of a Severely Mentally Retarded Child on Family Integration," *Monographs of the Society for Research in Child Development,* **24** (1959), 13.
[7] G. H. Zuk, "The Religious Factor and the Role of Guilt in Parental Acceptance of the Retarded Child," *American Journal of Mental Deficiency,* **64** (July, 1959), 145.

The *actual* situation in which a family finds itself may be less important in determining the behavior of the family members than the *imagined* situation, as Hansen and Hill have pointed out.[8] To an individual, his definition of what is occurring constitutes the real world. If a man thinks he can fly, in a real sense he can; this idea may even lead him to try it by jumping off a cliff. "Unfortunately," say Hansen and Hill in classic understatement, "although such definitions greatly influence the action he takes, the consequences do not flow from his definitions, and he may experience the impact of unexpected stress."

It is probable that the more successful families are the ones who can achieve the greater objectivity and thus greater reality in their definitions. Since cultural values vary so widely, it is also probable that, in the foreseeable future, there will not be universal standards by which an individual can measure the depth of the real crisis. But even if there were such objective measures, it is not very probable that any large number of people would use them. Conditioned values and personal anxieties would still operate to control behavior. In general, however, middle-class families, as Koos has shown, tend to have a greater sensitivity to crisis with a greater inclination to react (and sometimes overreact), than do lower- and upper-class families. Middle-class families recover more quickly and more often emerge with some positive benefit from their crises. Because of their less-adequate preparation, lower-class families are seldom really strengthened by what they define as crises.[9]

SUPPORTIVE HELP

Families meet crises more successfully and recover from them more quickly when relatives, friends, and neighbors are available to support them. This is a common observation. It is also validated by research data. In his war-separation study, Reuben Hill found that the families who were slowest to adjust to the separation were often solitary families who had moved often and to great distances from their relatives.[10] Stating it more positively, one study concluded that, "When the doors and kitchens of the neighbors are open to almost everyone, the long-term impact of stress may be resolved."[11]

Contemporary patterns of mobile and suburban living have many advantages, including new experience, greater self-reliance, and more independence from in-laws, relatives, and inquisitive neighbors. But there are disadvantages, too, and one of the greatest of these is the loss of comfort and support from people who really care in time of crises.

THE SOCIAL EXPECTATIONS

Families, like individuals, tend to behave the way they are expected to behave in the subcultural group in which they exist. Especially when under stress, families often take refuge in the rituals and customs that sustained their value system in the past, even if they gave little attention to those rituals and customs in

[8] Hansen and Hill, *op. cit.*, p. 805.
[9] Earl L. Koos, "Class Differences in Family Reactions to Crisis," *Marriage and Family Living,* **12** (Summer, 1950), 78.
[10] Reuben Hill, *Families Under Stress*, New York, Harper & Row, 1949.
[11] Hansen and Hill, *op. cit.*, p. 797.

noncrisis periods. This is especially true of religious ritual, but it is also true of community customs and social usage.

In those social groups in which it is appropriate for the widow to exhibit stalwart and stoic behavior at the funeral of her late husband, regardless of how she feels, the widow is likely to behave just that way. But in those subcultural groups where it is customary for the widow to express her grief animatedly, the performance of the stoic widow might be considered both curious and unfeeling.

In a family facing a crisis, the conditioned expectations of the partners are often heightened. Each partner becomes even more sensitive and more critical of the role behavior of the other. When under stress, family members can become devastatingly explicit in their accusations of how the other has failed to meet expectations.

Expectations have another way of affecting family problems, too. Parents who expect their adolescents to be difficult often have difficult adolescents. Parents who expect their child to have a religious "awakening" at puberty usually have a child who has a religious awakening at puberty. Families that have a self-expectation of pulling themselves out of crisis difficulties often do just that, and they will probably do it in just about the time that the social expectation says they should. For some, the expectation may require an extended period of grief and self-pity with a long, slow recovery period. In other families, this may mean an immediate effort on the part of all the members to face the situation realistically and set about restoring equilibrium. No one can really say which way is better. As with so many other things, a lot depends on what you're used to.

THE FAMILY GOALS

Family theorists and marriage counselors generally agree that the family that is well organized, has defined goals, and is steadily working toward them is far more likely to be successful than the family that has no purposeful direction.

The fact that many family members no longer have some of the goal satisfactions that families used to have may be, as we saw in Chapter 3, one important reason for today's high rate of marriage difficulty. Just producing enough to keep the family members alive was an important and satisfying achievement on the frontier, and being a "good provider" was a meaningful goal for a husband during the 1930s. These goals, however, derived from the necessities of living and did not have to be chosen in the same sense that family goals are chosen today.

In the present affluent society, short-range, pleasure-oriented goals are probably more easily attainable than at any time before. A new car, a color television set, or a European vacation can be procured by many individuals and families before these wishes have even attained the status of "fondest dreams." But it is the long-range, larger—yet less specific—goals, carefully chosen and diligently sought after, that enlarge family unity and provide a steadfastness of purpose. Such goals as a "good family life," a "college education for the children," or even a "successful marriage" can give meaning to all the sacrifices that are involved in achieving them. It would be hard to overestimate the importance of family goals in maintaining family unity and stability. Consider the following case:

"Sam said he is going to leave next Tuesday morning, four days from now, and nothing I could say will stop him," Mae told the counselor. "He's going out on a commercial fishing boat, and he'll be gone for three months. It isn't right. He promised five years ago that he would stay home forever if I would just marry him. We have two little babies now, and just when I need him most he's going back to fishing.

"It isn't as if he'd just be gone for these three months, either. As soon as they get back to port, they'll unload the catch and go out to sea again. I know all about fishing people. He'll only be home a few weeks out of every year from now on if I let him go.

"He was a fisherman when I met him, and I should have known better than to trust him. But he *promised* me. He promised that he would get a job in town. You tell him that he must live up to his promise. I'm entitled to some family life like the other girls I know. I need a man who will take me out once in a while. I need a man to walk up the street with me on Sunday, so that we can be a family. And the children need a father who is here. You believe in that kind of family life, don't you? Tell him not to go.

"There's something else, too. I know these fishermen, and they don't stay out at sea for the whole three months. They'll put in at some Mexican port. First thing you know, he'll be getting drunk and sleeping with one of those waterfront prostitutes down there. I'm sure he's been faithful to me ever since we've been married. But when he gets with those other fishermen, they'll shame him into being unfaithful. I won't have it—I just won't."

The counselor talked to Sam. "Yes, it's true," Sam said. "I did promise, and I did try. For five years I worked in a shipyard, and I hated every minute of it. In the shipyard, I was always competing with somebody. I didn't have any friends there. They had an incentive system, and it was cutthroat. You had to bolt so many plates, or you had to grind so many castings. I just can't work that way any longer.

"I know that I'll work longer and harder on the fishing boat. We'll be up before dawn, and we'll work until we drop, but every man will be working together. They're a bunch of good guys, and it's share and share alike. Everybody tries to help everybody else. I need that. I love that work, and I love that way. I don't care what Mae says or does. I'm leaving when that ship leaves on Tuesday.

"I've got a right to be happy. I'll provide for her and the kids better than I ever did before. I'll make a lot more money for her fishing than I ever did in the shipyard. In the end she'll thank me for it. But I can't tell her that now. All she keeps hollering is 'You're breaking your promise.' I didn't promise to be a miserable nobody, hating myself and hating her for the rest of my life. The way I see it, I promised to do the best thing for her I could. I thought then it might be working in the shipyard. I made a mistake. Now I'm leaving."

The counselor faced a difficult problem. What could be done in the next four days? As it turned out, several important things were accomplished, because, in this case, it was possible to restructure some family goals even in such brief a time.

The counselor worked closely with Mae and Sam for the next three days. First, each was allowed to ventilate all his hostile feelings. Then when they had totally exhausted their recriminations, they began to think positively about what could be done. The beginning of positive action came when the partners started to accept or eliminate possible superficial solutions to the problem. For example, it must have already occurred to every alert student that some compromise could be reached. Perhaps he could go out on short fishing trips for a few days at a time. But Sam, a real fisherman, totally rejected this as being both financially and statusfully inadequate. In his value system, only those who failed to make the grade as commercial deep-sea fishermen would join the "old men" on the short trips. Moreover, he argued, this would be lowering his family income instead of raising it.

But even as he talked, Sam gave indications of recognizing his responsibility to his family in ways other than just providing them with money. He began to think what he could do to provide a better recreational opportunity for his young wife and children while he was away, and how he could move her to a neighborhood closer to other fishermen's wives, where she would have some neighborly support during the long months when he was away from home.

On Saturday, Sam enrolled Mae in driving school, so that she would have some way of getting around while he was gone. (He insisted on giving her the first lesson himself.) Most important of all, Sam and Mae began to talk. By Sunday they were talking about the problem of infidelity when the ship put into a Mexican port. That Sam really reassured Mae was improbable; but the very fact that he was willing to talk with her about it made her feel that he understood her feelings. Then they talked about their long-range goals for the first time in their marriage. Ultimately, Sam and Mae agreed that they would put aside as much of the increased income as was possible, so that Sam might someday own a fishing boat of his own. When that day came, not only would be be able to provide the family with a handsome income that would take care of the children's college education, he might also be able then to employ a good skipper and miss a trip or two himself. Someday they could retire together with financial security and with the joint satisfaction of accomplishment.

Sam went fishing on Tuesday. In one sense Mae lost. But did she? Or did she perhaps gain something that was infinitely more important to her? And to Sam? And to the whole family?

PERSONAL MATURITY

When it is applied to humans, no one is quite sure what *mature* means. As a matter of fact, it implies different behaviors in different cultures. It is often used in its negative form—immature—to describe somebody who doesn't agree with us.

Although we can't define *mature*, all of us think of a mature person as one who behaves with calm decisiveness in difficult situations, who plans and solves problems intelligently, who seeks help from appropriate specialists when he needs it, and who is adaptable enough to change himself and so adjust to the realities of the situation that confronts him.

All of these behavior characteristics are crucial in effectively dealing with the difficulties in marriage and in family living that will inevitably arise. It is probable that a family will be successful to the degree and extent to which this kind of maturity exists in both of the marriage partners.

Even emotionally mature partners, though, must have a logical procedure in seeking a solution to their problems. Although specific reactions to specific marriage crises must be conditioned by the circumstances and the personalities involved, some general guidelines are suggested in the following section.

GUIDELINES FOR SOLVING
MARRIAGE PROBLEMS

Clearly the best way to solve any problem is to prevent it from ever arising. The best way to prevent a marriage problem from arising is careful choice of a mate. It isn't enough that he or she meets expectations while courting; it is even more important that he or she has the kind of flexible personality that can meet all of his partner's emotional needs for all the years to come. Even those partners who make a good choice will sooner or later have some rough spots in their marriage relationship. When trouble first arises, there are seven things to do.

1. First of all, assess the situation carefully. How much of it is real? How much are you imagining? Are you making a mountain out of a molehill? Will the problem disappear in a reasonable length of time if you do nothing about it?

2. Examine yourself and your own attitudes and expectations. What do you *really* want? In marriage counseling, it is common to find that when people are asked what solution they would like to have to their problem, they don't really know. Remember the classic marriage case in which the wife complained that her husband never comforted her when she cried. "Would you *be* comforted if he tried?" she was asked. She thought about this and then answered, "No, I think then I would feel that I really had something to cry about." Have clearly in your own mind what *will* resolve your difficulty.

3. Examine your partner's attitudes and expectations. Where could he possibly have gotten those ideas? How deeply are they conditioned into his personality? Is it *possible* that he *can* change, or would it be unrealistic to expect him to? What can you do toward meeting those expectations? Try to see the problem the way he sees it. The results are often surprising when a partner is asked by a marriage counselor, "What would your mate say if he were here and you weren't?" Some people begin to examine how their mate actually feels for the first time.

4. Communicate with your partner about the problem. This means, first, expressing your ideas clearly and calmly and in a way that is not threatening to him and, second, sticking to the essentials of the difficulty and not bringing in all sorts of extraneous arguments that have nothing to do with the problem.

Communicating also means listening carefully to him. It means providing a secure climate in which he can talk. And it means accepting what he says even though you cannot understand or agree with it. "I see it very differently, but yours is another point of view" is accepting. Shouting "You're crazy!" is *not* accepting. Remember that if you punish him for what he says—even by frowning, or crying, or withdrawing your love—it doesn't mean that he will stop doing what you don't want him to do, it merely means that he is going to stop telling you about it.

5. Try to work out some constructive "first moves." It isn't necessary to solve every problem all at once; in fact, sometimes it's impossible. Figure out what you can do now that will get both of you off dead center and will lead to some logical progress in problem solving.

6. Be determined, but be patient. There is a lot of living ahead, and there are very few things that have to be settled right now.

7. If, after a really determined trial for a reasonable length of time you cannot solve the problem, seek marriage counseling help. Often this involves an even greater emotional hurdle than ordinary help-seeking, for although modern Americans are conditioned to go to a physician, lawyer, banker, or mechanic when they need one, it is still difficult for them to seek help from a marriage counselor.

We have a long-standing middle-class tradition that people should be able to solve their own problems. In our earlier, less-complex agricultural society, this was even truer than it is today. Although this spirit of self-reliance undoubtedly helped to make America strong, it is possible that, over the years, more people might have been happier if they had sought more help in finding solutions to their difficulties.

MARRIAGE COUNSELING

Marriage counseling is as old as marriage. Today, however, trained professionals are available to replace the "granny," the tribal witch doctor, the bartender, and the beauty-shop operator.

Basically, marriage counseling combines tension reduction and education. Sometimes it is necessary to reduce tensions before education can take place. Sometimes it is necessary for some education to take place (*insight* is self-education in its finest sense) before any tension reduction can take place. But whichever comes first, both contribute to the ultimate goal of establishing new patterns of interacting that will replace old, nonadjustive patterns.

In a very simple way, everyone counsels himself. One voice inside will say, "I guess I'll park the car over there." But another voice will say, "Don't park there, the back end will stick out too far." Then the first voice may say, "All right, you're so smart, you find another place," and so on. If this kind of counseling reduces tension and leads to an acceptable solution of the problem, it is effective counseling.

Some problems, though, may be much too complex for anyone to solve himself. If he tries, he may find that he is giving himself so many arguments on both sides of the question and going over the same ground so often that he is merely creating additional inner tensions. He is pulled and pushed in all directions, and if he is not helped, ultimately he may fragment.

People can sometimes get out of this "tension box" by talking it over with another person. Usually the person they pick is a friend, and often a friend can be helpful. However, there are at least four things wrong with talking problems over with a friend:

1. By the very nature of things, we want to keep friends friendly, so we often alter the story just a little to make ourselves appear less guilty. Far from helping us, these adventures in fiction often just compound the problem.

2. The friend may have troubles of his own, and the last thing he wants to do is add ours to his worry list.

3. Often a friend cannot keep a confidence, and perhaps we shouldn't expect him to. After all, we didn't want to keep it to ourselves, either.

4. Usually a friend isn't any more competent to provide specialized help than we are ourselves. The number of problems of a similar nature that he has studied are as few as the number of problems we have studied. Often any discussion between friends is a matter of compounding ignorance.

So, if the problem is complex, and most marriage problems are, it is usually better to find a professional whom you can trust.

The thing that makes marriage counseling work—that makes any counseling or psychotherapy work—is the confidence that the people who need help have in the counselor they select. There are many different professionals who do marriage counseling—social workers, psychologists, clergymen, and even some physicians—in addition to the trained professional marriage counselors who have Ph.D.'s from recognized universities. Obviously, not all of them counsel in the same way, but any one of them who is able to engender and retain the confidence of the two partners involved can usually be helpful in some respect. At the very least, he can refer the partners to another specialist who has the competence and confidence to deal with whatever kind of specialized problem they may have.

The place to start seeking a marriage counselor is in the office of a trusted professional person: physician, minister, or teacher. In some communities, Family Service Agencies provide marriage counseling as a part of their regular service. In some communities, too, there are private professional marriage counselors who have had Ph.D. training and supervised postdoctoral experience. The American Association of Marriage Counselors can recommend the nearest member of the AAMC.

HOW MUCH DOES
COUNSELING HELP

There is no easy answer to the question of how much counseling helps. In one way, marriage counseling is more effective than it has any right to be, since by the time two individuals reach the marriage counselor, they have already taken the most important first step: They've agreed to try to solve their problem. In another way, though, the marriage counselor is faced with the most difficult task of all professional helpers, because often either one or the other of the troubled partners does not believe that he *himself* needs the counselor's service. A man may go to a doctor because he has a pain or to an accountant because he has a financial problem. But sometimes the partner who goes to the counselor doesn't think there is anything wrong with him; whatever is wrong, he thinks, is wrong with his mate.

Many times in marriage counseling, I have said to a complaining spouse, "If you could have anything you wanted as a solution to this marriage problem, what would you want?" The answer is often, "I want you to make him love me," or "I want you to make him make me happy."

No marriage counselor can *make* a marriage partner do anything, any more than his spouse can make him do anything. But the counselor can help the partner to create the kind of climate that will make the other mate *want* to love again. The counselor can help, that is, if the partner is willing to change himself enough to create this climate.

It was suggested above that perhaps the most important qualification of the mature person is his ability to change and so adjust to the realities of his situation. Nowhere is this more true than in solving marriage problems.

Usually any change of self involves some self-sacrifice, if only giving up long-standing notions about who or what is "right." In our culture, which is oriented to winning and to getting rather than to giving, this kind of self-sacrifice is exceedingly difficult. Somehow it just doesn't seem right to have to *give* something in order to *receive* love. Most feel they should get the love first and then do the giving, or else they will somehow be demeaned in the other person's eyes. In reality, though, there is nothing the least bit demeaning to the person who is willing to meet someone else's needs first and have his own needs met later. Back in Chapter 7, it was suggested that this is an evidence of strength, reserved for those people with superior self-respect and self-confidence. The insecure person is far too busy protecting his sensitive ego to be able to meet his partner's needs first.

Does this mean that you shouldn't expect to receive personal happiness in marriage, that it's all giving? No, indeed. There is nothing wrong with wishing for personal happiness. There has never been a more important goal since the beginning of mankind. But there is a widespread mistaken notion of how one arrives at that goal. Many believe that you find someone who *makes* you happy. This rarely happens. Happiness is a function of your own personality, and it develops *within* you. After many years of marriage counseling, I firmly believe that the only genuine happiness in marriage comes from anticipating the pleasure your partner will get from what you have to give, both physically and emotionally. It is that simple, yet that difficult.

ADDITIONAL
READINGS

Chapter 2

Andrews, Kenneth R., ed., *The Case Method of Teaching Human Relations and Administration,* Cambridge, Mass., Harvard Univ. Press, 1955.

Bernard, Jessie, Helen E. Buchanan, and William M. Smith, Jr., *Dating, Mating and Marriage,* Cleveland, Howard Allen, 1958.

Bowman, Henry A., Richard Kerckhoff, F. K. Dalvis, and Marvin B. Sussman, "Teaching Ethical Values Through the Marriage Course: A Debate," *Marriage and Family Living,* **19** (November, 1957), 325–339.

Christensen, Harold T., "The Intrusion of Values," in *Handbook of Marriage and the Family,* Chicago, Rand McNally, 1964, pp. 969–1006.

Clear, Val, "Marriage Education Through Novels and Biography," *Journal of Marriage and the Family,* **28** (May, 1966), 217–219.

Hinkle, R. C., Jr., and G. J. Hinkle, "The Quest to Make Sociology Scientific," in *The Development of Modern Sociology,* New York, Random House, 1954.

Hobart, Charles, "Commitment, Value Conflicts and the Future of the American Family," *Marriage and Family Living,* **25** (November, 1963), 405–412.

Klemer, Richard H., "The Empathetic Approach to Teaching Family Relations," *Journal of Home Economics,* **57** (October, 1965), 619–625.

Luckey, Eleanore, "Education for Family Living in the Twentieth Century," *Journal of Home Economics,* **57** (November, 1965), 685–690.

Rokeach, Milton, *Beliefs, Attitudes and Values,* San Francisco, Jossey-Bass, 1968.

Smarden, Laurence, "The Use of Drama in Teaching Family Relationships," *Journal of Marriage and the Family,* **28** (May, 1966), 219–223.

Somerville, Rose M., "The Literature Approach to Teaching Family Courses," *Journal of Marriage and the Family,* **28** (May, 1966), 214–217.

Chapter 3

Coudert, Jo, *Advice from a Failure,* New York, Stein and Day, 1965.

Cox, Frank D., *Youth, Marriage, and the Seductive Society,* Dubuque, Iowa, W. C. Brown, 1967.

Farber, Seymour M., et al., eds., *Man and Civilization: The Family's Search for Survival*, New York, McGraw-Hill, 1965.

Furstenberg, Frank F., Jr., "Industrialization and the American Family: A Look Backward," *American Sociological Review*, **31** (June, 1966), 326–337.

Levinger, George, "Marital Cohesiveness and Dissolution: An Integrative Review," *Journal of Marriage and the Family*, **27** (February, 1965), 19–28.

Nimkoff, Meyer F., ed., *Comparative Family Systems*, Boston, Houghton Mifflin, 1965.

Nye, F. Ivan, "Values, Family and a Changing Society," *Journal of Marriage and the Family*, **29** (May, 1967), 241–248.

Nye, F. Ivan, and Felix Berardo, eds., *Emerging Conceptual Frameworks in Family Analysis*, New York, Macmillan, 1966.

Parke, Robert, Jr., and Paul C. Glick, "Prospective Changes in Marriage and the Family," *Journal of Marriage and the Family*, **29** (May, 1967), 249–256.

Parsons, Talcott, and Robert F. Bales, *Family Socialization and Interaction Process*, New York, Free Press, 1955.

Pollock, Otto, "The Outlook for the American Family," *Journal of Marriage and the Family*, **29** (February, 1967), 193–205.

Queen, Stewart A., and Robert W. Habenstein, *The Family in Various Cultures*, 3rd ed., Philadelphia, Lippincott, 1967.

Rodman, Hyman, "Talcott Parsons' View of the Changing American Family," in Hyman Rodman, ed., *Marriage, Family and Society: A Reader*, New York, Random House, 1965, pp. 262–286.

Winick, Charles, "The Beige Epoch: Depolarization of Sex Roles in America," *Annals of the American Academy of Political and Social Science*, **376** (March, 1968), 18–24.

Chapter 4

Axelson, Leland, "The Marital Adjustment and Marital Role Definitions of Husbands of Working and Nonworking Wives," *Marriage and Family Living*, **25** (May, 1963), 189–195.

Blood, Robert O., and Donald Wolfe, *Husbands and Wives*, New York, Free Press, 1960.

Brenton, Myron, *The American Male*, New York, Coward-McCann, 1966.

Dunn, Marie S., "Marriage Role Expectations of Adolescents," *Marriage and Family Living*, **22** (May, 1960), 99–104.

Farber, Seymour M., and Roger H. L. Wilson, ed., *Man and Civilization: The Potential of Woman*, New York, McGraw-Hill, 1963.

Friedan, Betty, *The Feminine Mystique*, New York, Norton, 1963.

Goode, William J., *The Family*, Englewood Cliffs, N.J., Prentice-Hall, 1964.

Kammeyer, Kenneth, "The Feminine Role: An Analysis of Attitude Consistency," *Journal of Marriage and the Family*, **26** (August, 1964), 295–305.

Kirkpatrick, Clifford, *The Family as Process and Institution*, New York, Ronald Press, 1963.

Luckey, Eleanore, "Marital Satisfaction and Its Association with Congruence of Perception," *Marriage and Family Living*, **22** (February, 1960), 49–54.

Martinson, Floyd M., *Marriage and the American Ideal*, New York, Dodd, Mead, 1960.

Tallman, Irving, "Working-Class Wives in Suburbia: Fulfillment or Crisis?" *Journal of Marriage and the Family*, **31** (February, 1969), 65–72.

Chapter 5

Aller, Florence D., "Self-Concept in Student Marital Adjustment," *Family Life Coordinator*, **11** (April, 1962), 43–45.

Bennett, E. M., and L. R. Cohen, "Men and Women: Personality Patterns and Contrasts," *Genetic Psychology Monographs*, **59** (1959), 101–155.

Berelson, Bernard, and Gary A. Steiner, *Human Behavior*, New York, Harcourt, Brace & World, 1964.

Bossard, James H. S., and Eleanor Boll, *The Sociology of Child Development*, New York, Harper & Row, 1966.

Duvall, Evelyn, "Adolescent Love as a Reflection of Teen-agers' Search for Identity," *Journal of Marriage and the Family*, **26** (May, 1964), 226–229.

Fromme, Allan, *The Ability to Love*, New York, Farrar, Straus & Giroux, 1965.

Hamacheck, Don E., ed., *The Self in Growth, Teaching and Learning*, Englewood Cliffs, N.J., Prentice-Hall, 1965.

Klemer, Richard H., *A Man for Every Woman*, New York, Macmillan, 1959.

Luckey, Eleanore, "Marital Satisfaction and the Congruent Self-Spouse Concepts," *Marriage and Family Living*, **24** (November, 1962), 415.

McCandless, Boyd R., *Children: Behavior and Development*, 2nd ed., New York, Holt, Rinehart and Winston, 1967.

Moss, Joel, and Ruby Gingles, "The Relationship of Personality to the Incidence of Early Marriage," *Marriage and Family Living*, **21** (November, 1959), 373–377.

Prince, Alfred James, and Andrew B. Baggaley, "Personality Variables and the Ideal Mate," *Family Life Coordinator*, **12** (July–October, 1963), 93–96.

Chapter 6

Bell, Robert R., *Marriage and Family Interaction*, rev. ed., Homewood, Ill., Dorsey, 1967.

Bowman, Henry A., *Marriage for Moderns*, 5th ed., New York, McGraw-Hill, 1965.

Coombs, Robert H., "Value Concensus and Partner Satisfaction Among Dating Couples," *Journal of Marriage and the Family*, **28** (May, 1966), 166–173.

Dean, Dwight G., "Romanticism and Emotional Maturity: A Further Explanation," *Social Forces*, **42** (March, 1964), 298–303.

Goode, William J., "The Theoretical Importance of Love," *American Sociological Review*, **24** (February, 1959), 38–47.

Greenfield, S. M., "Love and Marriage in Modern America," *Sociological Quarterly*, **6** (Autumn, 1965), 361–377.

Heiss, Jerold S., and Michael Gordon, "Need Patterns and the Mutual Satisfaction of Dating and Engaged Couples," *Journal of Marriage and the Family*, **26** (August, 1964), 337–338.

Hunt, Morton M., *The Natural History of Love*, New York, Knopf, 1959.

Klemer, Richard H., *A Man for Every Woman*, New York, Macmillan, 1959.

Lantz, Herman, and Eloise Snyder, *Marriage: An Examination of the Man–Woman Relationship*, New York, Wiley, 1962.

Chapter 7

Banta, Thomas J., and Mavis Hetherington, "Relations Between Needs of Friends and Fiancés," *Journal of Abnormal Social Psychology*, **66** (April, 1963), 401–404.

Blood, Robert O., Jr., *Marriage*, 2nd ed., New York, Free Press, 1969.

Bolton, Charles D., "Mate Selection as the Development of a Relationship," *Marriage and Family Living*, **23** (August, 1961), 234–240.

Fromm, Erich, *The Art of Loving*, New York, Harper & Row, 1956.

Heiss, Jerold S., and Michael Gordon, "Need Patterns and the Mutual Satisfaction of Dating and Engaged Couples," *Journal of Marriage and the Family*, **26** (August, 1964), 337–338.

Lowrie, S. H., "Factors Involved in the Frequency of Dating," *Marriage and Family Living*, **18** (February, 1956), 46–51.

Maeher, M. L., J. Mensing, and S. Nafzger, "Concept of Self and the Reactions of Others," *Sociometry,* **25** (December, 1962), 353–357.

Stewart, R. L., and Glenn M. Vernon, "Four Correlates of Empathy in the Dating Situation," *Sociology and Social Research,* **43** (March–April, 1959), 279–285.

Chapter 8

Burchinal, Lee G., and Loren E. Chancellor, "Social Status, Religious Affiliation and Ages at Marriage," *Marriage and Family Living,* **25** (May, 1963), 219–221.

Coombs, Robert H., "A Value Theory of Mate Selection," *Family Life Coordinator,* **10** (July, 1961), 51–54.

Coombs, Robert H., "Reinforcement of Values in the Parental Home as a Factor in Mate Selection," *Marriage and Family Living,* **24** (May, 1962), 155–157.

Dinitz, Simon, Franklin Banks, and Benjamin Pasamanick, "Mate Selection and Social Class: Changes During the Past Quarter Century," *Marriage and Family Living,* **22** (November, 1960), 348–357.

Kephart, William M., *The Family, Society and the Individual,* 2nd ed., Boston, Houghton Mifflin, 1966.

Leslie, Gerald R., *The Family in Social Context,* New York, Oxford University Press, 1967.

Peterson, James A., *Education for Marriage,* 2nd ed., New York, Scribner, 1964.

Udry, J. Richard, *The Social Context of Marriage,* Philadelphia, Lippincott, 1966.

Chapter 9

Burchinal, Lee G., "Membership Groups and Attitudes Toward Cross-Religious Dating," *Marriage and Family Living,* **22** (August, 1960), 248–253.

Burchinal, Lee G., "The Premarital Dyad and Love Involvement," in Harold T. Christensen, ed., *Handbook of Marriage and the Family,* Chicago, Rand McNally, 1964, pp. 623–674.

Gordon, Albert I., *Intermarriage: Interfaith, Interracial, Interethnic,* Boston, Beacon, 1964.

Landis, Judson T., and Mary G. Landis, *Building a Successful Marriage,* 5th ed., Englewood Cliffs, N.J., Prentice-Hall, 1968.

Locke, Harvey J., G. Sabagh, and M. M. Thomes, "Interfaith Marriages," *Social Problems,* **4** (April, 1957), 329–333.

Rodman, Hyman, "Mate Selection: Incest Taboos, Homogamy, and Mixed Marriages," in Hyman Rodman, ed., *Marriage, Family and Society: A Reader,* New York, Random House, 1965.

Scott, John Finley, "The American College Sorority: Its Role in Class and Ethnic Endogamy," *American Sociological Review,* **30** (August, 1965), 514–527.

Snyder, Eloise, "Attitudes: A Study of Homogamy and Marital Selectivity," *Journal of Marriage and the Family,* **26** (August, 1964), 332–336.

Womble, Dale L., *Foundations for Marriage and Family Relations,* New York, Macmillan, 1966.

Chapter 10

Barron, Milton L., *People Who Intermarry,* Syracuse, Syracuse University Press, 1946.

Bowman, Henry A., *Marriage for Moderns,* 5th ed., New York, McGraw-Hill, 1965.

Burchinal, Lee G., and Loren E. Chancellor, "Survival Rates Among Religiously Homogamous and Interreligious Marriages," *Social Forces,* **41** (May, 1963), 353–362.

Gordon, Albert I., *Intermarriage: Interfaith, Interracial, Interethnic*, Boston, Beacon, 1964.
Heiss, Jerold S., "Premarital Characteristics of the Religiously Intermarried in an Urban Area," *American Sociological Review*, **25** (February, 1960), 47–55.
Kerckhoff, Alan, "Patterns of Homogamy and the Field of Eligibles," *Social Forces*, **42** (March, 1964), 289–297.
Vernon, Glenn M., "Bias in Professional Publications Concerning Interfaith Marriages," *Religious Education*, **55** (July–August, 1960), 261–264.
Zimmerman, Carle C., and Lucius F. Cervantes, *Successful American Families*, New York, Pageant, 1960.

Chapter 11

Cavan, Ruth S., *The American Family*, 3rd ed., New York, Thomas Y. Crowell, 1965.
Coombs, Robert H., "Sex Differences in Dating Aspirations and Satisfaction with Computer Selected Partners," *Journal of Marriage and the Family*, **28** (February, 1966), 62–66.
Hunt, Morton M., *The World of the Formerly Married*, New York, McGraw-Hill, 1966.
Ktsanes, Thomas, and Virginia Ktsanes, "The Theory of Complementary Needs in Mate Selection," in Robert F. Winch and Robert McGinnis, eds., *Selected Studies in Marriage and the Family*, rev. ed., New York, Holt, Rinehart and Winston, 1962, pp. 517–532.
Murstein, Bernard I., "Empirical Tests of Role, Complementary Needs, and Homogamy Theories of Marital Choice," *Journal of Marriage and the Family*, **29** (November, 1967), 689–696.
Pressey, Sidney L., and Raymond G. Kuhlen, *Psychological Development Through the Life Span*, New York, Harper & Row, 1957.
Rosow, Irving, "Issues in the Concept of Need-Complementarity," *Sociometry*, **20** (September, 1957), 216–233.
Schellenberg, J. A., "Homogamy in Personal Values and the 'Field of Eligibles,'" *Social Forces*, **39** (December, 1960), 157–162.
Strauss, Anselm, "Personality Needs and Marital Choice," *Social Forces*, **25** (March, 1947), 332–335.
Terman, Lewis M., et al., *Psychological Factors in Marital Happiness*, New York, McGraw-Hill, 1938.
Udry, J. Richard, "Complementarity in Mate Selection: A Perceptual Approach," *Marriage and Family Living*, **25** (August, 1963), 281–289.
Udry, J. Richard, "Personality Match and Interpersonal Perception as Predictors of Marriage," *Journal of Marriage and the Family*, **29** (November, 1967), 722–725.
Winch, Robert F., *Mate Selection: A Study of Complementary Needs*, New York, Harper & Row, 1958.

Chapter 12

Bell, Robert R., *Premarital Sex in a Changing Society*, Englewood Cliffs, N.J., Prentice-Hall, 1966.
Bernard, Jessie S., "The Fourth Revolution," *Journal of Social Issues*, **22** (April, 1966), 76–87.
Christensen, Harold T., "Cultural Relativism and Premarital Sex Norms," *American Sociological Review*, **25** (February, 1960), 31–39.
Duvall, Evelyn, and Sylvanus M. Duvall, eds., *Sex Ways in Fact and Faith: Bases for Christian Family Policy*, New York, Association Press, 1961.
Ehrmann, Winston, "Marital and Non-marital Sexual Behavior," in Harold T. Christensen,

ed., *Handbook of Marriage and the Family,* Chicago, Rand McNally, 1964, pp. 585–622.

Ferdinand, Theodore, "Sex Behavior and the American Class Structure: A Mosaic," *Annals of the American Academy of Political and Social Science,* **376** (March, 1968), 76–85.

Freedman, Mervin B., "The Sexual Behavior of American College Women: An Empirical Study and an Historical Survey," *Merrill-Palmer Quarterly,* **11** (October, 1964), 19–32.

Gagnon, John H., "Sexuality and Sexual Learing in the Child," *Psychiatry,* **28** (August, 1965), 212–228.

Pope, Holowell, and Dean Knudsen, "Premarital Sex Norms, The Family and Social Change," *Journal of Marriage and the Family,* **27** (August, 1965), 314–323.

Reiss, Ira L., *The Social Context of Premarital Sexual Permissiveness,* New York, Holt, Rinehart and Winston, 1967.

Chapter 13

Bell, Robert R., "Parent–Child Conflict in Sexual Values," *Journal of Social Issues,* **22** (April, 1966), 34–44.

Bernard, Jessie S., *The Sex Game,* Englewood Cliffs, N.J., Prentice-Hall, 1968.

Burchinal, Lee G., "The Premarital Dyad and Love Involvement," in Harold T. Christensen, ed., *Handbook of Marriage and the Family,* Chicago, Rand McNally, 1964, pp. 623–674.

Farnsworth, Dana, "Sexual Morality and the Dilemma of the Colleges," *American Journal of Orthopsychiatry,* **35** (July, 1965), 676–681.

Kirkendall, Lester A., "Values and Premarital Intercourse—Implications for Parent Education," *Marriage and Family Living,* **22** (November, 1960), 317–322.

Packard, Vance, *The Sexual Wilderness,* New York, McKay, 1968.

Poffenberger, Thomas, "Individual Choice in Adolescent Premarital Sex Behavior," *Marriage and Family Living,* **22** (November, 1960), 324–330.

Schur, Edwin M., *The Family and the Sexual Revolution,* Bloomington, Ind., Indiana University Press, 1964.

Chapter 14

Bowman, Henry A., "Dating Practices and Standards," in *Marriage for Moderns,* 5th ed., New York, McGraw-Hill, 1965, pp. 115–170.

Brill, Earl, "Sex Is Dead," *Christian Century,* **83** (August 3, 1966), 957–958.

Calderone, Mary S., "Sex and Social Responsibility," *Journal of Home Economics,* **57** (September, 1965), 499–505.

Duvall, Evelyn, *Why Wait Till Marriage?* New York, Association Press, 1965.

Fletcher, Joseph, "Ethics and Unmarried Sex: Morals Re-Examined," in Daniel O. Price, ed., *The 99th Hour,* Chapel Hill, N.C., Univ. of North Carolina Press, 1967.

Glassberg, B. Y., "Sexual Behavior Patterns in Contemporary Youth Culture: Implications for Later Marriage," *Journal of Marriage and the Family,* **27** (May, 1965), 190–192.

Hettlinger, Richard F., *Living with Sex: The Student's Dilemma,* New York, Seabury, 1966.

Kardiner, Abram, *Sex and Morality,* New York, Charter Books, 1962.

Kirkendall, Lester A., *Premarital Intercourse and Interpersonal Relations,* New York, Julian, 1961.

Klemer, Richard H., "Student Attitudes Toward Guidance in Sexual Morality," *Marriage and Family Living,* **24** (August, 1962), 260–264.

Mace, David R., "The Case for Chastity and Virginity," in Albert Ellis and Albert Abarbanel, *The Encyclopedia of Sexual Behavior*, 2nd ed., New York, Hawthorn, 1967, pp. 247–252.

Poffenberger, Thomas, "The Control of Adolescent Premarital Coitus," *Marriage and Family Living*, **24** (August, 1962), 254–260.

Smigel, Erwin, and Rita Seiden, "The Decline and Fall of the Double Standard," *Annals of the American Academy of Political and Social Science*, **376** (March, 1968), 6–17.

Chapter 15

Bernard, Jessie S., "The Adjustment of Marriage Mates," in Harold T. Christensen, ed., *Handbook of Marriage and the Family*, Chicago, Rand McNally, 1964, pp. 675–739.

Blood, Robert O., Jr., and Robert L. Hamblin, "The Effects of the Wife's Employment on the Family Power Structure," *Social Forces*, **36** (May, 1958), 347–352.

Blood, Robert O., Jr., and Donald M. Wolfe, *Husbands and Wives*, New York, Free Press, 1960.

Havemann, Ernest, *Men, Women, and Marriage*, Garden City, N.Y., Doubleday, 1962.

Heiss, Jerold S., ed., *Family Roles and Interaction: Anthology*, Chicago, Rand McNally, 1968.

Kenkel, William F., "Dominance, Persistence, Self-Confidence, and Spousal Roles in Decision Making," *Journal of Social Psychology*, **54** (August, 1961), 349–358.

Klemer, Richard H., and Margaret G. Klemer, *The Early Years of Marriage*, Public Affairs Pamphlet No. 424, 1968.

McGinnis, Thomas, *Your First Year of Marriage*, Garden City, N.Y., Doubleday, 1967.

Chapter 16

Berne, Eric, *Games People Play*, New York, Grove, 1964.

Blood, Robert O., Jr., *Marriage*, 2nd ed., New York, Free Press, 1969.

Blood, Robert O., Jr., "Resolving Family Conflicts," *Journal of Conflict Resolution*, **4** (June, 1960), 209–219.

Buerkle, Jack V., "Self Attitudes and Marital Adjustment," *Merrill-Palmer Quarterly*, **6** (January, 1960), 114–124.

Hawkins, James, "Associations Between Companionship, Hostility, and Marital Satisfaction," *Journal of Marriage and the Family*, **30** (November, 1968), 647–650.

Hobart, C. W., "Disillusionment in Marriage and Romanticism," *Marriage and Family Living*, **20** (May, 1958), 156–162.

Jacobson, Alver H., "Conflict of Attitudes Toward the Roles of the Husband and Wife in Marriage," *American Sociological Review*, **17** (April, 1952), 146–150.

Luckey, Eleanore, "Marital Satisfaction and Congruent Self-Spouse Concepts," *Social Forces*, **39** (December, 1960), 153–157.

Milt, Harry, *What Can You Do About Quarreling?* Public Affairs Pamphlet No. 369, 1965.

Mudd, Emily H., Howard E. Mitchell, and Sara B. Taubin, *Success in Family Living*, New York, Association Press, 1965.

Pineo, Peter C., "Disenchantment in the Late Years of Marriage," *Marriage and Family Living*, **23** (February, 1961), 3–11.

Schelling, T. C., *The Strategy of Conflict*, Cambridge, Mass., Harvard University Press, 1960.

Taylor, Alexander, "Role Perception, Empathy and Marriage Adjustment," *Sociology and Social Research*, **52** (October, 1967), 22–34.

Winch, Robert F., *The Modern Family*, rev. ed., New York, Holt, Rinehart and Winston, 1963.

Chapter 17

Brownfield, E. Dorothy, "Communication—Key to Dynamics of Family Interaction," *Marriage and Family Living*, **15** (November, 1953), 316–319.

Farber, Bernard, *Family: Organization and Interaction*, San Francisco, Chandler, 1964.

Handel, Gerald, ed., *The Psychosocial Interior of the Family*, Chicago, Aldine, 1967.

Howe, Reul, *The Miracle of Dialogue*, New York, Seabury, 1963.

Karlsson, Georg, *Adaptability and Communication in Marriage*, rev. ed., Totowa, N.J., Bedminster, 1963.

Navran, Leslie, "Communication and Adjustment in Marriage," *Family Process*, **6** (September, 1967), 173–184.

Rabkin, Richard, "Uncoordinated Communication Between Marriage Partners," *Family Process*, **6** (March, 1967), 10–15.

Satir, Virginia, "Communication: A Process of Giving and Getting Information," in *Conjoint Family Therapy*, Palo Alto, Calif., Science and Behavior Books, 1964.

Shapiro, Jeffrey G., "Responsivity to Facial and Linguistic Cues," *Journal of Communication*, **8** (March, 1968), 11–17.

Steinmann, Anne, "Lack of Communication Between Men and Women," *Marriage and Family Living*, **20** (November, 1958), 350–352.

Stroup, Atlee, *Marriage and Family: A Developmental Approach*, New York, Appleton-Century-Crofts, 1966.

Chapter 18

Brenton, Myron, *The American Male*, New York, Coward-McCann, 1966.

Brown, Daniel, and David Lynn, "Human Sexual Development: An Outline of Components and Concepts," *Journal of Marriage and the Family*, **28** (May, 1966), 155–162.

Crawley, Lawrence, and James Malfetti, *Reproduction, Sex and Preparation for Marriage*, Englewood Cliffs, N.J., Prentice-Hall, 1964,

Dengrove, Edward, "Sex Differences," in Albert Ellis and Albert Abarbanel, *The Encyclopedia of Sexual Behavior*, 2nd ed., New York, Hawthorn, 1967, pp. 931–938.

Henry, George, *Masculinity and Femininity*, New York, Macmillan, Collier, 1964.

Karen, Robert L., "Some Variables Affecting Sexual Attitudes, Behavior and Consistency," *Marriage and Family Living*, **21** (August, 1959), 235–239.

Kirkendall, Lester A., "Toward a Clarification of the Concept of Male Sex Drive," *Marriage and Family Living*, **20** (November, 1958), 367–372.

Krich, A. M., *Men: The Variety and Meaning of Their Sexual Experience*, New York, Dell, 1954.

Shuttleworth, Frank K., "A Bisocial and Developmental Theory of Male and Female Sexuality," *Marriage and Family Living*, **21** (May, 1959), 163–170.

Chapter 19

Anastasi, Anne, "Psychological Differences Between Men and Women," in William C. Bier, ed., *Women in Modern Life*, New York, Fordham University Press, 1968, pp. 42–43.

Dedman, Jean, "The Relationship Between Religious Attitude and Attitude Toward Premarital Sex Relations," *Marriage and Family Living*, **21** (May, 1959), 171–176.

Krich, A. M., *Women: The Variety and Meaning of Their Sexual Experience*, New York, Dell, 1953.

Lee, Margie R., "Background Factors Related to Sex Information and Attitudes," *Journal of Educational Psychology*, **43** (December, 1952), 467–485.

Maslow, Abraham H., "Self Esteem (Dominance Feeling) and Sexuality in Women," in Hendrik Ruitenbeek, ed., *Psychoanalysis and Female Sexuality*, New Haven, Conn., College and University Press, 1966, pp. 161–197.

Mead, Margaret, *Male and Female*, New York, Morrow, 1949.

Naismith, Grace, *Private and Personal*, New York, McKay, 1966.

Neisser, Edith, *Mothers and Daughters*, New York, Harper & Row, 1967.

Schur, Edwin M., ed., "The Woman Problem," in *The Family and the Sexual Revolution: Selected Readings*, Bloomington, Ind., Indiana University Press, 1964, pp. 200–316.

Tyler, Leona E., *The Psychology of Human Differences*, 3rd ed., New York, Appleton-Century-Crofts, 1965.

Chapter 20

Baruch, Dorothy, and Hyman Miller, *Sex in Marriage*, New York, Harper & Row, 1962.

Brecher, R. and E. Brecher, eds., *An Analysis of Human Sexual Response*, New York, New American Library, 1966.

Christensen, Harold T., and George R. Carpenter, "Timing Patterns in the Development of Sexual Intimacy: An Attitudinal Report on Three Modern Western Societies," *Marriage and Family Living*, **24** (February, 1962), 30–35.

Crawley, Lawrence, and James Malfetti, *Reproduction, Sex and Preparation for Marriage*, Englewood Cliffs, N.J., Prentice-Hall, 1964.

King, Charles E., "The Sex Factor in Marital Adjustment," *Marriage and Family Living*, **16** (1954), pp. 237–240.

Klemer, Richard H., and Margaret G. Klemer, *Sexual Adjustment in Marriage*, Public Affairs Pamphlet No. 397, 1967.

Masters, William H., and Virginia E. Johnson, *Human Sexual Response*, Boston, Little, Brown, 1966.

Udry, J. Richard, "Sex and Family Life," *Annals of the American Academy of Political and Social Science*, **376** (March, 1968), 25–35.

Wallin, Paul, and Alexander Clark, "Religiosity, Sexual Gratification and Marital Satisfaction in the Middle Years of Marriage," *Social Forces*, **42** (March, 1964), 303–309.

Chapter 21

Bossard, James H. S., and Eleanor S. Boll, *Why Marriages Go Wrong*, New York, Ronald Press, 1958.

Christensen, Harold T., "A Cross-Cultural Comparison of Attitudes Towards Marital Infidelity," *International Journal of Comparative Sociology*, **3** (September, 1962), 124–137.

Cuber, John F., and Peggy B. Harroff, *The Significant Americans*, New York, Appleton-Century-Crofts, 1965.

Ellis, Albert, "Sexual Promiscuity in America," *Annals of the American Academy of Political and Social Science*, **378** (July, 1968), 58–74.

Harper, Robert, "Extramarital Sex Relations," in Albert Ellis and Albert Abarbanel, *The Encyclopedia of Sexual Behavior*, 2nd ed., New York, Hawthorn, 1967, 384–391.

Levy, John, and Ruth Monroe, *The Happy Family*, New York, Knopf, 1945.

Mitchell, Howard E., James W. Bullard, and Emily H. Mudd, "Areas of Marital Conflict in Successfully and Unsuccessfully Functioning Families," *Journal of Health and Human Behavior*, **3** (Summer, 1962), 88–93.

Neubeck, Gerhard, and Vera M. Schletzer, "A Study of Extra-Marital Relationships," *Marriage and Family Living*, **24** (August, 1962), 279–281.

Chapter 22

Bigelow, Howard F., *Family Finance*, Philadelphia, Lippincott, 1953.

Blackburn, Clark, and N. M. Lobsenz, *How to Stay Married: A Candid Approach to Sex, Money, and Emotions in Marriage*, New York, Cowles, 1969.

Blood, Robert O., Jr., and Robert L. Hamblin, "The Effects of the Wife's Employment on the Family Power Structure," *Social Forces*, **26** (May, 1958), 347–352.

Bradley, Joseph F., and Ralph H. Wherry, *Personal and Family Finance*, New York, Holt, Rinehart and Winston, 1961.

Britton, Virginia, *Personal Finance*, New York, American Book, 1968.

Freeman, Ruth, and Jean Due, "Influence of Goals on Family Financial Management," *Journal of Home Economics*, **53** (June, 1961), 448–452.

Gross, Irma H., and Elizabeth W. Crandall, *Management for Modern Families*, 2nd ed., New York, Appleton-Century-Crofts, 1963.

Herrmann, Robert O., "Economic Problems Confronting Teenage Newly-Weds," *Journal of Home Economics*, **57** (February, 1965), 93–97.

Hofstrom, Jeanne L., and Marilyn Dunsing, "A Comparison of Economic Choices of One-Earner and Two-Earner Families," *Journal of Marriage and the Family*, **27** (August, 1965), 403–409.

Margolius, Sidney, *How to Make the Most of Your Money*, New York, Appleton-Century-Crofts, 1966.

Margolius, Sidney, *Family Money Problems*, Public Affairs Pamphlet No. 412, 1967.

Nickell, Paulena, and Jean Dorsey, *Management in Family Living*, 4th ed., New York, Wiley, 1969.

Riesman, David, and Howard Roseborough, "Careers and Consumer Behavior," in Lincoln Clark, ed., *Consumer Behavior*, New York, New York Univ. Press, 1955, pp. 1–18.

Schwabacher, Albert E., Jr., "The Repository of Wealth," in Seymour M. Farber and Roger Wilson, eds., *Man and Civilization: The Potential of Women*, New York, McGraw-Hill, 1963, pp. 241–254.

Chapter 23

Ackerman, Nathan, "Emotional Impact of In-Laws and Relatives," in Samuel Liebman, ed., *Emotional Forces in the Family*, Philadelphia, Lippincott, 1959, pp. 71–84.

Adams, Bert, *Kinship in an Urban Setting*, Chicago, Markham, 1968.

Albrecht, Ruth, "Intergeneration Parent Patterns," *Journal of Home Economics*, **46** (January, 1954), 29–32.

Bell, Robert R., *Marriage and Family Interaction*, rev. ed., Homewood, Ill., Dorsey, 1967.

Berardo, Felix M., "Kinship Interaction and Communications Among Space Age Migrants," *Journal of Marriage and the Family*, **29** (August, 1967), 541–554.

Duvall, Evelyn, *In-Laws: Pro and Con*, New York, Association Press, 1954.

Komarovsky, Mirra, *Blue Collar Marriage*, New York, Random House, 1964.

Mudd, Emily H., Howard E. Mitchell, and Sara B. Taubin, *Success in Family Living*, New York, Association Press, 1965.

Reiss, Paul J., "Extended Kinship Relationships in American Society," in Hyman Rodman, ed., *Marriage Family and Society: A Reader*, New York, Random House, 1965, pp. 204–210.

Shanas, Ethel, and Gordon Streib, eds., *Social Structure and the Family: Generational Relations*, Englewood Cliffs, N.J., Prentice-Hall, 1965.

Shlien, John M., "Mother-in-Law: A Problem in Kinship Terminology," *ETC*, **19** (July, 1962), 161–171.

Stryker, Sheldon, "The Adjustment of Married Offspring to Their Parents," *American Sociological Review*, **20** (April, 1955), 149–154.

Sussman, Marvin B., "The Isolated Nuclear Family: Fact or Fiction," *Social Problems,* **6** (Spring, 1959), 333–340.

Sussman, Marvin B., and Lee G. Burchinal, "Parental Aid to Married Children: Implications for Family Functioning," *Marriage and Family Living,* **24** (November, 1962), 320–332.

Sweetser, Dorrian, "Asymmetry in Intergenerational Family Relationships," *Social Forces,* **41** (May, 1963), 346–352.

Chapter 24

Bossard, James H. S., and Eleanor S. Boll, *The Sociology of Child Development,* 4th ed., New York, Harper & Row, 1966.

Brittain, Clay V., "Age and Sex of Siblings and Conformity Toward Parents Versus Peers in Adolescence," *Child Development,* **37** (September, 1966), 709–714.

Dager, Edward, "Socialization and Personality Development in the Child," in Harold T. Christensen, ed., *Handbook of Marriage and the Family,* Chicago, Rand McNally, 1964, pp. 740–781.

Ginott, Haim G., *Between Parent and Child,* New York, Macmillan, 1965.

Jenkins, Gladys G., Helen S. Shacter, and William W. Bauer, *These Are Your Children,* 3rd ed., Chicago, Scott, Foresman, 1966.

Koch, H. L., "The Relation of Certain Formal Attributes of Siblings to Attitudes Held Toward Each Other and Toward Their Parents," *Monographs of the Society for Research in Child Development,* **25**, No 4 (1960).

Kohn, Melvin, "Social Class and Parent–Child Relationships: An Interpretation," *American Journal of Sociology,* **68** (January, 1963), 471–480.

LaBarre, Weston, "Relation Between Parents and Children," *Child–Family Digest,* **19** (July–August, 1960), 5–16.

McCandless, Boyd R., *Children: Behavior and Development,* 2nd ed., New York, Holt, Rinehart and Winston, 1967.

Missildine, Hugh, *Your Inner Child of the Past,* New York, Simon and Schuster, 1963.

Smart, Mollie, and Russell Smart, *Children, Development and Relationships,* New York, Macmillan, 1967.

van der Veen, Ferdinand, "The Parent's Concept of the Family Unit and Child Adjustment," *Journal of Counseling Psychology,* **12** (Summer, 1965), 196–200.

Zunich, Michael, "Child Behavior and Parental Attitudes," *Journal of Psychology,* **62** (January, 1966), 41–46.

Chapter 25

Bailey, Margaret, "Alcoholism and Marriage: A Review of Research and Professional Literature," *Quarterly Journal of Studies on Alcoholism,* **22** (March, 1961), 81–97.

DeBurger, James E., "Marital Problems, Help-Seeking, and Emotional Orientation as Revealed in Help Request Letters," *Journal of Marriage and the Family,* **29** (November, 1967), 712–721.

Farber, Bernard, "Family Organization and Crisis," New York, *Monographs of the Society for Research in Child Development,* **25**, no. 1 (1960).

Fisher, Oliver, *Help for Today's Troubled Marriages,* New York, Hawthorn, 1968.

Goode, William J., *After Divorce,* Glencoe, Ill., Free Press, 1956.

Hansen, Donald A., and Reuben Hill, "Families Under Stress," in Harold T. Christensen, ed., *Handbook of Marriage and the Family,* Chicago, Rand McNally, 1964, pp. 782–819.

Hunt, Morton M., *The World of the Formerly Married,* New York, McGraw-Hill, 1966.

Johnson, Dean, *Marriage Counseling: Theory and Practice,* Englewood Cliffs, N.J., Prentice-Hall, 1961.

Klemer, Richard H., ed., *Counseling in Marital and Sexual Problems: A Physician's Handbook,* Baltimore, Williams & Wilkins, 1965.

Taylor, Donald, *Marriage Counseling,* Springfield, Ill., Charles C. Thomas, 1965.

Vincent, Clark E., "Mental Health and the Family," *Journal of Marriage and the Family,* **29** (February, 1967), 18–39.

INDEX

Accommodation in marriage, 185–186
Actuarial research, inappropriate, 6–7
Adams, John B., 87
Adjustments in marriage, 173–188, 189–200; accommodation, 185–186; adjustments before marriage, 174–176; aggression, 187; alteration as means of, 186–187; anticipation of, 187–188; bargaining position, 180–182; dominance, 178–180; equalitarian marriage, 182; idealization, 176–178; impediments to, see Impediments to marital adjustment; most important, 184–185; patterns of, changing, 199–200; process of, 183–184; sexual, see Sexual adjustment in marriage
Adult identification, 128
Adultery, see Extramarital sex
Affluence, premarital sex and, 141
Age, effect of in endogamous marriage, 108; mate selection and, 93–94
Aggression, adjustment in marriage through, 187
Aging problem, meeting and solving, 311–312
Allport, Gordon W., 6
Alteration, 186–187
   see also Adjustments in marriage
American Association of Marriage Counselors, 320
Approach to learning, empathetic, 1, 4–18; case for, 9–18
Asch, Solomon E., 169
Atomistic Family, 22
Attitudes, 2

Bachelors, see Unmarried adults

Baker, Luther G., Jr., 70, 140
Bargaining position in marriage, 180–181; effect of children on, 181–182
Barnett, Larry D., 89, 90
Barnlund, Dean C., 201
Barth, E. A. Thomas, 91
Baumrind, Diana, 305
Baur, E. Jackson, 15
Bell, Howard M., 102
Bell, Robert R., 57, 136, 167, 228, 229, 249
Bernard, Jessie S., 10, 197
Berne, Eric, 48, 196
Birch, Herbert G., 297, 298
Blackmail, 196–197
   see also Impediments to marital adjustment
Blaine, Graham B., Jr., 151
Blood, Robert O., Jr., 108, 110, 111, 155–156, 178, 182, 243, 262, 277, 286
Blumberg, Leonard, 167
Bolton, Charles D., 122
Bossard, James H. S., 86, 182
Bowman, Claude C., 6, 111
Bowman, Henry A., 165–166
Brainwashing, 196–197
   see also Impediments to marital adjustment
Brayboy, Thomas, 116
Brill, Earl H., 171–172
Bronfenbrenner, Urie, 221, 305
Budgeting, 271–275
   see also Spending problems
Buchanan, Helen E., 10
Bundling, 88

Burchinal, Lee G., 102, 122
Burgess, Ernest W., 99, 108, 137, 155, 223
Buying habits, specific, spending problem and, 264–265

Calderone, Mary S., 149
Carpenter, June, 44
Case material, analyzing and interpreting, 15–18
Castration anxiety, 218–219
Cervantes, Lucius F., 102, 118, 169
Chancellor, Loren, 102
Chase, Stuart, 190
Chess, Stella, 297, 298
Child–child relationships, 302–304
Child–parent communication, 300–302
Children, child–child relationships, 302–304; child–parent communication, 300–302; effect of on bargaining position in marriage, 181–182; husband–wife relationships after birth of, 291–293; parent–child communication, 298–300
Christensen, Harold T., 8, 247
Circumstantial adulterer, extramarital sex and, 256–258
Clear, Val, 10
Coleman, James C., 294
Collier, James L., 164
Commercialization of sex, 140–141, 149
Common-law marriage, 158
Communication in marriage, 201–214; ability to communicate, 202–204; child–parent, 300–302; desire to communicate, 204–207; parent–child, 298–300; reaction formation, 203–204; security in, 207–209; selectivity in, lack of, 209–211; sensitivity in, 211–214; sexual, see Sexual communication
Compensation, 51
    see also Defense mechanisms
Complementary-needs theory, 121–126
Compromise, 186
Contraceptives, 139–140
Cooley, Charles H., 45
Coombs, Robert H., 29, 45, 46, 73–74, 89, 109, 132, 143
Cottrell, Leonard S., Jr., 40, 99
Coudert, Jo, 25–26, 125–126, 133, 134, 210–211
Counseling, see Marriage counseling
Courtship customs, 88–89
Creative compromise, 186
Crises, 307–321; defining experience as, 313–314; family goals, 315–317; kinds of, 307–308; marriage counseling and, 319–321; personal maturity, 317; preparation for, 312–313; social expectations, 314–315
Crisis philosophy, premarital sex and, 143
Cuber, John F., 198, 199–200, 248, 249, 250, 251
Cultural differences, 97–100
    see also Mate selection
Cultural endogamy, 87
Cultural relativism, 5
Culture, 43–44

Customs, 2; courtship, 88–89

Dager, Edward Z., 305
Dangerous age, extramarital sex and, 255–256
Dating, factors influencing, 59–68
    see also Mate selection
Davies, Vernon, 45, 46
Davis, Allison, 97–99, 302, 303
Davis, Katherine B., 137
Davis, Keith E., 121
Defense mechanisms, 49–51; compensation, 51; identification, 50; projection, 50; rationalization, 49; reaction formation, 50; repression, 50–51
Dependency, and in-law problem, 280–282
Determination, change in, 22–23, 30
Deutsch, Helene, 179
Developmental tasks, 184
Disagreements, see Quarreling
Disguised feelings, 195–196
    see also Impediments to marital adjustment
Divorce, attitudes toward, 25; causes of, 185; rate, increase in, 20–21
Domestic Family, 22
Dominance in marriage, 178–179; effect of personality on, 179–180
Dunn, Marie S., 32
Duvall, Evelyn, 163–164, 183–184, 193, 271, 276, 277, 279

Education, effect of in endogamous marriage, 108–109; relationships, 2, 5–9; mate selection and, 93–94; sex, 170, 223, 232
Ehrmann, Winston, 7, 137, 220–221, 223
Eisenberg, Philip, 44
Electra complex, 230–231
Ellis, Albert, 146, 161, 250
Ellis, Evelyn, 70
Emotional needs, 46–49
Emotionally disturbed, the, extramarital sex and, 258
Emotionally indispensable, becoming, 76–78
Empathy, 4
Endogamy, 87; age for marital success in, 108; case against, 110–119; case for, 95–109; education for marital success in, 108–109; racial, marital success and, 107–108; religion, marital success and, 101–107; religious, 91–92; society's dilemma, 117–119; subcultural differences, 97–101; white–Oriental marriage, 114–116
Equalitarian marriage, 182
Escape, 127
Exogamy, 86–87
Expectations in marriage, 2, 31–39, 41; confused, 34–35; differing, 37–39; not enough, 35–36; too-great, 31–33
Expenditures, see Spending problems
Experiences, unique, determinant of personality, 44–45

336   Index

Extramarital sex, 246–261; afraid of missing something, 258; attitudes about, changing, 249–251; circumstantial adulterer and, 256–258; dangerous age, 255–256; dynamics of infidelity, understanding, 251–258; the emotionally disturbed and, 258; female involvement in, 248–249; libertine and, 252; marriage relationship, effect on, 251; middle-class male involvement in, 247–248; reaction of partners to, 258–261; the sexually deprived and, 252–255

Family, budget, see Spending problems; changes in, 21–22; functions of, changes in, 27–30; size of, decline in, 20
Family goals, problem solving and, 315–317
Family interaction concept, 296–298
Family-life cycle, spending and, 270–271; stages in, 183
Family-life education, 223, 232; early male, 218–220; self-confidence as factor in, 170
Family living, preparation for, 312–313
Family relationships, improving, 304–306
Farnsworth, Dana L., 154
Father role, see Roles in marriage
Fears, as inhibitors of communication, 208–209; lack of love motivation and, 62; of being left mateless, 126–127; sexual adjustment and, 240–242
Feldman, Harold, 103, 104, 206, 213, 293
Female sexual conditioning, 227–235; in a changing society, 231–235; psychosexual conditioning, importance of, 229–230; sex-role identification, 230–231
Ferdinand, Theodore, 143
Festinger, Leon, 81
Finances, see Spending problems
First impression, 72–73, 82
Fletcher, Joseph, 162
Flexibility, love and marriage and, 68–69
Folsom, Joseph, 57–58
Freedman, Mervin B., 136, 137–138
Freeman, Linton, 90, 116
Freud, Sigmund, 65, 166
Fromm, Erich, 81 n., 170

Galpin, C. J., 183
Gebhard, Paul H., 223
Ginott, Haim, 301–302
Glenn, Hortense M., 70
Glick, Paul C., 93
Goal-set, lack of love motivation and, 62–64
Goode, William J., 22 n., 29, 58, 185
Gordon, Albert I., 104–107
Gragg, Charles I., 17
Grandmother role, 35–36
Gruenberg, Sidonie M., 33

Habenstein, Robert W., 87
Habits, buying, spending problem and, 264–265; unrealized, 174–175
Hamburg, David A., 230
Hamilton, G. V., 137

Hampson, Joan G., 52, 53, 229
Hampson, John L., 229
Hansen, Donald A., 310, 314
Happiness, marital, 20, 22–23, 174, 321
    see also Adjustments in marriage
Harlow, Harry and Margaret, 218
Harper, Robert, 146
Harroff, Peggy B., 198, 248, 249, 250
Havighurst, Robert J., 302, 303
Heer, David M., 90, 182
Heider, Fritz, 16
Heiss, Jerald, 92
Hill, Reuben, 7, 193, 271, 310, 314
Hobbs, Daniel, 292
Hodges, Harold, Jr., 312
Hoehler, Alan, 21
Hollingshead, August, 91, 141
Homogamy, 87, 122–126
    see also Endogamy
Homosexuality, 64–65, 225
Howard, David H., 155
Hunt, Morton M., 58, 234, 249
Huntington, Robert M., 121
Hurlock, Elizabeth B., 292
Husband–wife relationships, after the children are born, 291–293; during pregnancy, 288–291
Hysterical personality, 52

Idealization, 176–178
Identification, adult, 128
    see also Defense mechanisms; Sex-role identification
Illegitimate births in the U.S. (1938 and 1965), 150
Immaturity, psychosocial, 52; spending problem and, 266–269
Impediments to marital adjustment, 189–200; blackmail, 196–197; brainwashing, 196–197; disguised feelings, 195–196; manipulative types and techniques, 197–199; passive resistance, 195–196; quarreling, 192–194; who's right?, question of, 189–192
Incest laws, 87
Income, see Spending problems
Infant sexual conditioning, male, 218
Infidelity, problem of, see Extramarital sex
In-law problem, 276–287; dependency, 280–282; extent of the problem, 276–277; helpfulness of in-laws, 286–287; mother-in-law problem, 277–279; other in-laws, 279–280; real interference, 282–286
Insidious problems, meeting and solving, 310–311
Interaction, symbolic, role theory and, 40
Interfaith marriage, 91–92
Intermarriage, see Racial intermarriage
Intersex contacts, increase in, 23–25

Jackson, Joan, 310
Johnson, Virginia E., 172, 227

Kanin, Eugene J., 155
Karlen, Arno, 158–159

New experience, need for, 76, 80
New family interaction concept, 296–298
Nicholson, Samuel O., 110, 111
Nimkoff, Meyer F., 19, 20
Nymphomania, 153

Obsessive-compulsive personality, 53–54
Odegaard, Charles E., 119
Oedipus complex, 65–66
Ogburn, William F., 19–20, 27 n.
Overcompensation, 51

Packard, Vance, 138, 139, 163
Parent–child communication, 298–300
Parent–child relationships, 293–296; faulty, summary chart of, 294
Parental confusion, premarital sex and, 144–147, 168
Parsons, Talcott, 22, 220, 221
Passive resistance, 195–196
    see also Impediments to marital adjustment
Peck, Robert F., 99
Pecking order, 179–180
Perceptions, changes in, 1
Personal confusion, premarital sex and, 148–159
Personal maturity, problem solving and, 317
Personality, development of, 42–43; effect on dominance in marriage, 179–180; hysterical, 52; spending problem factor, 265–266
Personality disorders, 52–56; hysterical, 52; obsessive-compulsive, 53–54; psychosocial immaturity, 52; sociopathic, 52–53
Personality in relationships, importance of, 41–56; culture, importance of, 43–44; defense mechanisms, 49–51; development of, 42–43; disorders of, 52–56; emotional needs, 46–49; experiences, unique, 44–45; hysterical, 52; obsessive-compulsive, 53–54; self-image, 45–46; sociopathic, 52–53
Petting, 167, 223
Pineo, Peter C., 32, 310
Poffenberger, Thomas, 163
Polyandry, 88
Pomeroy, W. B., 30, 137, 219, 220, 224, 229, 233, 246
Pregnancy, husband–wife relationship during, 288–291
Premarital sex, 135–147, 148–159, 160–172; affluence and, 141; attitudes toward, 152, 167; confusion about consequences of, 139; commercialization of sex and, 140–141, 149; crisis philosophy and, 143; future of, 170–172; live-togethers, 158–159; marital adjustment and, 155–158; new difficulties in, 152–158; next generation, what can be done for, 168–170; parental confusion about, 144–147, 168; personal confusion about, 148–159; public confusion about, 135–137; research evidence about, 137–144; secularization and, 140; self-confidence as factor in sex education, 170; self-fulfilling prophecy and, 143–144; sexual

equality for women and, 142; sexual restraints, abandonment of, question of, 160–168; situation ethics, 162–163; technology and changing, 139–140; traditional view of, 163–168; urbanization and, 140; value dilution and, 141–142
Problems, solving, 307–321; aging problem, 311–312; experience with, 313; family goals, 315–317; guidelines for, 317–319; insidious, 310–311; marriage counseling and, 319–321; personal maturity, 317; preparation for, 312–313; social expectations, 314–315
Projection, 50
    see also Defense mechanisms
Propinquity, 86
Psychological factors in mate selection, 120–134; adult identification, 128; escape, 127; fear of being left mateless, 126–127; need-meeting, 120–126; rebound, 128–129; revenge, 128–129; sexual attraction, 129; success and status, 129–132
Psychosexual conditioning, importance of, 229–230
Psychosocial immaturity, 52
Public confusion, premarital sex and, 135–137

Quarreling, 192–194
    see also Impediments to marital adjustment
Queen, Stuart, 87

Racial endogamy, marital success and, 107–108
Racial intermarriage, 89–91, 110, 114–119
Rapport, 71
Rationalization, 49
    see also Defense mechanisms
Reaction formation, 50
    see also Defense mechanisms
Rebound, 128–129
Recognition, need for, 76
Reik, Theodor, 203
Reiss, Ira L., 71, 72, 136, 138, 141, 142, 146, 150
Relatability, 71–84; first impression, 72–73, 82; improving, 82–84; needs, satisfaction of, 76–82; self-confidence, importance of, 73–74, 82; sex-appropriate friends, becoming, 74–76, 83
Relationships education, 2, 5–9
Relatives, see In-law problem
Religion, marital success and, 101–107
Religious endogamy, 91–92
Repression, 50–51
    see also Defense mechanisms
Resentments, sexual adjustment and, 240–242
Residential propinquity, 86
Response, need for, 76
Revenge, 128–129
Richardson, Arthur S., 92
Rokeach, Milton, 2 n.
Roles in marriage, 33–34, 40
    see also Sex-role identification
Romantic love, see Love
Roper Research Associates, 137, 151